The Public's Law

The Public's Law

Origins and Architecture of Progressive Democracy

BLAKE EMERSON

Oxford University Press is a department of the University of Oxford. It furthers the University's objective of excellence in research, scholarship, and education by publishing worldwide. Oxford is a registered trademark of Oxford University Press in the UK and certain other countries.

Published in the United States of America by Oxford University Press
198 Madison Avenue, New York, NY 10016, United States of America.

First issued as an Oxford University Press paperback, 2025

Library of Congress Cataloging-in-Publication Data

Names: Emerson, Blake, author.
Title: The public's law : origins and architecture of progressive democracy /
Blake Emerson.
Description: New York : Oxford University Press, 2019. | Based on author's thesis
(doctoral—Yale University, 2016) issued under title: Between public law and public sphere :
reconstructing the American Progressive theory of the administrative state. |
Includes bibliographical references and index.
Identifiers: LCCN 2018038830 | ISBN 9780190682873 ((hardback) : alk. paper) |
ISBN 9780197806845 (paperback)
Subjects: LCSH: Administrative law—United States—Philosophy. |
Public administration—United States—Philosophy. | Progressivism (United States politics)—
Influence. | Law—United States—German influences. | United States—Politics and government.
Classification: LCC KF5402 .E46 2019 | DDC 342.73/06—dc23
LC record available at https://lccn.loc.gov/2018038830

Paperback printed by Marquis Book Printing, Canada

For my parents,

Amy and Steve

CONTENTS

ACKNOWLEDGMENTS

The book before you grew out of my doctoral dissertation in Political Science at Yale University: "Between Public Law and Public Sphere: Reconstructing the American Progressive Theory of the Administrative State." While the spirit of the book remains the same, I have revised the content to clarify the connections between the Hegelian Progressives and Progressive legal thought more broadly, and to better articulate the normative theory that grows out of the intellectual and institutional history I present. In the Introduction and Conclusion, I have sought to situate this project in the difficult context of the Trump presidency, which flies in the face of Progressive democracy. I hope that my effort to recover Progressive ideas and institutions will help us to rebuild a state adequate to the requirements of individual and collective freedom.

This book would not have been possible without the support and influence of American and German civil society. When I was an undergraduate at Williams College, Joe Cruz, Monique Deveaux, Georges Dreyfus, Will Dudley, Nicole Mellow, Mark Reinhardt, Mark Taylor, and Robyn Marasco helped me to pursue my early interests in Hegel, political philosophy, and American politics. When I was a research assistant at the Aspen Institute Roundtable of Community Change, Anne Kubisch, Gretchen Susi, and Keith Lawrence introduced me to the importance of problems of economic and racial inequality, and the potential for government and community agencies to address them. The States of Connecticut and Baden-Württemberg supported a year of study at Heidelberg University, during which I began writing the dissertation, and took in the spirit of Southwest German constitutionalism. While I was in Heidelberg, Armin von Bogdandy generously provided me with a position at the Max Planck Institute for International Law and Comparative Public Law, where I was able to improve my German as a translator and present my research at institute colloquia. William Forbath helped arrange a visiting scholar position at the University of Texas School of Law, which allowed me to continue my work while living in the Lone Star State. Allen Fisher gave expert advice during my research at the Lyndon Baines Johnson Presidential Library. I received support from the Department of Government at the University of Texas at Austin to present a paper on German public law and the American Progressives at the University of Texas Graduate Conference in Public Law and from the Oscar M. Ruebhausen Fund to travel to Berlin for a conference organized by Dieter Grimm. The Max Planck Institute again provided support for me to return to Germany for a seminar on Marx and Legal Theory, organized by Benedict Vischer and Dana Schmalz, where I practiced my critique of Marx's *Critique of Hegel's* Philosophy of Right. Yale University supported my doctoral research in the Political Science Department. Peter Shane and Chris Walker hosted the Administrative Law New Scholarship Roundtable at The Ohio State University Moritz College of Law, where Jon Michaels, Nicholas Parrillo, Glen Staszewski, and others gave very helpful suggestions to revise chapter 2. The American Constitution Society hosted a Junior Scholars Public Law Workshop, where I received excellent feedback on chapter 2 from Edward Rubin and Mark Tushnet. The University of California, Los Angeles has supported the final stages of manuscript preparation.

Numerous friends, colleagues, and students have provided essential guidance and editorial help throughout the writing process. Jeremy Kessler met with me to discuss my early research on the Equal Employment Opportunity Commission, and helped me to puzzle through some of the darker crevices of administrative law doctrine. Andrew March, Steven Smith, Bryan Garsten, and Melvin Rogers provided useful feedback on my first attempts to engage with Du Bois and Hegel. Alice O'Connor, Jess Gilbert, and Spencer Wood helped me with my research on the agricultural New Deal. Professor von Bogdandy provided crucial suggestions in my study of German public law. Eldon Eisenach gave helpful comments on chapter 2. The members of Seyla Benhabib's *Doktoranden Seminar*—Umur Basdas, Adom Getachew, Stefan Eich, Devin Goure, Anna Jurkevics, and Erin Pineda—helped me to think through the argument in the early drafts. Members of Professor von Bogdandy's *Referentenbesprechung*—particularly Matthias Goldmann, Michael Ioannidis, and Dana Schmalz—provided important insights on my research on German administrative law and the concept of public authority. The American Political Development Workshop participants—especially David Lebow, Samuel DeCanio, and David Mayhew—helped me to think through my argument about the Progressives. Christian Rosser met with me in Bern to discuss our shared interest in the connections between Hegel, Goodnow, and Wilson. At my new home at the UCLA School of Law, my colleagues Beth Colgan, Kristen Eichensehr, Rebecca Stone, Richard Re, and Alex Wang have helped me to revise chapter 4. Stefan Eich, David Lebow, Travis Pantin, Laura Schaefer, Noah Rosenblum, Jason

Yonover, and Benedict Vischer read the final drafts of the dissertation carefully to provide corrections and suggestions. Judith Calvert was exceedingly patient and helpful with me as I delayed returning to law school while I finished the dissertation. Taylor Pitz provided great feedback on later drafts of the book, and Shane Farley's proofreading and indexing helped to finalize the manuscript. Jamie Berezin responded to my cold call to Oxford University Press, helped me to develop the book proposal, and has shepherded the manuscript to publication. Brooke Smith copyedited the manuscript.

The professors I worked with in the Political Science Department at Yale and at Yale Law School have shaped this project from top to bottom. Jerry Mashaw introduced me to the study of administrative law and provided feedback on chapter 2. Bill Eskridge's seminar on statutory interpretation helped me to develop my understanding of "the public's law." John Witt's seminar on legal historiography helped me to think through my historical argument and to flesh out the broader legal theory of the Progressive Era. Dieter Grimm's course on "Weimar Jurisprudence" provided me with crucial insights about German legal history, which helped me to compose the critique of German state theory I advance in chapter 1. Stephen Skowronek's course on "American Political Development" introduced me to scholarship on Progressivism and the American state that was absolutely formative for the approach I have taken—to think about ideas in and through the institutions in which they are embedded. The detailed feedback he has provided on all of the chapters has forced me to take institutional constraints yet more seriously; he has combined skepticism with encouragement in a way that has vastly improved the argument. Bruce Ackerman's *We the People*, which I read as an undergraduate, brought me to law school. His courses on "Constitution: Law, Philosophy, History," the "Civil Rights Revolution," and "The Foundations of Legal Scholarship" have defined my understanding of public law and its relationship to popular sovereignty. His unwavering support throughout this process, his formative advice, and the passion he brings to his teaching and scholarship have been an inspiration. Seyla Benhabib was the reason I chose to come to the Yale Political Science Department. Her course on "European Political Thought from Weber to Derrida" was the finest lecture I have ever attended and inspired me to pursue my interest in German political thought in the dissertation. She provided indispensable feedback, support, and careful reading of the drafts at every stage of the process. Her scholarship, combining Hegel's appreciation of the intersubjective core of law, Habermas's understanding of the moral substance of communication, and Arendt's concept of political action, has thoroughly shaped the normative perspective this book advances. I am truly honored and thankful to have studied under such an esteemed and generous group of mentors.

No ethical life is complete without family. My grandparents, Beatrice and Elizabeth and Edward, encouraged my early intellectual curiosity. Though I never met Blanchard, I am named after him, and carry his American spirit in my bones. My stepfamily, Jocko, Jenni, Anneka, and Kendra, have always given me a warm home and lively conversation in Haverford to come back to. My sister and religion scholar Abby has kept my spirits up with her love, her moral sense, and her intellectual spark. My father, Steve, who introduced me to philosophy, has always been there to talk with me about my research and about my life; I wouldn't be the scholar or the man I am if it weren't for him; he has taught me to "love this shot," even when the ball is underneath a tree, in a different time zone than the pin. My mother, Amy, indulged my early love for bureaucracy by ironing Ann Arbor Police Department insignia onto my blue Oxford shirts for my playground patrols. With her *OED* and *Fowlers* always handy, she has taught me the beauty of language; she has shown me how to live life with grace, independence, and liberal sentiments. My spouse, my love, Laura, has lifted me up in my moments, or months, of doubt and always been by my side even when we were far apart. In her work on death penalty clemency, she has taught me the dangers as well the virtues of executive discretion.

—Berlin and Los Angeles, Summer 2018

Introduction

The modern democratic state is an administrative state. Democracy requires administration to address the social problems the people identify. Some ethical and practical conflicts cannot be ascribed simply to the wrongful acts of individuals, but rather emerge from larger patterns of interaction. We confront vast inequalities of income, wealth, and opportunity that prevent citizens from participating equally as members of the political community; monopolistic firms, asymmetries of information, and transaction costs that impede fair exchange; industrial practices that degrade our environment and threaten our survival; institutions of education, employment, policing, and housing that entrench racial hierarchies; and cultures of gender domination in the school and the workplace that harm and humiliate students and employees. Because these problems arise from complex systems of social organization, they must be addressed through a complex system of political organization, namely bureaucracy. Public power must flow through authorities that gather and analyze information, make long range plans, and handle a mass of individual cases in a consistent fashion. Administrative agencies can deploy resources, personnel, and regulatory instruments in a way calculated to achieve collectively determined goals.

The administrative state, at the same time, appears not to be democratic. When we grant power to unelected officials to make decisions, we remove government from direct public oversight. When we delegate authority from the legislature to the executive, governance may lose that predictable, transparent, and discursive quality that is thought to attend liberal lawmaking. When we treat some members of our society as passive beneficiaries who are subject to official benevolence, discipline, and manipulation, we may deprive them of their status as authors of the laws that bind them. When we supplant deeply embedded and intimate forms of social order with alienated administrative power, we may drain the wellsprings of communal association that make collective action

The Public's Law. Blake Emerson.

possible. When we replace communicative reason, persuasive rhetoric, and good-faith argument over common ends with instrumental reasoning over the efficient application of power, we may enervate the public sphere in which democratic opinion is formed. Administration thus seems to threaten the very foundations for democracy, even as democracy requires administration.[1]

The apparent conflict between democratic politics and administrative organization is a tension internal to democratic order itself: between generally applicable laws and procedures sensitive to individuality; between the value of political accountability and the need to insulate decision-making from partisan opportunism; between the requisites for democratic life and the practice of democratic politics. These constitutive tensions do not render the modern democratic state untenable. They motivate its normative development. They furnish opportunities for institutional and conceptual adaptations that mediate the dialogue between public law and public opinion. By studying how law and discourse relate to one another, we can identify a general maxim to guide political progress: *structure the state to empower the public sphere.* Such a structure frames *the public's law*—the set of obligations that emerge from and guarantee a condition of shared freedom among all of the political community's members.

I construct this normative architecture from the intellectual history of the administrative state. The history begins with German public law scholars in the nineteenth century, whose ideas the American Progressives transformed at the dawn of the twentieth. This intellectual trajectory reveals the emancipatory tasks that motivated and legitimated administrative power on the European continent, and shows as well the great danger posed by bureaucracy without the involvement of the public in administration. That history foregrounds the democratic forms of administration that were imagined and implemented in the United States. The path of American legal and political development has partially realized the Progressive vision I reconstruct. We have developed participatory forms of administrative policymaking and bureaucracies capable of efficient service delivery, which reflect Progressive ideals. But today these institutional and ideological legacies have been marginalized, distorted, and undermined by the rise of technocratic theories of government and plebiscitary forms of democratic politics. I will argue for reforms in American public law and for alterations in public consciousness that would advance the project of Progressive democracy.

My turn to German thought may seem surprising to those American legal scholars steeped in our domestic tradition, the transnational roots of which seem to extend no further than English common law and constitutionalism. But this book will show how many of the American political theorists, social scientists, legal scholars, and statesmen who conceptualized and built up our administrative state did so with German theory and practice in mind. In particular, they learned from the German ideal of the *Rechtsstaat*—a "law state" that would guarantee individual freedom and promote social welfare with statutory authorization and through administrative action. To the extent contemporary theorists engage with this German background, their point of reference is usually the thought of Max Weber, who offered a pathbreaking account of bureaucracy and formal-legal authority in the early twentieth century.[2] Weber's vision of a state legitimated by statutory law, specialized scientific knowledge, and bureaucratic neutrality has shaped scholarly understandings of the American public law system.

I argue that this reliance on Weber has led to a truncated and distorted conception of the administrative state. His theory reflected a particularly unstable moment in German history when bureaucracy had lost its connection to substantive political values and instead took on a formal, instrumental cast. I turn back to the thought of G.W.F. Hegel to enrich our understanding of the purpose and structure of modern American government. I show how Hegelian ideas inspired Progressive thinking in the formative years of the regulatory state. Scholars such as John Dewey, Mary Follett, W.E.B Du Bois, Woodrow Wilson, and Frank Goodnow embraced Hegel's concept of a state committed to individual freedom, but enlarged it to encompass democratic values. I unearth this Hegelian background not merely because it is a contingent fact of intellectual history: more than this, Hegel's thought provides a firmer foundation for understanding the immanent relationship between public law and practical reason. I argue that we should reconsider Progressive Hegelianism as a model for the present, because it shows us how we might construct a state that furthers the freedom of citizens, both as individuals and as political consociates.

Recovering this Progressive theory of the democratic state is essential in the present moment. Though administrative law is prone to perpetual crises of legitimacy,[3] the presidency of Barack Obama saw particularly acute confrontations between liberal efforts to deploy the state to improve social welfare and vindicate civil rights, on the one hand, and conservative reaction against this trend on the supposed basis of constitutional principle, on the other. A significant strand of this reaction has targeted the Hegelian Progressives, in particular, arguing that they imported dangerous, proto-totalitarian ideas into American law.[4] The ongoing conservative project to uproot the legacy of Progressivism, the New Deal, and the Second Reconstruction has borne fruit in the Trump administration's attempted "deconstruction of the administrative state."[5] From financial regulation, to healthcare provision, to environmental protection, to sex equality, to the very independence of the civil service, the Trump administration has waged war on the regulatory state that has taken shape over the past century.

It is an open question, as of this writing, whether this project will succeed. Scholars, public officials, and citizens who wish to understand or respond to this reactionary agenda must first get to know the ideals and the institutions of the Progressive state, the remnants of which conservatives wish to expunge. My aim is therefore to retrieve the Progressive theory of democracy and its legacy for American political development so that these become available to us in the present. This project is not merely restorative, however. I want to help us build something new on the buried foundations of Progressivism—a political architecture that leans on its strengths and buttresses its weaknesses.

Before I explain my methods, I will situate my claims in the broader tradition of administrative critique in modern political theory. This wider survey will show how my claims relate to the treatments of bureaucracy in neighboring traditions of thought. By analyzing the most trenchant indictments of bureaucratic rule, we can discern the challenges my defense of administration must answer and the dangers administration must avoid.

I. THE SPECTER OF BUREAUCRATIC DOMINATION IN MODERN POLITICAL THEORY

Few have expressed the virtues of American democracy and the vices of European bureaucracy with greater eloquence than Alexis de Tocqueville. He observed that Jacksonian democracy was constituted by local forms of participatory government, economic equality, a dense network of civil associations, and the high esteem placed on law, courts, and attorneys. These together produced "the slow and quiet action of society upon itself" and a "state of things really founded upon the enlightened will of the people."[6] With limited powers delegated to the federal government and most authority held in local deliberative assemblies, he observed an "absence of what we term the Government, or the Administration."[7] The exercise of administrative power was transitory and illegible: "The authority which public men possess in America is so brief . . . that the acts of a community frequently leave fewer traces than the events in a private family. . . . But little is committed to writing, and that little is soon wafted away forever, like the leaves of Sybil, by the smallest breeze."[8]

While Tocqueville is frequently read as embracing America's administrative decentralization as a check to its democratic constitution,[9] his view was more complex. He argued that the American mixture of majority rule and impermanent administration could thwart the responsible exercise of democratic power. These institutions created a disparity between the strength of popular aspirations and the weak institutional framework that attempted to realize those aspirations: "by changing their administrative forms as often as they do, the inhabitants of the United States compromise the stability of their government. It may be apprehended that men, perpetually thwarted in their designs by the mutability of legislation, will learn to look upon the republic as an inconvenient form of society."[10] Here, Tocqueville compared the United States *un*favorably to the European governments, with their permanent administrative machinery. In America,

> as the majority is the only power which it is important to court, all its projects are taken up with the greatest ardor, but no sooner is its attention distracted, than all this ardor ceases; whilst in the free states of Europe, where the administration is at once independent and secure, the projects of the legislature continue to be executed, even when its attention is directed to other objects.[11]

A permanent, bureaucratic officialdom alone would be capable of amplifying democratic voice, extending law in time, and reshaping social relations according to public purposes.

Tocqueville's assessment of the continuities between the monarchical and the post-revolutionary state in France in his later work, *The Old Regime and the Revolution*, helps to clarify what he thought was indispensable and what was pernicious about bureaucracy. There, Tocqueville argued that the French Revolution radicalized political and social trends that were already underway during the monarchical regime. He described how the monarchy developed a centralized administration, unified in the *Conseil du Roi*, which exercised wide-ranging advisory, legislative, judicial, and administrative powers. The council exercised its power through public officials who implemented the national laws and policies at the local level. This officialdom enhanced the position of the crown against the aristocracy and paved the way for the revolution by placing all persons on an equal footing as the subjects of a central authority. The Royal Council would be reconstituted after the revolution and persist into the present day as the *Conseil d'Etat*—perhaps the world's foremost administrative institution.

By unsettling the patchwork of feudal authority, the system of absolutist administrative power thus facilitated "the most fundamental, the most durable, the truest portion" of the work of the revolution: "the natural equality of man, and the consequent abolition of all caste, class, or professional privileges, popular sovereignty, the paramount authority of the social body, the uniformity of rules."[12] Once administrative centralization treated all persons as equivalent, taxable objects, it was possible to reconstitute them as equal subjects; once administrative power made good on the king's claim to sovereignty, his person could be replaced with the body of the people; once the monarch had the bureaucratic capacity to realize his will across his territory, the general will could do the same; once broadly applicable laws and principles of administration were instituted, equality could become a political reality.

The despotic legacy of administrative power, however, was that it had not cultivated a capacity for political liberty. The feudal order it worked against had wrought a popular hatred of inequality but provided no experience with peaceful political participation. Absolutist bureaucracy likewise did not promote sentiments, skills, and institutions of public reason that would enable inclusive political engagement. The temporary fervor of the revolution for active political life therefore gave way to equal submission to centralized, imperial power under Napoleon Bonaparte.[13]

Tocqueville's indictment of post-revolutionary administration cannot be understood to reject bureaucratic institutions as a whole. In the case of America, he saw a democracy that lacked the institutional stability to realize democratic purposes, though the people were well versed in the practice of deliberative politics. In post-revolutionary France, he saw a democracy with awesome administrative power, which lacked customs and institutions of sustained political participation. Neither political order was adequate to the challenges of the new democratic age.

The challenge Tocqueville's studies together pose is how to marry administrative capacity with political liberty. While liberty without administration will result in frustration and disillusionment with republican government, administration without liberty will descend into despotism. For "nothing but liberty can draw men forth from the isolation into which their independence naturally drives them—can compel them to associate together, in order to come to a common understanding, to debate, and to compromise together on their joint concerns."[14]

It was precisely this spirit of joint venture that distinguished the American political project. As Hannah Arendt argued, the pilgrims who established the first colonies had "confidence that they had their own power . . . to combine themselves together into a 'civil body politick,' which, held together solely by the strength of mutual promise 'in the presence of God and one another', supposedly was enough to 'enact, constitute and frame' all necessary laws and institutions of government."[15] America had from the outset constituted itself by deliberative democratic practices that have relied upon the cohesive force of rational political engagement. Tocqueville's insight into the weakness of American administrative power suggested, however, that such practices of mutual promise and self-government would be a necessary but not sufficient condition for republican institutions. Modern democratic rule would require that mutual promise be born out by lasting bureaucratic performance, which would enforce those promises amidst a complex, resistant, and ever-changing social landscape.

What Tocqueville and Arendt failed to imagine, and what American Progressive thought and practice would first conceive, were forms of administration that cultivated rather than undermined political liberty. For Arendt, bureaucracy was a stultifying "rule by nobody," which eliminated the space for politics by "imposing innumerable and various rules, all of which tend to 'normalize' its members, to make them behave, and to exclude spontaneous action or outstanding achievement."[16] In its most extreme form, such a bureaucratic state becomes totalitarian: all space for the generation of common but contestable experience, discourse, and purpose is eliminated; moral judgment is reduced to meaningless clichés; the worst crimes are perpetrated by thoughtless officials who focus on problems of efficient management, become alienated from the consequences of their action, and cannot think from the perspectives of the persons they control.[17]

To avoid this dismal fate we must, as Arendt and Tocqueville suggest, maintain forms of rule that exercise power in a cooperative fashion, and widen public space in and through their operation. The problem we confront with bureaucracy is not, as Tocqueville thought, an overemphasis on equality at the expense of liberty or, as Arendt thought, a reduction of politics to social questions that are properly left to the private sphere. The problem is that we have not adequately realized the capacity of administrative institutions to bring the people into the state as partners in the interpretation and implementation of freedom. The solution I reconstruct from the American Progressives is to rethink administrative structures so they are capable of efficient action and yet remain open to the participation of the public in the formation of policy. If the public realm, where "men are together in the manner of speech and action," can extend into the interior corridors of the state, then the expansion of bureaucracy into society can avoid the pitfalls of democratic despotism and the nightmares of totalitarian rule.[18]

Recovering a sense of the democratic and emancipatory potential of administration requires attention to its location within the category of public law. It is typical among conservatives to see administration as a departure from law, as a modern form of extralegal prerogative, which is foreign to constitutional forms and values.[19] But the ubiquity of "administrative law" courses in the American law school curriculum, and the day-to-day production and implementation of law by federal and state administrative agencies testify to administration's legal character. So why does the legal status of administration remain so contested and ambiguous? Simple aversion to the welfare state and market regulation may motivate conservative indictments. But perhaps there also are deeper theoretical puzzles at the interface of law and administration.

Michel Foucault raised the problem of administration's legal status acutely with his concept of "governmentality." He described the development of an "art of government" in the eighteenth century, coeval with "the whole development of the administrative apparatus of the territorial monarchies."[20] This new political art, understood as a "right manner of disposing of things," sought to manage the "population" through the use of economics and statistics.[21] Because of this new emphasis on empirical knowledge and a social scientific turn in the practice of rule, the juridical frame of sovereignty receded into the background: "whereas the end of sovereignty is internal to itself and possesses its own intrinsic instrument in the shape of laws, the finality of government resides in the things it manages and in the pursuit of the perfection and intensification of the processes which it directs; and the instruments of government, instead of being laws, now come to be a range of multiform tactics."[22]

Though he was at pains to distinguish juristic sovereignty from administrative government, Foucault did not claim that governmentality somehow replaced sovereignty and law. Rather, he meant that governmentality consisted in "using laws themselves as tactics."[23] Laws were no longer merely related circularly to sovereignty, as institutions that originate in the claims of an ultimate political authority and then make that authority real through their operation. Rather, the laws had become instruments for the purposive disposition of persons and things and the discipline of thought and action.[24] Foucault thus acknowledged that government was not a fully comprehensive political concept but rather one that stood in relation both to juristic sovereignty and to disciplinary institutions.

Once it is conceded that tactical government does not replace law but instead uses laws as tactics, a space for critique and for public engagement opens up at the intersection between these political forms. Both in Europe and in the United States, the administrative *apparatus* has arisen hand in hand with administrative *law*, which affords affected persons the opportunity to contest the legality of state action.[25] Administrative law does not reduce administration to the juridical discourse of sovereignty and legal authorization; nor does it fully instrumentalize law so that it can be shaped to fulfill whatever disposition of persons and things the government seeks. Rather, it is a heavily contested domain where the logics of governmentality, disciplinarity, and law struggle with one another and overlap. Because these analytic frames coexist within administration, public *law* affords opportunities for the public *sphere* to test their congruity through litigation and other forms of participation.

At issue in such disputes is often precisely what is the "*right* manner of disposing of things." Foucault's use of the term "right" (*droite*) is significant, with its ambivalence between ethical judgment, legal entitlement, and factual correctness. Precisely these ambivalences make a deliberative rather than a purely technocratic form of administration possible and necessary. There are often administrative problems that are susceptible to more than one factually correct answer, depending on what ethical values we apply and what we interpret statutory rules to authorize, foreclose, or require. Administrative law is therefore at the heart of public law, not only in the sense that it concerns vertical relationships between the state and those subject to its authority, but in the sense that it situates this hierarchy within a web of discursive contestation. As Martin Loughlin has observed, "the 'public space' of public law is that which is needed for communication over matters of common existence. . . . Public law expresses a grammar of political conflict that flows through a system of shared understanding."[26]

To realize the practical force of this public legal discourse, we cannot think of government in the purely instrumental, economistic terms by which Foucault defines it or of law in the circular terms by which he analyzes sovereignty. Rather, government must be understood as fulfilling certain popular purposes that statutory law identifies and administrative authorities implement. Administrative law, properly understood, is the interpretation of these public purposes. It is therefore not quite the case, as Foucault suggested, that "the techniques of government have become the only political issue, the only real space for political struggle and contestation."[27] Rather, administrative law, as a liminal space between technique, ethics, and sovereignty, has become a (though not "the only") real space for political action.

The failure to recognize the truly public character of public law is a symptom of the prevailing belief that administration is a concealed and opaque form of rule—whereas publicity is something we encounter in constitutionalism, legislation, scholarship, journalism, political speeches, and conversations in venues such as salons, coffeehouses, and blogs.[28] We must resist this sharp, categorical boundary between bureaucracy and the public sphere. Political freedom consists in the interrogation of such institutional boundaries. Foucault himself, in one of his few explicit articulations of his political values, turned to Immanuel Kant's famous "What Is Enlightenment?" essay to argue that we must take up the "undefined work of freedom" by "grasping the points where change is possible and desirable, and to determine the precise form which this change should take."[29] The continuing requirement of enlightenment was to "work on our limits, that is, a patient labor giving form to our impatience for liberty."[30]

If we apply this liminal perspective to Kant's original essay, it becomes clear that administration itself is a threshold where such changes are conceivable. Kant's central claim was that for enlightenment "nothing is required but *freedom*, and indeed the least harmful of anything that could be called freedom: freedom to make *public use* of one's reason in all matters."[31] But Kant made an important proviso to this unrestricted use of reason:

> the private use of reason may . . . often be very narrowly restricted without this particular hindering the progress of enlightenment. But by "public use of one's reason" I understand that use which someone makes of it *as a scholar* before the entire public of the *world of readers*. What I call the private use of reason is that which one may make of it in a certain civil post or office with which he is entrusted.[32]

Kant's claim that bureaucratic reason was "private" reveals the limits of enlightenment in the context of Prussian absolutism. Though it is true that we too, in democratic states, expect public officials to obey the commands given to them by law and by their ministerial superiors, we do not think of such reasoning as "private." In carrying out a public purpose public officials exercise an open and contestable form of reason. This means that they cannot "behave[] merely passively."[33] They must state their reasons for action publicly. They must use their judgment to resolve any ambiguities in the laws that authorize and constrain their conduct. When they relate the general commands of law to the particular facts they confront in their official capacity, they must consult the sense of the community in exercising their own judgment. Only in this way does the performance of a legal duty remain a truly public thing, such that we can claim to live under a republican form government. By questioning the boundary between public law and public sphere, we engage in the patient labor of giving administrative form to our impatience for liberty.

Kant takes us to the trailhead of the intellectual path this book will follow. Hegel followed in Kant's footsteps in articulating the political requirements of individual freedom. He sketched a much more ambitious conception of the administration, not as a group of odedient royal servants, but instead as an official class and an institution that stood at the center of an organic constitutional order. He related this bureaucratic class to a specific political project, namely, the establishment and maintenance of a free social order. This vision would influence German public law and eventually inspire the democratic state theory of the American Progressives.

II. RECONSTRUCTIVE POLITICAL THEORY

This book *reconstructs* a normative vision of the administrative state from theoretical, institutional, and historical fragments.[34] I do not claim that we have achieved the ideal that I describe. Nor do I adopt an orthodox "philosophy of history," which would maintain that political development necessarily unfolds into higher forms of freedom and rationality.[35] I mean "Progressive" to denote a practical aspiration for the extension of social and political freedom, which originates in the teachings of our theoretical and institutional past. The Progressive theory I develop is grounded in a set of ideas that took form during the American Progressive Era, from the 1880s to the 1920s. I argue that this theory has continuing descriptive purchase and normative appeal today. My aim is to establish that the resources exist within our philosophical tradition, political history, and legal repertoire to better realize the Progressive conception of the democratic state.

The first step in this project is to recover the intellectual *origins* of Progressive democracy. I single out a particular line of intellectual development, beginning with Hegel and culminating in the American Progressives. Like Hegel, the Progressives sought to build an administrative state that would guarantee individual freedom. But unlike Hegel, they insisted that such a state must be democratic. This intellectual history shows what is cosmopolitan and what is specifically American about Progressive democracy. It locates a major aspect of our political tradition within a transatlantic discourse, thus rejecting the notion that American thought and practice can be understood apart from its broader context. At the same time, I show how the appropriation and transformation of German ideas resulted in distinctively American innovations that were in fact superior to the ideas that inspired them.

The second step in this reconstruction is to show how this intellectual strain has been at work in American political development. My account of the New Deal and the Second Reconstruction will show how the ideal of Progressive democracy was carried out in practice by administrative agencies during these periods of constitutional ferment. This study unearths the buried foundations for a political *architecture* that we might construct in our present—a common edifice that would "provide[] the community with a center or centers" and thus allow individuals to "gain their sense of place in a history, in a community, by relating their dwelling to that center."[36] This institutional reconstruction shows that Progressive conceptions are not only theoretically but also practically available to us. The various organizational configurations that arose in this period also tease out tensions within the Progressive tradition—tensions between the efficient provision of the requisites for democratic politics, on the one hand, and the broad-based participation of the people in the formulation of administrative policy, on the other. This history can then provide models and warnings for our present and future, helping us to build a state that engages the people in articulating their shared norms while effectively implementing a free and equal form of political association.

The third step is to reconstruct the values and structural properties that such a political project holds. It is possible, in principle, to develop such a normative theory of the administrative state without grounding it first in a single philosophical tradition. Henry S. Richardson has offered such an account, synthesizing contemporary liberal, republican, and democratic theory to explain under what circumstances bureaucratic power is legitimate.[37] His basic argument, with which I agree, is that administrators must use practical judgment and deliberate with affected persons when they exercise authority. Because of his focus on contemporary political theory, however, he does not engage with a set of essential questions that the Hegelian Progressive tradition discloses and makes tractable: What is the proper regulative relationship among the state, civil society, and the public sphere? How should the practice of administration *alter* our conception of legal rights and duties rather than merely operate within their fixed ambit? How can we sustain democratic legitimacy when laws and policies can rarely be fully justified by reasoned deliberation prior to their implementation? What are the costs of a fully rational public reason, and how might these costs be managed? These are the questions my normative theory sets out to answer.

III. THE PUBLIC'S LAW, CONSTITUTIONALISM, AND ADMINISTRATIVE LEGITIMACY

My account enters into a lively contemporary debate over the nature, legitimacy, and crises of the American administrative state. Some scholars have claimed that the administrative state is simply unconstitutional because it vests legislative and adjudicative power in executive institutions and more broadly threatens individual rights. According to this argument, the Progressives are largely responsible for our fall from constitutional grace. Philip Hamburger, for instance, argues that contemporary American administrative law is rooted partly in the Hegelian Progressives' "academic idealization of administrative power . . . and corresponding contempt for many of the formalities of constitutional law."[38] Hamburger worries that the Progressive theory and its instantiation in administrative law has undermined the Constitution's separation of powers and the protection of individual rights against governmental encroachment.

The Progressive account answers such concerns by turning to the fundamental place of democracy in our constitutional order. "We the people" are sovereign here, not some natural law sent down from a "brooding omnipresence in the sky."[39] Constitutional structures and individual rights must therefore be interpreted and delimited according to the fundamental requirements of collective self-government. The Progressive theory outlines such requirements. Democracy requires the equal freedom of all citizens. The meaning of freedom must be decided in argument and action among the people themselves, in a way that allows all voices to be heard and shared norms to emerge as the public's law—the "articulate voice" of the people.[40] Administrative bodies help to constitute the public's law, providing fora in which the abstract commands of statutes are constructed with due consideration of the entitlements, interests, and self-understandings of those the laws bind or otherwise affect. Constitutional values continue to play a role in Progressive thought. But they only provide the broad outlines for a democratic order, the details of which must be specified through legislation, administrative practice, and public participation in governmental processes. The Constitution can only tell us so much about what the state is and what it ought to do. Structured dialogue between the people and their officials tell us the rest.

Scholars sympathetic to the welfare state nonetheless continue to be deeply suspicious about Progressive democracy, in large part because of its German roots. Anne Kornhauser, for example, repairs to the liberal theory of John Rawls to avoid perceived threats of teutonic authoritarianism in the American administrative state.[41] Such a theory, much like its more conservative cousins, privileges the classical individual rights of private property, contract, and conscience above and beyond the requirements of social welfare.[42] The normative theory I reconstruct rejects any such serial ordering of rights and welfare. The Progressive theory reveals how relatively egalitarian scholars such as Rawls and Kornhauser have conceded the premises of political discourse to a libertarian philosophy that treats individuals as prior to society and privileges their private interests above those of the political community as a whole. I follow the Hegelian Progressives in arguing, by contrast, that the value of individual rights can only be understood by reference to their role in securing collective self-government. As a consequence, the rights of the individual cannot claim any absolute priority over the rights of the democratic public. They give individuals a sphere of independence from public power just so that the public's law can rely on their autonomous judgments to underwrite—or to challenge and ultimately fortify—its legitimacy.

Constitutional values sometimes play a more constructive role in scholarly accounts of the administrative state. Jon D. Michaels, for instance, has argued that the state draws its legitimacy from an "administrative separation of powers," in which political appointees play the role of the elected executive, the civil service substitutes for the judiciary, and civil society groups act like the legislature.[43] This system "situates the modern administrative state squarely within the constitutional tradition of pitting rivalrous, diverse institutional counterweights against one another to protect liberty, promote pluralistic, democratic governance, and assure fidelity to the rule of law."[44] The main threat to this order is the privatization of governmental functions, which threatens to upset the balance between these institutional players within government. Michaels's constitutional theory is consonant with the Progressive state defended here to the extent that it recognizes the administrative process as a forum for democratic politics, separates the logic of the state from the logic of the market, and rejects the decades-long project to outsource governmental functions to private contractors.

Progressivism, however, shifts emphasis from Michaels's theory of constitutional fragmentation to shared norms and centers of political coordination that give shape to the people's understandings of freedom. It privileges the formation rational democratic power over the contest between antagonistic institutions. For example, Michaels's observation that the participation of civil society groups in policymaking can function like the legislative power within the administrative process makes sense as an institutional aspiration, but it does not describe the current reality. Participation by well-financed corporate and public-interest groups, and occasional mass submission of generic comments from individuals, do not amount to a robust form of administrative parliamentarism. We must make good on the Progressive project of broadening public participation with new fora and shift the discourse within those contexts from exclusionary technocracy to inclusive political argument. The primary goal should not be to balance various power centers within the agencies against one another, but rather to increase administrative capacity in tandem with the public's access to administrative proceedings.

This does not mean that Progressivism dismisses the constraining function of law or embraces unilateral assertions of executive authority. Adrian Vermeule, in contrast to the Progressives, thinks the logic of constitutionalism itself has appropriately led to an abandonment of liberal legalism.[45] He argues that "law has leashed itself under the throne of the administrative state; and it has done so because the best internal understanding of legal arguments . . . has indicated that it should."[46] In particular, he notes that Congress created the administrative state by statute, the president has implemented it, and the courts have defined its workings with appropriate understanding of the limits of the judiciary's institutional competence. These accurate observations do serve to discredit high-altitude accusations of the administrative state's unconstitutionality. But they conceal a deeper and troubling political theology.

Vermeule is an enthusiast for wide executive discretion, arguing that a degree of "irrationality" is often necessary in administrative decision-making.[47] He embraces Carl Schmitt's critique of liberalism, arguing that modern states must rely on a president and administrative apparatus largely unconstrained by law.[48] He does not take seriously enough the dangers of executive authority and bureaucratic domination that Tocqueville and Arendt diagnosed. And the experience of twentieth century Germany has shown us that those concerns are not the overwrought handwringing of aristocratic liberals. They are real threats, even for states that currently live under democratic constitutions. The Trump administration's assault on the rule of law has lately shown that these risks remain live in the United States, even if descent into totalitarianism here remains a remote possibility. By drawing distinctions between the German thinkers such as Hegel who inspired the American Progressives and those later theorists such as Schmitt who midwifed the birth of the "total state," I aim to identify those continental influences that are appealing—and safe—for us to retain.

Hegelian Progressivism makes no virtue of an imperial presidency and does not revel in a bureaucratic bacchanal of discretionary decisions. It instead articulates deep connections among rationality, freedom, and the administrative process. To be sure, the president plays an important role in this process, bringing to bear a powerful distillation of public opinion in overseeing administrative decision-making. And agency discretion is another important piece of the puzzle, as public officials must have the space to interpret the law by reference to the input they receive from their political supervisors and from affected individuals and groups. But neither executive leadership nor administrative autonomy is an unqualified good. They serve the aims of the public's law, which are outlined in statute and remain accountable to independent norms of transparency, inclusiveness, and equality. The people must identify legislative solutions to shared problems, and administrative agencies must refine these solutions with expert observation of their consequences and broad-based discussion of the relevant moral values. This a pragmatic but ethically sensitive and inclusive form of governance, which aims to make good on the Constitution's promise of government by the people.

The viability of this Progressive policymaking project has been sharply put into question by Karen Orren and Stephen Skowronek, two of the leading scholars of American political development. They argue that Americans inhabit a "policy state" that exists in friction with a constitutional structure that disables coherent policy development and implementation.[49] The policy state's motive is to implement various goals authoritatively established (usually by statute) and accompanied by (usually administrative) guidelines that facilitate their accomplishment.[50] This description at least partially captures the Progressive state this book endorses. But the problem Orren and Skowronek identify is that "although the policy state opens government to a wider range of options, it also makes it less likely that government can be tied down to any one of them."[51] Particularly in our presidential constitutional system, where the executive has independent electoral and institutional authority from the legislature, and the courts hold the right not only to interpret but to invalidate statutes, the instrumental logic of policymaking conflicts with insoluble power struggles among the branches. As the policy motive erodes authority relations both within and without the government, governance becomes deeply disoriented, incoherent, and unsuccessful. Rational deliberation is pushed aside in favor of open conflict, heated rhetoric, and pitched regulatory battles. In response, some wish for an impossible return to classical constitutionalism. Others hope to profit from the inevitable collapse.

There is force to much of this diagnosis, and no one should doubt the obstacles Progressive democracy now faces. But despite their strong implication that the unspooling of democratic constitutionalism is ineluctable, Orren and Skowronek acknowledge that some "systematic approaches that recognize there are no magic bullets" might give us a way out.[52] Progressive democracy is that systemic remedy. It has channeled constitutional crisis into democratic consolidation twice before, in the New Deal and in the Second Reconstruction. In both cases, authority relations shifted, with the enactment of statutory rights and the creation of administrative institutions that uprooted social hierarchies. Political and administrative entrepreneurs in these periods made use of constitutional values—*as policy arguments* rather than as a set of stable rights and structures—to make good on the charter's promises of popular government, freedom, equality, and promotion of the general welfare.

But both of these constitutional moments also saw shortfalls in the democratic shape of policymaking—failures of institutional design and official comity that either excluded affected persons from participation, gave insufficient bureaucratic support and guidance, or did not acknowledge the moral character of administrative judgments. The next groundswell of Progressive energies can better entrench democratic norms in society and government if we are aware of the successes and failures of the past, the broad understandings of freedom that motivated them, and the reactionary retrenchment that usually comes in their wake. This study contributes to that historical, institutional, and ideological awareness. Progressivism does not expect or insist on a final, incorruptible allocation of authority. That is not achievable or desirable. It insists only on the improvement of the conditions for democracy. Such practical successes remain possible.

I am not alone in arguing that Progressive ideals and institutions are ripe for revival. At the close of the twentieth century, Richard Rorty drew on Hegelian motifs in the thought of John Dewey and Walt Whitman to argue for a pragmatist vision of American political progress, in which we "use democratic institutions and procedures to conciliate the various needs, and thereby widen the range of consensus about how things are."[53] However, apart from some suggestive remarks about "a constant need for new laws and bureaucratic initiatives," Rorty did not give an institutional account of what this Progressive democracy would look like.[54]

William N. Novak has likewise turned to Dewey's political thought to argue for a "democratic understanding of the nature and extent (for good or ill) of modern state power."[55] For Novak, however, German theory is a nonstarter for understanding American democracy. Weber and Hegel blend together in his account with their aristocratic, continental conceptualization of the state as a bureaucratic institution that is strictly separated from society. I will show that Hegel's thought had a more constructive influence on Dewey and the Progressives' democratic theory of the state. It enabled them to conceptualize the state as an ongoing relationship between government and society, rather than the government alone. This dynamic conception of the state helped them to envision a participatory administrative process in which officials and citizens would engage one another in practical reasoning about the requirements of freedom. The Progressives did indeed depart from Hegel in their commitment to democratic values. But they developed their normative conception of the state in reliance upon, and not merely in opposition to, the Hegelian model they had studied.

K. Sabeel Rahman has turned to some of the same Progressive theorists I examine to argue for a participatory form of market regulation that would counter social and economic "domination."[56] Like my study, Rahman's draws on the work of Dewey, as well as Louis Brandeis's, to articulate a vision of administrative politics that improves public understanding and equalizes social power through collective forms of policymaking. Like me, and the Hegelian Progressive Mary Follett, he is keen to emphasize that the administrative process must be sensitive to inequalities of power among social actors. It has "to include a more representative range of decision-makers, and to catalyze more active civic engagement."[57] We therefore must conceive "the regulatory state as *a site of democratic action*."[58]

Our agreement runs deep. And yet, the Hegelian Progressive account emphasizes the importance of *reason* and *deliberation* much more strongly than does Rahman's.[59] Rahman rightly notes that deliberative democracy sometimes focuses on exhaustive rational justification at the expense of equitable participation and transformative social intervention. I agree that a noisy and fractious process of public participation in administrative policymaking is often essential to popular empowerment. But if that process merely ends in a decision—say, to exclude certain classes of financial products from the market or to cap payday loan interest rates—without a written account of how that decision was reached or what makes it appropriate, such a regulatory intervention is likely to be quite ephemeral. Public memory of why such controls were needed and what kinds of values those controls expressed will, as Tocqueville put it, be "wafted away . . . by the smallest breeze." Hegelian Progressivism demands a historical-evolutionary development where we take into account what past publics have decided and reason self-consciously about whether we want to continue along that path or depart from it. That way, the administrative process will give ourselves and our posterity an understanding of who we are as a people and who we want to become, which will endure after periods of intense social mobilization have been exhausted.

This view necessarily gives a more central role to public officials in reviewing citizens' contributions to the regulatory process and attempting to give a best account of what citizens wanted and valued. Progressivism depends on an official culture that infuses public law with public needs and that adopts an egalitarian ethos in the exercise of discretion. Such a culture of reason-giving may in some cases slow down the pace of change. And the risk always remains that officials will misrecognize the claims of participants. But the ethically sensitive justification of policy nonetheless provides a record of public reasoning that renders officials' handiwork legible, open to critique, and resistant to arbitrary rescission. A democratic order requires such an authoritative, written discourse if it is to extend in time and work lasting changes in the lives of the people who constitute it.

IV. PLAN OF THE BOOK

This book begins with intellectual history, turns to institutional history, and then proceeds to normative reconstruction. Chapter 1 critiques German thinking about the administrative state that began with Hegel, blossomed in the public law scholarship of the nineteenth century, and eventually collapsed during the Weimar Republic. I show how Hegel inaugurated an essential line of inquiry into administration by linking public bureaucracy with the fundamental norm of individual freedom. Hegel argued that the state must not only protect the "abstract" liberal rights of property and contract but must provide comprehensive "police" services that afford individuals with basic goods and reduce the inequalities and antagonisms created by capitalist systems of economic production. I then show how this theory influenced major administrative law scholars of the nineteenth century: Robert von Mohl, Lorenz von Stein, and Rudolf von Gneist.

These Hegelian jurists developed a robust defense of administrative intervention in the name of individual self-determination. However, given the failure of the revolution of 1848, they did not consider how bureaucratic institutions could be guided by democratic will rather than by the authority of the monarch and his expert advisors. This antidemocratic thrust had disastrous consequences with the fall of the German Empire and the founding of the Weimar Republic. Public law scholars remained committed to an officialdom hermetically sealed from society and insensitive to democratic input. The social and political theory of Weber, which dominates today's legal and political thinking about bureaucracy, did not reflect a sociologically pure "ideal-type" of the modern state but rather this historically particularistic amalgam of liberal-democratic constitutionalism and strictly hierarchical administrative structure. The authoritarian constitutional theory of Carl Schmitt and the National Socialist administrative theory of Ernst Forsthoff that followed point to the extraordinary dangers of cabining administrative structure from public participation and identifying the legitimacy of the state with the decisive will of the chief executive. Though democratic ideals have re-emerged in Germany with renewed vigor from the ruins of the Nazi regime, German public law and theory remain committed to Weber's sharp distinctions between legislative democratic will-formation and instrumental bureaucratic performance.

Chapter 2 argues that the American Progressives painted a sharp contrast to this German development by appropriating but democratizing Hegelian state theory. W.E.B. Du Bois, Woodrow Wilson, John Dewey, Frank Goodnow, and Mary Follett were all directly influenced by Hegelian concepts of the state. But they saw administration as a democratic institution, in two interconnected respects. First of all, they argued that efficient administration was required to realize public purposes, such as social welfare provision and the regulation of monopolistic industries. Democratic control of society required giving authority to professionals who could grasp and manage complex problems through administrative, rather than judicial, techniques of conflict resolution. At the same time however, the Progressives stressed that administration required the participation of affected persons to function effectively. In the absence of such public consultation, administrators would not properly understand the tasks they confronted and would lose the confidence of the community. Some of the early administrative procedures at agencies such as the Federal Trade Commission and the Forest Service reflected this participatory vision.

Progressives thus sought to realize democratic goals through a democratic administrative process. But this deep commitment to collective action ran the risk that democratic processes might thwart the democratic purposes they were meant to achieve. This conflict between public ends and public means came into sharp focus over the question of racial civil rights, on which Du Bois and Wilson stood on opposite sides. Du Bois argued that bureaucratic authority was necessary to secure the conditions for inclusive, democratic self-government. Where some persons had been denied equality on the basis of race, government had to step in to enhance their social and political status so as to create the conditions for democratic politics in the future.

Wilson, by contrast, stressed the need to make administration sensitive to public sentiment and local control. In the context of his sympathies for the former Confederacy and his hostility to Reconstruction, the pernicious potentials of such accountability become clear. Where racist attitudes pervade a white majority, sensitivity to the current opinions of that majority is likely to undermine equality and institute a racialized conception of the political community. Wilson followed through on this white supremacist notion of American democracy by segregrating the civil service. I do not attempt to sweep Wilson's racism under the rug. Rather, I argue that a contemporary Progressivism must reject it, and instead embrace Du Bois's view that the state must delineate and protect the rights of subordinated groups against majority oppression. I nonetheless retain Wilson's view that the administrative process must be sensitive to public opinion for such an emancipatory state to have staying power. The people must participate in the administration of civil rights to be convinced of their legitimacy. We must abandon Wilson's racially exclusionary notion of the political community, and instead conceive of the democratic public as an association constituted by inclusive, rational discourse about the contents of our freedom and the entailments of our equality.

This demand took institutional shape in the New Deal and the Second Reconstruction, which furnished examples of the forms of administration the Progressives advocated. I consider these examples in chapter 3. This historical exploration elucidates the tension between the Progressive commitment to deliberative forms of administration, on the one hand, and the efficient maintenance of a democratic public, on the other. I first show how administrative agencies in the New Deal, under the direct influence of Dewey, created participatory forms of administration and sought to provide the material requisites for democratic citizenship. While participatory forms of administration successfully realized some of the deliberative ideals of Progressivism, they tended to exclude impoverished and minority groups from decision-making processes. Those programs that materially benefited these subordinated groups, by contrast, were not deliberative in structure and often acted paternalistically. The history of the New Deal thus shows the pitfalls of failing to provide for truly inclusive deliberation in the administrative process.

I then show how administrative agencies during the Second Reconstruction sought to combine deliberation and efficient social provision in new ways. The agencies that administered the Civil Rights Act of 1964 contributed ethical arguments to political and legal discourse over the meaning of the nation's commitment to equality. And the Office of Economic Opportunity sought to incorporate marginalized communities into the administration of the War on Poverty. These examples of democratic administration show that agencies are capable of contributing to value-based deliberation over the content of public policy. But they caution that deliberative administration must remain sensitive to issues of programmatic efficiency. The history of the Second Reconstruction also shows that Progressive democracy requires the judicial branch to recognize the ethical reasoning of administrative agencies, rather than mischaracterize official judgment as an exercise in technocracy.

In chapter 4, I build on the intellectual and institutional history developed in the previous chapters to reconstruct a normative theory of Progressive democracy. The usual accounts of administrative legitimacy—arguments from efficiency, constitutional norms, and republican theory—do not give fully satisfying accounts. In particular, each of these arguments reveals a troubling disconnect between the purposes they ascribe to regulatory institutions and the political structures in which those purposes would be operationalized. Some constitutional arguments, for example, hinge administrative legitimacy on the laws enacted by Congress and Congress's oversight of administration. And yet the fractured structure of the Constitution ensures that Congress's control over administrative agencies will be attenuated at best, with crosscutting authority emanating from the courts and the president.

The Progressive account of legitimacy differs from such arguments because it draws an intrinsic link between the purpose and structure of administration. The purpose of the Progressive state is to guarantee individual and collective freedom. These forms of freedom can only be achieved if the people engage in a deliberative process that generates, refines, and institutes shared norms. The structure of the state must therefore facilitate this process by channeling deliberation through the legislature, judiciary, executive, and the administrative agencies they jointly supervise.

We currently have a thin form of such a process in the Administrative Procedure Act's "notice-and-comment" rulemaking provisions.[60] But this procedure does not go nearly far enough in the extent of participation it affords, in its sensitivity to problems of unequal power, or in surfacing moral rather than merely technical questions in regulatory decision-making. The administrative process must be reworked to redress inequalities of information and power in civil society, giving voice, consideration, and institutional support for underresourced interests. It should not be dominated by the arbitrary will of the president, nor limited by judicial or official ideology to economistic reasoning. Administrative agencies must become sites to rationalize political conflict into an inclusive account of our shared obligations, and to institute these obligations in our social life.

This form of Progressive democracy is demanding. It would require significant alterations in our current institutional structure and political self-consciousness. But these changes are not impossible. The intellectual and institutional history I document show that Progressive threads lace through the patterns of our political order, even if those strands have been frayed by technocracy, market logic, and the strong winds of political reaction. We can weave these threads into a new, robust, and vibrant institutional fabric if we make our law truly public—a law that arises from and constitutes our commitments as a free and equal people.

My account is therefore addressed to several audiences within the democratic public: to the professors of administrative law and public administration who will educate the next generation of government officials in the procedures of policymaking; to the officials who enact, interpret, and implement public laws; to the critical theorists who identify social pathologies and openings for radical reform; to the political and legal philosophers who develop norms for collective action; to the social scientists who can help us to build institutions based on a practical understanding of their functioning; and to the citizens who ultimately must decide what laws and policies we need to become free.

1

Origins of Progressivism

German Theories of the State from Hegel to Habermas

I. INTRODUCTION

American political science and legal scholarship has been deeply influenced by German theories of the state. These theories inform the way Americans understand the structure and purpose of constitutional government, the role of the civil service, and the concentration of policymaking power in the executive branch. Much of this literature proceeds from Max Weber's conceptions of bureaucracy and legal-rational authority.[1] This Weberian view stresses that bureaucracy is and ought to be a technically superior, efficient, and value-neutral means for implementing statutory requirements. A related strand of research focuses on the American reception of the German idea of the *Rechtsstaat*—a constitutional state bound by the rule of law, which would grant binding authority to bureaucrats but constrain their discretion through statutory and judicial control.[2] A handful of other scholars locate the source of relevant German ideas not in Weber but in Hegel, who shared much of Weber's analysis of administrative power but emphasized the ethical function of the state above its monopoly over the instruments of violence.[3]

The specter of the *Staat* therefore looms large over the landscape of American public legal theory. For some, it provides an analytically useful framework for understanding what the modern state is and how it ought to function. Others believe the influence of German state theory has corrupted American political development with unconstitutional institutions and ideals. But the meaning of this continental conception of "the state" remains so obscure and variously conceived that such descriptive, normative, and critical accounts rest on tenuous foundations. This chapter will clear the way for a more accurate assessment of the links between German and American state theory, offering a

The Public's Law. Blake Emerson.

critical analysis of the evolution of German public legal theory from Hegel to Habermas. I will distinguish different phases in the theoretical and institutional development of the German state, so that the relevance of these configurations to the American context becomes definite.

I show that Hegel set out a compelling vision of the state as an institution that embodied and instituted the requirements for individual freedom. For Hegel, the administrative state had an emancipatory function in relation to the society it regulated. The state set out to uproot feudal privilege, to institute rights of property and contract, to provide for the public welfare through police functions, to mitigate antagonisms between social groups, and to provide a general normative framework in which people could understand and act in their environment. The civil servants who carried out these functions had an ethical vocation, as they attempted to implement the universal interest in individual freedom. In articulating this vision, Hegel outlined institutional dynamics that continued to unfold in later German public law scholarship and the reception of that scholarship in American Progressivism: the regulation of civil society by the state, the supplementation of private law with public law, and the interpretation and application of legislation by executive authorities as well as the judiciary. These aspects of Hegel's thought were indeed carried over into American Progressivism, where they provided crucial elements for the Progressives' novel, democratic theory of the administrative state. In this chapter, I will occasionally note the links between Hegelian thought and the Progressive theory that will be examined in greater depth in chapter 2 and the remainder of the book.

The democratic elements introduced by the American Progressives were totally foreign to Hegel and the German public law scholars who followed in his steps. Hegel's critique of popular sovereignty yielded a fractured constitutional architecture: administrative power was organized under the monarchical executive and was constrained by the legislature, which represented the interests of bourgeois civil society. Because of this unresolved bifurcation of social and sovereign interests within the state, Hegel's idea that administration was an ethical practice with freedom at its heart gave way to an alignment of bureaucracy with the conservative social paternalism of the executive, as against the economic liberalism of the legislative branch. When Germany suddenly adopted democratic constitutional arrangements in the Weimar Republic, administration nonetheless remained insulated from society, reactionary in its orientation, and subject to democratic control primarily through the decisive will of executive leadership. Germany's failure to develop a non-authoritarian form of administration was reflected in scholarship, such as Weber's, which treated democracy either as a matter of legislative control or of executive decision. Weber viewed bureaucracy as an alienated power that was as pernicious as it was necessary.

The collapse of the Weimar Republic and its descent into National Socialism suggest that there are great dangers in an administrative state that hinges its legitimacy upon charismatic executives and the technocratic competence of the bureaucracy. The recent turn to Carl Schmitt's critique of liberalism and the embrace of a strongly unitary executive in American administrative law scholarship is thus deeply troubling when seen in the context of German theory and history.[4] The dangerous German idea is not, as some commentators have suggested, the idea of an administrative *Rechtsstaat*, which the American Progressives indeed adopted from Hegelian legal theory.[5] Rather, the danger arises from the *loss* of the Hegelian theory's orientation toward individual freedom, the sundering of the connection between legal rationality and the exercise of bureaucratic power, and the rise of a plebiscitary form of administrative legitimacy. German legal theory therefore reveals both promising models and vivid warnings concerning crosscurrents in contemporary American administrative law and our broader understanding of the American state.

II. ADMINISTRATION IN HEGEL'S PHILOSOPHY OF LAW

Hegel is a suitable starting point for understanding the tradition of German state theory both because of his influence within this tradition and the more universal purchase of his philosophic insights.[6] Hegel understands the modern state as an ethical community committed to the norm of individual freedom. This norm required that the government underwrite but regulate a market economy. Regulation's purpose was to protect the common interest in fair and transparent markets, as well as to mitigate antagonism between social groups, provide basic services, and ameliorate poverty. These requirements were to be articulated in a constitutional structure that prioritized statutory authority and administrative discretion.

Hegel's *Philosophy of Right* sets out the basic value commitments of modern law and politics. In the Introduction, he states: "the will is free . . . and the system of right is the realm of actualized freedom."[7] Hegel understands freedom as self-determination, the process of the human will "giving itself content."[8] By saying "right" is based upon freedom in this sense, he means that law and other obligatory social relations facilitate the rational activity of individual subjects.[9] "The system of right is the realm of actualized freedom" because the modern legal order provides a social context in which freedom is not merely a mental hope or an individual striving but a way of life that is secured by stable rules and practices. Thus, whereas in Hegel's *Phenomenology of Spirit* the life-and-death struggle between master and slave fails to produce true freedom for either, in the modern state a framework of generally applicable laws enables such forms of full reciprocity.[10] Laws facilitate subjective freedom because they provide a shared background through which individuals can determine the content of their action by reasoning about it and justifying it to one another.

The starting point for this legal order is the classical liberal position of "abstract right," including most prominently the rights of property and contract. Hegel ascribes foundational importance to these rights because they enable each person to recognize every other as formally equal rational agents.[11] He describes the civil law as a statutorily codified system, in which the principles of private right become empirically actual and enforceable through the judiciary: "What is right *in itself* is *posited* in its objective existence, that is, it is determined through thought for consciousness and *known* as what is right and what is in force as right—it is *statute*; and right through this determination is *positive* right in general."[12] Positive law brings the principles of abstract right into public consciousness by making them known and enforceable. With shared universal legal norms to guide their reasoning, individuals recognize one another as participants in a joint social practice. As a consequence, individuals are able to reason about their actions and thus take ownership of their conduct in a way they could not otherwise. They are able to see one another as formally free and equal beings who are worthy of respect. As we shall see in chapter 2, W.E.B. Du Bois would later draw on this connection between mutual recognition and law in his account of the emancipatory efforts of the Freedmen's Bureau after the American Civil War.

Liberal rights and their codification in private law form the normative background for the social sphere of civil society (*bürgerliche Gesellschaft*) in which individuals are able to satisfy one another's wants through the "system of needs" of the market place.[13] Though civil society partially realizes the requirements of individual freedom, it also undermines it. Civil society and its law produce vast inequalities that prevent some individuals from attaining the prerequisites for self-determination. The liberal economy creates social divisions that make it impossible for individuals to recognize each other as a free and equal subjects. "When the activity of civil society is unrestricted . . . the specialization and limitation of work also increase, as do likewise the dependence and want of the class which is tied to such work; this in turn leads to the inability to feel and enjoy the wider freedoms, and particularly the spiritual advantages, of civil society."[14]

Economic development at the same time creates social linkages that make collective social consciousness possible. The rise of professional associations, unions, and other corporate bodies allows individuals to relate their own isolated actions and interests to those of similarly situated persons and to act with them to achieve shared purposes.[15] Civil society is therefore not merely a realm of contractual exchange and economic antagonism. It is also the space in which individuals form bonds of solidarity on the basis of their common interests.[16] John Dewey would draw on this Hegelian account of civil society to understand how the democratic "public" emerged from the externalities of market exchange.

But Hegel argues that without some overarching perspective from which to assess the validity of social relations, this social interconnectedness is bound to devolve into antagonism between opposed interests rather than coalesce into cooperative endeavor. The state provides the needed structural and normative unity. "The state is the actuality of concrete freedom," which is "both the law which permeates all relations within it and also the customs and consciousness of the individuals who belong to it."[17] It frames common social life with political bodies that set out the laws and provide social services. The state furnishes political unity through its constitution, which provides for a separation of powers: the legislative branch determines the statutory laws, the executive officialdom implements them, and the sovereign monarch represents the state's unitary will and ultimate decisions.[18]

Hegel describes the political constitution of the state as "organic," in the sense that the legislative, executive, and sovereign powers within the government are not totally separate, but rather interdependent elements of a system: "when we are dealing with the *constitution*, we are concerned solely with objective guarantees or institutions, i.e., with organically linked and mutually conditioning moments."[19] This understanding of the political organism is rooted in Hegel's concept of institutional rationality. The political institutions of the state are linked intrinsically because the value of each is based on the common principle of the free will, and the function of each can only be carried out in conjunction with the others. Woodrow Wilson and Frank Goodnow would adapt this Hegelian understanding of political organism to the American context, arguing that the American constitutional structure allowed a unified political purpose to form.

Hegel's understanding of organicism goes further, however, in construing the state itself as a meta-subject—a personality in which the free will of the individual finds ultimate expression. This second, stronger conception of political organicism leads Hegel into the dubious argument that the state requires a sovereign monarch who represents the unified personality of the state.[20] Hegel argues that because the principle of the free will is the foundation of the state, the state itself must be embodied in a natural free will. This personal conception of the state conflicts with the idea of popular sovereignty: "popular sovereignty is one of those confused thoughts which are based on a *garbled* notion of the people. *Without* its monarch and that *articulation* of the whole which is necessarily and immediately associated with monarchy, *the* people is a formless mass."[21]

Hegel's skepticism of popular sovereignty aligns with his critique of public opinion, which he says "deserves to be *respected* as well as *despised*."[22] For Hegel, public opinions that arise from experience within civil society are accidental forms of knowledge, as likely to lead to error as to truth. He thus assigns to the legislature the role of "permitting *public opinion* to arrive for the first time at *true thoughts* and *insight*" through representatives' rational deliberation.[23] The purpose of political representation is not to give voice to public opinion, but to educate the people about their common interests. Legislative debate and the framing of laws lead to generally valid norms in a way that mere private experience and discussion supposedly cannot.

Hegel gives no indication that state officials might be educated by the views of the public. Deliberative cultivation is a one-way street from the chambers of the legislature to private persons. There is no acknowledgment that the public domain might be constituted in interaction between citizens and officials of the state, nor that popular sovereignty might consist in the coherent, institutional articulation of that process. The subjective opinions of one person alone carry constitutional weight—those of the monarch.[24] It is in this respect that American Progressives such as Dewey, Follett, and Wilson would differ from Hegel most radically. They insisted instead upon a reciprocal, rather than hierarchical, relationship between the exercise of state power and the content of public opinion.

Hegel nonetheless minimizes the significance of arbitrary monarchical decisions within the constitutional state and instead emphasizes the centrality of the legislative power. He therefore assigns to the legislature the task of framing "the laws as such," and addressing "those internal concerns of the state whose content is wholly universal."[25] Though the monarch retains a formal power to approve legislation and the power to appoint and dismiss executive ministers, Hegel stresses that, in a "fully organized" constitutional state, the monarch is only

> the highest instance of formal decision, and all that is required in a monarch is someone to say "yes" and to dot the "I"; for the supreme office should be such that the particular character of its occupant is of no significance. . . . In a well-ordered monarchy, the objective aspect is solely the concern of the law, to which the monarch merely has to add his subjective "I will."[26]

The monarch's significance is thus primarily symbolic, whereas the substance of state rationality lies in the legislature and the civil servants who constitute the executive.

While the legislature frames the laws and the monarch symbolizes the unity and agency of the state, the executive power "subsumes" particular cases under the legislative universal.[27] Hegel therefore subordinates executive power to legislative power, as the statutory rule governs the treatment of any particular case that falls under it. But he diagnoses an essential ambiguity regarding the distinction between legislation and administration:

> It is possible to distinguish in general terms between what is the object of universal legislation and what should be left to the direction of administrative bodies or to any kind of government regulation, in that the former includes only what is universal in content—i.e. legal determinations—whereas the latter includes the particular ways and means by which the measures are *implemented*. The distinction is not entirely determinate, however, if only because a law, in order to be a law, must be more than just commandment in general . . ., i.e. it must be *determinate* in itself; but the more determinate it is, the more nearly capable its content will be of being implemented as it stands. At the same time, however, so far reaching a determination as this would give laws an empirical aspect which would necessarily be subject to alteration when they were actually implemented, and this would detract from their character as general laws.[28]

Legislation, in other words, must have some determinacy in order to retain its status as a norm that guides state action. But it must leave sufficient room for administrative adaptation in order to retain its generality and uniformity over time and across various realms of application.

This account of legislation and administrative implementation raises a crucial question with far-reaching consequences for both German and American legal thought: to what extent is the action of the executive predetermined by legal norms, and to what extent are executive officers free to interpret the meaning of statutory commitments? Upon the answer to this question depends the balance between legislation and execution in controlling the administrative functions of the state. Though Hegel stresses that the executive and its ministries must be subordinate to the legislature, he is unable to specify more precisely how much legal content should be determined by statute and how much should be left to administrative judgment. The matter is further complicated by the fact that Hegel positions the hereditary monarch at the apex of the executive power.[29] If the monarch holds the sovereign power and this power is aligned with the executive branch, then the subservience of this branch to the commands of the legislature is, at best, highly insecure.

The relationship between the legislature and executive, and their interaction with civil society, become clearer when Hegel turns to the administrative content of the executive branch. Hegel uses the terms "police" (*Polizei*) and "public authority" (*öffentliche Macht*) rather than "administration" (*Verwaltung*) to describe the portion of the executive that implements statutes and executive ordinances providing for security, utilities, and social welfare services.[30] What distinguishes administration from the judicial system, which Hegel also groups under the executive heading, is that courts decide cases of conflict between individual parties in accordance with legal rules. By contrast, the "police" function of the executive, which we would label administrative, is to resolve social conflict through more general regulations. The administration has the purpose of "upholding legality and the universal interests of the state" within the particular rights of the corporate bodies and "bringing these rights back into the universal."[31] It arbitrates "the conflict between private interests and particular concerns of the community, and between both of these together and the higher viewpoints and ordinances of the state."[32] The inequalities and antagonisms of civil society are therefore to be redressed through legally authorized administrative action, such as provision for food, health, education, and security, as well as market regulation.

Hegel's understanding of administration incorporates a strong notion of "the public," not only as the target of regulation, but as an entity entitled to the state's protection against the inequalities and injustices of civil society. Hegel thus defends economic regulation, not as a utilitarian measure to maximize wealth and efficiency, but rather as a *right*, held by the public, to transparent and thus freedom-preserving contractual relations. He ascribes to the administration a "right to regulate" the market when goods "are offered not so much to a particular individual as such, as to the individual in a universal sense, i.e. to the public."[33] The administration's right to regulate flows from the "public's right" to fair commercial relations as a "common concern."[34] Hegel here suggests that there is an intrinsic connection between administrative regulation and the public sphere. The public holds the right to control market exchanges that go beyond intimate, private transaction and come to have broader effects and meanings for the community as a whole. This entitlement in turn grounds the state's authority to regulate such relations through law.

Regulation thus serves to address complex forms of economic organization that cannot be properly understood by private persons: "The main reason why some universal provision and direction are necessary is that large branches of industry are dependent upon external circumstances and remote combinations whose full implications cannot be grasped by the individuals who are tied to these spheres by occupation."[35] When individuals are subjected to powerful and antagonistic social forces that cannot be understood, engaged, or countered by means of property and contract, their self-determination requires a public authority that implements their shared interests and redresses their collective harms.

Hegel's critique of public opinion is therefore not to be confused with a more profound rejection of the concept of the public in general. He understands the public as a realm of common concern, which can only be adequately defended through the use of public law and administrative management as opposed to private law and judicial adjudication. The public arises from the externalities of market relations and the inadequacy of the form of freedom embodied in classical liberal rights. The economic and ethical costs of market externalities can be critiqued according to the concept of right, which identifies the impediments civil society poses to individuals' rational agency. The remedies for such impediments to individual freedom must then be institutionalized in statutory norms, which are interpreted and realized by the administrative arm of the state. We will see a similar, but democratized, understanding of publicity in Dewey's notion of "the public and its problems" and Mary Follett's understanding of "creative administration." For now, the essential feature of Hegel's view to keep in mind is that public interests are not, and cannot be, adequately known by private individuals themselves, but can only be grasped by state officials who transcend market actors' limited perceptions of the problems. Without a state, the dimensions of the public sphere and the rights of the public cannot be known.

Hegel describes the corps of public officials that administers public rights as a "universal estate," which has the "universal interests of society as its business."[36] The bureaucracy is universal, first, in the sense that it applies the general laws passed by the legislature. Second, it is universal because it attempts to identify general interests that are shared by competing groups in order to make justified regulatory determinations. In this way, the officialdom seeks to overcome conflicts between narrow social interests through norms that all might endorse. Third, dealing with matters of common concern has the effect of educating public officials to think from the perspective of the community as a whole rather than from the self-interested perspective of market actors. As Hegel put it in his essay on the Estates Assembly of Württemberg:

> The sense of the state is acquired above all in habitual occupation with universal concerns, which gives occasion not only to discover and acknowledge the infinite worth which the universal has in itself, but also to experience the intransigence, hostility, and disingenuousness of private interest and to struggle with its obstinacy in cases where it is posited in the form of right.[37]

Administration thus does not merely reduce conflict between opposing interests but also struggles against particular interests that falsely clothe themselves in an absolute right. This struggle requires an intellectual habit of solving problems based on a comprehensive view of the public interest.

The fourth and strongest sense in which Hegel ascribes universality to the bureaucracy is its institutional orientation toward "public freedom," "the self-determining universality of the will."[38] The bureaucracy specifies and enforces the general norms that individuals need in order to think and act rationally. Insofar as such administration makes the concept of freedom actual in the social field, "the universal is the end of its essential activity."[39] Administrative officials therefore require "direct *education in ethics and in thought*, for this provides a spiritual counterweight to the mechanical exercise and the like which are inherent in learning the so-called sciences appropriate to these [administrative] spheres."[40] The ability to fashion rules to decide conflicts between opposed interests within civil society requires a form of practical reason that can effectively grapple with the values at stake. Civil servants must consider the meaning of the law with reference to its application and effect. The content of legal norms evolves as the social situation shifts, just as the social order evolves in response to the rules that govern it.[41]

Administration is in this sense the contact point between the normative unity of the constitutional order and the empirical diversity of the social realm to which it applies. The question of the relationship between legislation and administration thus ties into the further question of the relationship between state and society. The purpose of Hegel's state is at once to preserve civil society and to transcend it by bringing citizens alienated from one another as economic actors into a common political life. Through the state, the principles of classical liberalism are in one sense realized and in another sense transformed. They are realized insofar as the state remains bound and committed to the recognition, codification, and protection of the rights of property, contract, and individual conscience. Classical liberalism is transformed through the state, however, to the extent that the administration complements these liberal rights with public rights or, more radically, limits the scope of liberal rights relative to those of the public. The ideal is to preserve, but rationalize, the tension between private and public rights in a coherent political order. In the state, "the contradiction between rights as abstract freedom and the fulfilled particular content of welfare is negated but preserved [*sei aufgehoben*]."[42] The ambiguity of this speculative claim sets out the terms for the conflictual but interdependent relationship between civil society and state and between law and its administration.

In chapter 2, I will describe how the American Progressives embraced Hegel's understanding of the administrative state as a guarantor of freedom. The Progressives would turn away from Hegel, however, in contemplating an active role for public opinion in the administrative process and emphasizing that the modern state must be democratically legitimate. Hegel's vision of constitutional monarchy, by contrast, reflected a non-democratic constitutional order, in which liberalizing bureaucrats would attempt to emancipate civil society within an authoritarian political structure. German thought and practice would remain bound to this tension between social and political freedom until the sudden and ultimately cataclysmic introduction of democracy in the Weimar Republic.

III. HEGEL AND GERMAN ADMINISTRATIVE HISTORY

While Hegel's *Philosophy of Right* provides general conceptual tools for thinking through the administrative state—the centrality of individual freedom, the relationship between state and society, and the distinction between legislative universality and administrative particularity—his work also engages with a particular moment in German political history. Exploring this context illuminates the thrust of Hegel's project and the institutional constraints it confronted. As Gertrude Lübbe-Wolf has shown, Hegel's work can be understood as his proposed "constitutional plan" in the early nineteenth-century Prussian constitutional struggle.[43] Hegel offered a proposal for national representation, in which the various estates of the Prussian social order would be represented in a bicameral legislature.

Hegel's proposal remains of little direct relevance today given the decisive turn toward modern representative democracy. But his attempt to develop a form of representation that would move Prussia toward a constitutional state underscores the central importance he placed upon legislation. Hegel sought a form of representation through which legislation could truly reflect the universal interests of society and thus work against the dominance of particular interests that impeded the exercise of individual freedom. At the same time, however, he remained committed to a monarchical executive, which would underwrite the symbolic authority of the head of state with the political judgments of the highest public officials. And he remained skeptical that public opinion ought to guide either legislation or administration.

Hegel's historical context underscores that he understood bureaucracy to have an emancipatory function. His account of the universal class was an idealization of the efforts of the Prussian civil service to thwart feudal authority, assert liberal private law, and provide for social welfare in the years following the establishment of the Prussian General Code.[44] Hegel incorporated into his political thought the thrust of the reforms of Prussian statesmen Baron Karl vom Stein and Karl August von Hardenberg, who sought to rationalize the legal order, increase central state control, and reform local arms of government.[45] The goal of this administrative reform was not to eliminate local corporate governance but rather to integrate municipalities into the state structure, so that they would mediate between the universal interests of the community as a whole and the particular interests of individuals.[46] Hegel's idea of the bureaucratic universal class—an "estate of generalizers"—thus embraced the reformers' project of comprehending and rationalizing German civil society and incorporating without eliminating the insular, autonomous political orders of local government.[47] Such an increase in centralized bureaucratic power, which originally grew out of the fiscal-military needs of the state, fostered a certain unified, egalitarian national consciousness amongst members of the German states.[48] Administrative reform thus went hand in hand with the forging of a modern, national liberal order.

This socially transformative orientation was, however, fragile because it remained ensconced within an authoritarian, unresponsive, and undemocratic political structure. The *Philosophy of Right* expressed the spiritual and constitutional dilemmas of Prussian bureaucratic reformers who attempted to liberalize Prussian society. Hegel's idea of the administration as a "universal class" having "the universal interests of society as its business" sketched, in Reinhart Koselleck's analysis, "not merely the idea that the Prussian officials had of themselves, but of the actual situation itself."[49] In the absence of a fully developed constitutional state and in the face of a judiciary that only halfheartedly implemented the egalitarian clauses of the General Code, the bureaucratic reformers took on this socially transformative task themselves: "protected by internal state law, the administration won a monopoly to create, guarantee, and enforce general statutes: city ordinances, commercial regulations, agrarian reform, and taxation were all in the department of the central administration. . . . The unity-building power went over from the General Code and the judiciary to the administration."[50]

The concentration of reform energies on the bureaucracy created a tension between the administrative means of liberal reform and the constitutional structure in which the administration operated.[51] The bourgeois political class was increasingly suspicious of administrative reform, as they, like the land barons the administration sought to undermine, developed vested interests in their property rights: "in order to implement urgent general laws—such as the corporation law, the railway law or the law for the protection of works—the ministries avoided prescribed procedural forms—for all laws concerned personal and property rights—and hid behind the sovereign claim of the monarch. If the bureaucracy wanted to be effective, it bred the suspicion of illegality."[52] Thus, at the same time that the reformist bureaucrats unleashed a liberal society, they created bourgeois-revolutionary energies hostile to their monarchically legitimated power. Bourgeois bureaucrats were placed in the paradoxical situation of relying upon the power of the monarchical state to advance their agenda at the same time as they were forced to acknowledge the failure of this state to recognize liberal constitutional norms.[53] According to Koselleck, this development was one source of the revolution of 1848, which, though it failed to establish a democratic constitutional state, did advance the economic position of the bourgeois middle class without robbing the bureaucracy of its prominent role in the state.

The revolution attempted to achieve German unification, protect fundamental rights, create a nationally representative and politically potent legislative authority, and develop an administrative body bound by its commands. But despite the politically liberal thrust of the bourgeois revolutionary forces, the revolution was not an attempt to deprive the state of its administrative capacity to provide for social welfare. As Michael Stolleis observed, "the liberal demands" of the 1848 revolution were "primarily oriented towards the limitation of the monarchical principle, basic rights, separation of powers, and parliamentary representation of the property owning and educated classes, not however against welfare-state intervention."[54] This could be seen in the work of the theorists who participated in the revolution of 1848 and developed the field of administrative law.[55]

It was in this period that the theory of the *Rechtsstaat*—a state under the rule of law—came into ascendancy. The norm of *Rechtsstaatlichkeit* entailed binding executive power to statutorily codified, generally applicable rights and duties. It emphasized both a sphere of individual independence against state power and the legitimacy of legislatively authorized welfare and regulatory interventions. Thus Robert von Mohl insisted like Hegel that "the freedom of the citizen is the foundation of the whole *Rechtsstaat*."[56] Mohl understood this to mean both that the state must ensure that individuals "will not be forcefully disturbed in the pursuit of the rational . . . development of their powers"; and the state must also "complement the insufficiency of individual powers to achieve rational life-goals through the use of the comprehensive authority entrusted to it."[57] The revolutionary claim, which placed Mohl beyond the ambit of Hegel's philosophy, was the emphasis on constraining the exercise of public power by constitutionally defined rights. Though Hegel's political philosophy might be read to create such actionable guarantees against public power, he was less clear about the entitlements individuals held against the state than the entitlements they held against one another.

The revolution would founder in part on the question of the degree of monarchical power and hence on the relative autonomy of executive administration from legislative control. Beyond the reactionary power of aristocratic forces, the failure of the revolution stemmed in part from the opposition between revolutionary liberals and democrats over the question of monarchical power and thus of the independence of the executive.[58] To the extent the conflicting political models of the revolution placed varying emphasis upon the monarchical principle versus the legislative power of popular representatives, they also reflected differing conceptions of the role of administration in the modern state. Greater power for the monarch would come along with greater discretion for his executive functionaries and lesser subjection to legislative command. Without a powerful independent monarch, the legislature would strictly control the administration.

Karl Marx had been the most radical philosophical proponent of this latter democratic vision. In his critique of Hegel's *Philosophy of Right* in 1843, he interpreted the Hegelian state as a mere reflection of the pre-revolutionary Prussian state. He saw this as a principally "bureaucratic" organization that was separated from the real experience of individuals and committed to a false bifurcation of social and political emancipation.[59] The legislature served as a passive instrument that simply protected the current shape of civil society through the refinement of civil law. The alternative Marx posited was that "the democratic element should be . . . the actual element that acquires its rational form in in the whole organism of the state."[60] Such a legislative democracy would mean the abandonment of the separation of state from society: "The drive of civil society to transform itself into political society, or to make political society into the actual society, shows itself as the drive for the most fully possible universal participation in legislative power."[61] In this early period, Marx believed that the transition to legislative democracy would lead to the overcoming of class domination in civil society, for "civil society would abandon itself if all its members were legislators."[62]

As Marx's critique of Hegel in the years preceding the revolution suggests, the alternatives at hand at the time could be understood through varying interpretations of Hegelian political theory. For Hegel had recognized that the relationship between abstract legislation and concrete administration was unstable. An arrangement that gave greater power to the monarchical executive would increase the particularism of state action and loosen the constraint of general norms. An arrangement that diminished monarchical power and its administrative subordinates would strengthen the universal element of the legislature, as well as its connection to broader social interests. Hegel himself understood that, in a fully developed state, the monarch himself should have little power and serve a mostly symbolic role, representing the unified personality of the state.[63] But this position did not fully resolve the question of the relationship between legislation and administration, for in Hegel's view, the highest-ranking administrators rather than the monarch would take on the tasks of execution. Hegel's symbolic monarch did not imply an impotent executive; rather it elevated the highest ranking civil servants to paramount importance.

For reformist bureaucrats, the appeal of such a Hegelian constitutional monarchy was clear: it would support their authority in the state and enable them to use their discretion to address social problems not adequately foreseen or addressed by the legislature.[64] The monarch would give them independence from the legislative organ and thus enable them to steer the social order according to their conception of the necessary requisites for rational personal development. At the same time, the existence of a bona fide elected legislature would situate administration within constitutional constraints and provide it with the political legitimacy that it had lacked, at least in Prussia, in the period leading up to the revolution.

IV. THE SURVIVAL OF HEGELIAN PUBLIC LAW IN THE WAKE OF REVOLUTIONARY FAILURE

Hegel's concept of the state, and the tensions between legislation and execution that he had identified, would persist after the failure of the 1848 revolution. Two Hegelian legal scholars in particular—Rudolf von Gneist and Lorenz von Stein—expressed the public philosophy of the non-democratic but constitutional state that developed in Germany in the latter half of the nineteenth century. As I discuss in chapter 2, these thinkers would be studied and cited by Woodrow Wilson and Frank Goodnow, who developed some of the earliest American conceptions of the administrative state. Though Gneist and Stein did not share these American scholars' emphasis on democracy, they imparted to the Progressives the Hegelian ideal of welfare-promoting, legally accountable administrative action.

Despite the immediate failure of the revolution, the order of constitutional monarchy that had existed in the southern German states prior to the revolution continued and expanded to Prussia once the hopes for liberal-democratic unification had been vanquished. This "constitutional monarchy was based upon the monarchical principle, but bound the exercise of monarchical authority to a greater or lesser degree to the constitution and the constitutionally established participation rights of parliamentary popular representation. The government was accountable to the monarch and only to a limited extent to the parliament."[65] German constitutionalism therefore continued to insulate executive administration partially from legislative control. Administrative courts, which could protect individual rights against unlawful administrative action, developed in the German states from 1863 onward.[66]

Under the Reich Constitution of 1871, this constitutional order was largely replicated at the national level, as the king of Prussia and his chosen Reich chancellor controlled the imperial administration.[67] Executive administration was principally restricted by legislative and judicial control in matters where the state intruded upon property or personal freedom. Independent administrative courts served to bind executive administration to statutory law, developing a principle of "proportionality" that required administration to use the least intrusive means to achieve statutory ends where private rights were infringed.[68] But administration generally had a free hand where it supplied some kind of positive public service or good and did not directly interfere with private property or personal liberty.[69] This "dualistic constitutional monarchy" represented an uneasy compromise between monarchical sovereign and the executive administration, on the one hand, and the legislature and bourgeois civil society, on the other.[70]

Under the control of the Prussian monarch, the administration increasingly developed a conservative political orientation that was hostile to the liberal and social democratic forces in the legislature. Beginning with a purge of liberals from the civil service following the failure of the 1848 revolution, the bureaucracy evolved from an institution of egalitarian social reform into a bulwark against it.[71] The liberal ideology of early nineteenth-century bureaucratic reform was thus pushed aside after the quest for democratic constitutionalism had failed. This late nineteenth-century public officialdom was not conservative in the American sense that it was opposed to state intervention. To the contrary, official conservatism sought to deploy state power to reduce the attraction of socialism, promote political stability, and foster nationalistic solidarity. It provided for social welfare services, such as workplace injury compensation, in order to bolster the legitimacy of the Crown and to thwart political participation and dissent.[72]

This unique German blend of liberal constitutionalism and politically conservative administrative intervention would find theoretical reflection in the theory of the state and administrative law. Lorenz von Stein and Rudolph von Gneist both participated in the 1848 revolution and in the development of German administrative law and theory in the mid-to-late nineteenth century.[73] Their scholarship elaborated Hegelian themes of the relationship between state and society and the embedding of the administration in the separation of powers. For both of these theorists, the necessity of an active state administration that would address the insufficiencies and injustices of antagonistic civil society became a dominant concern. The relationship between legislation and administration remained a fraught question, reflecting not only the struggles of German constitutional history but also the difficult conceptual distinction between legislative generality and administrative particularity. The absence of any practical possibility for democratic constitutionalism continued to lead to a sharp contrast between the quasi-democratic legislature and a powerful, unelected monarch at the head of the bureaucratic organization.

Stein fastened on the Hegelian idea that administrators could further social progress. He developed a thoroughly Hegelian theory of a monarchical administration that would guarantee social freedom.[74] As Carl Schmitt noted, "Lorenz von Stein is the foundation of nineteenth-century German thinking on constitutional theory (and, simultaneously, the conduit through which Hegel's philosophy of the state remains vital)."[75] The key Hegelian features of Stein's view of administration were his dialectical conception of the relationship between state and society, his understanding of the unstable distinction between legislation and execution, his vision of administrative social reform, and his understanding of freedom as a foundational value that the state was bound to foster. Like Hegel, Stein saw the state as an organic unity that could mediate the antagonisms of civil society:

> Between these two great factors—the particularity of actual existence, which pervades the state, and the unity of the will of the state, which rules over such particularity—there takes place a continual, never ceasing struggle, in which the two elements reciprocally fulfill one another in service of the highest idea of personal development, with or without consciousness.[76]

Stein emphasized that state action at once reflected and transformed the interests of social movements in civil society, turning these interests into statutory commands which would guide administrative action. Stein, like Mohl, posited a distinction between the "statute" (*Gesetz*) and the "ordinance" (*Verordnung*), with the one having precedence over the latter: "according to its higher essence, the statute always stems from the entire consciousness of state life and, therefore, also always intends to achieve its goals," whereas the ordinance derives from the "distinctiveness and . . . changing character" of the factual condition it regulates.[77]

Stein described the "administration of social progress" as a primary task of the administration.[78] Administrative authorites had to ease the tension between capital and labor and provide the working classes with all the "*pre-requisites* of development, which they cannot create on their own, due to their lack of capital as well as physical and intellectual earning capacity, while leaving the actual acquisition of capital to the workers themselves." [79] In Stein, many of the classical aspects of the *Rechtsstaat* are thus combined with a sense of the significance of the "social question" Hegel had recognized much earlier on—namely the extent to which the institutions of bourgeois civil law created class inequalities and perceptions of injustice.

Stein offered a socially reformist and yet institutionally conservative defense of constitutional monarchy. In his view, the administration served to implement the commands of statute and to unify society under the monarch. Despite this monarchical emphasis, constitutional scholar Ernst-Wolfgang Böckenförde would observe in 1972 that Stein had accurately foreseen the "actuality of the modern state," insofar as he anticipated the "legitimation of the state not so much from the constitution, as from the active, social-guaranteeing administration; the determination of the content of politics by the social; welfare assistance and appropriate participation in social production as a means to securing real freedom; and progressive dissolution of traditional political structures and their mediatization in favor of socialization."[80]

Stein resolved the ambiguous Hegelian relationship between legislation and execution by arguing that administration, while bound to respect statutory limits, had an active role to play even without clear statutory authorization: "for the executive power, the simple execution of existing law does not suffice, rather . . . at almost all points it goes beyond the law, and thus has a law-fulfilling and in part law-substituting function."[81] As Peter Badura has observed, this active role meant that "the administration could not content itself with knowledge of positive administrative law. It required a scientifically developed administrative theory in contrast to mere service of statutory administrative law. This, however, meant that the administration must itself take on all those powers and laws that dominate actual life; 'it must constitute administrative law from the essence of that which is to be administered.' "[82] As I will show in chapter 2, Woodrow Wilson would draw on this idea as he described the relationship between legislation and execution in the American context, arguing that administrative authorities must go beyond the strict terms of the law to implement the public interest. For Stein, however, this invocation of administrative values autonomous from legislation was bound up with the role of the monarch as a neutral power standing above the antagonism of civil society. The administration acted as the agent of this neutral power, attempting to realize the common social good while respecting any clear limitations established by statute.

This vision of "social kingship" became a second-best alternative for social democrats, such as Gustav Schmoller, who lacked significant power in the legislature but nonetheless believed the king might protect their interests. They hoped that "just as liberalism and the German administrative- and military-monarch once together accomplished reforms, so too will it be with socialism. . . . The Prussian state, because it has the strongest monarchical constitution and administration, is also able to carry out social reform most wisely."[83] The palliative social reforms of Bismarck could satisfy the socialists as to the "reformist" capacity of the state without, however, realizing their deeper concern for political emancipation and the structural inequality between labor and capital. W.E.B. Du Bois's defense of the Freedmen's Bureau's role in defending the rights of African Americans after the American Civil War would draw on this German idea of socially progressive but nonetheless paternalistic administration.

Gneist adopted Stein's Hegelian conception of the relationship between state and society in his work on the *The* Rechtsstaat *and the Administrative Courts in Germany*. He maintained that "the 'state' is independently posited in the ethical nature of humanity, whereas society is grounded in the system of human needs."[84] Like Hegel and Stein, Gneist emphasized that the state provided a normative unity capable of regulating and reducing the economic inequalities and antagonisms of society. He did not seek the total control of society by the state but rather recognized that freedom required individual independence as well as the public provision of social needs. Gneist therefore described the basic tasks of the state as "the protection of rights and at the same time the uplifting of the weaker classes."[85] This conception of the *Rechtsstaat* gave a double significance to law: "law should not only regulate the external life of the subjects under its commands; it also protects the sphere of rights of the individual against authority."[86]

Administrative law therefore had to mediate between the claims of the individual and the claims of the community to pursue social policy. The individual would not be granted absolute protection from state intrusion, but rather could hold administrative authorities accountable by appeal to special administrative courts:

> Administrative law concerns an objective order, which is independent of the petition of parties, in order to handle public law and welfare. Consequently all controls of the state administration are determined for the protection of the collective as well as the individual. When in contested questions this order grants subjects a legal hearing . . . this happens (as in the criminal process) to secure a corresponding implementation of the law. One recognizes the interests of the parties concerned as a legal claim, but in another way than when the legal protection of individual rights is the first aim and object of official actions.[87]

Gneist thus articulated a special relationship among judicial adjudication, individual rights, and administrative law: the judicial defense of individual rights would not limit the operation of regulatory laws, but rather ensure that administrative authorities adhered to the relevant statutory requirements. Administrative courts would have statutorily determined jurisdiction to review administrative action on certain enumerated issues to ensure officials' conformity to law.[88] Individuals whose legal rights had been infringed could contest official action in special courts, but so long as the administrative action remained within the bounds of legal authority, the action would stand. Individual rights were to be granted by legislation, without independent constitutional foundation. Gneist's understanding of administrative legal claims was instrumental in the development of a separate administrative jurisdiction in Prussia.[89] They would also inform Frank Goodnow's suggestion for reforming the American administrative process, as I will describe in chapter 2.

Whereas Stein sought to insulate bureaucratic action from social pressure by shielding administration under the authority of the Crown, Gneist emphasized the need to integrate the state with civil society at the local level. He argued that Germany should adopt a form of the English system of local "self-government" by justices of the peace.[90] "Honorary officials" would implement state laws on such municipal issues as roads, hospitals, and common lands.[91] His hope was that the combination of administrative courts and local self-administration would establish "a new foundation for the relationship between state and society, in which the legislature is not the sole representative of the social interest, but rather society can itself perform the obligations of the state in administration and in judicial judgments."[92]

Gneist therefore sought to retain at least a shadow of the liberal spirit of 1848 through administrative courts that would protect individual rights, social welfare provision that would reduce social antagonism, and local self-administration that would give the propertied and the educated a role in the performance of state functions. His conception of local self-government came the closest amongst the German Hegelians to the Progressives' democratic reconstruction of administration. His proposals did not, however, contemplate a deep engagement of the broader public in the formulation of administrative rules at the national level. Gneist only sought to give local notables and the bourgeoisie some discretion over the administration of their communities.

Though their institutional emphasis deferred, both Gneist and Stein envisioned a *Rechtsstaat* that was defined not only by legal rationality but by a concrete ethical commitment to preserving freedom in modern civil society. This political content of the *Rechtsstaat* would fade with the turn to legal positivism.

V. FROM THE SUBSTANTIVE TO THE FORMAL *RECHTSSTAAT*

Mohl, Gneist, and Stein followed Hegel in describing a social welfare administration within the context of a *Rechtsstaat*. The positivist jurisprudence at the dawn of the twentieth century would systematize these developments in describing an administrative state authorized and constrained by legislative power. But with the turn to positivism, the Hegelian state was gradually drained of ethical content. This positivist approach set the stage for the purely instrumental conception of bureaucracy espoused by Max Weber.

The fullest expression of administrative legal positivism at dawn of the twentieth century was Otto Mayer's *German Administrative Law*, which had a dominant position in its time and to a great extent long after.[93] His approach was positivist in the sense that he described the logical structure of administrative law in relation to other elements of the broader German legal system, while claiming not to rely upon any ethical or political judgments to compose this order. For Mayer, the rule of statutory law over executive administration action was the foundation of the *Rechtsstaat*.

Mayer remained under the influence of Hegel but in a far more formal and removed sense than Gneist and Stein.[94] The general commonality between Mayer and Hegel was the belief in the formal-rational nature of legal concepts. As Mayer wrote in the preface to his second edition of *German Administrative Law*, he held a "belief in the power of universal legal ideas, which appear and unfold in the diversity of actual law, but at the same time change and progress through history. In my view, it aligns with the Hegelian philosophy of law . . . that I might venture to pursue such ideas in the disjointed and unfinished German administrative law, in order to uplift and exhibit them."[95] Mayer's attempt to construct a system out of German administrative law thus derived its inspiration from Hegel's view that law had an inherently rational, universal structure. Mayer would develop this Hegelian position into a legislation-centered concept of administration. This variety of Hegelianism was distinct from Stein's in describing administration through a purely legal, rather than social and ethical, lens. With the emptying out of the substantive, emancipatory thrust of Hegel's conception of the state, only Hegel's emphasis on the coherence and intelligibility of state action remained.

Mayer did not understand the state, as Hegel did, as the "actuality of concrete freedom." Rather, "the state," as Mayer defined it, "is a commonwealth capable of action, in which the people is bound together under a sovereign authority. Administration is the capacity of the state to realize its ends."[96] This presupposed a separation between the "administering state" and the aggregate of persons who were its subjects: "across from the administering state stand the mass of individuals, the subjects. Administrative law is only conceivable when a relationship of the subjects to the state is put in question."[97] Mayer thus emphasized a bilateral relationship between the state and the individual, jettisoning Hegel's corporate conception of society and his normative commitment to bringing about a condition of reciprocal recognition between individuals. Administration for Mayer was merely the application of political ends to individuals through law. Whereas civil law concerned the relationship between subjects within civil society, administrative law concerned the relationship between the members of this society and the state.

Mayer's systematic account of German administrative law succeeded by restricting the scope of its analysis to a concept of police command (*Polizeibefehl*) rooted in the principles of classical liberalism. Whereas *Polizei*, for Hegel as well as for Mohl, had designated a relatively encompassing state capacity to provide material support for individual development, Mayer limited *Polizei* to state acts that intervened into the private legal rights in order to preserve the freedom of individual actors.[98] This narrow concept did not reflect an absence of welfare-state activities in the German state practices of Mayer's time.[99] National and municipal government provided various forms of social insurance and social services—public utilities, operation of forests and ironworks—none of which could be grasped through a narrowly individualist conception of police intervention.[100] But the classical-liberal blinders on Mayer's positivism made it impossible for him to adequately systematize these far-ranging welfare and commercial interventions.[101]

VI. MAX WEBER'S THEORY OF BUREAUCRACY IN CONTEXT

Max Weber articulated the sociological counterpart to this positivist conception of administrative law. As I noted in the introduction to this chapter, the Weberian view has exercised decisive influence over American political science and administrative law scholars. But Weber's thought did not figure prominently among the American Progressives who provided the intellectual groundwork for our own administrative state. Instead, Hegel and the mid-nineteenth-century public law scholars who followed in his footsteps were their point of reference within the German tradition. The next chapter will show how their American adaptation of Hegelianism led to a distinctive understanding of the state, with a greater stress on democratic procedure and the substantive requisites for public participation. Here, however, I describe how Weber's understanding of the administrative state represented a historically particular and institutionally unstable constellation of political structures, rather than a universally applicable ideal type. This should caution against embracing Weberian understandings of bureaucracy in the American context.

Weber's legal sociology took as his starting point for analysis the "two-sided" state theory of Georg Jellinek. In this theory, the state was on the one hand a legal entity, which could be presented as a coherent system of norms, and on the other hand a sociological entity, whose historical emergence, institutional durability, and psychological acceptability were not legally cognizable.[102] The legal quality of the state arose from the "self-obligation" of the monarchical administration to legal norms.[103] Weber focused on the sociological aspect of Jellinek's theory of the state, showing how the formal system of legal norms he described functioned as a system of social rule.[104] Weber thus distinguished a particular kind of rule, "legal authority," which was grounded not upon the charismatic aura of an individual or the reassuring embrace of communal heritage but rather proceeded through the enactment "by imposition or agreement" of a "consistent system of abstract rules" that provided for the "continuous rule bound conduct of official business."[105]

Legal authority was based on "rational grounds," in the sense that it systematized commands into a coherent structure of abstract rules.[106] This required, as Talcott Parsons puts it, that "a system of legal norms itself must become relatively *universalistic*. It must be organized in terms of general principles so that to some significant degree particular decisions come to be derivable from these general principles when related to more particular facts."[107] Such applications of principles to facts then required a technical treatment of regulated persons and things such that they fit into formal legal categorizations.[108] The positivist system of formal law was thus treated by Weber as a peculiarly modern, rationalist system of authority. It corresponded to a world disenchanted of fixed religious values, instead facilitating the efficient, instrumental-rational behavior of individuals.

Within this formal-rational system, the bureaucracy functions as the concrete social-political organization that made commands efficacious. The bureaucratic staff provided the most effective, instrumentally rational means to carry out the law. Several particular features contributed to bureaucracy's instrumental rationality. Officials were employed according to their technical merit and paid in fixed salaries, both of which made bureaucrats' employment dependent upon their efficient performance of their tasks. They were "organized in a clearly defined hierarchy of office" and each was "subject to strict and systematic discipline and control in the conduct of his office."[109] A system of hierarchical control ensured that the implementation of law had a rational structure which reflected the rational structure of the legal norms. The decision-making power of each official was clearly delimited and subject to the control of a superior in a chain of command that enforced the commands of statute.

As an agent within this formal hierarchy, the bureaucratic official himself exhibited "a spirit of formalistic impersonality. . . . The dominant norms are concepts of straightforward duty without regard to personal considerations. Everyone is subject to formal equality of treatment; that is, everyone in the same empirical situation."[110] The continuous functioning of the system required that the logical structure of legal rules and the bureaucratic hierarchy together determine the outcomes, to the exclusion of any autonomous value judgments by the bureaucrat himself. In order to subsume empirical situations under the abstract commands of law, bureaucratic officials applied technical skill and empirical data. In this sense, "[b]ureaucratic administration means fundamentally domination through knowledge. This is the feature of it which makes it specifically rational."[111]

The incentives created by the bureaucratic implementation of law induced social action that mirrored the formal rational structure of legal norms and the instrumental activity of the bureaucratic system that implemented them.[112] For this reason, purely bureaucratic administration was "capable of attaining the highest degree of efficiency and is in this sense formally the most rational known means of exercising authority over human beings."[113] The success of the bureaucratic implementation of legal authority was so great, in Weber's view, that it had become extraordinarily difficult to displace: "Once fully established, bureaucracy is among those social structures which are the hardest to destroy. Bureaucracy is *the* means of transforming social action into rationally-organized action."[114]

The disparity between this Weberian vision of bureaucracy and the Hegelian account is remarkable. Hegel and Weber described the same general kind of institutional phenomena—a merit-based public officialdom carrying out the laws, organized in a hierarchical, functionally differentiated system. But for Hegel this administrative staff was permeated with substantive normative commitments. Its purpose was to advance social freedom through public welfare provision, a contextually sensitive implementation of law, and a careful adjudication of social antagonisms and conflicts. Public law for Hegel was the means by which individuals were able to recognize one another as members of a common political project and community. The officials who implemented this law were therefore engaged in the interpretation and maintenance of the public rights held by this community. For Weber, by contrast, administration had become a purely instrumental form of rule. The law it implemented was distinguished by its formal generality, which was open to any substantive content. The ethic of the bureaucratic staff and the structure of bureaucratic organization both aimed to facilitate the efficient application of these statutory commands, whatever they happened to be. The bureaucrat did not think so much as calculate and obey.

In the mirror of these contrasting visions of the administrative state, we can see the historical shift from the dashed hopes for administrative social reform in the early nineteenth century to eventual acquiescence in paternalistic and authoritarian forms of rule. Unwilling to embrace in theory and unable to achieve in practice robust forms of democratic constitutionalism, Germany's early experience with state-led emancipation gave way to a state legitimated by shrewd executive politics, efficient administrative performance, and the legislative codification of liberal law.

This convergence of legal positivism and legal sociology in the waning years of the German Empire upon a legal-rational conception of bureaucratic authority, however, pointed to a structural tension within the German state. Though administration was in theory bound by legislative command, it remained aligned with an executive that was bound to the law for the most part only negatively. The law erected a sphere of negative rights around individuals that protected them from state intervention. But bureaucratic officials were guided by formal legal principles only as the general authorities behind and limits upon their discretion. Within this zone of discretion, they were guided not by formal law but by reason of state: the need for the preservation of the existing order of rule.[115] The non-legal determinants of executive-bureaucratic action, and those forms of administrative action that could not neatly be described as intervention into the private sphere of the individual, fell outside of legal doctrine as supplements that had as yet escaped categorization and control. The structural conflict in German history between legislative and executive power would become explosive when this uneasy institutional settlement became destabilized by the First World War and the state was thrust suddenly into the new context of constitutional democracy.

VII. THE *RECHTSSTAAT* IN CRISIS

In the Weimar Republic, democratic values took institutional form in one of the most liberal, democratic, and socially conscious constitutions of the modern world. At the same time, however, the tension between executive administration and parliamentary legislation only intensified, ending in the collapse of the constitutional structure into a totalitarian party-administrative apparatus. The causes of this collapse extended far beyond constitutional theory and practice. But by tracing the theoretical reflection of the political crises of this period, we can see the dangers of an administrative theory that rests upon a combination of presidential leadership and technocratic competence. The path from Weber's "leadership democracy," to Carl Schmitt's "governmental state," to Ernst Forsthoff's "total state" shows how a purely hierarchical form of administration, steered by the unilateral will of an executive claiming ultimate popular authority, risks the destruction of democracy, the rule of law, and human freedom. This intellectual history serves as a foil for the American Progressive theory of the state I will develop in the following chapters, which instead anchored administrative power in broad-based, deliberative, and participatory popular control.

In the third edition of *German Administrative Law*, which appeared in 1923, Otto Mayer claimed that while "constitutional law passes away, administrative law persists."[116] Mayer meant that the constitutional change from the *Kaiserreich* to the Weimar Republic did not entail a shift in the basic norms of administrative law, as a system in which administrative action was authorized and bound by statute, and citizens had rights to contest the legal foundations of administrative action in court. But because Mayer had excluded forms of state action that did not fit the model of forceful intervention from his systematic approach, significant changes in the content and extent of administrative intervention and in the constitutional allocation of regulatory powers were beyond his grasp.

The political turbulence of the Weimar period threw into sharper relief the tensions in the formal *Rechtsstaat* ideal of the legality of administration. The Republic would simultaneously and suddenly see a growth in democratic political competition, an expansion and nationalization of social welfare administration, and an increase in economic pressures. The First World War had both widened administrative intervention in the labor market and created new demands for social support for veterans. The Weimar Constitution opened the way for broad-scale social legislation not only through the general equality clause but through specific authorizations for parliamentary action on labor and social law.[117] In its early and middle years, the parliamentary coalition was politically attuned to such "social questions" and passed several laws codifying the social insurance system, notably the Reich Law on the Responsibility to Provide Social Welfare Assistance (1924). The establishment of the Reich Labor Ministry, the institution of special labor courts to settle disputes between employers and employees, administrative mediation of labor conflicts, and the extension of youth and housing administration, exemplified the growing egalitarian intervention into civil society.[118]

While state action expanded, the *Rechtsstaat* ideal of parliamentary supremacy did not keep pace with the growing demands. As Franz Neumann observed, in the Weimar Republic "the modern mass-democratic state changed into an intervention state, which led to a transformation of the legislative state into an administrative state. At the same time the bureaucracy made itself independent from the control of the parliament."[119] As the economic circumstances became more dire, while political conflict immobilized parliament, the administrative state was increasingly governed not by legislation but by presidential and cabinet-level decrees, administered by the civil service. The public officialdom, which was retained from the Empire, was largely hostile to the social-democratic thrust of the early Republic and sought instead to solve political problems through their specialized knowledge. The legislature's extensive use of enabling laws, which granted discretionary governing power to the president and the cabinet, served to diminish traditional rule-of-law guarantees and increase relative administrative power.[120] As Karl Dietrich Bracher noted, "[a] steadily expanding bureaucracy, with its pre-democratic traditions, thus persisted in the modern administrative state in latent opposition to parliamentary democracy, to parliament, to the parties and to their direct organs. . . . Their tendency and their objective essentially was to reduce political problems to technical administrative tasks."[121] The Republic thus settled upon a form of rule whose legitimacy was grounded upon the plebiscitary democratic mandate of the president and the technical competence of the administration. The legal rationality of state action became of secondary importance.

Weber's political writings on the eve of the Weimar Republic anticipated this state of affairs. He attempted to make a virtue of the sharp cleavage between decisive executive authority and bureaucratic instrumentality. Weber advocated for a strict separation of the proper role of the political leader from the bureaucratic official. "The difference" between the two lies "in the kind of *responsibility*" that attaches to each role.[122] "An official who receives a directive which he considers wrong can and is supposed to object to it. If his superior insists on its execution, it is his duty and even his honor to carry it out as if it corresponded to his innermost conviction, and to demonstrate in this fashion that his sense of duty stands above his personal preference."[123] The hierarchical structure of bureaucracy depended upon such obedience as a primary principle of organization, and such official obedience was at the core of the state's legitimation. The subservient attitude that made bureaucracy function rendered bureaucrats unsuited to decide upon the ultimate ends that the legal system enforced. Whereas the bureaucrat was bound to obey, "[a] political leader who behaved in this way would deserve contempt. . . . 'To be above parties'—in truth, to remain outside the realm of the struggle for power—is the official's role, while this struggle for personal power, and the resulting personal responsibility, is the lifeblood of the politician as well as of the entrepreneur."[124]

The political leader and the bureaucrat thus related to one another as master and servant. The politician gave the orders, and the official followed them without question. For such a scheme to succeed, the bureaucrat had to be apolitical: "he should engage in impartial administration."[125] The rational legitimacy of the state then combined with the charismatic legitimacy of the elected leader. Statutes embodied the substantive values advanced by politicians, which the bureaucracy carried out through formal rational processes under the supervision of politically accountable superiors. In this way, the tension that Weber noted in legal history between formal procedures and substantive ethical commitments became articulated into the separation of politics from administration.[126]

Weber sought to subordinate bureaucracy to charismatic champions of political ideology because of his philosophic ethic. For Weber, in a modern disenchanted world without overarching religious or metaphysical commitments, "the ultimately possible attitudes toward life are irreconcilable, and hence their struggle can never be brought to a final conclusion. Thus it is necessary to make a decisive choice."[127] Given this unavoidable conflict, various conceptions of value could only struggle against one another for dominance. Following Nietzsche, Weber believed that human life gained meaning through existential struggle between exceptional individuals to advance worldviews between which no rational arbitration was possible.[128] These heroes' ethic of responsibility would ensure that political charisma translated into consistent policy, according to clearly defined values. Democratic politics then combined the emotional attachment of the people to the statesman with the statesman's own irrational, but steadfast, choice of values. While Weber thus sought to undermine the political conservatism of the officialdom Weimar had inherited from the empire, he sought to retain its technocratic emphasis and ensconce it firmly under the leadership of a democratically elected chief executive.

Though Weber's proposal to combine plebiscitary democratic authority with legal-bureaucratic rationality was an ingenious effort to compartmentalize the severe political pressures facing the nascent German Republic, it was also inherently contradictory. For plebiscitary rule depended not upon reason but upon a charismatic aura. The alignment of bureaucracy under the decisive will of the executive, rather than under determinate statutory norms, would undermine the predictability that Weber prized in bureaucratic rule. It would succeed only at the expense of the rationality codified in statute and concretized by a law-bound bureaucratic officialdom. If bureaucracy remained bound to legal duty, as opposed to the hierarchical command within the ministry, this would short-circuit the capacity of a plebiscitary president to implement his democratic mandate.

Carl Schmitt, who Jürgen Habermas once called a "'legitimate pupil' of Weber's," would eventually resolve this contradiction in favor of authoritarian, executive-oriented rule.[129] Whereas in *Constitutional Theory* (1928), Schmitt had expounded a vision of the Weimar Constitution as a "decision for the bourgeois *Rechtsstaat*,"[130] in *Legality and Legitimacy* (1932) he argued that the structural exceptions to this ideal in the Constitution would, and should, lead to the dissolution of the *Rechtsstaat* in favor of a new order. This order centered on the authoritarian rule of the executive administration, legitimated by the popular acclamation of the president.[131] The substantive content of this regime was not, as for Hegel, a matter of normative elaboration but instead instituted an existential choice to recognize "the substantive characteristics and capacities of the German people."[132] It was based around an agonistic, even violent, conception of politics, in which a categorical distinction between the "friend" and the "enemy"—both without and within the state—was the foundation of legitimate power.[133]

Schmitt correctly understood the liberal *Rechtsstaat* to be a legislative state in which administrative interventions into individual freedom and society at large had to be authorized by statutes passed by parliament. On this model, which could be seen in the positivist administrative legal theory of Mayer, the executive administration was made subservient to the legislative authority and derived its legitimacy from statutory mandates. Schmitt observed, however, that the positivist transformation of the ideal of the *Rechtsstaat* from a substantive commitment to individual freedom into a merely formal principle of statutory authorization already paved the way for a transition from the legislative state to the "governmental" or "administrative" state:

> when it is transformed into an empty functionalism of momentary majority decisions, the normative legality of a parliamentary legislative state can be linked with the impersonal functionalism of bureaucratic, regulatory necessities. In this peculiar, though practical alliance of legality and technical functionalism, the bureaucracy in the long run remains the superior partner and transforms the law of the parliamentary legislative state into the measures of the administrative state. The word "*Rechtsstaat*" should not be used here.[134]

What distinguished the administrative state from the *Rechtsstaat*, for Schmitt, was the collapse of the distinction between durable, general legal norms with a substantive commitment to bourgeois values, on the one hand, and temporary administrative measures undertaken pursuant to those norms, on the other: "When the concept of law is deprived of every substantive relation to reason and justice, while simultaneously the legislative state is retained with its specific concept of legality concentrating all the majesty and dignity of the state on the statute, then any type of administrative directive, each command and measure . . . can be made legal and given the form of law."[135] Of particular interest to Schmitt were the president's decree powers under Article 48 of the Weimar Constitution, which united legislation and execution in one person. With this provision, which was activated to address political and economic emergencies, the always unstable distinction between legislation and administration fell away, and with it, the structure of the classical *Rechtsstaat*.[136]

Schmitt thus paved the way for Ernst Forsthoff's National Socialist administrative theory in *The Total State*. Forsthoff observed that "the system of rule of the national socialist state is distinguished by the connection between the national socialist order and the bureaucratic administration."[137] In this total state, the dialectical relationship between state and society that Hegel had diagnosed vanished, as society became totally dominated by a party-administrative apparatus claiming to act in the name of a unified *Volk*. The connection between legislation and administration had also been lost, as the total state fulfilled the transformations Schmitt had diagnosed in *Legality and Legitimacy*. With ultimate authority resting in the dictator's will, the *Rechtsstaat* distinction between legislative statute and administrative ordinance disappeared. In this context of the collapse of legislation and administration and between state and society, "freedom is today politically discredited, in as much as one identifies it with individual freedom, with the security of the individual against the grasp of the state. This freedom, a postulate of human thought, has been overcome."[138]

It is no coincidence that Forsthoff's administrative theory dispensed with freedom at the same time as it dispensed with the separation of powers and the idea of statutory authority. Since Hegel, German administrative theory had recognized that freedom could only be guaranteed if state actions took on a predictable and transparent form. The rational structure legislation in turn facilitated individuals' practical reasoning—their ability to determine their own ends and the best means to achieve them. An administrative theory relying upon the will of the leader to express the "substantive" characteristics of the German people (whatever those might be) could not have this rational, predictable quality. The German state thus devolved from one of constitutional reason to dictatorial will.

National Socialism was therefore in no sense the realization of the Hegelian state, though some Anglo-American theorists drew this connection.[139] Rather, it was categorically opposed to Hegel's basic normative commitments and institutional structures. As Franz Neumann observed in *Behemoth*, his path-breaking account of national socialist rule,

> Hegel cannot be held responsible for the political theory of National Socialism. . . . For no one can doubt that Hegel's idea of the state is basically incompatible with the German racial myth. . . . Hegel's theory is rational; it stands for the free individual. His state is predicated upon a bureaucracy that guarantees the freedom of the citizens because its acts on the basis of rational and calculable norms. This emphasis on the rational conduct of the bureaucracy, which is, according to Hegel, a prerequisite of proper government, makes his doctrine unpalatable to national socialist "dynamism."[140]

In Neumann's view, the Nazi regime could not be called a state at all, precisely because it had jettisoned the Hegelian commitment to law-based administrative action in service of the underlying ideal of individual self-determination. The form of bureaucratic rule ushered in by the collapse of Weimar constitutionalism was not only devoid of the formal strictures *Rechtsstaatlichkeit* but diametrically opposed to the emancipatory spirit of Prussian social reform that Hegel held up as exemplary.

While it is therefore plainly false to associate Hegelian ideas with Nazi rule, it would also be erroneous to attribute the rise of Nazism to the decline of Hegelian thought and institutions. The origins and motivations for totalitarianism stretch far beyond this narrow aspect of German legal history.[141] The legacies of anti-Semitism, racism, and imperialism were secular trends, which, when combined with a bureaucratic power divorced from the guarantees of the rule of law, lay the basis for totalitarianism.[142] The worst forms of bureaucratic domination were facilitated by a constellation of institutional and ideological developments: the decline of legislative control; the rise of plebiscitary presidential legitimacy; the hollowing out of ethical administrative judgment and its replacement with purely technical calculation. As I will argue in chapter 4 and in the Conclusion, these pathologies remain dangers in the American context as well. But they are symptomatic not of Hegelian statism but rather of a political order that has lost touch with the immanent connection between practical reason, individual freedom, and public law that Hegel had identified.

The most significant failure of the Hegelian tradition of German state theory, with its emphasis on a welfare state bound by the rule of law, was that it did not appreciate the need to democratize the state as a whole and the administrative process in particular. Hegelian legal scholars did not adequately recognize that individual freedom would require active popular involvement in the exercise of public power if the principle of self-determination were to have real purchase. When the state had finally been democratized under Weimar, this occurred only at the level of the parliament and the president. With the decline in parliamentary control, the "democratic" nature of administration was thus identified with the plebiscitary mandate of the president rather than with deliberation in the public sphere, in parliament, or within administrative bodies themselves.

The history of Weimar should thus give us pause about hinging state legitimacy on presidential power and technocratic competence. Those in America who adhere today to the presidentialist conception of the state hope to reduce the complexities of modern political life by the application of decisive political choices through an obedient bureaucratic apparatus. They reject the more circuitous but less treacherous alternative: to recognize the administrative core of the modern state as a forum for public reasoning.

VIII. ADMINISTRATIVE LAW IN THE FEDERAL REPUBLIC

In postwar German political theory and law, the democratic ideal of rational will-formation has indeed been institutionalized in constitutional law. But it has remained mostly external to the administrative apparatus itself. German constitutional and administrative law thus insist strongly on individual rights and democratic values but largely continue to treat administration in Weber's terms as an instrument for policies fully determined by other constitutional authorities.

The Basic Law states that Germany is a "democratic and social federal state."[143] In the early years of the Federal Republic, the meaning of the "social state" provision of the Basic Law was a subject of sharp dispute among constitutional and administrative law scholars.[144] Forsthoff, who abandoned Nazi ideology and became one of the most prominent administrative law scholars of the Federal Republic, argued that the idea of the social state and the *Rechtsstaat* were compatible only if they were placed at different levels of constitutional order: "The guarantees of the *rechtsstaatliche* constitution have their own logic, specified by the logic of the statutory concept: they are in the first instance exclusions."[145] The social state, by contrast, "has the structure of a positive intervention: social-legal guarantees go in the first instance not towards exclusions but rather towards positive performance, not to freedom, but rather to participation."[146] These positive interventions must, according to the principle of the *Rechtsstaat*, have legal authorization and respect statutorily established limitations and formal subjective rights. But the social state's emphasis on planning and distribution must permit great administrative discretion to interpret the broad welfare requirements identified by the legislature. The social state was thus an open-ended political concept rather than one of strict constitutional law and judicial enforcement. Forsthoff conceived administration as an instrument of democratic political choices, rather than as part and parcel of the process by which such political choices are made and elaborated.

The Marxist constitutional law scholar Wolfgang Abendroth argued, against Forsthoff, that the idea of the social state was indeed an essential constitutional principle, "leaving open the future development of social democracy" and allowing the thoroughgoing reconstruction of the economy along egalitarian lines.[147] But, like Forsthoff, he was not anxious to give the judiciary much authority in interpreting and implementing the social state. Both sought to shift the weight of constitutional power to the political branches. They differed in how they ordered political accountability. Whereas Forsthoff stressed that the social state meant a privileging of the executive, Abendroth stressed that the legislature must assume the primary role in defining the nature of the state's welfare commitments. "In a democratically organized order, society is subjected to the immediately democratically determined organ of the state, namely the legislature."[148] The other powers remain largely subservient to the legislature under this constitutional scheme: "leadership falls to statutorily-framed directives of state activity made by parliament, to whose will the formative activities of administration and the judiciary are adapted."[149] The judiciary could only "correct the democratically legitimated legislature when it widely trespasses the outer boundaries that the legal norms of the Basic Law have placed upon it."[150] For both Forsthoff and Abendroth, therefore, the democratic and social state is formed at the level of the political branches of government.

Fritz Werner offered a noteworthy alternative, suggesting that administrative law be understood as "concretized constitutional law."[151] Werner argued that the idea of a social and democratic state should be operationalized in the administrative process. He described a pluralistic kind of democracy in Germany, in which "the nation is not understood as an unstructured mass, but rather as a number of structured bodies."[152] In this context, "the administration comes more and more into the role of mediator. It is called to find and maintain social equilibrium, so that the individual is not ground to dust by the associations or struggles between associations."[153] Werner thus argued that the administrative process itself could and should realize the constitutional ideal of democracy, not merely by acting as an arm of democratically elected branches, but rather as a forum for mediating conflicts between the group interests into which society had become articulated. In this way, he gave a democratic gloss to Hegel's view of administration as a mediating institution between antagonistic social bodies. The approach of the Progressives I examine in the next chapter is very much in consonance with Werner's proposal.

The development of German public law, however, has not fully embraced the vision put forward by Forsthoff, Abendroth, or Werner. Neither Abendroth's vision of legislative supremacy in administration, nor Forsthoff's vision of executive supremacy, nor Werner's effort to internalize democracy within administration gained traction in the ensuing doctrinal development of German administrative law. From roughly 1958 to 1990, German administrative law underwent a thorough constitutionalization, which confirmed the direct applicability of fundamental rights to administrative action and further developed the principle of proportionality to assess the constitutionality of administrative actions that interfered with such rights.[154] In order to immunize the new republic from the dangers of totalitarian dictatorship, German public law put fundamental rights and the judiciary at the core of the legal order.[155] On this vision, the constitutional foundation of the *Rechtsstaat* was not simply that administrative acts were bound by statute but that individuals were protected, even from legislatively authorized action, by judicially enforceable constitutional rights. In addition, administration would remain strictly subordinate to the legislature.[156] The German constitution provides that when the legislature delegates rulemaking power to administrative bodies, "the content, purpose and scope of the authority conferred shall be specified in the law," thus limiting the discretionary power of administrative bodies and reserving the "essential" decisions to the legislature.[157] On the whole, these developments submit administration to extensive judicial and parliamentary control.

The principle of democratic will-formation in German public law, however, is completely prior to the process of administrative implementation. The constitutional principle that "[a]ll state authority is derived from the people" does not require, and in some cases limits, direct popular participation in the administrative institutions of the state.[158] Understood as the unity of all citizens, the people's control over state authority may be imperiled by the participation of specific affected persons in administrative implementation, for this may distort or dilute the application of the abstract popular will upon its members.

German administrative law thus identifies democracy with an "unbroken chain of legitimation" that stretches from the people, to their elected representatives, to the public officials who have been authorized to perform public tasks.[159] There are relatively few "independent" agencies lying outside the ministerial bureaucracy.[160] The strongly instrumental, Weberian conception of bureaucracy thus remains deeply entrenched in German administrative law, despite some recent efforts in scholarship and arguably some recent constitutional court decisions, which adopt a more disaggregated and pluralistic concept of popular sovereignty.[161] Werner's early argument that the constitutional principle of democracy must be concretized through participatory administrative procedures thus remains marginal to the doctrinal mainstream, as it is in tension with a unified and abstract *Volk* as the source of all state authority.

Habermas, who has been called the "Hegel of the Federal Republic,"[162] has largely embraced contemporary German public law's separation of the process of democratic will-formation from the administrative means by which it is implemented. His habilitation, published as *Structural Transformation of the Public Sphere*, sought to recover the tradition of rational discourse from nineteenth-century bourgeois liberalism in order to ground the democratic constitutionalism of the Federal Republic. Drawing explicitly on Forsthoff's understanding of the dissolution of the boundaries between state and society and his mentor Abendroth's defense of the egalitarian reconstruction of society as a constitutional command, Habermas argued forcefully that democracy must be grounded upon critical public discourse rather than mere mass manipulation, administrative welfare provision, and corporatist policymaking.[163]

Habermas's ensuing philosophical career has repeatedly puzzled through the problem of preserving the integrity of public deliberation in the face of necessary but potentially corrosive extensions of administrative power. In *Legitimation Crisis*, he argued that the great expansion of the welfare state's crisis management functions must be grounded in "rationally motivated agreement," which would provide reasons for the exercise of governmental authority that could be accepted by all affected persons.[164] Echoing Weber's critique of the alienated forms of reasoning produced by purely bureaucratic rule, Habermas insisted that "*there is no administrative production of meaning*."[165] Though he departed from Weber in insisting that politics can and must be based on public reason, rather than existential struggle and irrational choice, he adhered closely to Weber's separation of bureaucratic authority from such communicative forms of reason.

In *A Theory of Communicative Action*, Habermas similarly distinguished between those aspects of law that are aligned with the social "lifeworld" from those that merely serve the reproduction of the economic "system." Constitutional and criminal law fell under the former realm, as legal institutions that "need substantive justification, because they belong to the legitimate orders of the lifeworld itself and, together with informal norms of conduct, form the background of communicative action."[166] Commercial law and administrative law, by contrast, were only formally rational. They were justified only by their role in circulating of economic and political power.

In Habermas's systematic exposition of his political theory, *Between Facts and Norms*, he continued to insist that "legitimate law is generated from communicative power and the latter in turn is converted into administrative power via legitimately enacted law."[167] In his most famous formulation of this discourse principle, political legitimacy must ultimately be rooted in "the unforced force of the better argument."[168] As I shall show in chapters 2 and 4, and as Habermas himself acknowledges, John Dewey's concept of the public in many ways anticipated this understanding of democratic legitimacy.[169] But for Habermas, unlike Dewey, the deliberative process took place only in the public sphere and its relationship to the legislative branch. Administration, by contrast, was merely an instrument for the purposes identified by the legislature. Thus, the basic divide in Habermas's social theory between system and lifeworld unfolded again in a sharp distinction between communicative and administrative power: "The administration is not permitted to deal with normative reasons in either a constructive or reconstructive manner. The norms fed into the administration bind the pursuit of collective goals to pre-given premises and keep administrative activity within the horizon of purposive rationality."[170] His concern was that administrative agencies might become "self-programming," thus sundering the chain of legitimation that led from collective will-formation in the public sphere to the administrative act.

Though Habermas has continued to adhere to this strict separation between constitutional and administrative law and between instrumental and deliberative reason, he has also admitted that these categorical demarcations may not be tenable as a practical matter. With the expansion of the welfare state, it became impossible to deprive administrative agencies of at least some access to normative reasons. Given that agencies must have recourse to such reasons as they interpret open-textured statutes, and given that such norms must ultimately arise from the communicative processes of the public sphere, Habermas remained open to a "'democratization' of the administration that, going beyond special obligations to provide information, would supplement parliamentary and judicial controls on administration from within."[171] He thus endorsed experimenting with different forms of "participatory administrative practices," echoing Werner's earlier call for concretizing the constitutional norm of democracy within the administrative process.[172] But in describing such practices, he turned to the *American* example of procedures of public participation in administration, as described by the legal scholar Jerry Mashaw.[173]

Habermas's late recognition of the possibility that the administrative state itself might contribute to the process of democratic will-formation remained under-theorized and was not developed at length. His communicative addendum to Weberian bureaucratic theory left open a host of unanswered questions: Who should be included in participatory procedures for bureaucratic decision-making, and in what way should they participate? What is the proper relationship between the opinions expressed in legislative acts and those given voice in administrative regulation? What role, if any, ought the political executive play in guiding administration? If bureaucrats ought to be participants in deliberation, how ought we characterize their role in this process?

IX. CONCLUSION

In the next chapter, I will introduce a set of American thinkers who developed this deliberative understanding of administration much earlier on and provided the insights necessary to answer these questions in a coherent fashion. In the late nineteenth and early twentieth century, they introduced an understanding of the state that embraced the *Rechtsstaat* ideals they had learned from their study of Hegelian public law scholars. But they sought to reform the administrative state they had discovered in Germany by increasing the scope of democratic input. They set out not from Weber's idea of bureaucracy as a technical instrument for fulfilling any desired substantive purposes, but rather from Hegel's idea of a state in which administrative agencies and their officials reason together about the requirements of individual freedom.

The great obstacle for these thinkers would be Hegel's opposition to democracy. As we have seen, Hegel was hostile to democratic theories of the state and suspicious of the influence of public opinion on lawmaking and the state as a whole. Not only his disenchantment with popular revolution in the wake of the Reign of Terror, but also his understanding of the proper role of philosophy foreclosed him from imagining a constitutional *and* democratic state. Political philosophy, for him, was a historically limited endeavor. It was "its own time apprehended in thought."[174] In his historical context, democracy meant the unmediated, undifferentiated will of the masses; thus it could make no happy partner for the institutional rationality of the state. But Hegel also realized that freedom was an unfinished project. The political repertoire of his present could be remade as history unfolded. "America," Hegel thought, "is the land of the future."[175] It is to this future that we now turn.

2

The Hegelian Progressives

Democratic Spirit in the New American State

I. INTRODUCTION

The age of administration came relatively late to the United States. There were certainly examples of federal administrative governance, as well as substantial regulation at the state and local level, prior to the Civil War.[1] But these early forays were both quantitatively and qualitatively distinct from those introduced during the Progressive Era. In the first half of the nineteenth century, there was as yet no national consciousness of "the state"—of an overarching political structure that embodied and expressed the sovereignty of the American people. The creation of such a state would face both institutional and philosophical obstacles. In the years after the end of Reconstruction, the courts interpreted the Constitution to constrain legislative interference with the private realm of property and contract.[2] The dominant public philosophy understood the individual to be normatively prior to both society and government and endowed with certain inviolable natural rights.[3]

As the American Progressives sought to challenge such philosophical and institutional assumptions, they found abundant resources in European political thought. With the growth of major cities and industrial capitalism, Americans now found themselves sharing with Europeans "new landscapes of fact and intertwined landscapes of mind."[4] The legal and political philosophy of Hegel was one powerful stream of this vast watershed, in which continental ideas flowed into the American political imagination.[5] As I noted in the last chapter, Hegel had argued that the modern state was nothing less than the "actuality of concrete freedom."[6] He meant that the state institutionalized the principle that individuals must be the authors of their own deeds. Hegel's vision of constitutional government accordingly codified classical liberal entitlements that enabled people to interact on a formally free basis. But he argued that this order of property and contract was insufficient on its own to guarantee full self-determination. The external consequences of private economic transactions created gross inequalities of wealth, persistent poverty, and intense antagonism between social groups. These social pathologies prevented many persons from acting autonomously. The state therefore needed to perform a robust set of welfare and regulatory functions—from basic services, to consumer protection, to the adjudication of conflicts between economic interest groups. These functions were necessary to give people the resources to act as purposive agents within a competitive and complex society. A professional civil service would carry out these tasks, using not only technical skill but also ethical judgment to further the state's interest in the freedom of its constituents.

This Hegelian theory enabled the Progressives to refashion Anglo-American constitutional ideals of liberty, the rule of law, and self-government. It offered the Progressives an interactive conception of individual freedom, constituted by egalitarian social conditions and institutions rather than given by divinity or natural right. It provided an organic theory of political association, in which laws and political structures expressed the interdependent identities of the individuals who composed society. It furnished a historical conception of normativity, in which moral values corresponded to the needs of a dynamic society rather than to static ends divorced from experience. And it treated the state as an institution capable of realizing these modern conceptions of freedom, community, and worth. The basic shape of this Hegelian vision was eloquently expressed by Richard T. Ely in his proposed mission statement for the American Economic Association in 1886: "We regard the state as an educational and ethical agency whose positive aid is an indispensable condition of human progress. While we recognize the necessity of individual initiative in industrial life, we hold that the doctrine of laissez faire is unsafe in politics and unsound in morals; and that it suggests an inadequate explanation of the relations between the state and its citizens."[7]

This Hegelian inheritance has long drawn the ire of those who remain committed to classical liberal constitutionalism. Scholars such as Friedrich Hayek, and more recently Philip Hamburger and Jean Yarbrough, have sought to discredit the contemporary American administrative state and its progenitors by associating them with Hegel's supposedly odious, un-American understandings of history, politics, and freedom.[8] They suggest that Hegel and his American disciples sought to undermine individual liberty, the separation of powers, and limited government with their expansive conception of the state and a positive understanding of liberty.[9]

Scholars more sympathetic to Progressivism at the same time show some embarrassment at Hegel's influence. At the mid-twentieth century, Richard

Hofstadter sought to rebut Hayek's and other conservatives' association of Hegelian ideas with American statism by insisting upon the thoroughly domestic pedigree of Progressive ideology.[10] More recently, James Kloppenberg has suggested that Progressivism's true insights shone forth from "beneath a layer of Hegelian jargon," and Marc Stears has sought to identify the pragmatic core of Progressive political theory through the "haze of quasi-Hegelian metaphysical philosophy."[11] Kloppenberg and Stears do acknowledge that Hegel's ideas about history and the social constitution of individuality were important for Progressive thinkers. They have not, however, paid sufficient attention to the institutional dimensions of Hegel's concept of freedom and the ways these informed Progressive thought.

As the last chapter has shown, Hegel's understanding of the state did not reject but rather reformulated liberal constitutional ideals. While he critiqued natural-law reasoning, he nonetheless recognized that private rights were indispensable for individual agency.[12] For Hegel, these entitlements were fundamentally relational, guaranteeing conditions of equality, reciprocity, and recognition between persons rather than erecting boundaries between their insoluble wills. Though he rejected an absolute separation of powers as an untenable fiction, he insisted the state's functions needed to be differentiated to guarantee rational, lawful, and coherent state action. The Hegelian state did not turn to monarchical discretion to secure administrative legitimacy; instead, it relied on statutory authorization and a professional civil service to advance liberty, social welfare, and the rule of law.

The Progressives sought to integrate this institutional émigré into the American political project. They did not merely reiterate Hegel's ideas, but rather transformed them along democratic lines. While both Hegel and the Progressives stressed the active role of the state in promoting social freedom, Hegel rejected the idea of popular sovereignty and derided public opinion's contingency and one-sidedness. The Progressives, by contrast, looked to public opinion as an essential reference point for administrative action. As Herbert Croly argued, "[i]n so far as the exercise of popular political power in a democratic state is dissociated from the exercise of merely coercive methods, and derives its authority from the consent of public opinion, administrative action cannot very well become an agency of oppression."[13] This emphasis on public opinion reflected the contemporaneous expansion of national political journalism and the growing influence of broad-based reform movements on national legislation.[14] The coalescing mass public experienced a perilous civil society in which individuals had lost their capacity to recognize themselves in the laws and patterns of social organization that governed them.[15] The application of democratic control to social life might restore self-government, but only if the methods of administration were themselves popular: "the administration itself must be democratized at once by its organization, its methods of recruitment, its behavior, its sympathies and ideals."[16] Administrative specialists would engage in ethical reasoning, not as a cloistered group of enlightened experts, but rather as partners with affected persons in the elaboration of statutory norms.

This chapter explores this vision through five prominent American Hegelians: W.E.B. Du Bois, Woodrow Wilson, John Dewey, Mary Follett, and Frank Goodnow. What unites these thinkers is an understanding of *the state as an institutional articulation of the public*. That is to say, the state referred to the ongoing interaction between collective deliberation, on the one hand, and the political institutions that expressed and enforced the conclusions of such deliberation, on the other. But each of these theorists emphasized different aspects of this understanding, sometimes in ways that were in tension with one another. Du Bois developed an account of the Reconstruction period that stressed the role of the state in guaranteeing the freedom of African Americans. His account centered on the administrative provision of requisites for the creation and maintenance of a future democratic political order. Wilson, by contrast, stressed the need for administrative responsiveness to public opinion. While Wilson's thought is indispensable in understanding Progressive theory, his theory and politics included undeniably racist elements. Rather than deny this aspect of his legacy, I argue that Wilson's theory of racially constituted social unity must be supplanted by Du Bois's concern for civil rights and Dewey's early formulation of deliberative democracy.

Dewey argued that rational public discourse required extensive social intervention by the state. But he maintained that the state's welfare functions must themselves be guided by an articulate, associative public. Follett buttressed Dewey's concept of the public with a Hegelian theory of democracy, in which individuals would develop cooperative power through egalitarian participation in administrative decision-making. Goodnow emphasized the connection between administration and popular sovereignty and explored how individual rights could be respected within the administrative process. Together, these Hegelian Progressives established the intellectual foundations for a state that aimed to realize individual autonomy in and through collective autonomy, as it was expressed in public law, and carried out in administrative action.

I am hardly the first to suggest that German theory may shed light on American public law. As I noted in the Introduction and first chapter, scholars today often think of administrative agencies in Max Weber's terms as bodies that apply "power on the basis of knowledge."[17] The Progressive defense of administration, in particular, is typically treated as a Weberian effort to promote bureaucratic efficiency and instrumental rationality.[18] Some scholars, by contrast, have insisted that the American administrative state is and ought to be governed not primarily by statutory fidelity and scientific knowledge but rather by the dictates of presidential will.[19] Their model is not Weber's, but Carl Schmitt's.[20]

These perspectives, however, provide at best incomplete and at times dangerous conceptions of administrative legitimacy. Under the Weberian view, bureaucracy is an inherently alienating form of rule that can do no better than to implement the commands of statutory law efficiently. Administrative agencies in this model are characterized by their technical know-how, their obedience to hierarchical command, and their ineluctable tendency to undermine human dignity and democratic self-rule. The Weberian framework of statutory positivism runs out, however, when the law leaves significant policymaking discretion to the executive branch. In that case, the Schmittian view recommends itself: the agency ought to follow the commands of the president. This presidentialist account of democratic accountability risks an unstable and even arbitrary form of rule, in which regulatory policy is guided not by the public purposes that brought agencies into being but instead by the short-term political calculations or preferences of the president. Where executive decrees upset serious reliance interests or conflict with the values held by large swaths of the population, ever deepening legitimation crises are likely to result.

The Progressive Hegelian view, by contrast, emphasizes an ongoing, constitutive relationship between administrative agencies and the people at large. It posits that the function of the administrative state is to enable individual and collective freedom in a material rather than merely formal sense. The state must provide the social and economic requisites people need to live their lives freely. But, on the Progressive view, the concrete meaning of freedom must be determined through collective deliberation rather than by expert fiat or philosophical contemplation. Progressivism therefore licenses deep transformations in the social order but requires that such reforms be authorized and specified through an institutionally disaggregated, participatory, and rational process.

Throughout this chapter, I will relate the thought of the Progressives Hegelians to broader themes in Progressive legal thought, as well as institutional developments during the Progressive Era. Progressivism is sometimes painted as opposed to constitutionalism or even legal formalism generally.[21] But the relationship between Progressivism and law is much more complementary and complex, as Progressives embraced certain conceptions and sources of law while disfavoring others.[22] Progressives rejected hierarchical conceptions of constitutional order, which placed courts at the apex of government. Legislative lawmaking instead came to center stage as an expression of democratic will. Administrative law—including both the orders and regulations of agencies, and the judicial review thereof—then served to facilitate and rationalize popular deliberation. The usual story, that participatory forms of administration were latecomers to American public law, is therefore myopic.[23] It is only when administrative law is studied from the narrow perspective of judicial review of administrative action, rather than in the broader context of actual administrative procedure and its theoretical background, that such a view can plausibly be maintained.

This recovery of Progressive Hegelian political theory is meant to situate salient features of our current public law into a normative understanding of what the state is and what the state ought to do. The administrative production and protection of rights, public participation in administrative rule-making, administrative due process, presidential leadership, and statutory priority were all part and parcel of Progressive Era theories of the state. But a reconsideration of Progressivism shows that these ways of proceeding were in the service of a substantive aim: the equal liberty of all members of the political community. A Progressive state could provide the material goods and institutional structures in which each person would see themselves, and one another, as participants in the construction of a free and fair form of human association.

II. W.E.B. DU BOIS'S BUREAU OF FREEDOM

Du Bois is a challenging but essential figure for the Progressive Hegelian tradition. He is challenging because, unlike the thinkers to follow, he does not offer direct statements of his concept of the state, in general, or administration, in particular. Du Bois is nonetheless essential, because he draws a direct link between bureaucratic governance and the norm of freedom. From Du Bois we can see the emergence of the administrative state as an institutional solution to the Hegelian struggle for equal recognition. Beginning with Du Bois in this way frames the Progressive project differently than does the usual narrative. It traces Progressive aspirations not merely to the civil service reforms of the Pendleton Act and the regulatory interventions of the Interstate Commerce Commission but further back, to the ephemeral effort of the federal government to protect the rights of freed African Americans in the southern states in the wake of the Civil War. This change in perspective reveals the underlying logic of later bureaucratic efforts to promote civil rights, which will be discussed in the next chapter.

Du Bois drew from Hegel a conception of freedom defined as equal and reciprocal recognition between individuals. And he argued as Hegel did that bureaucratic intervention could furnish the institutional and material conditions that make such recognition possible. But Du Bois went beyond Hegel in arguing that this form of freedom and this practice of administrative intervention could lay the groundwork for a racially inclusive democratic society. Du Bois's

Hegelianism thus captures American Progressivism's lasting concern with civil rights and its use of the administrative state to define and vindicate those rights. At the same time, it highlights a significant tension within Progressivism between the administrative protection of minority interests, on the one hand, and popular self-government, on the other.

The ethical stakes of Progressive Hegelianism become clearer when the problem of domination and the requirements of freedom are placed at its foundation. Progressives were generally concerned with the way modern social life could produce domination—the exercise of arbitrary power by some persons or groups over others.[24] But the Progressive movement of the early twentieth century had a poor record on questions of racial equality, with policies aimed at advancing labor and the middle class often advancing side by side with the perpetuation and deepening of the racial caste system.[25] Wilson, as we shall see, was particularly prone to coupling Hegelian political conceptions to theories of racial essentialism and exclusion. Du Bois's thought offers a rejoinder to these pathologies of the early Progressive movement.

Beginning with Du Bois's account of Reconstruction also highlights the links between the rise of the national state, individual rights, and bureaucratic intervention. The modern welfare state is sometimes portrayed as an assault on liberal rights.[26] In fact, however, rights-focused constitutionalism and federal administrative intervention were often co-original.[27] Reconstruction is a paradigm case for this simultaneous expansion of bureaucratic power and private right. Under the aegis of the Thirteenth and Fourteenth Amendments, Congress empowered the Reconstruction agencies to defend the civil rights of emancipated African Americans against hostile state and local governments. The rise of the administrative state is therefore not a simple story of public power curtailing individual rights but also of the simultaneous production of rights by the state itself. This history demonstrates the Hegelian insight that rights are political institutions that enable egalitarian social relationships rather than freestanding moral values that secure the individual against outside interference.[28] Such an understanding of reframes administrative action as a means for expanding entitlements instead of constricting them.

1. From Double-consciousness to Bureaucratic Emancipation

Du Bois's intellectual background in German idealism helped him to grasp this imminent connection between individual rights and state authority. Scholars have already noted that Du Bois's groundbreaking concept of black "double-consciousness" had its roots partly in Hegel's idea of the struggle for recognition.[29] Double-consciousness referred to a black person's "sense of always looking at one's self through the eyes of others, of measuring one's soul by the tape of a world that looks on in amused contempt and pity."[30] Du Bois argued that African Americans could not be free under conditions where "systematic humiliation" and "personal prejudice" forced them to see themselves through the downward glancing eyes of whites.[31] They could not recognize themselves as free because of the unequal power dynamics of a racially stratified society that persisted after the formal demise of slavery. Du Bois in this way adapted Hegel's insight that, between a master and a slave, any recognition could only be "one-sided and unequal" and "enmeshed in servitude."[32] True freedom would require conditions of equal and reciprocal recognition between blacks and whites.

Du Bois's Hegelian inheritance goes further than his concept of double-consciousness, however. When he turned to the role of the federal government in attempting to secure black equality, this move from the perspective of individual consciousness to the institutional requirements of freedom also had a Hegelian impulse. Hegel had observed that "the ineligibility of the human being in and for himself for slavery . . . is an insight which comes only when we recognize that the idea of freedom is truly present only as *the state*."[33] For Hegel, freedom would be a mere mental longing or personal striving, sure to end in anguish, if legal conditions were not in place to secure the autonomous agency of each of society's members. He therefore embraced the liberalizing reforms of the Prussian civil service in the early nineteenth century, which undermined feudal authority, established rights of property and contract, and provided welfare services.

Du Bois would have been familiar with this statist perspective on liberty from his study at Humboldt University in Berlin. There, he took a course on "Prussian constitutional history" with Gustav Schmoller, the preeminent scholar of the "social question" in the historical school of economics, and another on "Prussian reforms" with Rudolf von Gneist, one of the most prominent theorists of the administrative *Rechtsstaat*, who followed Hegel in emphasizing the state's dual commitment to individual rights and social provision.[34] Studies with Adolph Wagner and Heinrich von Treitschke introduced him to their more conservative Hegelian defense of the welfare state.[35]

Max Weber also briefly taught Du Bois as a substitute lecturer.[36] However, there is no evidence that Du Bois developed his understanding of bureaucracy from Weber. Du Bois' account of the Freedmen's Bureau did not address themes distinctive to Weber's account of bureaucracy, such as formal hierarchy, value-neutrality, or technical knowledge. It rather resonated with Hegelian idealist strands in the late nineteeth century German academy's study of law, history and political economy, which emphasized the positive role the bureaucratic state could play in guaranteeing positive freedom. When Du Bois interpreted the legacy of the Freedmen's Bureau, he refracted its history through the lens of this German tradition, which had witnessed liberal social order emerge through the interventions of enlightened bureaucracy.

The Bureau of Refugees, Freedmen, and Abandoned Lands was established by Congress in 1865 with immensely broad jurisdiction to "control all subjects relating to refugees and freedmen from rebel states . . . under such rules and regulations as may be prescribed by the head of the bureau."[37] The Freedmen's Bureau was therefore a relatively neglected early example of the federal welfare state, equipped with broad discretionary powers that would be carried out through administrative regulations.[38] With this power, Commissioner Oliver Otis Howard directed the Bureau to focus on support for black schooling, to "systematize and facilitate" the work of Northern educational associations.[39] When the Bureau was reauthorized, Congress specified that its purpose was to "aid" the freedmen "in making the freedom conferred by proclamation of the commander-in-chief, by emancipation under the laws of States, and by constitutional amendment, available to them and beneficial to the republic."[40] To achieve this mission, Congress provided for the use of federal administrative tribunals to adjudicate employment contract disputes, where ordinary courts had failed to recognize the entitlements of black workers.[41]

Du Bois intended his account as a rebuke to the predominant interpretation of the Bureau at the time, which saw it as an outrageous usurpation of white Southerners' rights, and an impediment to national reunification.[42] Du Bois, instead, drew a direct connection between the Bureau and the American political project of individual freedom: "[T]his tale of the dawn of Freedom is an account of that government of men called the Freedmen's Bureau,—one of the most singular and interesting attempts made by a great nation to grapple with the vast problems of race and social condition."[43] He described the Bureau's attempts to address these problems, quoting from Bureau circulars:

> "It will be the object of all commissioners to introduce practicable systems of compensated labor" and to establish schools. Forthwith nine assistant commissioners were appointed. They were to hasten their fields of work; seek gradually to close relief establishments, and make the destitute self-supporting; act as courts of law where there were no courts, or negroes were not recognized in them as free, establish the institution of marriage among ex-slaves, and keep records; see that freedmen were free to choose their employers, and help in making fair contracts for them.[44]

The requirements of freedom Du Bois identified in the work of the Freedmen's Bureau paralleled those outlined in Hegel's *Philosophy of Right*. As in Hegel's account, the purpose of these institutions is to enable each person to see every other as a free and equal being.

Du Bois's ultimate assessment of the Bureau was mixed.[45] He observed neglect and favoritism amongst Bureau personnel—often, according to Du Bois, in favor of the freedmen. Mostly he found that the context of severe racial domination, along with the extreme resistance of southern states and President Johnson, made the Bureau's work next to impossible. But despite the Bureau's failure, Du Bois draws from its history an institutional ideal:

> Had political exigencies been less pressing, the opposition to government guardianship of Negroes less bitter, and the attachment to the slave system less strong, the social seer can well imagine a far better policy—a permanent Freedmen's Bureau, with a national system of Negro schools; a carefully supervised employment and labor office; a system of impartial protection before the regular courts; and such institutions for social betterment as savings-banks, land and building associations, and social settlements. All this vast expenditure of money and brains might have formed a great school of prospective citizenship, and solved in a way we have not yet the most perplexing and persistent of the Negro problems.[46]

In advocating such a permanent Bureau, Du Bois may have had in mind the provisions of the second Freedmen's Bureau Bill, which had been vetoed by President Andrew Johnson.[47] This Bill would have extended the Bureau's life indefinitely. As Mark Graber has argued, it offered a model for a legislatively authorized administrative state that would have provided the "means and policies that best enabled former slaves to develop the capacities necessary to exercise the rights of full and equal citizens of a democratic republic."[48] Such a permanent Bureau would have facilitated equal recognition between black and white citizens and helped to assemble an inclusive American people.

2. The Democratic Purposes and Deficits of Reconstruction

Du Bois's discussion of the Freedmen's Bureau highlights the ways in which bureaucracy might be deployed for emancipatory purposes. The Freedmen's Bureau set about to establish certain necessary conditions for the legal and social freedom of African Americans. Its intervention into the labor market, social services, and public education were systematically related to one another as so many attempts to furnish forms of interpersonal recognition that make free activity possible. Du Bois emphasized the comprehensiveness of the Bureau's functions as a virtue: only such a multi-institutional approach could hope to address the deep problem of racial subordination, as its roots stretched across the grounds of social life.

The value of democracy, which would be of such moment to the other Hegelian Progressives, had a precarious place in Du Bois's thought. His reinterpretation of Reconstruction was intended as a contribution to democratic discourse, drawing on white persons' sympathy to enlarge their conception of the American popular sovereign to include African Americans.[49] Much of Du Bois's early work was directed in this way to alter white social consciousness. In *The Philadelphia Negro*, for example, he combined cutting-edge sociological analysis of African American conditions in the city with a plea for a "radical change in public opinion" to redress the segregation of even educated blacks to menial labor.[50] Du Bois sought to present the African American experience, both in literary and scientific form, in a way that would change the white majority's attitudes. He hoped that "when Right is reinforced by calm and persistent Progress . . . in the end it must triumph."[51] This was a preeminently Progressive effort to inform public opinion with a sense of both social justice and social-scientific knowledge; to bring about equality through interracial sympathy and empirical understanding.

The implicit radicalism of Du Bois's account of Reconstruction, however, was that the Freedmen's Bureau was in many respects a coercive intervention rather than a merely deliberative exercise. As Du Bois acknowledges, the Bureau was created by an act of Congress without the participation of representatives of the southern states, which remained occupied by federal armed forces.[52] The Bureau thus operated as an arm of military government, attempting—with only occasional success—to protect the rights and interests of the freedmen against the wishes of white Southerners.[53] The prerequisites for black political freedom could only be furthered through the temporary deprivation of their former masters' political freedom. Moreover, black persons were often treated as wards of the Bureau rather than as citizens who had an equal stake in republican government.[54] The Bureau thus figured as a democratically impoverished effort to pave the way for democracy, providing the requisites for self-governance in a time to come.

Some thirty years later, Du Bois would describe the Bureau as imposing a temporary "dictatorship" over property that would enable social democracy more broadly and not merely formal racial equality.[55] In the midst of the New Deal, he endorsed a democracy of ends, not a democracy of means—a suspension of ordinary political accountability and judicial process in order to achieve the egalitarian social conditions under which a future democracy could flourish. As I describe in greater detail in the next chapter, Du Bois saw a clear connection between the Freedmen's Bureau and Progressive New Deal agencies, which he believed would democratize the rural South through extensive supports for tenant farmers.[56] Du Bois was nonetheless aware that such a bureaucratic vanguard for a democratic future was necessarily limited by broader public views about the worth of the project. He lamented "the utter inability of the American mind" to grasp the ethical significance of Reconstruction and the "indifferent public opinion of the whole nation" to the condition of African Americans.[57] Without a discursive transformation in public views on questions on race, class, and property, the administrative transition from "aristocracy to industrial democracy" could not be maintained.[58]

Du Bois's analysis points to a real tension within the Progressive Hegelian political theory. On the one hand, the Progressive state must provide the *requisites* for democratic governance: it must provide the legal protections and the material goods that make equal and rational contribution to public opinion possible. On the other hand, the state must provide *contexts* for democratic governance within the state: it must enable public opinion to be efficacious, not only in framing the laws, but in their administration. Otherwise, bureaucratic intervention loses its democratic legitimacy and cannot long endure. But where social domination prevents the formation of rational public opinion on an egalitarian basis, public participation in the state threatens to undermine the bureaucratic provision of the means for democratic life. It may work to reproduce the forms of inequality that administrative intervention seeks to remedy. The case of the Freedmen's Bureau raises this issue acutely because of the strength of racial domination, racist public opinion, and the many institutional requisites for political freedom of which the freedmen and women had been forcefully deprived.

III. WOODROW WILSON'S DEMOCRATIZATION OF THE HEGELIAN STATE

As Du Bois sought a state that would enable the future formation of a free and democratic public, Wilson sought one that would reflect the will of the people in the present.[59] The juxtaposition of Du Bois and Wilson here is provocative, given the Wilson administration's infamous segregation of the federal government. Rather than ignore Wilson's racism, I contrast Du Bois's racial egalitarianism and Wilson's segregationist policies purposefully to show a tension between democratic populism and democratic equality in Progressive political thought. Du Bois championed non-participatory, vanguardist forms of bureaucratic intervention in the midst of a deeply unjust society. These transformative administrative policies would allow a future democratic public to flourish. Du Bois acknowledged, however, that this kind of revolution from above could not be sustained for long without popular support. Wilson, by contrast, sought to subject administrative intervention to the control of contemporaneous public opinion. While this approach would ensure that the administrative state was subject to popular influence, it also had reactionary consequences in a society permeated by racial prejudice. The question Du Bois and Wilson together pose is how regulatory intervention can maintain sufficient distance from the current social situation to critique and remedy its injustices, while at the same time remaining accountable to and legitimate in the eyes of those it binds.

Linking Du Bois and Wilson's thought to their common Hegelian roots not only helps to surface this problem, but also points the way toward a solution. Both Wilson and Du Bois were captivated by the German model of a welfare state staffed by morally upright professionals who would supply conditions for free agency that private action alone could or would not.[60] But unlike Hegel and Du Bois, Wilson was convinced that administration in the democratic context must maintain a popular ethos throughout, remaining open to public opinion not only by way of legislative commands but also through direct contact with affected parties. Du Bois's unassailable concern to protect the interests of subjugated social groups suggests that this process of public participation would need to be structured in a way that would counter the existing constellation of power in society. These themes will be developed further in the next chapter through examples from the New Deal and the Second Reconstruction.

1. The Study of Administration

Wilson's landmark essay, "The Study of Administration," was inspired by the movement for civil service reform, which sought to supplant the system of party patronage with a professional civil service.[61] The first significant victory for this movement was the Pendleton Act of 1883, which established a Civil Service Commission under the control of the president to supervise competitive examinations for 10 percent of the federal civil service.[62] Civil service reform was a halting and lengthy process, in which Wilson himself would later play an ambivalent role as president, as Progressive reformers sought to reconstitute the American state with a salaried and professional officialdom.[63]

Wilson began his treatment with a seemingly objective statement: there are things that government can "properly and successfully do" and the purpose of the study of administration is to discover "how it can do these things with the utmost possible efficiency."[64] Quickly, however, this initial question of objectively proper ends and efficient means gave way to a much subtler inquiry into the kind of ends and means suitable to a democratic constitutional state. This exploration of democratic administration was guided by Hegel's conception of historicity and Lorenz von Stein's Hegelian conception of the role of administration.[65] Wilson cited Hegel's *Philosophy of Right* for the proposition that philosophy is "nothing but the spirit of that time expressed in abstract thought" to explain why administrative science had come so late on the scene: "The question was always: Who shall make the law, and what shall the law be? The other question, how the law should be administered with enlightenment, with equity, with speed, and without friction, was put aside as 'practical detail' which clerks could arrange after doctors had agreed on principle."[66]

These questions of the "Who," "What," and "How" of law had interconnected answers. Democratic constitutionalism settled the question of the "Who" by placing sovereign authority in the people themselves. But the democratization of lawmaking also meant that "where government once might follow the whims of a court, it must now follow the views of a nation. And those views are steadily widening to new conceptions of state duty."[67] Democratization opened the possible content of legislation to the wide array of concerns of the people at large, under circumstances of increasing economic complexity, labor unrest, financial speculation, and monopoly.[68]

Democracy not only changed the ends for which law should be deployed, it also changed the way that law should be implemented. "The idea of the state and the consequent ideal of its duty are undergoing a noteworthy change; and 'the idea of the state is the conscience of administration.' Seeing every day new things which the state ought to do, the next thing is to see clearly how it ought to do them."[69] The unattributed quotation is from Lorenz von Stein.[70] As discussed in chapter 1, Stein developed Hegel's concept of the bureaucratic state into an influential vision of "the administration of social progress." Stein argued that the "idea of the state" provided the administration with "a free view into the future" amidst the ambiguities of social conflict in the present.[71] Wilson endorsed this Hegelian conception of administrative decision-making, even as he remained sensitive to concerns with official efficiency, impartiality, and expertise that Hegel and Weber shared. While "the field of administration is a field of business," it was nonetheless "raised very far above the level of mere technical detail by the fact that through its greater principles it is directly connected with the lasting maxims of political wisdom, the permanent truths of political progress."[72]

Wilson, however, democratized the ethical orientation of Hegelian bureaucracy. Because the scope of state duty was ultimately determined by the popular sovereign, the "conscience of administration" must be shaped by public opinion: "administration in the United States must remain sensitive at all points to public opinion. . . . The ideal for us is a civil service cultured and self-sufficient enough to act with sense and vigor, and yet so intimately connected with popular thought, by means of election and constant public counsel, as to find arbitrariness or class spirit out of the question."[73] Wilson did not mean to equate administration with politics or to elevate it to the realm of constitutionalism.

On the one hand, "administration lies outside *politics*. Administrative questions are not political questions."[74] He wished to distinguish administration from politics on the grounds that politics settled the greater policy issues, and administration concerned the details of their implementation. But both "politics" and "administration" might make up the work of one and the same public institution: "no lines of demarcation, separating administrative from non-administrative functions can be run between this and that department of government."[75]

2. The Sources of Social Organism: Racial Homogeneity or Egalitarian Discourse?

To grasp Wilson's conception of the relationship between politics and administration, it is helpful to consider Wilson's broader political theory. Like Hegel, Wilson had an organic political theory, meaning he emphasized supra-individual forms of organization and identity. But unlike Hegel, Wilson located the organic principle in society itself, rather than in political institutions. As he put it in the *The State*, "[g]overnment is merely the executive organ of society, the organ through which its habit acts, through which its will becomes operative, through which it adapts itself to its environment and works out for itself a more effective life."[76]

Wilson's understanding of the "social organism" is both underdeveloped and profoundly problematic, as it was rooted in both ascriptive and communicative commonality. In an unpublished essay on "The Modern Democratic State," he at one point relied on racial identity to delimit the social organism, arguing that "democratic institutions depend upon homogeneity of race and community of thought."[77] Here, Wilson adopted a racialized conception of the social organism, which was widespread in the founding period of American political science, particularly among other Hegelian scholars such as John Burgess.[78] Though racial identity had played no role in Hegel's own political philosophy, these theorists blended his organic conception of the state with race "science" and theories of social evolution in order to analyze political development according to the intrinsic political "genius" of racial groups. Such a racially exclusionary concept democracy was not idle speculation for Wilson. In his campaign for president he had courted the support of black leaders such as Du Bois, promising improvement on civil rights issues; but upon assuming office, Wilson approved the segregation of positions in the Post Office, Bureau of the Census, and Treasury Department.[79] In Wilson's hands, the recently minted federal bureaucracy was transformed into an instrument of white supremacy.

In a furious open letter to Wilson on the pages of *The Crisis*, Du Bois described the segregation of the civil service as "the gravest attack on the civil liberties of our people since emancipation."[80] Greater than the routine violence, grinding material want, and the day-to-day indignities of Jim Crow was the Wilson administration's physical separation of black from white employees and its removal of black professionals from positions of authority over whites. Du Bois described the resulting "personal insult and humiliation" in vivid terms: "We are told that one colored clerk who could not actually be segregated on account of the nature of his work has consequently had a cage built around him to separate him from his white companions of many years."[81] The democratic promise of the civil service—not only to deliver professional government, but also to further emancipation and interracial solidarity—had been dashed in Wilson's nationalization of white supremacist institutions and ideology. It is a testament to the esteem in which Du Bois held the federal civil service in the wake of Reconstruction that this event could even rival the lynch mob in the annals of the civil rights violations suffered by the African American community, much less constitute the "gravest attack" on black civil rights since slavery. And it is a testament to Wilson's and the nation's bigotry that this public trust could be so swiftly betrayed.

This episode should not be treated only as an ugly stain on Wilson's political legacy, however. It is also instructive about the theoretical and practical dilemmas of Progressive democracy. Where society is riven by prejudicial sentiments and conditions of deep social inequality, a Wilsonian effort to subject administration to the social philosophy of his own political party may simply reproduce those same pathologies. The federal reinforcement of institutionalized racism might have been "democratic" in the shallow sense that it allowed the sentiments of a political majority to guide both the making and implementation of law. But it was undemocratic in the deeper sense that it prevented each member of the political community from contributing as an equal to political will-formation.[82]

Du Bois's theory therefore offers a necessary rebuttal to the racist elements of Wilson's thought and practice, thus dissociating a normative theory of Progressivism from the Progressive movement's historical solicitude for white supremacy. Progressive democracy, as I understand it here, requires state action that is based not merely upon majority will but also upon an inclusive, egalitarian, and rational public sphere. The state must not allow the preferences of the contemporary populace to undermine conditions under which all persons can contribute as equals to public discourse. Administration must therefore be sensitive to popular thought but not dominated by it. The government should remain relatively autonomous from society, so that it can remedy and not merely reflect its current ethical failings. "Progress" can occur in the interchange over time between the public's influence on government and the government's influence on public opinion. The interaction between public opinion and public policy can advance freedom, however, only if the state's institutional structure and professional culture are geared to counter the unequal distribution of resources and voice within society. A Progressive state that combines the best elements of Wilson's thought with Du Bois's would require administrative procedures that ensure marginalized groups are adequately heard by public officials who use their discretion to promote egalitarian outcomes.

Traces of this understanding of administration can be found in Wilson's own writings, though it would await fuller theorization by Dewey and Follett. While Wilson at times embraced racial nationalism, he nonetheless relied more heavily on "community of thought" than he did on racial identity to underwrite democratic unity: "[T]he influences which make all sources of information common to all men alike, which scatter broadcast the world's thought and the world's news, are sure to put an end to the conditions under which the many will receive without question the thought of a ruling few . . . . They multiply infinitely the number of voices which must be heeded in legislation or in executive policy."[83] Rational public discourse must regulate administration, not only indirectly through the legislative control, but directly, through public participation in the administrative process: "Liberty consists in enlightened *authoritative* public opinion—consists in the realization of the purposes of active, directive popular thought. Liberty lives and moves and has its being in self-government."[84]

3. The State and Law

Self-government required a democratic state. The concept of "the state" was of crucial importance to Progressivism and represented both the most fundamental and most elusive aspect of its Hegelian inheritance. As Eldon Eisenach points out, "What is most problematic about . . . Progressive paeans to the state is the uncertainty of its location."[85] In *The State*, Wilson covered topics ranging from anthropology, to social organization, to constitutional structure, to legal arrangements, to other governmental functions. This was not merely a matter of imprecision. The state, for Wilson and other Progressive Hegelians such as Burgess, did not simply mean official political bodies; rather, it referred to society's relationship with governmental organs.[86] In saying that "law is the will of the state," Wilson therefore did not embrace a naive legal positivism that would equate law with whatever the government commanded.[87] Rather, law was the will of the political community, expressed authoritatively by its governmental institutions, but ultimately rooted in a more fundamental social consciousness. In treating the state as designating the relationship between government and society rather than government alone, the Progressives followed Hegel, who stated that "the state . . . is both the law which permeates all relations within it and also the customs and consciousness of the individuals who belong to it."[88] This Hegelian view of the state emphasized the imminent connections between political institutions and social processes. A similar perspective was shared by W.W. Willoughby, who maintained that for the national state to come into being, "an essential psychological element must first exist subjectively in the minds of the people, and then becomes objective in laws and institutions."[89]

Such a comprehensive conception of the state was particularly powerful in the context of public finance. As Ajay Mehrotra has shown, economists such as Richard Ely and Henry Carter Adams and legal scholars such as Edwin Seligman relied upon German conceptions of the "organic or collective nature of the state" to argue that taxation ought to be based upon "ability to pay" rather than the material "benefit" the taxpayer received from government services.[90] In a country founded in opposition to taxation without representation, this formulation was necessary to recast taxation as a positive social good rather than as a necessary evil. As Adams put it, "a sense of organic unity and of interdependence and consciousness of common rights and duties go along with the idea of [tax] contribution."[91] Seligman likewise insisted that "we pay taxes not because the state protects us, or because we get any benefits from the state, but simply because the state is a part of us; . . . it is interwoven with the very fibers of [our] being."[92] These claims may strike our ear as totalitarian, since we are accustomed to equate the state with government. But the Progressives meant to express the more general point that social relationships, and the political institutions that express and enforce them, constitute individuals' identities, rights, and obligations.

The subtle but essential difference between this Progressive conception of the state and Hegel's was that Hegel had treated political institutions as the source of social unity. He understood the "organism of the state" to refer to the dynamics of the differentiated legislative, executive, and sovereign powers, which were related to each other as stages of a rational process—the creation of a "universal" rule, its application to a "particular" case, and the "ultimate decision" that unites these moments.[93] Civil society lacked this organic unity because it was characterized by antagonism between individuals and amongst social groups.

The Hegelian Progressives, by contrast, understood constitutional structures as the articulation of an underlying social identity or process. Wilson observed that there was a more fundamental "law which makes the Constitution possible, . . . which makes us conscious of our oneness as a single personality in the great company of nations; conscious of a common interest, a common vocation, and a common destiny."[94] Willoughby likewise understood the Constitution only as kind of "physical frame" for the organism of society.[95] The effect of this amendment to Hegelian state theory was to reduce, but not eliminate, the autonomy of political institutions from civil society. As Charles Edward Merriam observed, the political theories of Wilson and Willoughby embraced the German theory in which "the purpose of the state" was "expanded from the 'police theory' to the general care of the interests of the community," but they assimilated this enlarged political authority to a domestic political tradition that was "essentially democratic."[96] Merriam could therefore speak interchangeably of "governmental control or regulation" and "regulation by the people."[97] In place of Hegel's enlightened bureaucracy that was insulated from popular opinion, the Progressives insisted that administrative procedures transform public sentiments into actionable and rationable political programs.

4. Public Law and Individual Liberty

Wilson understood individual rights to lie at the core of constitutional government, and he placed significant faith in the judiciary as their guardian. But Wilson did not think the meaning of liberty remained the same across time: "Liberty fixed in unalterable law would be no liberty at all. Government is a part of life, and with life, must change, alike in its object and in its practices."[98] The Constitution therefore had to allow for substantive legal changes that would give force to the people's evolving conceptions of freedom: "The object of constitutional government is to bring the active, planning will of each part of the government into accord with the prevailing popular thought and need, and thus make it an impartial instrument of symmetrical national development."[99] The structures of government "organized" public opinion, making it a "concert of thought" that would authorize and circumscribe the exercise of political power.[100] The relationship between "the atmosphere of opinion" and government would remain lawful and non-arbitrary because the processes of lawmaking, execution, and adjudication would "make the requirements of opinion . . . clearly formulated and understood."[101]

While Wilson was influenced by German conceptions of the state, he also remained committed to an Anglo-American view of the rule of law. Wilson therefore treated the judiciary as the "balance-wheel of our entire system; it is meant to maintain that nice adjustment between governmental powers and individual rights which constitutes political liberty."[102] But he nonetheless recognized that the primary source of law in a government constituted by public opinion must primarily be legislation. The "validity" of constitutional rights depended not merely upon their general statement in the Amendments but also upon "the careful running of definite lines of positive law which shall separate those invasions of individual right by executive power which are necessary to the order and energy of the State from those which are unnecessary, arbitrary, and tyrannical."[103] Common law adjudication could work micro-adjustments in historically entrenched notions of entitlement, obligation, and liability. But the judiciary had neither the proper incentives nor the primary duty to articulate the current self-understandings of the people.

There was a risk, therefore, that the courts might impede popular legislation through spurious statutory and constitutional construction. As Roscoe Pound argued, when the judiciary "assumes to stand between the legislature and the public and thus . . . to protect the individual from the state, it really stands between the public and what the public needs and desires, and protects individuals who need no protection against society which does need it."[104] For this reason, "courts are less and less competent to formulate rules for new relations which require regulation. They have the experience of the past. But they do not have the facts of the present."[105] Statutes enacted by elected officials were instead the preeminent mechanisms of historical adaptation. Wilson observed that through such "deliberate formulation of new law," the public could reshape social relations to address the concerns that had arisen through public discourse.[106] Legislation was the instrument the people could use to form society according to their broad "and broadening" interests.[107]

5. Legislative Democracy and Administrative Discretion

Democratic governance, though expressed in legislation, was not limited to it. Locating normative motivation in the organism of society required regulatory techniques that were continually responsive to the present needs of the people. Administration channeled current social understandings into the implementation of law. In his "Lectures on Administration" at Johns Hopkins, Wilson observed: "The *scope of administration* is . . . *all the necessary and characteristic functions of the State*, largely defined and regulated and always limited . . . by the laws, to which it is of course subject; *but serving the State, not the law-making body* in the State, and *possessing a life not resident in statutes*.[108] Administration's "life" was bound to the underlying social processes that gave rise to its legislative mandate. When administrative officials interpreted the commands of a statute, they were mediating between the institutionalized opinions and needs of a past public and the inchoate opinions and needs of a present public: "*Law is always a summing up of the past*: its result, the conclusion from its experience . . . . *Administration* . . . is *always in contact with the present*: it is the state's experiencing organ. It is thus that it becomes a *source of law*: *directly*, by the growth o[f] administrative practice and tradition . . . *or indirectly*, by way of suggestion and initiative."[109] Administration could become a "source of law" because every exercise of state "will" was a more-or-less proximate expression of popular consciousness. Administrative regulations could adjust to shifts in common understanding more quickly than statutory or common law could.

Willoughby similarly rejected a hierarchical view of the public legal order, with the constitutional law at the apex and administrative law at its base. Instead he insisted that an administrative ordinance was of "equal legal validity with the more general and formal mandates of the State," so long as it was within "the legal competence of the authority uttering it."[110] The Constitution established Congress's jurisdiction to legislate, and legislation established the administrative agency's jurisdiction. But, according to Willoughby, an ordinance, regulation, or adjudicative order that fell within the sphere of an agency's delegated powers had the same degree of legal authority as a statute, judicial common law, or constitutional law.

This view drew on certain strands of nineteenth century administrative law, which treated regulations as "binding on all within the sphere" of the "legal and constitutional authority" under which it had been issued.[111] By the last decades of the century, the Court found that a regulation could bind private persons as well, so long as the regulation was consistent with the statutory scheme.[112] This approach still maintained a formal hierarchy of statutory and administrative law, with the courts prepared to strike down regulations that exceeded the scope of authority Congress had delegated to the agency.[113] But giving a regulation the force of law tended to destabilize this normative hierarchy. The Constitution granted to Congress the power to "make laws necessary and proper for carrying into Execution" its powers.[114] Investing an administrative official with the power to issue regulations in furtherance of such powers would sometimes be appropriate. At that point, regulations issued by the officer might be treated as mere extensions of legislative power, entitled to the same deferential standard of judicial review as the statute itself. The Supreme Court thus observed in *Boske v. Comingore* (1900) that "[i]n determining whether the regulations adopted . . . are consistent with law, we must apply the rule of decision which controls when an act of Congress is assailed as not being within the powers conferred upon it by the Constitution; that is to say, a regulation should not be disregarded or annulled unless in the judgment of the court it is plainly or palpably inconsistent with law."[115] Along this line of reasoning, a regulation might in effect determine the meaning of an ambiguous statute, rather than leave the interpretation of law exclusively to the judiciary.

This approach migrated even into constitutional challenges to administrative orders, in which the fact-finding of the agency might be treated in the same way as the fact-finding of the legislature itself.[116] Affirming the constitutionality of a rate-setting order by a state railroad commission, for example, Justice

Hughes observed in 1899 that "[t]he rate-making power necessarily implies a range of legislative discretion; and so long as the legislative action is within its proper sphere, the courts are not entitled to interpose upon their own investigation of traffic conditions and transportation problems to substitute their judgment for that of the legislature or of the railroad commission exercising its delegated power."[117] It was necessary to treat administrative findings on parity with legislative findings in constitutional matters if statutory standards were to have an independent effect on the conduct and judicial review of administrative bodies. Otherwise every question of administrative law would be challenged and settled by generic principles of constitutional law rather than according to the statutory scheme in which the agency operated.[118]

Wilson's striking claims that administration had "a life not resident in statutes" and could become a "source of law," and Willoughby's claim that a regulation had "equal validity" with statutes and the Constitution, thus had support in American judicial case law. But because of their immersion in German state theory, Wilson and Willoughby were able to situate this legal doctrine in a more comprehensive conception of the role of administrative agencies in democratic government. Regulations were the contact point between political institutions and the civil society they ruled. They might serve to maintain a concrete, rather than merely formal, connection between citizens' self-conscious understandings and the legal norms to which they were bound. Giving full scope to this connection required elevating administrative norms to the full rank of law proper.

6. The Rhetorical Presidency and Delegated Execution

Though administration was authorized by legislation, the Constitution placed responsibility for the execution of the law on the president.[119] And where statutes left some discretion as to their implementation, the political legitimacy of such choices would seem naturally to stem from the president's independent constitutional stature and electoral mandate. Hegel's chief executive—a hereditary monarch—was to do little more than "say 'yes' and dot the 'i'" and was meant merely to symbolize national sovereignty.[120] The American president, by contrast, had unique democratic-constitutional authority that might justify administrative conduct. And indeed, the presidency did play a major role in Wilson's thought and practice, as an office that could give shape and energy to national political programs. But he did not believe that the president ought to control administrative action directly, preferring a more pluralistic and participatory executive process.

The Progressive Era marked a radical reconceptualization of the office of the president that has carried through to the present. As Sidney Milkis observes, in the 1912 election contest both Wilson and Theodore Roosevelt "downplayed the importance of their respective party platforms, stressing instead a vital connection to popular will," and catalyzing "a shift from a decentralized public to a mass democracy."[121] Wilson placed a premium on the presidency as a "unifying force in our complex system" of checks and balances.[122] He argued that, by the beginning of the twentieth century, the president had become "the guide of the nation in political purpose, and therefore in legal action."[123] It was his duty to be the "spokesman for the real sentiment and purposes of the country" as "the only spokesman of the whole people."[124]

The magnified role Wilson claimed for the presidency was primarily in relation to congressional legislation. He was to serve as an "originator of policies" rather than the mere executor of them.[125] It would be a mistake, however, to equate Progressivism's concern with democratic administration with extensive presidential control of the administrative apparatus. The Progressive presidency did not operate according to a strongly "unitary" theory of the executive, which would subject executive officers throughout the administrative hierarchy to the president's direct command.[126] On the contrary, Wilson asserted that "as legal executive, his constitutional aspect, the President cannot be thought of alone. He cannot execute the laws. Their actual daily execution must be taken care of by the several executive departments and by the now innumerable body of federal officials throughout the country."[127] Wilson therefore suggested that most executive authority be delegated to cabinet positions, which the president should fill with "eminent representative citizens, selecting them rather for their special fitness for the great business posts to which he has assigned them than for their political experience, and looking to them for advice in the actual conduct of the government rather than in the shaping of political policy."[128]

This form of executive government by "commission" opened up yet another channel for public influence on administration.[129] Though Wilson conceived the cabinet members as performing an administrative rather than political role, he recognized that the president might nonetheless seek their "political advice," not because of their "intimate contact with politics," but rather because of "their natural good sense and experienced judgment, . . . their knowledge of the country and its business and its social conditions, . . . [and] their sagacity as representative citizens of more than usual discretion."[130] Secretaries responsible to the president might therefore be political, not in the sense of partisanship or electoral contest, but in the sense of making value judgments rooted in an informed understanding of the means by which the president and his party's broad goals might be implemented.

These theoretical commitments were born out in practice. Wilson pioneered the "rhetorical presidency," using his speeches to influence legislation and national public discourse.[131] He took presidential leadership over Congress as "the legislation of the New Freedom poured fourth at an unheard-of pace,"[132] including regulatory statutes such as: the Keating-Owen Child Labor Act,[133] which empowered the attorney general, the secretary of commerce, and the secretary of labor jointly to promulgate rules to prevent the interstate shipment of goods produced by child labor; the Federal Reserve Act,[134] which established an independent commission to supervise banks and determine monetary policy; and the Federal Trade Commission Act,[135] which established an independent agency to prevent unfair competition.

Wilson thus pressed for and won landmark Progressive legislation that would grant administrative discretion to solve major social problems. But he did not seek systematically to control its exercise. Wilson carried out a "theory of devolution" and "consciously avoided discussing the affairs of other agencies when dealing with a single department head."[136] His executive was much more plural than unitary. In this respect, Wilson's presidency realized the Progressive effort to carve out a space for administrative decision-making not immediately subject to partisan politics and yet responsive to public input and social scientific judgment.

IV. JOHN DEWEY'S COMMUNICATIVE CONSTITUTION OF THE ADMINISTRATIVE STATE

In *The Public and Its Problems*, Dewey quoted Wilson's presidential campaign platform, *The New Freedom*: "Yesterday, and ever since history began, men were related to one another as individuals. . . . To-day, the everyday relationships of men are largely with great impersonal concerns, with organizations, not with individuals. Now this is nothing short of a new social age, a new age of human relationships, a new stage-setting for the drama of life."[137] While Dewey criticized the historical exaggeration of Wilson's claim, he agreed that "the contrast which Mr. Wilson had in mind is a fact."[138] Like Wilson's "New Freedom," Dewey advocated for a "new individualism," in which personal freedom would reemerge through the democratic, experimental, and administrative control of the massive social organizations and forces into which persons had become submerged in the process of industrialization. But Dewey also shared with Du Bois a concern to ensure that the government provide the institutional and material goods to establish a democratic public.[139] For Dewey, democracy required broad governmental support to ensure that the people was constituted by free individuals who had realized their personal capacities to the fullest.

For many of these ideas, Dewey, like Wilson and Du Bois, was deeply indebted to Hegel.[140] Even once he moved away from Hegelian metaphysics and embraced the pragmatic philosophy of William James, Dewey acknowledged that Hegel had "left a permanent deposit in [his] thinking."[141] Dewey's understanding of the relationship between individual and community, between moral judgment and laws and institutions, and ultimately his conceptions of the relationship between the public and the administrative state each bear the marks of Hegelian philosophy. Dewey reworked Hegel's ideas, however, by developing a conception of the state as an institutional reflection of public discourse about shared social problems. This pragmatic conception of the state rejected Hegel's tendency toward metaphysical formulations of politics without adopting Wilson and Burgess's racially circumscribed conceptions of social organism. Dewey in this way provided a theory of the administrative state that placed collective deliberation at its core.

1. Hegelian Institutionalism, Generalized Individualism, and Social Legislation

In his 1897 lecture at the University of Chicago on "Hegel's Philosophy of Spirit," Dewey observed that for Hegel government "constitutes the State where the individual identifies himself with the will manifested in the community in which he lives and thus gets beyond his mere individuality and becomes a member and organ of the whole. The state is then completed objective spirit; the externalized reason of man."[142] This concept of the state as "externalized reason" provided a foundation for Dewey's later understanding of the state as an institutional articulation of the public. But Dewey argued that Hegel's account of the political constitution was the "most artificial and the least satisfactory portion of his political philosophy."[143] He seemed to object most strongly to Hegel's claim that a constitutional monarchy was the highest form of the state. Hegel, Dewey implied, had not realized the superiority of the democratic principle. Importantly, Dewey did not subject to the same criticism Hegel's description of the civil service: "The class having charge of the general interests of civil society, the educators, the priests, and the civil authorities . . . devote themselves more specially to the higher spiritual interests and to the control of society."[144]

Dewey also followed Hegel in seeing the individual as a socially and institutionally formed being. In *The Ethics of Democracy*, Dewey embraced a conception of the democratic community as a "social organism," in which "the citizen is a member of the organism, and, just in proportion to the perfection of the organism, has concentrated within himself its intelligence and will."[145] Dewey's organic concept of society did not entail submersion of the individual within the democratic whole. Rather, he argued for the "sovereignty of the citizen," since each citizen embodied in microcosm the whole of the democratic sovereign.[146] Likewise, in *Outlines of a Critical Theory of Ethics*, which was explicitly indebted to Hegel's *Philosophy of Right*,[147] Dewey offered the following "ethical postulate": "In the realization of individuality there is found also the needed realization of some community of persons of which the individual is a member; and, conversely, the agent who duly satisfies the community in which he shares, by that same conduct satisfies himself."[148] Individuals' freedom would be achieved in and through equal participation in a shared social life. This co-realization of the individual and the community took place through the family, church, and "the city, state, and nation."[149] Because such institutions "are expressions of common purposes and ideas, they are not merely private will and intelligence, but public will and reason."[150]

This Hegelian conception of individuality and institutionalism motivated Dewey's account of public administration. In his 1908 treatise *Ethics*, written with James Tufts, Dewey emphasized the technical need to "increase administrative efficiency," but he quickly turned to the substantive areas that required administrative regulation, such as municipal social services.[151] Dewey acknowledged that American political ideology was resistant to such forms of state activity. But he argued that the present realities required a reformulation of individualist ideals:

> American cities and states find themselves confronted with the same problems of public health, poverty and unemployment, congested population, traffic and transportation, charitable relief, tramps and vagabondage, and so forth, that have troubled older countries. We face these problems, moreover, with traditions which are averse to "bureaucratic" administration and public "interference." Public regulation is regarded as a "paternalistic" survival, quite unsuited to a free and independent people. It would be foolish, indeed, to over-look or deny the great gains that have come from our American individualistic convictions. . . . But it is certain that the country has reached a state of development, in which these individual achievements and possibilities require new civic and political agencies if they are to be maintained as realities. Individualism means inequity, harshness, and retrogression to barbarism (no matter under what veneer of display and luxury), unless it is a *generalized* individualism: an individualism which takes into account the real good and effective—not merely formal—freedom of *every* social member.[152]

The formal freedom of the market needed to be complemented by a principle of positive freedom that would ensure that all individuals could in fact exercise their capabilities. This was a more expansive, Hegelian conception of individual freedom than the contractual, juridical freedom of classical liberalism.

For Dewey, individuality was at the core of democracy itself, which was the "embodiment of the moral ideal of a good which consists in the development of all the social capacities of every individual."[153]

He therefore argued for "constructive social legislation," which would secure a "*generalized* versus a *partial* individualism" thus "making individual liberty a more extensive and equitable matter."[154] Such social legislation would establish new "public agencies of inspection, supervision, and publicity" to address the social problems and inequalities created by an increasingly complex society.[155] Dewey's repeated emphasis on administration as a means of "publicity" arose from a notion similar to Wilson's that administration was government's "experiencing organ." He suggested that administrative bodies could bring to light problems of which citizens were unaware. This meant that administration's proper role was not merely to execute clearly circumscribed functions that the public had already endorsed. More than this, public authorities would raise into common consciousness previously unrecognized social failings that merited political intervention.

2. Science, Democracy, and Planning

Deweyan administration was more than a matter of expertise. It required a practical ability to determine what questions were of moral significance to the public among the mass of potential topics of administrative inquiry: "The problems which fall to the lot of the proper organs of administrative inspection and supervision are scientific problems, questions for expert intelligence conjoined with wide sympathy. In the true sense of the word, they are political questions: that is, they relate to the welfare of society as an organized community of attainment and endeavor."[156]

Politics and science were not opposed but rather intrinsically linked, with administration mediating between the two. As Hillary Putnam observes, "For Dewey, the scientific method is simply the method of experimental inquiry combined with free and full discussion—which means, in the case of social problems, the maximum use of the capacities of citizens for proposing courses of action, for testing them, and for evaluating the results."[157] To be sure, a truly scientific experiment would isolate some independent causal variable and identify its effect on some dependent variable. But this level of precision would not be possible in public discourse, elections, or even expert administration. Instead, public discussion provided the more fluid and open ground in which hypotheses might be raised and in which the practical and moral consequences of empirical information could be weighed. Dewey did not see this as a purely instrumental process in which normative ends would be chosen and scientific means adapted to those ends. Instead, the results of testing various means would feed back into the discussion of values. He suggested that "policies and proposal for action be treated as working hypotheses, not as programs rigidly adhered to and executed. They will be experimental in the sense that they will be entertained subject to constrained and well-equipped observation of the consequences they entail when acted upon, and subject to ready and flexible revision in light of observed consequences."[158]

Such experimental social planning was necessary because of contradictions in the ideological and institutional structure of advanced industrial society. The coherent classical liberal model combining small-scale capitalism, individualism, natural rights, and common law legalism had given way to an incoherent model combining large-scale corporate capitalism with an individualist law and ethic premised upon classical bourgeois political economy. Beholden to these anachronistic ideals, "we glorify the past, and legalize and idealize the *status quo*, instead of seriously asking how we are to employ the means at our disposal so as to form an equitable and stable society. . . ."[159] Dewey thus argued that the "old" individualist philosophy needed to be replaced with a "new" one, grounded upon the reciprocal relationship between individual freedom and social institutions that he had elaborated in his earlier writings. Americans would have to "cease opposing the socially corporate to the individual."[160]

In this respect, Dewey shared with the Progressive movement a preoccupation with "para-state" institutions, such as trade and professional associations, unions, universities, charitable foundations, religious organizations, advocacy groups, and research centers, which could mediate between the interests of the isolated individual and the broader national community.[161] This tradition drew on Hegel's vision of vocation-based "corporations," which served as an "ethical root of the state" by providing individuals with a "universal end" shared by the members their trade.[162] Such bodies could synthesize individual interests into an organized institutional apparatus and so enable the state to reconcile and harmonize the conflicting values within society. Para-state educational and research institutions could also disseminate knowledge more widely to enhance the quality of public engagement in policymaking. By bringing science and technology under the purview of the democratic public, these institutions could help individuals develop their interests and capacities.

The para-state formed a crucial link between individuals and the administrative apparatus itself.[163] The two often shared organizational logics, professional orientations, collective purposes, and subject-matter emphases that facilitated communication between private persons and officers of the state. Noting such agencies as the Interstate Commerce Commission, Federal Reserve Board, and Farm Relief Board on the eve of the New Deal, Dewey therefore suggested that "the probabilities seem to favor the creation of more such boards in the future, in spite of all concomitant denunciations of bureaucracy and proclamations that individualism is the source of our national prosperity. . . . The problem of social control of industry and the use of governmental agencies for constructive social ends will become the avowed center of political struggle."[164] If democratically responsive, such governmental agencies could promote the new individualism by identifying social problems, elaborating political purposes, and generating consciousness of the interconnectedness of personal fates.

3. The Public and the State

To understand how Dewey imagined reformulating administrative agencies along democratic lines, we must turn to Dewey's foundational conception of "the public." Dewey's *The Public and Its Problems*, much like Hegel's *Philosophy of Right*, sought to diagnose and resolve problems stemming from the legal and economic structure of modern social life. Hegel had recognized that the "right of property" provided a kind of "formal" freedom but that the "private use of property also has external relations . . . which can wrong or harm other people."[165] Complex industrial economies are "dependent on external circumstances and remote combinations whose full implications cannot be grasped by . . . individuals."[166] Because these implications could impact society at large, the "individual in a universal sense, i.e. the public," has a "right to regulate" them.[167] Dewey shared Hegel's concern that relations in privity could cause harm to third parties—what economists today call the problem of "externality."[168] The perception of these externalities gave rise to the public: "transactions between singular persons and groups bring a public into being when their indirect consequences—their effects beyond those immediately engaged in them—are of importance."[169]

Dewey went beyond Hegel, however, in arguing that democracy was the core political norm of a society that placed moral value on individual freedom. He argued that classical liberalism gave rise to the legitimate demand that the officers of the state should be controlled by the collective voice of citizens. However, the legal implementation of free markets also set forces in motion that impeded democracy: turbulent economic cycles, large-scale industrial concerns, and complex patterns of organization over which the citizenry had no conscious control. Such conditions "demand the utilization of government as the genuine instrumentality of an inclusive and fraternally associated public. The new age of human relationships has no political agencies worthy of it. The democratic public is still largely inchoate and unorganized."[170]

The theory of the democratic public that Dewey advanced here had evolved significantly from his earlier social organic theory.[171] In this later phase, Dewey retained but reworked the Hegelian notion of institutional rationality. Whereas Hegel had understood institutional rationality to consist in the political constitution's embodiment of the principle of individual freedom, Dewey understood institutional rationality as a more pragmatic capacity to understand and resolve "problems" that arose through social interaction.[172] He therefore departed from Hegel in arguing against what he saw as a "magnified idealization of the State," which had the tendency to place political institutions out of the reach of popular influence.[173] The Progressives often criticized this authoritarian aspect of the Hegelian concept of the state, especially in the years surrounding World War I.[174] Dewey observed that "Hegel found it 'superficial and absurd to regard as objects of choice' social constitutions; to him 'they were necessary structures in the path of development.' To us [Americans] they are the cumulative result of a multitude of daily and ever renewed choices."[175]

Dewey understood constitutional government not as an inherently rational institutional architecture, as Hegel did, but rather as an experimental and always imperfect effort to reassemble a fractured social consciousness: "The lasting, extensive consequences of associated activity bring into existence a public. In itself it is unorganized and formless. By means of officials and their special powers it becomes a state. A public articulated and operating through representative officers is the state; there is no state without government, but also there is none without the public."[176] Dewey thus followed Wilson, Willoughby, and Burgess's comprehensive understanding of the state, designating the relationship between society and government rather than government alone. His major innovation was to discard the concept of social organism as a basis for political unity, which often aligned with a racially exclusionary view of political identity. He replaced this social unity with a "public" that was brought together in discourse concerning market externalities. "The state" referred to the ongoing linkages between this discourse and governmental action. As Elizabeth Anderson explains, "Dewey took democratic decision-making to be the joint exercise of practical intelligence by citizens at large, in interaction with their representatives and other state officials. It is cooperative social experimentation."[177]

Dewey followed the broader Progressive tradition in understanding public opinion not as the arbitrary outburst of the crowd or as the mere tallying of individual preferences. It was, rather, a condition of what Frank Giddings called "rational like-mindedness."[178] Opinion only became truly "public" when it aimed at reasoned understanding, when it was informed by experience and experiments, and when it was open to revision on the basis of discussion and the observation of consequences. "Opinions and beliefs concerning the public presuppose effective and organized inquiry. . . . Opinion casually formed and formed under direction of those who have something at stake in having a lie believed can be *public* opinion only in name."[179] This did not mean that rational public opinion needed to be unanimous or that no reasonable differences about the means or ends of politics could exist. Rather, as Melvin Rogers has argued, Dewey's "public" was a plural concept, allowing the relationship between social groups and bureaucratic power to evolve over time in at once complementary and conflictual fashion. Rogers observes that Dewey held "a view of the public sphere that is internally differentiated. This differentiation accounts for the smooth substantive inclusion of the demands of specific publics into the administrative apparatus of the state, even as it defends publics that emerge in a more oppositional relationship to state power."[180] Where truly "public" opinion remained inarticulate, political and administrative institutions could facilitate its advancement through the provision of knowledge, resources, and egalitarian deliberative conditions.

4. The Public, the "Public Interest," and the "Science of Common Action"

Dewey's notion of "the public" both reflected and influenced public legal discourse. In the classical constitutional discourse of the late nineteenth century, individual rights of property and contract constituted a private sphere into which the state could not generally intrude, except in the exercise of certain "police" functions relating to public health and welfare.[181] The Supreme Court held in *Munn v. Illinois* (1877) that property "affected with the public interest" nonetheless lay presumptively within the bounds of police regulation.[182] Though such property could be identified in cases of monopoly or "virtual monopoly," the scope of the category was potentially elastic: "Property does become clothed with a public interest when used in a manner to make it of public consequence, and affect the community at large."[183] The public's legitimate interest in private property took on increasing importance in Progressive administrative reforms, as state-level commissions sought to set rates charged by railroad and utility companies.[184]

Progressive legal scholars sought to broaden the public utility concept, arguing that there was no justiciable boundary line between private property affected with public interests and "purely" private property. As Robert Hale argued, "There is scarcely a single advantage possessed by a business affected with a public use which cannot be matched in the case of some unregulated concern."[185] Instead of leaving the scope of permissible regulation to judicial determination, they argued that the extent of the state's regulatory power should be determined primarily by public opinion. Justice Oliver Wendell Holmes, for example, contended that "the Legislature may forbid or restrict any business when it has sufficient force of public opinion behind it," providing compensation only when the regulation went so far as to constitute a "taking" of private property.[186] Thomas Reed Powell likewise criticized the Court's restrictions of wage regulations by arguing that "the wage relation is a subject of public concern and that, therefore, the field in which minimum wage legislation operates is a proper field of government activity."[187]

Dewey followed in this Progressive legal tradition in understanding "the public" as a community constituted by discourse concerning economic and social problems created by purportedly "private" interactions. "Public interest" from this perspective was not a circumscribed legal category, such as a property interest, but a malleable expression of the people's concern with how the rights of some had come to infringe upon the interests of others without contractual agreement. Dewey therefore rejected any categorical demarcation between purely private property and the public interest, insisting that "the line of demarcation between actions left to private initiative and management and those regulated by the state has to be discovered experimentally."[188]

Dewey's concept of the public and its problems in turn influenced administrative law scholar John Dickinson's argument for administrative regulation. Dickinson cited Dewey for the proposition that "the study of social order . . . must begin with the concrete phenomena of human interactions. The activity of one human being may reinforce, or cooperate with, the activity of another, or it may interfere with it. . . . When such interference frustrates what is felt by the other as an interest, the material is present for conflict and disorder."[189] Dickinson concluded that in a complex of modern society, such conflicts could not be settled by custom or voluntary adjustment. Drawing an analogy to vehicle traffic in densely populated areas, he argued that chaos would ensue without "the presence and directing activity of a specialized agency in the form of a policeman."[190] Dickinson's point was not merely that in a congested society, efficiency required third-party coordination in public spaces. Rather, the fundamental problem the traffic metaphor sketched was a clash of interests that could not adequately be resolved through contract or ex post determinations of liability. Instead, "concentration of the directing function in a single center is imperative."[191]

Dickinson like Dewey saw the need for centralized administrative control as arising from the insufficient knowledge and capacity of individuals to remedy harms. He argued that, "Such are the relations between individuals to-day that, if one person fails to make timely insistence on his rights, the result may often be damaging to many others. . . . There must be some agency to initiate action on behalf of the public in such cases, based on wider information than private individuals generally have, and the action must be more summary in form than a proceeding at law."[192] Dickinson concluded that where the public interest could not be adequately represented by private action, it had to be represented by "the intelligent and flexible discretion of a responsible directing mind."[193]

This is not to say that Dickinson sought to remove legal control altogether. His treatise, *Administrative Justice and the Supremacy of Law in the United States*, held out an important role for the courts in settling matters of law at the boundaries of agencies' discretionary judgment. Though "the knife of policy alone" could make an "artificial cleavage at the point where the court chooses to draw the line between public interest and private right," he insisted that the judiciary must draw such practical limits to maintain a measure of social and institutional stability in the sea of administrative experimentation.[194]

While Dickinson drew from Dewey the connection between social conflict and administrative government, he had not noted the deeper relations between the public sphere and the organization of administrative bodies. As administrative law scholar Bruce Wyman observed, "the fundamental condition" in administration is that "many officers are found together. The purpose of the law of administration is obvious, then; it is the science of common action."[195] He thus detailed how "internal administrative law," including principally the regulations governing inferior officers' exercise of statutory authority, regularized and constrained the discretion of each person within the bureaucratic apparatus.[196] Understood as a "science of common action," administrative law was the science of Dewey's public—a process by which the "common interest" perceived by those affected by social activity can be "organized and made effective."[197]

The difference between Wyman and Dickinson's administrative science and the science that Dewey proposed was that the former was characterized by hierarchically delegated power and official discretion. Wyman and Dickinson articulated the conventional legal view that public officials operated under authority given by legislation and by the orders of officers higher up the executive's chain of command. Officials would deploy their authority to regulate the behavior of private persons under the watchful eye of the judiciary. Dewey, by contrast, stressed the need for a more porous form of administration that opened the deliberations of inferior officers to the various groups and interests in the affected community.

5. Democratizing Administrative Procedure

The Public and Its Problems emphasized the dangers of an administration geared only toward technical competence. Dewey's main target in this work was Walter Lippman's critique of public opinion and his argument for government based upon elite expertise.[198] Lippman argued for the use of "intelligence bureaus" to develop understandings of complex social problems, "so as not to burden every citizen with expert opinions on all questions, but to push that burden away from him towards the responsible administrator."[199] But Dewey argued that expert management could not solve the public's problems on its own: "[I]n the absence of an articulate voice on the part of the masses . . . the wise cease to be wise," because it was impossible for administrative experts "to secure a monopoly of such knowledge as must be used for the regulation of common affairs."[200] Thus, "[n]o government by experts in which the masses do not have a chance to inform the experts as to their needs can be anything but an oligarchy managed in the interests of the few. And the enlightenment must proceed in a way which forces the administrative specialist to take account of the needs."[201] Dewey did not deny the role of expertise but rather sought to guide administration with popular input. Such administrative institutions could then serve several communicative functions: they could address problems of common concern; provide institutional settings for citizens to influence policy and for officials to educate citizens; and represent, symbolize, and concretize the public, embodying the shared commitments that had arisen through political discourse.

Dewey's vision of participatory forms of administration was not a mere fantasy or detached ideal. Rather some administrative practices in the Progressive Era anticipated Dewey's vision. For example, before issuing regulations under the Federal Water Power Act of 1920, the Federal Power Commission was required to hold hearings.[202] The Department of Agriculture, similarly, held hearings, above and beyond those required by statute, in implementing the Plant Quarantine Act of 1912.[203] The most expansive examples of public participation were at the Forest Service, which sent out draft regulations for grazing on public lands for comment and held week-long, deliberative meetings with grazing associations before finalizing the regulatory provisions.[204]

In his analysis of these participatory rule-making practices, political scientist John Preston Comer argued that they were in some respects more effective than the legislative process in bringing "group opinion" to bear on policymaking: "The Executive is better organized to reach out for the more timid and modest opinions, and for the sifting of the bolder and more aggressive types."[205] At the same time, he did not suppose group opinion would determine or dominate administrative decision-making:

> Pressure groups must not be looked upon merely as expressing their opinion to an administrative legislator whose only desire is to effectuate their every wish. . . . It is the larger aspect of the question of executive checks that is to be emphasized, i.e., the compelling force of organized opinion to make a careless or arbitrary officer respond to, and to bring a sympathetic officer into harmony with, the groups affected.[206]

This aspect of Progressive administrative procedure aligned with Dewey's conception of the modern democratic state. He offered a vision of administration as the articulation of public purposes, as a means by which social intelligence could be operationalized and brought to bear upon social reality. This account of administration gave a doubled importance to democratic values. First, democratic values created the need for administration. Democracy required equitable social conditions, which often had to be furnished through administrative measures. Second, democratic principles structured the administrative processes. Affected interests and the community at large had to inform administrative officials, at the same time as specialists enhanced the public's understanding of its problems.

In 1930, Felix Frankfurter would answer Dewey's exploration of "the public and its problems" with his lectures at Yale Law School on "The Public and Its Government."[207] Though he did not cite to Dewey himself, the future Supreme Court justice offered a spirited Deweyan defense of the civil service on a democratic basis. Despite his enthusiasm for the expansion of federal administrative capacity, he worried that "government by experts" was "prone to abuse unless its exercise is properly circumscribed and zealously scrutinized. For we have greatly widened the field of administrative discretion and thus opened the door to arbitrariness."[208] Frankfurter's answer to the threat of bureaucratic domination was not, however, a reduction in administrative activity, a strict specification of administrative powers within statutory limits, or a return to the rule of judicial common law. Rather, he added to Dewey's scientific and democratic faith a lawyer's commitment to fair process: "safeguards largely depend on very high standards of professional service, an effective procedure (remembering that 'in the development of our liberty insistence upon procedural regularity has been a large factor'), easy access to public scrutiny and a constant play of alert public criticism, especially by an informed and spirited bar."[209] Frank Goodnow would further elucidate Frankfurter's lawyerly emphasis on procedural legitimacy. But first the shape and substance of "public scrutiny" deserve closer examination.

V. MARY FOLLETT'S THEORY OF CREATIVE ADMINISTRATION

Though Mary Follett is less well known today than the other Progressives considered so far, she was a major figure in the Progressive movement and has had lasting impact on theories of public administration.[210] Political theorists and legal scholars are also beginning to reawaken to her significance.[211] Deeply influenced by the British neo-Hegelians Bernard Bosanquet and T.H. Green, she adapted Hegel's concept of the state and his social conception of individuality to the problem of democratic governance in industrial society. Her theory complemented Dewey's with a deeper sensitivity to questions of power. She argued for administrative procedures that would draw on citizen experience to develop cooperative solutions to social conflict. Her account is essential to the Progressive Hegelian theory because of her critique of interest-group pluralism. She argued that administration must not be dominated by social interests but instead provide a setting in which disputes between them could be rationally reformulated and equitably resolved.[212] The state could gain "spiritual authority" only through "its citizens in their growing understanding of the widening promise of freedom."[213]

1. The Hegelian Critique of Pluralism

Follett's theory of the democratic state grew out of a sympathetic critique of British pluralism. Pluralists such as Harold Laski understood political society to be composed of various associations, which struggled with one another for political power.[214] Follett wholly accepted the pluralists' emphasis on groups as forms of public identity. Her concept of politics was based upon what she called the "group principle," the notion that "individuals are created by reciprocal interplay."[215] Democracy was the institutional embodiment of this psychological and philosophical truth: "To be a democrat is not to decide on a certain form of human association, it is to learn how to live with other men."[216]

Follett understood freedom in the Hegelian sense as a form of self-relation achieved through social interaction and participation in social life. "That we are free only through the social order, only as fast we identify ourselves with the whole, implies practically that to gain our freedom we must take part in all the life around us: join groups, enter into many social relations, and begin to win freedom for ourselves."[217] She did not mean to say that freedom meant giving up individual particularity to social wholes. Rather, the formation of any whole had to preserve the dynamic interplay of personal difference, never stifling the creative growth of individual personalities. At the same time, the quest for personal freedom could only be achieved through interpersonal recognition: "there is only self-in-and-through-others."[218] This meant that group membership and participation were essential for individuals to understand themselves as free and to act as such.

Follett nevertheless rejected the anarchic consequences of group pluralism as an ultimate institutional structure. On the vision of pluralists such as Laski, the state became only one form of association among other associations of equal status, such as trade unions. Follett argued that such pluralism led to an untenable condition where each association battled with the others and no higher form of cooperation could emerge.[219] As she explained: "The outcome of group particularism is the balance of power theory, perhaps the most pernicious part of the pluralists' doctrine. The pluralist state is to be composed of sovereign groups. What is their life to be? They are to be left to fight, to compete, or, word most favored by this school, to balance."[220] "The practical outcome of the balance theory will be first antagonistic interests, then jealous interest, then competing interests, then dominating interests—a fatal climax."[221] Follett's concern to avoid "dominating interest" revealed her concern with fostering social equality. Her vision of democracy required that powerful groups not be able to control less powerful ones in social life, in politics, or in law.

2. An Egalitarian and Coordinate Conception of Power

Follett developed this Hegelian conception of social freedom into a unique, proto-Arendtian conception of power.[222] She argued that "genuine power is power-with, pseudo-power, power-over."[223] Power-with referred to "a jointly developed power, a co-active, not a coercive power."[224] Such power only existed where two or more individuals agreed on and enacted a common purpose and succeeded in "creating new values, a wholly different process from the sterile one of balancing."[225] Illegitimate power existed where one person or group imposed the genuine power they had created within themselves upon another person or group. She rejected pluralism in part out of a concern that the balance between groups could not be sustained—that one group would achieve illegitimate "power-over" vis-à-vis others.

Follett sought to use groups in a constructive rather than antagonistic way. Like Hegel and Dewey, she argued that various forms of local, vocational, and political association served to mediate between individual identities and the state as a whole. But whereas Hegel had ultimately located state sovereignty in the identity of the monarch, Follett adopted the American constitutional principle of popular sovereignty. She answered the fundamental question of democratic theory—"how can the people be the sovereign power of the state?"—by arguing that "there must be two changes in our state: first the state must be the actual integration of living, local groups, thereby finding ways of dealing directly with its members. Secondly, other groups than neighborhood groups must be represented in the state: the ever-increasingly multiple group life of today must be recognized and given a responsible place in politics."[226]

The democratic state Follett envisioned was also rooted in the American constitutional tradition of federalism. Like Wilson, she argued that administrators needed to be attuned to local forms of identity and association, as well as the broader national concerns they were charged with implementing. Interestingly, Follett argued that federalism, properly understood, was a Hegelian principle.[227] A pluralist form of federalism, in which the states were separate entities with stable rights free from outside interference, was a false federalism: "The political pluralist whom we are now considering, believing that a collective and distributing sovereignty cannot exist together, throw overboard collective sovereignty. . . . The true Hegelianism finds its actual form in federalism."[228] This "true Hegelian" federalism meant that the partiality of state groupings had to be respected as a basis on which individuals developed their social personalities. States were thus to function as a spatial version of Hegel's corporation. Individuals would develop common purposes—and thus power—on the basis of their shared regional interests and desires. But Follett, like Hegel, did not believe the differentiation of interests at the level of plural social groups could be a stopping point. The differentiation paved the way for states to find ways of developing "power-with" one another at the national level.

The existing federal structure of elected representation was not sufficient to realize the constitutive importance of states and other social groups. In part this was because Follett recognized that there were many other forms of association—particularly economic—that transcended geographic boundaries. Like Hegel, she recognized that individuals develop group affiliations on the basis of their work and material interests, which in America had been accorded no direct political representation. In addition, Follett was skeptical that majority voting really satisfied the democratic impulse toward developing collective power, for "all pure majority power is getting power over. Genuine power is activity between, not influence over."[229] Of course, to the extent that political representation could become a deliberative process of developing new common interests above and beyond local, state, economic, and other loyalties, it could help to constitute legitimate power. But the "A or B" structure of elections could not fully satisfy Follett's wish for a politics of "both/and." Methods beyond and in addition to election would therefore be required to achieve democratic power on a national scale.

3. A Responsive Concept of Administration

Administrative efforts to rework originally antagonistic interests provided a fruitful alternative. Follett did not believe that administration and democracy were at all opposed principles. She observed that

> the tendency to transfer power to the American citizenship, and the tendency towards efficient government by the employment of experts and

> the concentration of administrative authority are working side by side in American political life to-day. These two tendencies are not opposed. . . . [A]dministrative responsibility and expert service are as necessary a part of genuine democracy as popular control is a necessary accompaniment of administrative responsibility.[230]

Like most Progressives, Follett had great faith in scientific expertise. The complex problems of modern society could not be solved without empirical insight, which took great training and experience to generate. But such expertise needed to be subject to popular influence. This did not mean mere consent, which was only the illusion of popular sovereignty: "The problem of democracy is how to develop power from experience, from the interplay of our daily concrete activities. The expert cannot dictate and the people consent. This is the voice of the wax doll; it has no reality."[231] Because legitimate power could only be generated through shared understandings, administrative expertise could not be deployed paternalistically and by fiat upon a passive public. It would have to arise from a deliberative interchange between the people—already disaggregated into groups with internally legitimate power—and the administration. Administrative processes that managed to bring about new understandings and conceptions of self-interest among conflicting groups would serve to create an ever-greater democratic power amongst the particular clusters of interest that constituted society.

Follett's concrete suggestion for achieving this administrative generation of democratic power was an "experience meeting" between experts and the public. "The first step in these would be to present the subject under consideration in such a way as to show clearly its relation to our daily lives. . . . The second step would be for each one of us to try to find in our own experience anything that would throw light on the question."[232] The point of this exercise would be to give administrators a better grasp on the problem at hand by seeing how it had been perceived by those affected by it. At the same time, for the public, the process of learning about the problem and thinking about their lives in relation to it would help them to "begin to observe and analyze our experience much more carefully than we do at present."[233] Experience meetings would educate both the administrative expert and the citizen, thus serving to create public power, not solely within groups outside the official institutions of the state, but between those institutions and the people together.

The proposal of experience meetings clarified Follett's conception of public opinion. Follett agreed with Hegel that public opinion was often mistaken and in need of education, but she nonetheless thought it had much to contribute to the formulation of administrative policymaking: "We no longer declare a mystic faith in a native rightness of public opinion; we want nothing from the people but their experience, but emphatically we want that. Reason, wisdom, emerge from our daily activities. It is not the *will* of the people we are interested in but the *life* of the people. Public opinion must be built from concrete existence."[234] She agreed with Dewey that participatory forms of administration were needed to make this experience intelligible: "We are not now the master of our experience; we do not know what it is and we could not express it if we did. We need an articulate experience."[235] Just as Dewey understood the state as a "public articulated," Follett understood deliberative forms of administration as a means for crystallizing and systematizing individual and collective experience. Experience would be made articulate by bringing it into direct contact with administrative decision-making. Through such meetings, individuals would come to think of their personal experience as a matter of public concern, and the activity of government would become motivated by the reflectively understood activity of its citizens:

> When the process of cooperation between expert and people is given its legitimate chance, the experience of the people may change the conclusions of the expert while the conclusions of the expert are changing the experience of the people; further than that, the people's activity is a response to the relating of their own activity to that of the expert. Here we have the compound interest of all genuine coöperation. Industrial and political organization will take different forms when we understand cooperation not as addition, but as *progressive* interweaving.[236]

Administrative expertise, mediated by the experience of citizens, would stitch together a democratic social fabric out of the rough but tenacious threads of collective power within society.

Because Follett understood administrative processes as potential sites for the generation of democratic power, she also understood that administrative agencies had an important role to play in the development of law. Follett was deeply influenced by the sociological jurisprudence of Roscoe Pound, which saw the law as embodying particular constellations of interest and social purposes.[237] However, Follett went beyond this description to put the law at the service of her project of generating public power, as clashing groups found forms of dynamic interaction that could produce "power-with." Follett followed Pound in arguing that "[t]he key-word for jurisprudence and politics as for psychology is desire." "But," she pointed out, "this desire can be the desire of a dominant class or the unifying desires of all classes, all men. It is for us to choose."[238]

For Follett, the choice was clear: a pluralist system ending in anarchy or the dominance of powerful interests would be a society of illegitimate power-over.

Follett thus proposed that law be reformulated so that it was not a matter of reactively deciding between the claims of one party or the other but instead of actively reformulating the legal interest of the parties to make them harmonious: "Law is to find the way of uniting interests. It is to seek to limit the area of mutually exclusive interests, but it is to do this not by arbitrary declaration, but by suggesting and encouraging those activities which will produce interests that are capable of uniting. Law should seek far more than mere reconciliation; it should be one of the great creative forces of our social life."[239] This did not mean that all legal disputes ought to end in some kind of settlement rather than a victory for one party or the other. It meant a creative jurisprudence, which, by resolving a particular dispute in a forward-looking fashion, would set the stage for more complementary social dynamics in the future.

Follett recognized that administrative agencies offered a new and promising setting for such legal developments to unfold. She understood administrative agencies to have a certain situational flexibility, which allowed them to restructure social conflict so as to produce the possibility of broader forms of public power. Like Hegel and Wilson, she realized that the need for and promise of administration lay in the necessary generality and retrospective origin of legislative enactment:

> When the Interstate Commerce, the Federal Trade or Tariff Act came to be administered, it was found that those laws were made for such varying factors that wide discretion must be used in their administration; that is, as law cannot vary we have administrative commissions which can. Here we see clearly what we have called the evolving situation: the interweaving of varying activity and what is practically, through the possibility of different interpretations by the administrative commissions, a varying law. We have found the basis of creative experience is circular response. Nowhere do we see this more steadily than in the history of law, and here in our administrative commissions is a very striking instance of circular response; between legislative enactment as administered by these commissions and the activity in question.[240]

Administrative agencies applied given rules to varying fields of activity, with different groups at play. As Hegel had argued, public officials had to find a way to reconcile the statutory universal with particular facts. They therefore developed contextually sensitive judgments, through which the law developed. There was a process of "circular response" between administrative law and social activity, in which the law responded to the social facts it regulated, adjusting them at the same time that it adjusted itself.

Follett's circular response theory had real parallels in contemporaneous regulatory procedure. The Federal Trade Commission, for instance, consulted with industry groups to learn about trade practices about which it had received complaints. These "trade practice submittals"

> consisted of an invitation, which is in no sense a summons, for the whole industry or its representatives, to meet together in the presence of the Commission to discuss the merits and demerits of practices which have been complained of to the Commission and any other practices which may be brought to the attention of the meeting. At the end of the discussion, each of the practices which have been examined are taken up separately, are submitted to the industry for an expression of opinion as to their fairness or unfairness, their usefulness or harmfulness.[241]

If the opinion of the industry was "practically unanimous" it would be given "great weight" by the Commission in determining whether such practices were unlawful.[242] In this way, the deliberations of affected parties might inform the conclusions of the Commission, if only in an advisory manner.

Reserving the final decision to the Commission, rather than actually delegating authority to a private body, had important corrective potential. Administrators had to consult the communicated experience of regulated groups in order to understand their divergent understandings of the problem at hand. They had to find ways to bring these differences into a coherent relationship that would produce greater legitimate power between them. To do so, however, the threat of "power-over" had to be kept in mind to ensure that forms of collaboration were not mere domination in disguise. Administrators had to be sensitive to questions of social equity. They could bring law's authority to bear to facilitate interaction on equal terms, and mitigate inequalities of resources and voice that prevented the creation of genuine democratic power.

VI. FRANK GOODNOW'S DEMOCRATIC *RECHTSSTAAT*

While Follett developed this egalitarian and participatory theory of administration, Frank Goodnow aimed to harmonize politics and administration so that the aims of the people could be realized efficiently. Goodnow's "thinly veiled Hegelianism" consisted in his personification of the state as an agent with a "will" and an administrative apparatus that would carry this will into action.[243] Like his fellow American Hegelians, he sought to apply this concept to a democratic context, where the will of the state had to be the will of the people, and the rights of the individuals within this sovereign authority had to be maintained. He therefore argued that democracy required legislative authorization of administrative action, administrative due process, and impartiality in the execution of law. His theory of the state was particularly prescient in recognizing the overlaps between judicial and administrative authority, as both institutions adjudicated claims arising under statutory law. Unlike Wilson, Dewey, and Follett, he did not focus on broader forms of public participation within the administrative process. Nonetheless, his view of administration was compatible with theirs because he admitted that politics might legitimately influence the higher reaches of administration.

1. The Discovery of Administrative Law

Though administrative law existed throughout the nineteenth century, in terms of regulations and orders issued by administrative bodies and principles of judicial review, it was not then recognized as a distinct field of law. As Frankfurter later noted, Goodnow, alongside Ernst Freund, was a "pioneer" in recognizing the existence of this special branch of public law.[244] Goodnow defined administrative law as a system of law that "fixes the organization and determines the competence of authorities which execute the law, and indicates to the individual remedies for the violation of his rights."[245] The aims of administrative law were "governmental efficiency, individual liberty, and social well-being, as interpreted by the body representative of public opinion."[246] Goodnow thus sought to treat administrative law, not merely as an extension of constitutional principles, but as the enterprise of balancing democratic will and individual right.[247]

Goodnow's interest in administrative law was prompted by the fact that, in America, the question of "social well-being" and the role of the government in its promotion had increased so profoundly in importance with increasing industrialization and rapid urbanization. He thus sought to examine the legal validity of administrative efforts regarding commercial regulation and public welfare provision. This survey of administrative law touched on constitutional questions, since the Supreme Court had set boundaries upon the capacity of the federal government and the states to legislate in the interests of the social welfare: "[T]he Supreme Court of the United States has really become a political body of the supremest importance. For upon its determination depends the ability of the national legislature to exercise powers whose exercise is believed by many to be absolutely necessary to our existence as a democratic republic."[248]

Goodnow argued for an approach to constitutional interpretation that would make it adaptable to the political and social needs of the present rather than beholden to an outmoded political philosophy. "What we need more than anything else at the present time is a consistent theory of constitutional interpretation, which will permit our orderly development as a nation in accordance with our economic and social needs, and is not confined within the political and legal conceptions of a century or more ago."[249] Goodnow thus sought to separate the philosophy of classical liberalism—especially the doctrine of natural rights, the social contract, and the tripartite separation of powers—from the project of constitutional interpretation. Like Hegel, he found the doctrine of natural rights to ignore the historical and social nature of entitlements. The social contract, likewise, was in fact a feudal vestige that had little bearing upon the principles underlying democratic republics.[250] And the strict separation of powers turned an analytically plausible distinction among legislative, executive, and judicial functions into the untenable notion that these functions could be neatly assigned to three separate departments of government.

In each of these Hegelian arguments, Goodnow was not arguing against individual rights or against the rule of law or the Constitution. On his interpretation of early Supreme Court precedents, "the constitution did, as a matter of fact, give to the federal government a sphere of action whose limits are to be laid down, not as a result of an acceptance of the historical tradition of constitutional power of the last sixty or seventy years, but rather as a result of consideration of the present needs of the country."[251] The generality of certain clauses, particularly regarding the federal government's power to regulate commerce,[252] permitted the abstract commands of the Constitution to be adapted toward current understandings and circumstances. Goodnow also found flexibility in the constitutional scheme of the separation of powers, insofar as Congress might delegate legislative powers to executive agencies, so long as it "lays down the general principles which will control the subject in question"—principles which a court could use to review the legality of administrative action where it affected private rights.[253] Goodnow thus saw in the Constitution a framework in which administration might lawfully proceed—governed by statute, specified by the executive officials, and policed by the courts.

2. Legislation and Execution, Politics and Administration

Goodnow's understanding of administration, like Du Bois's, Wilson's, Dewey's, and Follett's, was grounded in Hegelian understandings of the state. As Christian Rosser has shown, through intellectual intermediaries such as Burgess, Stein, and Gneist, "Goodnow partly anchored his writings in the Hegelian intellectual tradition, sharing its organic notion of the state and its emphasis on an influential administrative apparatus. Goodnow was positive that a body of well-educated public servants would promote individual and collective welfare."[254] In addition, the constitutional structure of the *Rechtsstaat*, as interpreted by Hegelian public law scholars, powerfully influenced Goodnow. Hegel had emphasized that administration must relate to legislation as particular to the universal; statutory law must always authorize, frame, and constrain administrative action while affording public officials discretion to interpret and apply open-textured statutory norms. Hegel therefore did not embrace Montesquieu's conception of the separation of powers, which distinguished among legislative, executive, and judicial functions. Instead, he distinguished among legislative, executive, and "sovereign" powers, with the sovereign monarch representing the unity of the state's separate functions, but lacking significant political authority.[255] Both judicial and administrative authorities were forms of executive power, because each concerned the application of law, either to particular "cases" (judicial) or to various "spheres" of social life (administrative).[256] Stein translated Hegel's distinction between the legislative universal and the executive particular into the "will" and the "deed" of the state, observing that "the most universal principle of the state" was that "the deed must be subordinated to the will."[257] Gneist then argued for administrative courts to control administration by providing "consistent maxims governing the scope of discretionary powers, which police regulations leave open at innumerable points."[258] The common thrust of this *Rechtsstaat* ideal was that statutory law must authorize administrative action and judicial review must control it, so as to enable active government regulation while preventing arbitrary infringements on private rights.

Following in Hegel and Stein's footsteps, Goodnow distinguished between politics as the expression of the "will" of the state and administration as its "deed."[259] He embraced the *Rechtsstaat's* subordination of administrative action to legislative maxim, but for a different reason than German thinkers had provided. The German liberal constitutionalist tradition had explained the subordination of the executive to the legislative power in terms of the demand that public power take rational form. Particular cases needed to be subsumed within a coherent, codified system of legal obligations, both in the domain of civil and criminal justice and in the domain of police regulation. Such a framework would protect the individual by ensuring that the private sphere could only be invaded on an intelligible statutory basis. Goodnow, by contrast, rooted the priority of legislation directly in democratic principles: "Popular government requires that it is the executing authority which shall be subordinated to the expressing authority, since the latter in the nature of things can be made much more representative of the people than can executive authority."[260] Legislation must precede and control administration so that the popular will expressed in statute would control administration rather than be controlled by it. If rationality could not be guaranteed by the general form of legislation alone, it would have to be secured through an administrative system that ensured that governmental action was well-reasoned and responsive to legitimate private interests.

3. Multiple Expressing Organs: Congress, the President, and Appointed Officers

When he referred to the "expressing authority," Goodnow meant primarily Congress. This body, composed of representatives of localities and of the states, and requiring the assent of bicameral majorities to legislate, could claim unique democratic credentials. It therefore had the popular legitimacy to act as the "regulator of administration."[261] But Goodnow recognized that the function of expressing political will was not solely restricted to the legislature: "The organ of government whose main function is the execution of the will of the state is often, and indeed usually, entrusted with the expression of that will in its details. These details, however, when expressed, must conform with the general principles laid down by the organ whose main duty is that of expression. That is, the authority called executive has, in almost all cases, considerable ordinance or legislative power."[262]

This point had special force in the American constitutional structure. In a system where the president had an independent electoral constituency, there could be no strict and exclusive equivalence between "expression" and "Congress," on the one hand, and "execution" and the "president" on the other: "The rule that the legislature is the regulator of the administration does not mean, in the case of the national government, that the executive may act only in the execution of the law, and that it possesses no discretion."[263] Rather, the president might also "express" the will of the state, provided his interpretation of that will was authorized by and consistent with the statutory framework. Expressions of state will might then extend further down the administrative hierarchy. Goodnow argued that "if questions of policy are to be determined in accordance with popular will," the "higher divisions" of the executive departments and administrative agencies should not have permanence of tenure but rather be subject to political appointment.[264] Political influences thus impinged deeply upon the administrative apparatus, even as Goodnow sought to insulate ministerial responsibilities from political meddling.

In such a system of distributed policymaking power, conflict might arise between presidential and congressional will. Such "lack of harmony between the law and its execution results in political paralysis."[265] Goodnow argued that parties ought to be strengthened to ensure policy continuity between the executive and the legislature. But this proposal failed to account for the possibility that the president's party might differ from the party in control of Congress.[266] In a constitutional system where two actors could claim independent democratic mandates, some means of "harmonization" other than partisanship would be required.

The courts could play an important role in this respect. In cases where the president or an executive department promulgated a regulation, a reviewing court might "examine into the ordinance for the purpose of determining whether the authority which issued it was under the law competent to issue it."[267] Another method of harmonization, which Goodnow did not consider but which Dewey, Follett, and Wilson had converged upon, would have been to expose executive determinations of policy to wider public influence. Participation by affected parties might strengthen the highly attenuated links between votes cast and the particular policy determinations of executive officials, which might have little salience in the minds of the electorate. If significant questions of policy could be exposed to the input of all affected, then executive-branch policymaking might claim a firmer foundation in the diverse interests of the populace than in the strained ties of electoral representation. To avoid the replacement of the general interest with that of particular constituencies, however, Follett's principle of "power-with" would have to be adhered to: administrative policymaking could not merely replicate the existing constellation of power and interest but would have to reformulate it on a more egalitarian basis.

4. Two Faces of "Administration": The Judiciary and the Bureaucracy

The constitutional theory of the *Rechtsstaat* that Goodnow adapted distinguished fundamentally between two powers—legislation and execution—and understood the judiciary and the administrative apparatus as two distinct but related aspects of execution. In Goodnow's hands, this German constitutional theory revealed how American constitutional structures would adjust to the expansion of administrative authority. Defined generically as the carrying out of the will of the state, administration encompassed both the work of the federal judiciary and of the bureaucratic officialdom. Both of these bodies were concerned with implementing the law. It was therefore necessary to insulate the officials who performed these tasks from electoral politics: "The tendency of the body in the state possessing the power to express the state will is, however, always to make use of its powers of control over the execution of state will. . . . The law ceases to be administered impartially, and is administered solely or largely in the hope of influencing directly or indirectly the future expression of state will, and frequently in the interest of certain classes in the community."[268]

Goodnow thus disparaged the spoils system in which administrative offices had been filled by party functionaries whose loyalty lay to their partisan benefactors rather than to the law itself. Like life tenure for federal judges, the civil service system inaugurated by the Pendleton Act could ensure that once the policy position of the public had been articulated by law and regulation, it would be administered faithfully and impartially. "The fact is . . . that there is a large part of administration which is unconnected with politics, which should therefore be relieved very largely, if not altogether, from the control of political bodies. It is unconnected with politics because it embraces fields of semi-scientific, quasi-judicial, and quasi-business or commercial activity—work which has little if any influence on the expression of the true state will."[269] Goodnow's conception of nonpolitical "quasi-business" administration drew him into the movement for budget reform, which aimed to make public finances more professional, transparent, and efficient, which ultimately bore fruit in the Budget and Accounting Act of 1921.[270]

The *Rechtsstaat* alignment of the judiciary and the civil service as institutions of impartiality was useful in diagnosing the increasing overlap between the tasks of the constitutional executive and those of the judiciary. On the one hand, the bureaucracy took on "quasi-judicial" tasks, such as the adjudication of tax, pension, land, and patent claims. On the other hand, as agencies assumed more and more such tasks from 1877 onward, the federal judiciary assumed a more intensive role in reviewing their actions.[271]

The courts could justify this shift in part because of the affinity they observed between the "sciences" upon which Progressive administrative legitimacy depended and the newfound "science" of law. At the same time as the German conceptions of academic science were transforming the disciplines of politics and economics at Columbia and Johns Hopkins, this scientific practice also influenced the study of law at Harvard.[272] Understood as yet another science, law might have some purchase on the practices of other sciences within administrative agencies. Thus, in allowing judicial review of the decisions of the patent commissioner, the Court observed that "the investigation of every claim presented involves the adjudication of disputed questions of fact upon scientific and legal principles, and is therefore essentially judicial in character, and requires the intelligent judgment of a trained body of skilled officials, expert in the various branches of science and art, learned in the history invention, and proceeding by fixed rules to systematic conclusions."[273]

Chief Justice Melville Fuller later quoted this language in affirming the constitutionality of the statutory scheme that permitted judicial review of the Commission's decisions.[274] Wyman described this holding as a "surprise"—a startling and improper departure from the nineteenth-century jurisprudence under the prerogative writs, which had left executive officers wide discretion so long as they remained within the scope of their statutory authority.[275] But with the rise of the Progressive faith in accredited knowledge, matters assigned to administrative officials were no longer merely "political questions" on which the law could have little grasp; they were subject to a kind of rational analysis that the courts could recognize as cognate to law. The rise of administrative government thus saw courts and agencies increasingly engaged with one another in partnership and struggle, as the meaning of law more and more became "mixed" with the social scientific facts upon which agencies and courts would render judgment. Administrative agencies and the courts would have to deliberate together over the content of policy, rather than remain in totally separate constitutional spheres.

Though the federal courts asserted broad power to review and remedy the abuse of administrative discretion, they allowed Congress to circumscribe the scope of review. Courts had granted little to no deference to the Interstate Commerce Commission (ICC) under its 1887 organic act, which had treated ICC rulings as "prima facie evidence of the matters therein stated," but required the Commission to seek enforcement in a federal circuit court, which would "hear and determine the matter."[276] In response to agrarian populist criticism of the judiciary's apparent solicitude for railroad interests in such cases, Congress passed the Hepburn Act of 1906, which shifted authority back to the agency.[277] Commission orders would automatically "take effect" thirty days after their publication unless "suspended or set aside by a reviewing court of competent jurisdiction."[278] The Court got the message and relaxed its standards of review.[279] While the judiciary would retain jurisdiction over questions of law and constitutional power, when it came to a "mixed question of law and fact," the Court would not "examine the facts further than to determine whether there was substantial evidence to sustain the order."[280] Courts in this way adopted an appellate approach in the review of administrative action, which allowed them to decide pure questions of law while deferring to some extent to an agency's findings of fact and application of the law to facts.

5. Rudiments of Administrative Due Process

By treating administrative orders as quasi-judicial judgments akin to trial verdicts, the courts disentangled the requirements of due process from those of the separation of powers. In the traditional nineteenth-century understanding, the question of whether an administrative procedure violated due process was sometimes treated as equivalent to the question of whether the legislature had the power to confer jurisdiction over the relevant persons and subject matters to an executive agency, or whether instead the dispute had to be adjudicated by an ordinary court.[281] The process due was either judicial or otherwise open to legislative and executive definition. Summary procedures in police regulation were therefore commonplace, as courts refused to impose internal procedural requirements on their factual findings.[282] Goodnow argued that stringent judicial review was justified in such cases by the "informality of existing administrative procedure."[283]

But in its public utility jurisprudence during the Progressive Era, the Supreme Court insisted upon certain elementary protections of "notice" and a "hearing" within administrative procedure at the same time as it admitted deferential review of factual findings.[284] Goodnow hoped for a broader application of this approach:

> When we develop an administrative procedure which is reasonably regardful of rights, e.g. notice and a hearing to the person affected by the administrative determination, it may well be that the courts will change their attitude and come to the conclusion that the changed and complex conditions of modern life . . . should have an effect both on the constitutional rights of individuals and on the powers and procedures of administrative authorities.[285]

Instead of "pricking out a line" beyond which the exercise of police power "becomes an invasion of the guaranty of liberty," the courts might allow the ambit of regulatory power to expand only on condition of appropriate procedural safeguards.[286]

John Dickinson likewise embraced procedural frameworks that accorded discretion in exchange for basic elements of due process. His paradigm case was state workmen's compensation. Workmen's compensation had been one of the principal avenues for Progressive reform, in which state-level administrative judges adjudicated claims between employers and employees under the supervision of the ordinary courts.[287] From such schemes Dickinson reconstructed a "more intelligent doctrine of review" that he thought might apply to police regulation in general. The courts should accept agencies' factual findings so long as there was "evidence reasonably to support them" and individuals had been afforded "proper notice and hearing in the course of administrative proceedings."[288] Dickinson thus concurred with Goodnow in the effort to replace the highly discretionary, paternalistic, and localized practices of nineteenth-century police regulation with a procedurally rigorous administrative state that would be respectful of individual autonomy.[289]

The due process innovations that Goodnow observed and urged onward distinguished the American *Rechtsstaat* from its German ancestor. While German administrative law scholars had sought to model administrative orders on judicial judgments, they had not argued for the replication of quasi-judicial procedures as requisites to lawful administrative action.[290] The Progressives followed the German model in admitting that the judiciary and the administration were two complementary and interlocking aspects of the process of implementing the law, rather than categorically distinct spheres of governmental power. But more so than their contemporaneous civilian counterparts, they sought to bring procedural rigors into the executive administration of law.

As a consequence, American public law came to prize the reasoning of administrative actors in justifying their actions. If the administrative state could be expected to proceed in some respects like a court, so too should it be expected to explain itself like one. Thus, in comparing the Federal Trade Commission (FTC) and the ICC, Gerald Henderson concluded that courts more often rejected the FTC's rulings than those of the ICC because, in the case of the FTC, "reasons for the decisions are never given."[291] The Progressive state, like the Hegelian state, would hinge its reputation on rationality. But whereas German idealist rationality was instinct in the structure of institutions, American pragmatist rationality had to be on the record and available for public criticism and engagement.

VII. CONCLUSION

Without the background of the Hegelian political theory they shared, the scholarship of Du Bois, Wilson, Dewey, Follett, and Goodnow might appear only loosely associated by a set of common concerns. But when we consider this set of thinkers through a Hegelian lens, it becomes possible to reconstruct a coherent picture of the Progressive state. They each drew from Hegel the basic notion that the state could provide the conditions for modern liberty, and they each sought to apply and adapt Hegel's ideas to a democratic context.

Du Bois maintained that the American state had an emancipatory task, providing the requisites for free and equal citizenship through the administrative provision of rights and social services. He adapted Hegel's interpretation of liberalizing administrative reform in Prussia to the context of the Reconstruction South, showing how the Freedmen's Bureau set about to build an egalitarian civil society in the wake of slavery.

Despite his abysmal record on civil rights, Wilson nonetheless shared with Du Bois a commitment to the administrative construction of a democratic society. Concerned not with problems of racial domination but rather with monopoly, unfair competition, and degrading working conditions, he argued that a professional civil service would equip the American state to reform industrial society. Whereas Du Bois had emphasized the administrative provision of the requisites for democratic politics, Wilson underscored the need for administrative structures that were permeated with popular thought. Administration mediated between the formality, retrospectivity, and stability of law and the evolution of an organic American people.

Dewey translated Wilson's racialized language of organicism into a discursive understanding of the democratic public. The public was formed through discussion about market externalities and articulated in the institutions of government. The state therefore had to provide the resources necessary for the rational and equal formation of public opinion. At the same time, administrative decision-making had to be open to the influence of such opinion.

Follett clarified the norms of public participation in the Progressive state and explained the way law ought to be understood within it. She argued that individual freedom could only be achieved in and through group membership—that the groups that composed the democratic public had to engage with one another on equal terms, so that they together exercised "power-with," rather than wielded or suffered under "power-over," one another. She saw administrative procedure as a means of working out egalitarian forms of cooperation and social development.

Goodnow adapted the institutional structure of *Rechtsstaat* to the American context: he argued that the administrative "deed" had to remain subject to the political "will" of legislation and that agencies had to afford individuals affected the opportunity for a hearing. Administrative and judicial action would not be categorically distinct but rather would overlap, as agencies regularized their procedure into quasi-judicial forms and courts deferentially reviewed the findings made through such procedures. Courts and agencies would become partners in carrying the will of the state into action. They would have to reason together about the meaning of the public's law.

Together, these thinkers outlined a vision of a state in which the public sphere would become politically efficacious in and through administrative governance. The government would not serve merely as a neutral channel for the application of public sentiment to society. Rather, it would structure the formation of public opinion through the provision of the requisites for democratic life and through rational deliberation between private citizens and the administrative officials who acted in their name.

This concept of the Progressive state was not without its tensions. The administrative establishment of democratic requisites might be undermined by administrative processes that empowered the voice of inegalitarian, uninformed, and distorted popular views. But administrators could only fully grasp what people required to participate in democracy by consulting the public's self-understandings. The substance and the procedure of democracy therefore had to complement and constrain each other. The challenge would be to identify forms of administrative governance that were autonomous enough from the existing constellation of social power to remedy its injustices, while sufficiently informed by public opinion to enhance the perceived and actual legitimacy of state action. These challenges were taken up by public officials during the New Deal, as they acted under the direct influence of Hegelian Progressive thought.

3

The Institutional Architecture of Progressive Democracy

From the New Deal to the Second Reconstruction

I. INTRODUCTION

The Hegelian Progressives crafted a democratic conception of the state. This state would provide the material and institutional requisites for a vibrant public sphere. Social welfare provision, consumer protection, and corporate regulation would guarantee sufficient social equality to underwrite democratic politics. But the Progressives' state could not truly claim to be "democratic" unless the people themselves determined the content and the format of regulatory protections. The government would have to pursue democratic ends by democratic means. This chapter will show this ideal's programmatic legacy, from the New Deal through the Civil Rights Era. The diverse administrative arrangements that flourished over this period variously attempted to enact democratic discourse in their procedures, to foster an egalitarian civil society, and to combine deliberative and bureaucratic forms of social provision. By studying how such interventions were conceived and structured, where they succeeded, and where they failed, we can see how the normative tensions instinct in Progressive thought re-emerged in institutional architecture. More than this, these examples help to point the way forward for a Progressive public law in the present. If we are mindful of the internal dilemmas of Progressivism, we should be better positioned to build on its impressive but imperfect handiwork.

Recall how the Progressive ideal was forged in American thinkers' encounter with German state theory. The Hegelian vision of the state stressed administration's emancipatory function. Hegel articulated and defended the spirit of Prussian administrators who sought to replace the feudal order with the beginnings of a classically liberal society.[1] He understood these bureaucrats as bourgeois reformers who sought to free the serfs, institute rights of property and contract, and provide basic public goods and welfare services. The form of emancipation Hegel and the Prussian "universal class" envisioned, however, was not democratic but purely civil and economic. It neither contemplated nor emerged from a popular process of contestation, debate, and participation. Theirs was a paternalistic kind of social reform, relying upon the practical judgment and discretion of administrators to advance Enlightenment social values and the interests of the German middle class. After the failed revolution of 1848, this antidemocratic feature of Hegelian state theory remained deeply embedded in German public law scholarship.

By the turn of the twentieth century, the emancipatory task of administration had fallen by the wayside. The main line of German administrative law scholarship turned to positivism and thus eschewed any immanent connection between the system of administrative law and the political functions it ought to serve. When democracy arrived in Germany with the founding of the Weimar Republic, administrative law and organization did not adapt to the new constitutional circumstance in which it operated. The bureaucracy remained insulated from society, politically conservative, and bound to the authoritarian form of rule inherited from the empire.[2] Weber's account of bureaucracy, centering on formal legality, instrumental reason, hierarchical control, and official obedience was symptomatic of this peculiar amalgam of democratic constitutional forms and hierarchical administrative structures. As political and economic crises shifted the center of constitutional gravity from the paralyzed legislature to the independent executive, administration became equipped with ever more powers, the legitimacy of which could only be grounded in the decisive will of the chief executive.[3] The combination of plebiscitary presidentialism, increased administrative discretion, and legislative incapacity in the Weimar Republic thus opened the door for the totalitarian developments that followed. Without a democratic reformation of administration to accompany the shift to democratic constitutionalism, the emancipatory administrative state that Hegel had envisioned was particularly liable to turn into its opposite.

As I argued in chapter 2, the American Progressive adaptation of Hegelian ideas distinguished itself from its German counterpart by stressing the democratic foundations of administrative legitimacy. Du Bois, Wilson, Goodnow, Follett, and Dewey sought to imagine, build, and legitimate an administrative state in which the democratic public would liberate itself from conditions of economic and social domination rather than passively benefit from government benevolence. Like Hegel, these Progressives argued that individual freedom had legal, social, and material requisites that the marketplace could not furnish and that the state must somehow provide. And they too saw bureaucratic discretion as a key element of social reform. They departed from Hegel and his German intellectual progeny, however, in insisting that individual freedom entailed the collective self-determination of the people as a whole rather than the merely symbolic representation of such autonomy in the person of a monarch. They therefore outlined how the state could best incorporate, express, and give binding force to the concerns of the public sphere.

There were two distinct, but interrelated visions of how the democratic spirit of administration was to be institutionalized. On the one hand, Progressives stressed the social and material *requisites* of democratic life. Thus, Du Bois would uphold the work of the Freedmen's Bureau after the Civil War in ushering in a "dawn of freedom" for southern blacks by providing the very kinds of institutions that Hegel had posited as the foundations of modern liberty: rights of property and contract, marriage licenses, employment, and education.[4] Dewey, Goodnow, and Wilson likewise proposed various forms of social legislation that would regulate the economy so as to curtail the excesses of industrial capitalism. This kind of democratic administration differed from the Hegelian *Rechtsstaat* not in the substance of the services the government would provide but rather in the function these services were thought to serve. The Progressives thought of administration as providing background conditions not merely for individual agency nor merely for the habitual experience of a communal life but, more fundamentally, for the active political engagement of all members of the democratic public in discussing their common problems and determining solutions. Only a materially secure and educated citizenry could hope to take on the task of collective self-government under conditions of rapid economic and social change. The Progressives therefore argued for administrative institutions at the local, state, and national levels to furnish the goods, services, and regulatory functions that would equip the people for active democratic engagement.

On the other hand, the Progressives also aimed at democratic administration in a procedural sense. They sought to create *contexts* for popular deliberation and participation within the government as a whole and the administrative process in particular. Goodnow thus argued that legislation must control administration so that democratic will would determine the activities of government. Wilson stressed that administration must be "sensitive at all points to public opinion," arguing that "elections and constant public counsel" would discipline administration to conform to the popular spirit.[5] Dewey likewise underscored the need for public consultation in bureaucratic practice, and Follett advocated "experience meetings" where members of the public would contribute their practical knowledge to administrative decision-making.[6] The Progressive state they outlined derived its legitimacy not merely from legislative authorization or presidential supervision but also from the discursive interaction of the branches of government in fleshing out public purposes, and from the engagement of the public in administrative decisionmaking. This understanding of administration recognized the indeterminacy of legislative norms, the imperfect capacities of executive management, and the limits of judicial competence. It emphasized that the inequalities and antagonisms of civil society undermined the political and judicial branches' capacity to hear the claims of the people. The Progressives therefore turned to mechanisms that would enable the public to influence administrative deliberations directly.

Though the requisites and contexts for democracy were mutually constitutive, they were also in tension with one another. The contrast between Du Bois's and Wilson's assessments of Reconstruction illustrates the point acutely. Whereas Du Bois upheld the Freedmen's Bureau as an example of bureaucratically led democratization, Wilson saw Reconstruction as the North's oppressive intervention upon the local forms of rule that existed in the South at that time.[7] Seen in the context of his white supremacist inclinations, Wilson's plea for an administrative state that would be "intimately connected with popular thought" had more sinister connotations.[8] Though he treated the national consciousness that emerged from the Civil War as a salutary historical development, Wilson was glad to have seen the socially and politically transformative efforts of Reconstruction stifled. For him, the racist mores of the white public were legitimate expressions of their local, "democratic" culture.

We should take care, however, not to reduce fully the distinction between the Progressive administrative thought of Du Bois and Wilson to their opposite views on racial equality. For they also set out two contrasting visions of how administrative reform should reflect democratic will. Du Bois's defense of the Freedmen's Bureau suggested that democratic life required certain universal entitlements, which the state must furnish, irrespective of the corroding influence that these interventions would have on local political control, popular folkways, or majoritarian prejudices. Wilson, by contrast, was more interested in a gradual, reformist kind of Progressive administration, which would draw on and reinforce the local wellsprings of democratic politics and cultivate a common ethic through participatory forms of decision-making. In this respect, at least, his approach to Progressive administration was fully in line with that of Dewey and Follett, who did not seem to share his racial prejudice.

The relevant contrast, for our purposes, is therefore not between a true model of Progressive administration and a false one, but between the conflicting demands for the efficient provision of goods, services, and regulation, on the one hand, and deliberative and participatory techniques of administrative implementation, on the other. Participatory forms of administration promise to legitimate governmental authorities in the eyes of the public they serve, to draw on widely dispersed knowledge and insight, and to incorporate the views of affected parties into the administrative interpretation of legislative aims. But the more administration is subject to the critique, influence, and control of the affected public or to the endorsement of the coordinate branches, the greater the costs of providing the requisite goods and the greater the risk that the best organized, most powerful interests will have a decisive say in delimiting the scope of administrative interventions. The social pathologies the Progressive state seeks to remedy always threaten to undermine the democratic integrity of the administrative process by which such remedies are conceived and implemented.

This chapter documents this normative tension as it took institutional shape over the course of the twentieth century. I will describe how New Deal agencies such as the Tennessee Valley Authority and the Agricultural Adjustment Administration sought to provide democratic contexts within the state, providing for the participation of farmers in the administration of land use planning. The Farm Security Administration, by contrast, sought to provide impoverished farmers with democratic requisites. I will then show how, during the Second Reconstruction, the state sought to combine democratic requisites and democratic contexts in different ways. The Department of Health, Education, and Welfare combined formal bureaucratic requirements with intensive deliberation between the executive and the judicial branches to provide educational requisites to African Americans. The Office of Economic Opportunity engaged in expansive public-sphere deliberation, giving citizens significant control over community action agencies. The Equal Employment Opportunity Commission combined deliberation with civil society groups and interventions in judicial discourse to inscribe its critical interpretations of discrimination into binding law.

I do not choose these institutions because they are the only examples of Progressive administration in our political history. Examples of participatory forms of administration abound. In particular, the notice-and-comment process established by the Administrative Procedure Act of 1946 (APA) is the statutory cornerstone of public participation in regulatory policymaking today. The APA requires that, when agencies issue regulations with the force of law, they must "give interested persons an opportunity to participate in the rule making through submission of written data, views, or arguments with or without opportunity for oral presentation."[9] This requirement has become a routine element of administrative procedure, practiced by agencies ranging from the Environmental Protection Agency to the Federal Communications Commission to the Securities and Exchange Commission. I will touch on this procedure briefly in this chapter and explore it in greater detail in the next. But my aim here is to recover a wider array of administrative practices, which together might expand our conception of the democratic capacities of administrative procedure.

I choose examples from the agricultural New Deal because of their ideological links to the Progressive Era. These links show that Progressive concepts of administration were in fact institutionally efficacious. I then turn to examples from the Second Reconstruction to demonstrate that, even after the direct intellectual influence of Progressivism has waned, the impulse toward deliberative democratic statehood continued to be politically vital and socially formative. These examples, which fall outside the usual canon of administrative law scholarship, serve to decenter our understanding of the state—away from technocratic management and toward democratic and emancipatory forms of administrative action.

II. PROGRESSIVE ADMINISTRATION IN THE AGRICULTURAL NEW DEAL

The contrast between democratic requisites and democratic contexts in Progressive administration was starkly demonstrated in the New Deal's efforts to regulate and reform American rural society. New Deal bureaucrats, under the influence of Progressive administrative thought, developed participatory and cooperative forms of administration in the Agricultural Adjustment Administration (AAA) and the Tennessee Valley Authority (TVA). While these forums for democratic planning successfully engaged members of the public in interpreting and implementing agricultural reform policies, they almost invariably privileged the interests of upper- and middle-class farmers at the expense of impoverished farm tenants and sharecroppers, who were disproportionately African American. By contrast, the Farm Security Administration (FSA) provided much-needed financial support to poor farmers and was less discriminatory toward African Americans. But the FSA was for the most part not participatory in structure. Rather, it was highly bureaucratic and hierarchical, relying upon the centralized implementation of an egalitarian agenda from the national administrative offices, with very little in the way of local control or deliberative democratic engagement. Thus, the New Deal institutionalized the tension in Progressive thought between the administrative provision of democratic requisites and the construction of democratic contexts within the state.

1. The Tennessee Valley Authority

Among the many innovative administrative experiments of the New Deal, the TVA has long captivated the intellectual imagination. In 1950, Henry Steele

Commager described it as the "proving ground . . . of a dynamic democracy. Here was tested the broad construction of the Constitution, large-scale planning, the recasting of federalism along regional lines, new techniques of administration and new standards of civil service, the alliance of science and politics, and the revitalization of democracy through a calculated program of economic and social reconstruction."[10] This explicitly Progressive theory of dynamic democracy was hardly recognizable in the text of the TVA Act, but instead grew out of the philosophies and practices of TVA administrators.

The TVA was established as a public corporation by Congress in 1933 to control flooding and support agricultural and industrial development in the Tennessee River Valley.[11] It had the power to acquire and lease property, to construct dams and reservoirs, to produce and sell electricity, and to "cooperate with National, State, district, or county experimental stations or demonstration farms, with farmers, landowners, and associations of farmers or landowners" to develop and experiment with fertilizers and erosion-prevention techniques.[12]

The TVA's lasting economic contribution to its area of operation and to the national economy as a whole was its infrastructural improvements.[13] But the cooperative aspect of its activity has become its most famous ideological feature. The cooperative mandate was interpreted by David Lilienthal, who was a commissioner and later the chairman of the TVA from 1933 to 1946, as a far-reaching authorization of "grassroots" democracy in regional planning: "Working at the grassroots is the surest guarantee of that day-to-day adjustment to needs and aspirations of the people which is the liveliest form of public accountability."[14] In expounding this notion of democratic planning, Lilienthal quoted at length from Dewey: "American democracy can serve the world only as it demonstrates in the conduct of its own life the efficacy of plural, partial, and experimental methods in securing and maintaining an ever-increasing release of the powers of human nature, in service of a freedom which is co-operative and a co-operation which is voluntary."[15] By engaging affected farmers in administrative decision-making, the TVA hoped to bolster its legitimacy and its efficacy, drawing on the knowledge and authority of local agents.

The grassroots ideology, however, concealed more profound social and political conflict as the TVA adapted to its local environment. As Philip Selznick argued in his classic sociological study of the agency, the TVA won support from local elites for its public power program by giving substantive control over its fertilizer programs to politically conservative agriculture departments in state land-grant colleges and their allies in the American Farm Bureau—a lobby for upper- and middle-class farming interests.[16] While the farm demonstration programs were relatively participatory and deliberative amongst this agricultural elite, they tended to exclude the voices and interests of poor and minority farmers.[17] As James C. Scott notes, the experience of the TVA showed that "working through local institutions, when those institutions reflect great inequalities in property, education, income, and political access, means accepting and reinforcing those inequalities."[18] The grassroots approach of the TVA therefore extended only to the greener pastures of the social landscape, leaving its parched tracts untended.

2. The Agricultural Adjustment Administration

Similar dynamics were at work in the Agricultural Adjustment Administration (AAA). The AAA was established within a week of the TVA in 1933 to "relieve the existing national economic emergency by increasing agricultural purchasing power."[19] To address plummeting agricultural prices, the Act provided that the federal government would pay farmers to reduce their output and tax agricultural processors to pay for the subsidies.[20] Despite legal setbacks, this was one of the most "successfully institutionalized" parts of the early New Deal, owing in large part to the well-developed administrative capacity of the Department of Agriculture and its links to state and local governments.[21]

The proposal for production controls was the brainchild of institutional economists such as M.L. Wilson and Rex Tugwell, both of whom were deeply influenced by Dewey's philosophy of democratic planning and critique of laissez-faire ideologies.[22] The AAA not only grew out of Deweyan Progressive thought but also relied institutionally upon a system of administrative federalism that had been developed under the Wilson administration. Wilson signed into law the Smith-Lever Act of 1914, which gave legislative backing to the Department of Agriculture's education and technical assistance programs.[23] These programs worked through the Agricultural Extension Service, which provided federal assistance through a network of state land-grant colleges and county agricultural agents, who were appointed by state extension offices with local advice.[24] This federal grant program kept Wilson's philosophical commitment to a federal state that was responsive to local needs and interests. The extension service also mirrored Mary Follett's defense of "federalism as the integration of parts," in which local and national interests would inform one another, as opposed to a false "mechanical federalism," in which state and federal authority would be categorically separate.[25] The extension service, land-grant colleges, and county agents provided the organizational backbone for the drive to reduce farm production under the AAA.[26] Local farmers acted as "co-administrators" alongside the county agents, serving on County AAA Committees that determined the production allotments within their jurisdiction.[27] Local farmers subject to the adjustment program elected representatives to serve on these committees.

In the later, more experimental phases of the New Deal, the extension service continued to provide the foundation for a program of much more comprehensive participatory planning. The Department of Agriculture's County Land Use Planning Committees were organized by the state extension service and composed of a substantial majority of "representative" farmers, as well as officials from relevant federal and state agencies.[28] By 1941 this program had organized almost 200,000 farmers and nearly 20,000 local, state, and federal officials into local committees that developed and implemented land-use, healthcare, and education reforms.[29] As Jess Gilbert's landmark study documents, Progressive officials at the Department of Agriculture set up "a national network of local organizations," in which "citizens, scientists, and bureaucrats joined together in discussion-based education and action."[30] While this effort sought to modernize rural farming with advanced techniques, the approach was conciliatory rather than oppositional. As M.L. Wilson put it, "the best way to modify a whole cultural system is for the educational processes to work within it, not to attack it broadside. The most effective way to work within any cultural group is to show how a program developed cooperatively by the group and the experts contributes to the solution of the problems of the persons and groups involved."[31]

Complementing this local, participatory planning initiative was an adult education program at the Department for extension workers, with lectures on themes such as "individualism, democracy, and social control," "unity and diversity in society," and " 'progress' and the philosophy of history."[32] If the influence of Progressive Hegelianism on the agricultural New Deal was not already obvious enough, one course went so far as to explore the question: "Was Hegel right, that the spiritual factors have in the main controlled historical trends, or was Marx right, that it is the physical and economic factors which drag the spiritual and cultural in their wake?"[33]

For organic intellectuals' committed to Deweyan democracy and social planning rather than economic determinism, the choice between Marx and Hegel was clear. Reflecting Dewey's Hegelian critique of classical liberalism in *Individualism Old and New*, the lecture outline suggested that " 'natural rights' and the ownership of 'private property,' . . . served their purpose . . . by securing individualism, but they are fast becoming institutionalized at the expense of social welfare."[34] The lectures thus sought to frame the problems confronting rural society, without dictating to the extension workers any particular solution:

> In what is obviously a transition age, will the future be determined by forces beyond our control—by material conditions, or a mass psychology which is largely emotional—or is the human mind capable of controlling

> developments, largely by planning and foresight . . . ? What are the objects towards which we should direct our efforts in order to create a 'great society' in accordance with desirable human and social patterns?[35]

The disciples of Dewey and the inheritors of Wilsonian institutions thus advanced the Progressive Hegelian project of social transformation guided by critical social theory and deliberative democratic engagement.

But precisely because of their reliance on local decision-makers and institutions, the "low modernists" in the Department of Agriculture tended to replicate and in some cases worsen social and economic inequalities within the agricultural economy.[36] The extension system through which production controls and local planning programs were implemented gave great discretion to the states in how to implement the program, thus allowing the racial prejudices of southern agricultural elites a free hand.[37] The AAA's local committees in the South were composed of white, propertied farmers who represented the interests of their own class almost exclusively; they failed to enforce the obligation of landowners to distribute a share of federal subsidies to their tenants and, in violation of AAA regulations, evicted already-impoverished black and white tenants from their lands to meet production requirements.[38]

In the later, more politically Progressive phases of democratic planning, the class bias of the agency was less severe but still real. Many of the midwestern, middle-class intellectuals who developed the program were relatively blind to the issues of class and race inequality that permeated American agriculture.[39] More important, the extension service upon which the cooperative planning system was built remained a conservative institution. It favored the dominant agricultural interests of the American Farm Bureau, which the service's architects believed were better positioned to accrue and convey technical knowledge and productive benefits.[40] As a consequence, the use of the extension service as an instrument of planning restricted participation to the white, bourgeois farmer, even while it engaged this group in otherwise exemplary forms of deliberative democratic engagement and provided some ancillary material benefits to impoverished whites and blacks.[41]

3. The Farm Security Administration

The administrative interventions of the Farm Security Administration stood in sharp contrast to those of both the TVA and the AAA. While the core activities of the FSA were mostly not deliberative or participatory in format, the agency provided essential goods and services to the agricultural underclass. And it benefited African American clients more than did the programs that engaged in democratic planning amongst landed farmers.

Like those of the TVA and AAA, many of the FSA's programs were not dictated in detail by Congress, but were rather the product of administrative creativity and experimentation. The FSA's institutional progenitor was the Resettlement Administration (RA), which was established by an executive order from President Franklin D. Roosevelt to administer funds appropriated by Congress for "rural rehabilitation and relief in stricken areas."[42] Roosevelt tasked the RA with the administration of resettlement programs for tenant farmers who had been displaced as a result of the AAA production controls, with land-use planning, and with a farm tenant loan program for equipment and purchase of lands.[43] The Bankhead-Jones Farm Tenant Act of 1937 gave legislative support for some of the RA's programs, providing for tenant home ownership through long-term mortgage loans and a host of other rehabilitation measures: short-term loans for livestock and equipment, grants in aid, a debt reduction program, and federal purchase of submarginal lands.[44] Following the recommendations of his Committee on Farm Tenancy, Roosevelt then reconstituted the RA as the FSA to administer these programs within the Department of Agriculture.[45] Most of the FSA's funds and efforts went not toward the farm mortgage lending program stressed by Congress but rather toward various rehabilitation initiatives originally conceived by the public officials in the RA, the President's Committee on Farm Tenancy, and the FSA itself, as well as representatives of the radical Southern Tenant Farmers Union.[46]

Unlike the TVA and AAA, the FSA carried out these rehabilitation initiatives through a relatively bureaucratic, hierarchical, and centralized structure. Though the farm mortgage program was explicitly structured by Congress to mirror the AAA, with local committees making loan decisions, the FSA did not extend this model to most of its rehabilitation programs.[47] In the bulk of its activities, the FSA operated not by soliciting the participation of affected parties in shaping agency policy but rather by providing goods, services, and legal, technical, and organizational assistance to impoverished farmers. In his seminal study of the FSA, Sidney Baldwin observes that FSA administrators "had little faith in the panacea of local administration through committees of farmers, and they viewed . . . federal-state collaboration as an invitation to irresponsibility."[48] Instead, "[t]he central unifying principle in the Washington office . . . was the concentration of effective policy-making and control powers in the hands of the Administrator."[49]

This organizational centralization served to permeate the agency with the political purposes of its leadership: to furnish the conditions for democratic equality by lessening the dependency of agricultural tenants upon their landlords. As Keith Kenneth Conkin observes, "The Farm Security Administration . . . was a militant defender of the small farmer and laborer. It constantly stressed the lack of economic and social justice for the small farmers who were unable to participate in American democracy, contrasting them with the large farmers who were becoming more and more separate from those at the bottom."[50] The FSA's official guide for staff, *Toward Farm Security*, which was distributed to all county offices, stated that the "immediate objectives" of the agency were not only to "relieve the suffering and misery among rural people" and to "increase real income" but also to "weave into the general fabric of community living all the families which are at present gradually forced out of the general community life by their low incomes."[51] Moreover, "[o]f all the Farm Security objectives the most important is the desire, ultimately, to open up the gates of opportunity to all its families on an equal basis with the rest of the rural community."[52] This emphasis on furnishing such material, democratic requisites, rather than maximizing administrative participation, insulated the FSA from the power dynamics and prejudices of the rural political economy to a greater extent than the TVA and AAA. Because of its hierarchical bureaucratic structure and the commitment of agency leaders C.B. Baldwin and Will Alexander to racial equality, the FSA had the best record amongst agricultural programs in serving African American farmers, even though disparities persisted.[53]

The FSA relied on Dewey to expound its administrative philosophy, just as David Lilienthal had in explaining the philosophy behind the TVA. But the selection from Dewey in *Towards Farm Security* reveals telling differences in administrative orientation: "The means have to be implemented by a social-economic system . . . for the production of free human beings associating with one another on terms of equality."[54] Whereas Lilienthal drew upon Dewey's ideas about voluntary "co-operation" in administration, the FSA cited Dewey's thoughts on the administrative "production" of individuals capable of participation in democratic life. In the agency's view, "*[t]he people who need supervision most, need the Farm Security Administration most.*"[55] FSA loans and grants were thus accompanied by a fairly invasive process of budget consultation and home visits to ensure that borrowers and grantees were practicing sound household management, as understood by the administration.[56]

The democratic requisites the agency furnished were not limited to loans, grants, and technical assistance for individuals and families. The FSA also sought to support and to create new forms of social cooperation, which it hoped would prepare their participants future, more transformative social change. In this respect, the FSA approach aligned with the institutional structure of Hegelian ethical life. It provided administrative support not only for property, contract, and the family, but also to forms of corporate membership, wherein farmers could develop a sense of common purpose.

The FSA inherited and expanded the RA's experiments with rural settlement communities, ultimately administering roughly two hundred such settlements. FSA cooperatives were chartered as corporations, in which farmers collectively owned or leased and worked the land with financial support from the FSA and an option to purchase their own plots in the future.[57] These collective farming associations would later draw the wrath of conservative members of Congress and their elite agricultural allies, who derided them as "communistic."[58] But the far more extensive programs were cooperatives wherein farmers pooled resources with the FSA's financial assistance to purchase services or capital goods. The vast majority of the 25,000 cooperatives survived at least until the FSA was abolished in 1946, with 63 percent repaying their loans to the government in full.[59] Perhaps the most farsighted of these experiments were the medical care cooperatives, wherein farmers received subsidized loans from the FSA to buy into health insurance pools administered by the agency.[60] The program reached 615,000 clients at its peak in 1942.[61]

The purpose of these cooperative ventures was not simply to provide relief to impoverished farmers, but to inspire a kind of collective social consciousness amongst this social class. As Sidney Baldwin puts it, "the leaders of the agency hoped that such associations would significantly promote a sense of solidarity among the clientele, and weld them into a politically more formidable power base for the FSA."[62] With its support for cooperatives the FSA aimed to build up the economic, social, and political capacity of low-income farmers, so that the FSA and its constituency could reinforce one another's precarious positions in their respective bureaus and communities. The FSA therefore supported novel forms of social organization amongst farmers, even while it excluded the poor farmer from any significant participation in the administrative decision-making process of the FSA. Whereas the TVA and AAA had fostered deliberative democratic forms of administrative action amongst property-owning farmers, the FSA sought to equip tenant farmers with the economic and social capital necessary to acquire political agency. It furnished the requisites for democratic participation in civil society, rather than providing contexts for democratic participation within the administrative state itself.

If the AAA was the institutional embodiment of Wilson's plea for democratic participation in administration, the FSA captured Du Bois's hope that administrative provision could lay the groundwork for the democratic reconstruction of society. In an article on "Federal Action Programs and Community Action in the South," Du Bois treated the New Deal's intervention in the southern rural economy as an attempt to establish in public consciousness "a direct connection between politics and industry, between government and work, between voting and wages, such as the South was born believing was absolutely impossible and fundamentally wrong."[63] Du Bois like Dewey and Holmes was conscious of the historical development whereby the line between state and society, between a public realm and a private realm, could no longer be drawn categorically. Capturing at once the promise of the FSA and the class bias of the AAA, Du Bois urged

> the necessity in the South of facing new problems of democracy, of harking straight back to that attempt made in Reconstruction to include all human beings in the realm of democratic control. If this be not done then the South, still prisoned and controlled by old bars and patterns including not only the color line but the eighteenth century conception of freedom of industrial enterprise, becomes the pensioner of a Federal Government with all the difficulties of local administration in a region where local government is neither democratic nor efficient.[64]

The New Deal's interventions had the capacity to sow the seeds of radical political change in the South. But such interventions needed to avoid becoming mired in local governments that were inegalitarian, exclusionary, and lethargic. While Du Bois was inspired at this point in his career by Marxian class analysis, he retained a Hegelian faith in the capacity of a relatively autonomous state to advance the cause of dominated economic and racial classes through programmatic action. Du Bois therefore concluded that, with the most recent relief work of the federal government,

> the South will be more compelled to put politics in industry, to reconstruct government so as to give and direct work, and to make that government democratic. I feel that the South is more or less consciously thinking of these things and groping towards a solution; and that this thinking is not so much the work of its intellectual leaders, of its colleges and writers, as of the man to whom the federal government has given bread.[65]

By providing basic goods and services to the southern poor, the FSA provided nourishment for social change. The precondition for democratic life, where it was as yet stunted, was a bureaucracy that provided for the poor rather than one that privileged their participation in administration.

4. The Death and Life of Progressive Administration

This dream of social transformation was, however, deferred. The demands of the Second World War lessened financial support and public enthusiasm for the most Progressive New Deal programs, at the same time as southern Democrats and propertied farmers increasingly resisted attempts to upset the rural political economy. Congressional conservatives and the American Farm Bureau rightly saw the FSA as a threat to the system of white supremacy and economic domination. Appropriations were therefore reduced from 1942 onward, and at the end of the war the FSA was dismantled after a scathing report from the Senate Agricultural Committee on the bureau's finances and ideological aims.[66] Likewise, the democratic planning program of the Department of Agriculture ran into a dead end in the face of stiff resistance from the American Farm Bureau and congressional conservatives; the Department failed to institute many recommendations of the local planning committees and reduced the influence of the Deweyan civil servants.[67]

The administrative politics of agriculture reflected a broader conservative reaction to the Progressive elements of the New Deal. As agencies such as the National Labor Relations Board and the Securities and Exchange Commission challenged financial and employer interests and government lawyers wielded administrative procedures to the disadvantage of the corporate bar, business elites turned to the values of due process and separation of powers to protect their position.[68] Roscoe Pound acted as the foremost intellectual spokesman for this movement, labeling as "administrative absolutism" the "highly centralized administration set up under complete control of the executive for the time being, relieved of judicial review, and making up its own rules."[69] Though Pound during the Progressive Era had been an ardent proponent of legislative rather than common law legal development, he was even then concerned with the proliferation of "executive justice," in which administrative bodies would take on the responsibilities of courts in settling disputes between private parties.[70] Now, as these trends hit full steam, Pound led the American Bar Association in advocating for a firm legislative response to reassert judicial prerogatives.[71] In 1939, Congress passed a bill that built upon the bar's proposals, including requirements of extensive hearing procedures for both adjudicatory orders and regulations and an expansion of judicial control over the administrative process.[72] President Roosevelt, however, vetoed this bill. Following the studies of current bureaucratic practices by the Attorney General's Committee on Administrative Procedure, the Administrative Procedure Act of 1946 (APA) instead provided a general template for administrative adjudication, rulemaking, and judicial review of administrative action.

While the APA represented a modest retrenchment from the heights of bureaucratic discretion during the New Deal, it at the same time endorsed the participatory practices that had been at the heart of Progressive understandings of the state. As the Attorney General's Committee recognized and the previous chapter demonstrated, public participation in policymaking had been a frequent aspect of administrative procedure since the early twentieth century at agencies such as the Federal Reserve Board, Federal Trade Commission, and the

Forest Service.[73] The Committee recommended "wider use of these methods of obtaining the knowledge, views, and criticism of outside interests in the process of rulemaking . . . in the light of the conscious policy of encouraging the participation of those regulated in the process of making the regulation."[74]

The APA built upon this existing practice with its now famous "notice and comment" provisions. It required that when agencies issue regulations, they "give interested persons an opportunity to participate in the rule-making through submission of written data, views, or arguments with or without opportunity for oral presentation. After consideration of the relevant matter presented, the agency shall incorporate in the rules adopted a concise general statement of their basis and purpose."[75] Thus, at the same time as the APA constrained administrative adjudication to mimic judicial proceedings, it licensed and extended the Progressive effort to incorporate the voice of the diffuse public into the administrative process. It codified in statute Goodnow and Dickinson's proposal to condition judicial deference to administrative judgment on agencies' provision of public notice and a hearing to affected parties.

The notice-and-comment provision of the APA was nonetheless a thin form of participation relative to the more radical forms of public involvement in agricultural land-use planning, or the iterative, deliberative hearings of the Forest Service mentioned in chapter 2. They required only an opportunity for written comments rather than the kind of local, face-to-face deliberation the most experimental phases of the Progressive Era and the agricultural New Deal had put into practice. In the wake of war with Nazi Germany and at the beginning of the Cold War with soviet communism, the robust theory of the state that had animated Progressive thought had lost its appeal.[76] Instead, more conservative, society-centered, and private-rights-regarding approaches to administration came into ascendance. Theories of interest-group bargaining came to supplant the more participatory and socially transformative understanding of the state that the Hegelian Progressives had advocated and the low modernists at the Department of Agriculture had implemented.[77] Planning democracy survived only as a shadow of its former self. But this shadow has stretched across the full institutional edifice of the administrative state. In the next chapter, I will suggest how the deliberative democratic capacities of this rulemaking procedure might be deepened, so as better to reflect the transformative spirit of the New Deal.

As the APA codified a threadbare form of Progressive administrative procedure, the substantive interventions of the New Deal provided the rudiments for the future democratization of civil society. The material requisites furnished by the Farm Security Administration, in particular, left significant ideological and institutional legacies. In his groundbreaking treatise on racial problems in the United States, which would be cited by the Supreme Court in *Brown v. Board of Education*,[78] Gunmar Myrdal offered a detailed discussion of the FSA's interventions on behalf of low-income farmers in the South, concluding:

> Nobody who has had any contact with those doing field work for the Farm Security Administration can escape becoming impressed by these attempts to rehabilitate farm families. . . . The Farm Security work, after this period of rather diversified experimentation, has provided the kind of practical administrative experience which would be needed for a major reform of land and tenure conditions.[79]

Though the "major reform" of the sort Myrdal hoped for did not come to pass, its "diversified experimentation" yielded significant material benefits for the emerging civil rights movement and related interventions in the War on Poverty during the 1960s. The FSA resettlements in the rural South created small groups of landed black farmers, as well as safe settings for mobilization, which empowered them politically in the struggle for racial equality.[80] Institutions furnished by the FSA provided the economic and social capital necessary to underwrite the Mississippi Freedom Democratic Party, which challenged the white primary in the state, leading to the election of the first black Mississippi state representative since Reconstruction.[81] As Spencer Wood has argued, "by helping southern sharecroppers purchase their own farms the FSA planted the seeds of independence that matured for more than a generation, eventually bearing their most bountiful harvest during the civil rights movement."[82] The combination of subsidized landownership and encouragement of solidaristic social practices thus set up crucial bulwarks against the powerful forces of white supremacy that beset the civil rights movement on all sides.[83]

Nor were the contributions of the FSA limited to landownership in the Delta. The FSA's rural health operatives were both institutionally and ideologically influential for similar efforts conducted by the Office of Health Administration at the Office of Economic Opportunity (OEO) in the 1960s, as officials modeled their program on the FSA's medical cooperatives,[84] and built upon local institutional capacities nurtured by the FSA.[85] Likewise, FSA loans to rural cooperatives became the model for a similar program sponsored by the OEO, despite the resistance of southern congressional conservatives to the idea.[86] All of these discrete examples amounted to a substantial institutional legacy for the bureau in furnishing democratic requisites for the rural poor and providing models for future efforts at social transformation.

While the FSA provided institutional infrastructure for the southern civil rights movement, the AAA's crop reduction programs significantly accelerated black migration from the rural South to northern cities. Incentivized to reduce their output and allowed by landlord-friendly adjustment committees to violate tenancy rights, white landowners shed their tenants and invested in capital goods to replace farm labor.[87] The result was greater concentration of African Americans in urban ghettos and the beginnings of white flight from the cities.[88] The twin arms of the civil rights movement—the struggle to end de jure discrimination in the South and to end de facto discrimination in the urban North—were thus linked to the qualified successes and partial failures of the rural New Deal.

These historical connections go to show how administrative interventions reshape society in ways that facilitate and structure new forms of social order and antagonism. The dynamics of this development are neither the same in every instance nor predictable in advance. But in retrospect, we can see their basic contours. The partial and sporadic democratic requisites furnished by the FSA provided important resources for African Americans who remained in the South and buttressed their successful efforts to end Jim Crow segregation. At the same time, the compromised democratic contexts of agricultural adjustment transformed structures of social and racial domination in the South by uprooting and modernizing the practically feudal system of cotton tenancy. Many African Americans were thus cast off the land and thrust into new urban landscapes, setting the stage for the northern civil rights mobilization and urban unrest. At the same time, the conservative reaction to the New Deal elevated the status of the courts as the guardians of individual rights, which positioned them to play a more active role in protecting the interests of African Americans.[89] In the Second Reconstruction, the courts and civil rights agencies would then engage in a constructive dialogue over the meaning and requirements of racial equality.

III. PROGRESSIVE ADMINISTRATION IN THE SECOND RECONSTRUCTION

Second Reconstruction was a period of intense social and administrative mobilization, in which the resources of the public and its government coalesced to uproot segregation and promote racial equality. Just as the New Deal had challenged the stable boundaries between state and civil society with its administrative interventions into economic life, Second Reconstruction subjected forms of private economic organization and local government to unprecedented federal regulation in order to protect the entitlements and enlarge the opportunities of African Americans. The federal government in many respects realized Du Bois vision of a "permanent Freedmen's Bureau" with a panoply of agencies, offices, and commissions tasked with civil rights enforcement.[90]

This emancipatory state built upon the administrative capacities and legal doctrines that had been generated from the Progressive Era through the New Deal.[91] Recall that Goodnow had understood that courts and administrative bodies would have overlapping roles in the implementation of regulatory law, as they each had the responsibility to translate legislative will into official deeds. This situation gave rise to qualified judicial deference to agencies' judgments, as courts sought to respect Congress's allocation of authority to agencies, and to incorporate administrative policy determinations into their own jurisprudence. The judiciary thus came to accept agencies' interpretation of law where the proper construction of the statute was within the scope of the agency's delegated authority, its subject-matter competence, and its experience.[92] The civil rights era would extend this judicial adoption of administrative reasoning to new social spheres. Administrative agencies became the fulcrum for *inter-branch deliberation*, providing administrative rules and guidelines that moved the courts toward more expansive understandings of the ills of racial discrimination and the demands of equal protection. The requisites for democratic equality were furnished in a collaborative process among Progressive legislators, bureaucrats, judges, and civil society groups.

In the War on Poverty, the administrative state provided even more extensive democratic contexts in which excluded groups could participate. These community action programs institutionalized *public sphere deliberation* in the provision of material requisites for democratic life. Second Reconstruction thus offered another iteration of Progressive administration that recombined democratic ends and democratic means in novel institutional forms.

1. The Department of Health, Education and Welfare

Inter-branch deliberation was essential to the implementation of school desegregation in the South. The Department of Health Education and Welfare (HEW) deployed its statutory authority to comprehend the broader social context in which school desegregation operated. This in turn gave courts the impetus to uproot the dual school system that operated in the southern states.

In *Brown v. Board of Education* (1954), the Court had explained that education had become a key requisite to democracy: "Today education is the most important function of state and local governments. . . . It is the very foundation of good citizenship."[93] But despite the Supreme Court's renunciation of the "separate but equal" doctrine, ten years later only 2.25 percent of black children in the former Confederate States and only 10.9 percent in the entire South attended schools with white children, with more than half of the region's 3,000 school districts still completely segregated.[94] This was due to the massive resistance of southern localities to desegregation, the federal courts' adherence to the gradualist logic of integration "with all deliberate speed," and the limits of constitutional enforcement through private litigation alone.[95]

With the Civil Rights Act of 1964, Congress authorized a powerful new administrative tool to address the problem.[96] Section 601 of the Act provided that "[n]o person in the United States shall, on the ground of race, color, or national origin, be excluded from participation in, be denied the benefits of, or be subject to discrimination under any program or activity receiving Federal financial assistance."[97] To effectuate this requirement, Congress authorized and directed "each Federal department and agency which is empowered to extend Federal financial assistance" to issue "rules, regulations, and orders of general applicability."[98] Because of its use of capacious undefined concepts such as "discrimination," "exclu[sion]," "participation," and "benefits," Title VI gave great discretion to administrative agencies to delineate the scope of the statutory command.

HEW accordingly issued a regulation in 1964 that stated that a school system would be found to be in compliance with Title VI if it "submits a plan for . . . desegregation . . . which the Commissioner of Education determines is adequate to accomplish the purposes of the Act . . . and provides reasonable assurance that it will carry out such plan."[99] This provision empowered HEW officials to determine whether school desegregation plans were adequate or whether districts were shirking their responsibilities. In an effort to win political support for compliance with the regulation, HEW consulted with members of Congress and governors across the nation, in addition to civil rights groups, prior to promulgating them.[100] But this effort did not eliminate local resistance, even if it may have for a time blunted vocal opposition from some state and national officials. Many southern states and localities simply submitted rote compliance statements without detailing plans to achieve desegregation; HEW replied that such statements of compliance were insufficient.[101] To address southern foot-dragging, HEW elaborated on these requirements in successive guidelines in 1965 and 1966.[102] By issuing "guidelines" rather than a "rule," which by the terms of Title VI would have required presidential approval,[103] HEW assumed direct responsibility for its desegregation policy.[104] This decision exemplified the Progressive conception of democratic statehood, which untethered administrative legitimacy from the democratic authority of the president and re-anchored it to direct exchanges between the agency and other political actors.

Though the 1966 Guidelines followed judicial precedent in allowing "freedom of choice" plans, which provided that parents could determine which school their children would attend, it went beyond the jurisprudence of the time in emphasizing that "[a] free choice plan tends to place the burden of desegregation on the Negro or other minority group students and their parents. . . . [T]he very nature of a free choice plan and the effect of long-standing community attitudes often tend to preclude or inhibit the exercise of a truly free choice by or for minority group students."[105] Accordingly, HEW shifted the burden to the local governments, stating that it would "scrutinize with special care the operation of voluntary plans" and set target percentage increases for black enrollment, which increased inversely to each school's rate of desegregation in the previous year; the Commissioner reserved discretion to reject such plans if he "concludes that such steps would be ineffective."[106]

The Guidelines' recognition that "community attitudes" and the "burden" that freedom-of-choice plans placed upon minorities tended to "inhibit . . . truly free choice" was a normative judgment and not merely a search for nails by a hammer-wielding agency.[107] HEW's approach to these problems harkened back to the Progressive Hegelian critique of classical liberalism, emphasizing that individual choices occur within a social landscape and that such choices cannot be truly free in circumstances where the community does not recognize the equal moral and political status of all of its members. HEW officials arrived at this conclusion not through the direct influence of Progressive thought but rather through the encounter between civil rights ideologies and administrative experience. Based on their previous evaluations of voluntary plans, HEW staffers came to realize that the mere removal of legal barriers to integration would be insufficient to establish real educational freedom for southern blacks.[108]

In addition to this pragmatic experience, HEW officials were motivated by a moral understanding of the American political tradition. Derrick A. Bell Jr., who was Deputy Director of the Office of Civil Rights (OCR) at HEW from 1965 to 1968, stated that the "morality aspect" of Title VI and its implementation at HEW "should not be overlooked. Behind American institutions—law, statutes, legal precedents in case rulings—lies a tradition[], at least in theory, of ordering society according to basic principles of morality, fairness, justice. This is so despite patent betrayals of principle in [the] relationship between the races."[109] At OCR, Bell, Peter Librassi, David Seeley, Elaine Heffernan, and other staff put this general moral consciousness to work as they sought to understand and to reconstruct the social spheres in which black students and their families made educational choices.[110] Bell and Librassi, who directed OCR, were both ideologically and institutionally aligned with the civil rights movement and brought its ethos to their work in the Department.[111] Their ideals of freedom, fairness, and equality were synthesized with administrative experience. This encounter between universal norms and their particular social application produced new understandings of what those ideals meant and required: not merely de jure desegregation, but a more thoroughgoing transformation of southern civil society along racially egalitarian lines.

With its innovative Guidelines, HEW stepped beyond contemporaneous judicial precedent to establish a new, results-oriented test of school district compliance.[112]

The courts followed HEW's lead, as the Fifth Circuit, beginning in *Singleton v. Jackson Municipal Separate School District* (1965),[113] relied on Department guidelines to determine whether schools districts were maintaining segregated systems in violation of the Fourteenth Amendment.[114] In explaining the court's deference to HEW's administrative standards, Judge John Minor Wisdom expressed a discursive understanding of the separation of powers:

> We attach great weight to the standards established by the Office of Education. The judiciary of course has functions and duties distinct from those of the executive department, but in carrying out national policy the three departments of government are united by a common objective. There should be a close correlation, therefore, between the judiciary's and the executive department's standards in administering this policy. Absent legal questions, the United States Office of Education is better qualified than the courts and is the more appropriate federal body to weigh administrative difficulties inherent in school desegregation plans.[115]

Judge Wisdom recognized that administrative agencies and courts had a special relationship when it came to the implementation of public rights, such as the right of the public established by Title VI to non-discrimination in the distribution of federal education grants. The branches were here "united by a common objective," with the administrative agency playing the role of primary interpreter of statutory norms.

Judge Wisdom's constructive, deliberative understanding of the separation of powers was reminiscent of Justice Frankfurter's statement that "[c]ourts and public agencies are not to be regarded as competitors in the task of safeguarding the public interest. Courts no less than administrative bodies are agencies of government. Both are instruments for realizing public purposes."[116] The courts would ensure that administrative interpretations were within the boundaries of the law; if they were, courts would be prepared to give these administrative determinations binding force and elaborate on the social judgments administrators reached.

HEW's critique of socially constrained individual choice fundamentally shaped not only the courts' interpretation of the Civil Rights Act, but of the Constitution itself.[117] As the judiciary gave great weight to the judgment of the agency in its interpretation of the very meaning of Title VI, the courts and the agency engaged in inter-branch dialogue to articulate the public purposes of non-discrimination and equal protection. The lower federal courts did not replace spiritless number-crunching with social-theoretic values of their own making but rather fleshed out, enforced, and constitutionalized concepts of freedom and social domination that HEW officials had previously articulated in their internal deliberations and administrative guidelines.[118]

2. The Equal Employment Opportunity Commission

Administrative efforts to address discrimination in the labor market combined deliberation among the legislature, the agency, and the courts with direct exchanges between the agency and the public sphere. Through these exchanges, the Equal Employment Opportunity Commission (EEOC) would craft powerful understandings of discrimination that continue to shape legal doctrine today.

As the 1963 "March for Jobs and Freedom" demonstrated, members of the civil rights movement saw an immanent connection between legal and material equality, with marchers carrying signs demanding "equal rights *NOW*!" alongside "jobs for all *NOW*!" side by side.[119] Freedom and employment were not seen merely as independent goods but as interrelated "promises of democracy."[120] Title VII of the Civil Rights Act of 1964 sought to make one of those promises real by declaring: "It shall be an unlawful employment practice for an employer . . . to fail or to refuse to hire or to discharge any individual, or otherwise to discriminate against any individual with respect to his compensation, terms, conditions, or privileges of employment, because of such individual's race, color, religion, sex, or national origin."[121]

While it was clear Congress sought to prevent intentional and explicit discrimination, it was unclear whether discrimination "because of" an individual's race might be read to include employment practices with discriminatory effect but lacking in explicit racial animus.[122] The scope of the prohibition would be shaped through a process of inter-branch elaboration between the courts and the agency Congress established to implement Title VII: the EEOC. EEOC's powers were extremely limited. Because congressional Republicans wanted to avoid the creation of another National Labor Relations Board with adjudicatory powers, they demanded the Commission have only technical assistance and complaint investigation functions. EEOC nonetheless served as a site for civil rights mobilization. The NAACP Legal Defense Fund strategically inundated the office with employment discrimination complaints, with hopes of showing the need for more potent legislation.[123]

EEOC responded by issuing guidelines that interpreted its antidiscrimination mandate expansively. The Commission "reasoned that it is an unlawful practice to fail to or refuse to hire, to discharge, or to compensate unevenly, or to limit, segregate and classify employees on criteria which prove to have a demonstrable racial effect without clear and convincing business motive."[124] The Commission's experience with discrimination complaints and its collection of racially disaggregated data on employment showed that employment tests had a particularly negative impact upon black employment. Though Title VII specifically stated that it would not "be an unlawful employment practice for an employer to give and to act upon the results of any professionally developed ability test,"[125] the EEOC issued a guideline stating that the Commission "interprets 'professionally developed ability test' to mean a test which fairly measures the knowledge or skills required by the particular job or class of jobs which the applicant seeks. . . . The fact that a test was prepared by an individual or organization claiming expertise in test preparation does not, without more, justify its use within the meaning of Title VII."[126]

EEOC's interpretations of Title VII were motivated by its critical evaluation of the social context in which it operated rather than a perhaps futile search for the "true" congressional intent. As EEOC attorney Alfred Blumrosen later put it, "the legislative history set limits beyond which administrators could not go in carrying out the statutory mandate, but it did not dictate the course of administration. . . . This view of legislative history requires the administrator to develop ideas, policies, and procedures which derive from an informed understanding of the dynamics of the social problem and the role of government in its resolution."[127] EEOC's experience with the problem of black exclusion from the labor market over the first three years of its existence would convince it to shift from an individualist to an institutional, systemic understanding of the problem. EEOC Commissioner Samuel C. Jackson thus observed that

> [d]iscrimination is becoming less often an individual act of disparate treatment flowing from an evil state of mind. Discrimination is more institutionalized—the application of a system of personnel selection, assignment, promotion, layoff, transfer, or discharge. We at EEOC have reasoned that it is unlawful practice to fail to hire or to refuse to hire, to discharge or to compensate unevenly, or to limit, segregate, and classify employees on criteria which prove to have a demonstrable racial effect.[128]

Chairman William H. Brown III likewise stated in an EEOC public hearing in 1970 that "discrimination is a condition of pervasive exclusion. It does not matter whether exclusion is the result of a deliberate act of discrimination or the maintenance of a traditional community pattern of employment or the perpetuation of past discrimination."[129] EEOC leadership in this way interpreted discrimination to mean not only making decisions consciously on the basis of race but a broader condition of social "exclusion." This was a concept of racism that concerned not primarily individual prejudice but rather the social power of dominant groups and its manifestation in the structures of society. Equal employment meant the empowerment of minorities against an entrenched racial hierarchy.[130]

EEOC's interpretation was not the isolated work of bureaucrats but was rather a synthesis of official practical judgment, information gathering, and input from regulatory beneficiaries. In November 1965, EEOC announced that it would require all employers with over one hundred employees—118,000 in all—to submit "EEO-1" reports on their minority hiring practices.[131] EEO-1 reports assembled data on employment disaggregated by race and sex. Such reporting requirements were adopted after a White House conference where some business representatives expressed concern that the requirement was overly intrusive, and some civil rights advocates worried that reporting on the racial identity of employers might actually enable further discrimination.[132] EEOC published its reports, revealing highly unequal patterns of employment, particularly in white-collar jobs.

EEOC employment reports also served as the catalyst for a series of hearings with employers in different industries and regions to shed light on unfair employment practices and encourage voluntary compliance with Title VII. The hearings created a setting for further public reflection on the meaning of the nation's commitment to racial equality. The 1968 New York City hearings on white-collar employment were perhaps the most successful of these meetings. The goals of hearing were to "focus public attention on the problem of discrimination" and to "serve notice on all concerned of EEOC's determination to exercise its legal authority imaginatively and aggressively" and "to discover, and lay a basis for, Commission action to remedy entrenched discrimination practices in white collar hiring and upgrading."[133] The hearings gained significant publicity, with a front page *New York Times* article declaring "Business Job Bias in City Is Charged" and citing the Commission's finding that "56 of 100 major corporations in New York City 'had not a single Negro serving as official or manager.' "[134] EEOC Chairman Clifford Alexander, Jr. also observed that a few firms had indeed hired African Americans and Puerto Ricans for white-collar jobs; this, he argued, undermined the claim that there were no viable minority candidates for such work.[135] Herbert Hill, labor secretary for the NAACP, complimented the EEOC's hearing for having exposed the "rigid pattern of exclusion" in New York's white-collar employment market.[136] EEOC thus provided both the information and the forum to rethink the nature of discrimination—to understand racial inequality not merely as a problem of intentional malice but also of systemic barriers.

In all the EEOC's activity, the opinions and interests of civil rights organizations and their clientele received particular attention. As Luther Holcomb, Vice-Chairman of EEOC from 1965 to 1971, attested, the Commission treated the NAACP and its president Roy Wilkins as a "partner," and "the NAACP and the

Urban League played a major role in the development of the EEOC."[137] But the EEOC was in no sense captured by civil rights groups, as historian Hugh Davis Graham has suggested.[138] Its staff was not unanimously aligned with civil rights organizations,[139] and its statistics-based approach to identifying and remedying discrimination was initially resisted by some members of civil rights community.[140] Eventually, however, EEOC and civil rights organizations "collaborate[d] . . . in pursuing race-conscious remedies for employment discrimination in a variety of local-level forums."[141]

The option had been open to EEOC to take the path of least resistance—routine processing of complaints according to the intent-based understanding of discrimination that Congress had unambiguously sanctioned. But EEOC officials felt the obligation to take a more proactive approach. In its effort to find a solution to the problems demonstrated in the avalanche of employment complaints registered with the Commission, EEOC had to rework the intentional understanding of discrimination initially embraced by civil rights groups into an effects-based, structural perspective. The eventual embrace of this turn in the meaning of discrimination by the civil rights community should not be read as a capitulation to administrative pragmatism. It was rather the result of the dialogic process Dewey and Follett had envisioned: arguments advanced in the public sphere interacted with the judgment and expertise of administrative officials to forge new solutions to pressing social problems.

The critical judgments that emerged from the EEOC's public-sphere interactions proved crucial in a landmark Supreme Court case on employment discrimination law: *Griggs v. Duke Power* (1971).[142] *Griggs* was an employee suit against a company that had "openly discriminated on the basis of race" prior to the passage of the Civil Rights Act, and had subsequently introduced high school education and testing requirements for many of its departments.[143] The tests the company used were professionally prepared in an apparent attempt to comply with section 703(h) of the Civil Rights Act, which allowed the use of certain "professionally developed ability tests."[144] The Supreme Court rejected the lower court's determination that the tests were permitted under the Act because there was no "showing of a racial purpose of discriminatory intent."[145] On the contrary, the Court held that

> the Act proscribes not only overt discrimination but also practices that are fair in form, but discriminatory in operation. The touchstone is business necessity. If an employment practice which operates to exclude Negroes can not be shown to be related to job performance, the practice is prohibited.[146]

To reach the conclusion that the Civil Rights Act targeted racially unequal consequences of employment practices and not merely discriminatory intent, the Court explicitly relied upon EEOC guidelines: "The Equal Employment Opportunity Commission, having enforcement responsibility, has issued guidelines interpreting §703(h) to permit only the use of job-related tests. The administrative interpretation of the Act by the enforcing agency is entitled to great deference."[147]

EEOC's decision to issue testing guidelines, and the doctrine of judicial deference to administrative interpretations, therefore led to a broad construction of the statute. In adopting the EEOC's interpretation, the Court applied the persuasive force of a previously non-binding administrative opinion, finding that the Commission's Guideline "comports with congressional intent."[148] The Commission thus deployed its powers of rational argumentation, rooted in discourse with the public sphere, to expand the power of the courts to redress discrimination in the absence of direct evidence of intentional bias.

3. The Office of Economic Opportunity

The War on Poverty was administered with unprecedented public participation. The Office of Economic Opportunity's decentralized and collaborative approach supported the development of the urban black public sphere and channeled social unrest into political mobilization.

Congress had passed the Economic Opportunity Act of 1964[149] in response to growing public and presidential concern about "poverty in the midst of plenty" and unrest in urban ghettos.[150] While the Economic Opportunity Act explicitly targeted poverty and benefited poor whites as well as blacks, it was widely understood at the time as an integral element of the civil rights struggle.[151] President Johnson certainly considered civil rights and the war on poverty to be interconnected, as he referred explicitly to the economic opportunity programs in his speech presenting the Voting Rights Act in 1965:

> The bill that I am presenting to you will be known as a civil rights bill. But in a larger sense, most of the program I am recommending is a civil rights program. . . . Because all Americans just must have the right to vote. . . . But I would like to caution you that to exercise these privileges takes much more than legal right. It requires a trained mind and a healthy body. It requires a decent home and a chance to find a job, and the opportunity to escape from the clutches of poverty.[152]

Johnson understood the connection between democratic requisites and democratic contexts: one cannot effectively participate in democratic life if one does not have the economic and social wherewithal to do so.

The Economic Opportunity Act established the Office of Economic Opportunity (OEO) in the Executive Office of the President, thus locating the War on Poverty's command center outside of and above the established departments and government agencies. While providing for rural rehabilitation loans similar to FSA programs, job training, and employment incentives, the core of the Act provided that OEO would approve and provide grants to "community action programs" (CAPs) in cities and other localities to develop and implement comprehensive anti-poverty programs.[153] Congress defined a "community action program" as a program that "provides services, assistance, and other activities of sufficient scope and size to give promise of progress towards the elimination of poverty or a cause or causes of poverty"; that was "conducted administered by a public or private non-profit agency"; and that was "developed, conducted, and administered with the maximum feasible participation of residents of the areas and members of the groups served."[154]

The "maximum feasible participation" requirement would become the most contentious and politically significant aspect of the War on Poverty. The language was drafted by the President's Task Force in the War on Poverty.[155] Members of the Task Force thought the phrase had numerous, overlapping meanings, including coordination between local government and private organizations, symbolic or real involvement of the poor in program administration, and support for transformative political action.[156] It was drafted as an ambiguous phrase to allow administrative flexibility later on.[157] Daniel Patrick Moynihan, however, subsequently argued that the phrase "was intended to do no more than ensure that persons excluded from the political process in the South and elsewhere would nonetheless participate in the *benefits* of the community action programs in the new legislation."[158] He thus took the more expansive form of community action that OEO in fact implemented to depart from legislative intent.

Moynihan's interpretation, which has dominated scholarship on the community action program, not only differs from the admittedly ambiguous intent of its drafters, but, more important, from statutory text and legislative history. Moynihan neglected to mention that the Act required that community action programs be "*developed, conducted, and administered with* maximum feasible participation of the residents of the area and members of the groups served."[159] This multidimensional participation requirement plainly contemplated more than participation in the benefits. Nor did the legislative history support his reading. The Report of the Senate Committee on Labor and Public Welfare stated that "it is expected the widest possible range of community organizations will participate."[160] Likewise, the Report of the House Committee on Education and Labor claimed that the community action program was "based upon the belief that local citizens know and understand their communities best and that they will be the ones to seize the initiative and provide sustained, vigorous leadership."[161]

"Seize the initiative" is precisely what they did. When mayors and other local governments proposed CAPs that provided very little or no representation to minority and impoverished residents in the governance structure, they met with a swift backlash from civil rights organizations.[162] OEO responded to the protests of the newly organized urban poor by interpreting the statutory requirement of maximum feasible participation program broadly, requiring in guidelines that one-third of the governing boards be chosen by "traditional democratic approaches and techniques."[163]

These community action agencies served to support the urban black public sphere. In Harlem, for example, the HARYOU-ACT community action agency sponsored Black Arts poet Amiri Baraka's "school of cultural history," which taught the "political philosophy of the black man in America," as well his street theater productions, which drew audiences in the thousands.[164] J. David Greenstone and Paul E. Peterson argue that, in cities that saw destructive and violent unrest in the black communities, "community residents active in CAPs worked to focus and to make concrete those demands which rioters articulated."[165] In these and similar contexts, such as in Syracuse and Newark, the community agencies were quite radical, serving as rallying points for direct and sometimes hostile challenges to the local government and OEO itself.[166] Even in these cases, however, "the activity of the relatively large number of blacks involved in the more participatory CAPs involved concrete demands articulated within the framework of the existing *political* regime, even though these activists sought major *social* transformation, namely the elimination of racial inequality."[167] In most other cases community action agencies combined strategies of conflict and cooperation with local government and social service agencies, eventually retreating into more conventional roles of service providers and neighborhood advisory boards for welfare agencies.[168]

The Community Action Program thus aimed both to furnish democratic requisites and to provide democratic contexts within the administrative process. This stood in contrast to the New Deal, when administrative contexts for deliberative democracy had excluded impoverished and minority farmers, whereas agencies that provided the requisites for democratic participation had not included the poor in the decision-making process. The War on Poverty, instead, sought to incorporate impoverished and minority citizens into the administrative apparatus of a program that would provide them with benefits. It synthesized the two dimensions of the Progressive state.

IV. ASSESSING THE ADMINISTRATIVE LEGACIES OF THE SECOND RECONSTRUCTION

The administrative implementation of Second Reconstruction saw new configurations of the twin Progressive requirements of providing the requisites for a democratic society and creating contexts for democratic participation within the government. HEW's efforts to provide educational requisites through school integration primarily took the form of inter-branch deliberation: it mediated between the broad norms established by elected representatives and judicial judgments. EEOC combined inter-branch deliberation with public sphere engagement in an effort to provide economic requisites to minority participation in democratic life. OEO sought to synthesize democratic ends with democratic means, fostering public sphere deliberation over the control and content of the anti-poverty program. In this section, I review the legacies of these administrative efforts. I conclude that in the case of inter-branch deliberation, the provision of democratic requisites is more likely to be sustained if courts explicitly engage with and adopt agencies' critical judgments. This history also suggests that the creation of democratic contexts within administration will not efficiently furnish democratic requisites without significant bureaucratic support, supervision, and training.

1. Community Action: Political Empowerment and Economic Poverty

The OEO's community action program sought to combine democratic requisites and democratic contexts by giving excluded, low-income African Americans a significant say in program implementation. This synthesis proved imperfect, however. On the one hand, community action succeeded in increasing black political power at the urban level. This process was a symbolic, ideological struggle, in which the discourse of "maximum feasible participation" mobilized, challenged, and altered social roles in urban politics.[169] The urban public sphere was transformed by the new claims African Americans could raise to full membership in the local political community. OEO's support for grassroots black organizing not only enabled urban blacks to thwart some of the most disastrous attempts at "urban renewal" in the Model Cities program[170] but also led to increased black political representation at the local and national level.[171]

Although community action succeeded in facilitating black political organization and representation, it had only meager immediate effects on the material condition of impoverished Americans.[172] Because of a failure to train or prepare local leadership for programmatic responsibility, community action agencies were ill-equipped—financially, organizationally, and professionally—to effectively deliver desperately needed material support to the communities they represented.[173] Those programs that succeeded and became an entrenched part of the welfare state, such as Head Start, were not primarily the product of input from community members but rather were contrived at the national level.[174] While the community action agencies attempted to overcome the tension between democratic contexts and democratic requisites, the conflict between efficient implementation and the inclusion of all segments of the public in decision-making thus re-emerged. Because it dealt with many of the most dominated, excluded, and under-resourced people, "maximum feasible participation" imposed significant transaction costs for the allocation of programmatic benefits. The Economic Opportunity Act's core concern with economic poverty, as opposed to black political empowerment, likely would have been addressed better through a conventional, bureaucratic allocation of goods and services to the poor.

The War on Poverty is therefore to be credited with attempting, more so than any government program in the past, to reconcile the demands for democratic requisites and democratic contexts. Not all the blame for its insignificant effects on economic poverty should be cast on its participatory process: the failure to provide requisites was as much a function of the paltry resources dedicated to the program as of its inclusive administrative structure.[175] But the example of the OEO goes to show that conflicts between administrative efficiency and deliberative democratic legitimacy are difficult to fully eliminate.

The challenge is to develop administrative forms that, in the spirit of the Community Action Program, attempt to combine democratic contexts and democratic requisites in untried but promising institutional shapes. Greater technical and administrative support, combined with more cabined discretion for community action agencies, might have increased the success of the program. If OEO had done more to provide bureaucratic staff to community action agencies and to train local leaders to administer the program, and if it had provided such agencies with a clear menu of policy choices, it might have provided democratic requisites more efficiently while simultaneously serving as a venue for political empowerment. Though the tension between democratic requisites and democratic contexts cannot be eradicated, it can be better mediated through administrative structures that are alive to the genuine conflicts between them.

2. Disparate Impact and the EEOC: Judicial Deference and Institutional Durability

The institutional consequences of the inter-branch deliberations of EEOC and HEW in providing democratic requisites show the importance of genuine discourse between agencies and courts rather than formulaic deference to technocratic expertise. Though the concrete effects of EEOC policy on black unemployment rates are difficult to discern, EEOC policy enhanced the quantity and likelihood of success in discrimination suits, at least up until the early 1980s.[176] These gains partially receded during the Reagan administration. Under the leadership of Clarence Thomas, EEOC rejected the institutional approach to discrimination developed by the early Commission and reverted to a more narrow focus on cases where direct evidence of intentional discrimination was available.[177] An increasingly conservative Supreme Court subsequently rolled back the expansive, effects-based understanding of discrimination the Court endorsed in *Griggs*.[178]

EEOC's critical evaluations of social context endured this period of conservative reaction, however. In response to the Supreme Court's narrowing of EEOC and the *Griggs* Court's effects-based interpretation of discrimination, Congress passed the Civil Rights Act of 1991.[179] The Act states as a "finding" that the "the Supreme Court[] . . . has weakened the scope and effectiveness of Federal civil rights protections."[180] The purpose of the Act is therefore to "codify the concepts of 'business necessity' and 'job related' enunciated by the Supreme Court in *Griggs*" and to "confirm statutory authority and provide statutory guidelines for the adjudication of disparate impact suits under Title VII."[181] The Act accordingly reinstituted a modified form of the disparate-impact theory developed by EEOC and the *Griggs* Court. The legislation was the result of a decade-long struggle among a conservative executive, an increasingly reactionary Supreme Court, and civil rights groups and their liberal allies in Congress.[182] EEOC's innovative, institutional understanding of discrimination had thus won the full-throated support of the civil rights community, providing a civil society constituency to counter the rearguard action to limit the meaning of the legal commitments of Second Reconstruction.

EEOC's reinterpretation of the meaning of discrimination was recently enshrined by the Supreme Court in another sphere of social regulation: housing. *Texas Department of Housing and Community Affairs v. Inclusive Communities Project, Inc.* (2015)[183] addressed the question of whether the Fair Housing Act of 1968 (FHA)[184] barred housing practices and policies that produced a racially disparate impact in addition to those that evinced racially disparate treatment. Lower federal courts[185] and the Department of Housing and Urban Development (HUD)[186] had previously interpreted the FHA to prohibit disparate impact. As Justice Kennedy noted in his majority opinion, HUD's regulations explicitly analogized their interpretation of the FHA to the disparate impact interpretation of Title VII set forth in *Griggs*.[187] He endorsed this analogy from the sphere of employment to the sphere of housing, holding that "[t]he FHA imposes a command with respect to disparate impact liability" and that such an understanding of discrimination was an essential part of "our Nation's continuing struggle against racial isolation."[188]

Though Justice Kennedy did not credit EEOC with the disparate impact theory, Justice Clarence Thomas, in his dissent, did: "The author of disparate impact liability under Title VII was not Congress, but the Equal Employment Opportunity Commission."[189] For Thomas, the EEOC's authorship was an indictment of the law of disparate impact liability, as he believed the early EEOC had gone beyond the explicit terms of Title VII. Thomas was right that the "author" of disparate impact was the EEOC. But the agency was an author tasked by Congress with articulating the broad purposes it had set out. In *Griggs*, the Court reviewed the agency's elaboration of public purposes and confirmed it in judicial judgment.

The institutional durability of the disparate impact analysis inaugurated by the EEOC owes itself in large part to this explicit incorporation of the agency's analysis into judicial precedent. By agreeing with the EEOC that "Congress directed the thrust of the Act to the consequences of employment practices, not simply motivation,"[190] the *Griggs* Court clearly set out a disparate impact theory of liability that subsequent courts could weaken, but that was very difficult to overturn once established. Though administrative guidelines come and go, like arguments in the public sphere itself, once they are embraced and remade into legal commands by the Supreme Court, they have lasting power—not only within the domain where they apply but in new areas to which the highest court's precedents may be extended.

3. Desegregation at HEW: Judicial Erasure of the Department's Social Theory

In the school segregation context, by contrast, the Court failed to articulate the trenchant analysis of the problem of segregation developed by HEW and endorsed by the Fifth Circuit. In *Green v. County School Board* (1968),[191] it held that a "freedom of choice" plan in a historically segregated school district in eastern Virginia was not sufficient to meet the desegregation requirements imposed by *Brown I* and *Brown II*. But, as Bruce Ackerman notes, Justice Brennan's opinion in *Green* offered a "formulaic opinion that replaced discussion of fundamental values with the language of imperial command. . . . Once stripped of basic principle, all that remained in *Green* was a dramatic show of impatience, a broad approval of technocratic measures of compliance, and a caution that lower courts should temper desegregation demands with common sense."[192] The Court thus failed to explicitly embrace HEW's administrative determination that "the very nature of a free choice plan and the effect of longstanding community attitudes often tend to preclude or inhibit the exercise of a truly free choice by or for minority group students."[193] It therefore did not enshrine in legal precedent the agency's thoughtful engagement with the social determinants of individual agency.

As a result of this judicial lacuna, and an increasingly conservative Supreme Court bench, jurisprudence on school desegregation has swung back to classical liberal understandings of school choice, with the Court holding unconstitutional local plans to achieve desegregation through race-conscious student assignment plans.[194] As Chief Justice Roberts put it, "[t]he way to stop discrimination on the basis of race is to stop discriminating on the basis of race."[195] Contrary to the chief justice's claim, it was only by taking into account the racial composition of southern schools that HEW and the federal courts were able to achieve such great gains in desegregating the South.[196] The Court's erasure of the history of the implementation of Title VI and of the Fourteenth Amendment owes itself in part to the failure of Justice Brennan to write that administrative history firmly into Supreme Court precedent. The contrast between EEOC's durable articulation of economic requisites and HEW's quiescent articulation of educational requisites thus goes to show that inter-branch deliberation only succeeds when the courts acknowledge and inscribe into precedent agencies' critical interpretations of the public's law.

V. CONCLUSION

The democratic vision of administration that was first developed by the Progressives, and has been most fully implemented during the constitutional moments of the last century, continues to provide important ideological and institutional resources with which to confront the problems of our present. As we grapple with the threats posed by climate change, with the challenges of immigration, with the violent abuse of police power, with sexual assault and harassment, and with the discursive transformations of the internet, the twin demands of democratic contexts and democratic requisites must continue to guide our administrative practice. We must expect and demand that public officials regulate society with a critical and ethical, rather than merely instrumental, mindset. The examples of the FSA, AAA, EEOC, and HEW show that administrators are capable of this combination of social-theoretic sophistication—that they can be more than mere technocrats whose highest calling is to perform a regulatory impact analysis or to find ways to nudge and manipulate the public into efficient behavior.[197] A crucial element of this social recognition of administrative capacity is for courts to solicit and respond to value-based arguments from agency officials when such officials explain their resolution of statutory ambiguities. If courts explicitly engage with the social judgments agencies make, they will often fortify these interpretations to weather the reactionary storms that tend to follow moments of constitutional change and administrative creativity.

If public will coalesces for another great era of constitutional revolution and critical administrative intervention, we must also learn from the participatory structures exemplified by the TVA, AAA, and OEO. We must ensure that deliberative democratic forms of administration include all affected persons on equal terms. We must not commit the monumental error of the rural New Deal in providing democratic contexts for propertied farmers while excluding the poor from the determination of their social environment. At the same time, we must ensure that such fully inclusive forms of democratic planning have sufficient administrative support, technical assistance, and programmatic guidance to deliver efficiently the requisites for a fully inclusive public sphere. We must ensure that all citizens are capable of participating as equals in constructing the public's law. In this way the state will better realize the requirements of individual freedom and more clearly articulate the stifled voice of public opinion.

4

The Normative Architecture of Progressive Democracy

Reconstructing the Administrative State

I. INTRODUCTION

This chapter reconstructs a normative theory of the administrative state on the basis of the intellectual and institutional history presented thus far. The intellectual history presented in chapters 1 and 2 addressed the common misconception that Progressivism merely called for expert and apolitical administrative policymaking. I have shown that there was much more to this vision, focusing on a prominent group of Progressive thinkers who democratized Hegel's theory of the state. These thinkers adopted Hegel's view that the classical liberal regime could not secure freedom on its own, that the state must guarantee freedom through regulatory and welfare laws implemented by public-spirited officials. But unlike Hegel they argued that the meaning of freedom must be specified by the people themselves and therefore that citizens must meaningfully participate in the administrative process.

The institutional history presented in chapter 3 has shown that this vision was not idle speculation, but rather a practical discourse that has been at work in American political development. In some cases, such as the agricultural New Deal, Progressive ideas directly influenced the administration of social programs and the self-conceptions of public officials. In other cases, such as the public-participation requirements of the Administrative Procedure Act, or the implementation of civil rights in the 1960s, we can interpret the significance of public laws in light of Progressive understandings. Such interpretations are permissible because of Progressivism's ideological influence on the regulatory state such laws grew out of, and because of the fit between actual institutional

The Public's Law. Blake Emerson.

practices and Progressive conceptions. Hegelian Progressivism thus provides an analytically useful prism through which to study the American administrative state and its history.

But this historical excavation does not establish that the Progressive conception is a normatively appropriate perspective from which to understand, criticize, and reform our current administrative state. The fact that Progressivism has been a potent political ideology does not necessarily mean it is well justified. The history of the Progressive state establishes its pedigree as a credible candidate to guide our thinking and practice today. But history does not, without more, establish validity.

In this chapter, I argue that the Progressive theory provides a compelling framework through which to assess and fortify the legitimacy of the contemporary American administrative state. This problem of legitimacy has been a central preoccupation of administrative law scholarship for generations.[1] The question is why, and under what conditions, it is appropriate for unelected officials and administrative organizations to exercise political authority. Some tell us: because it's efficient. Others: because it's constitutionally permitted. Still others: because it prevents some people from being dominated by others. There is truth in each of these accounts. Each captures intuitions about what government ought to do and how it ought to do it. But none of them successfully connects the purpose of regulation with its structure. They do not tell us how the policy goals of regulation—efficiency or non-domination, for example—are to be advanced by an institutional setting that is arguably inefficient or vulnerable to arbitrariness.

The Progressive account provides an overarching framework that connects the why and how of the administrative state. On this view, administrative power is legitimate to the extent that it enables us to be free, in the sense of determining our own commitments and plans. In a context deep social interdependency, such freedom requires jointly authoring shared norms, and turning these shared norms into shared social conditions. The *structure* of administrative power is then to be judged by its ability to facilitate rational deliberation over the meaning of public norms that are presumptively valid, yet not fully specified. The *purpose* of administrative power is to make these norms efficacious elements of the social world. Because rational deliberation about shared norms requires information about how the norms will function in practice, the structure and the purpose of administration are intrinsically linked. The implementation of a regulatory norm is part and parcel of deliberation about our shared commitments. It allows us to see how the rule plays out when it is put into action, and then reassess the rule's validity according to how it works in the world around us.

This is a summary of a more elaborate story—one I have intimated in the intellectual and institutional history presented thus far. Property and contract create economic and normative externalities felt by people beyond the immediate parties to the exchange. These externalities at the same time bring into existence a public that jointly perceives them and deliberates about their ethical significance. Such discourse can be concretized into institutional rules that give common interests binding force. But deliberation in the social sphere, as well as in representative bodies, remains distorted by the very externalities it seeks to diagnose and remedy. Inequalities of resources and insufficient understandings of the relevant social problems foreclose the expression of a fully rational, inclusive, and egalitarian debate prior to legislative enactment. It is therefore necessary to complement the electoral-political system with an administrative system that is geared to remedy these deficiencies in the course of interpreting and implementing the law. The administrative system must synthesize the partial distillations of public opinion that come before it in the form of statutes, presidential directives, and input from the affected public. It must do so in a way that is calculated to counter and redress the unequal distribution of argumentative resources that otherwise dominate social and political processes. When this system operates adequately, it promotes an improvement of social conditions in tandem with an improvement in political discourse.

This Progressive theory offers three fundamental critiques of our current public law system. The first is that the administrative process is often insufficiently attuned to the inequalities of information and power that pervade civil society. Progressive administration would increase public involvement in the administrative process while taking steps to increase the salience of marginalized interests and the presence of excluded groups in policymaking. The second problem with our current system is that the judiciary polices administrative action in a way that promotes technocratic explanations and discounts value judgments arrived at by deliberative procedures. A Progressive system of judicial review, by contrast, would allow agencies to address fundamental political and ethical questions, but require them to do so in a way that promotes egalitarian public deliberation in the administrative process. The final problem is that presidential control over administration threatens to undermine the integrity of agencies' deliberative processes. The Progressive theory would admit a significant role for the president in shaping the regulatory process but would not seek to anchor administrative legitimacy exclusively in the president's electoral mandate and managerial control.

Before elaborating these claims, I will critique arguments that purport to justify the administrative state on the basis of efficiency, constitutional norms, and republican political theory. The Progressive theory situates aspects of these theories within a coherent understanding of regulatory purpose and structure. Its critique of property, contract, and the marketplace embraces but goes beyond economic concerns with inefficiency and republican concerns with domination. Its account of the public law system as a means to articulate public discourse specifies the relationships among the legislature, the executive, and the judiciary in the administrative process. Its account of freedom links the conditions of social justice with the conditions of political legitimacy.

II. ARGUMENTS FROM EFFICIENCY

Some arguments for regulation are premised on the role of administrative action in promoting efficiency, in the sense of net-utility improvement. There are two related efficiency arguments that together justify a certain kind of regulatory state. The first is that there are various kinds of "market failure," in which private exchange does not deliver utility-improving results.[2] These are cases in which some of the costs of an activity are "external" to the transaction, are not factored into its price, and therefore impose uncompensated harms on society at large.[3] There are also cases in which some sellers or buyers may possess "market power," and can therefore extract a rent above the price that would obtain under conditions of perfect competition.[4] And there are cases where information is imperfect and asymmetrical, so that parties do not come to mutually advantageous bargains.[5] Government regulation of some form can be used to address these market failures, by taxing underpriced activities, breaking up monopolies, forbidding certain kinds of deceptive practices, or requiring disclosure of crucial information.

A second efficiency argument suggests that administrative agencies are the appropriate bodies to conduct these kinds of efficiency-promoting interventions. Administrative agencies can be staffed by experts, focus investigation on a particular subject matter, exclude arbitrary political meddling, make rules more swiftly than Congress, and adjudicate cases more swiftly than courts.[6] It is therefore argued that they are more cost-effective institutions for carrying out efficiency-promoting regulations than other governmental bodies. Goals other than mere efficiency itself can also be programmed into the regulatory output of such organizations. Regulatory purposes, such as promoting equality or dignity, can be understood as preferences in individuals' utility functions, such that satisfying these preferences through efficient administrative regulation would improve net utility.

These arguments from efficiency run into difficulties, however, because other kinds of efficiency concerns cut strongly against administrative regulation. For example, there is the problem of administrative "shirking" or "agency costs."[7] Suppose the aggregate social utility function indicates that a particular regulation would have efficient results—enough utility would be generated to compensate for the disutility it created. If there were an omnipotent, omniscient, and purely altruistic regulatory dictator, this efficient regulation would be implemented. None of these conditions is remotely plausible, however, given the limits of human knowledge, power, and character. The more plausible system is to authorize agents who have incentives to follow their principals' preferences. But there are always significant information and monitoring costs to these arrangements—the representative options voters have to choose from may track their preferences very imperfectly, and it takes time and resources to observe these agents and ensure they are doing their job.[8] Moreover, in the case of an administrative body, we have an agent whose principal (or principals) is itself an agent of the people, creating multiple opportunities for distortions and discontinuities between the social utility profile and the regulation implemented. In this kind of a system, there is a substantial risk that administrative regulation will depart widely from the preferences of the society in whose name it acts, and so implement inefficient policies.

The efficiency theory is also vulnerable because of the privileged status it gives to the perfectly competitive market as a means to achieve social welfare. The analysis assumes that frictionless transactions between fully informed, self-interested, rational agents would yield the most desirable social outcome. It proceeds to look at how our current arrangements fail to fulfill those requirements, and then corrects the arrangements so that they better meet the requirements. This view takes the utility of an individual as the unit of analysis and thus treats all social and collaborative norms as parasitic upon the satisfaction of those preferences. This approach rhetorically, though not logically, supports the conclusion that individuals are best positioned to act on the basis of local knowledge, and that the government planners generally lack the fine-grained understanding of interests, needs, and obstacles that private contracting parties possess.[9] With this assumption of the general, comparative efficiency of private over public law, the case for regulation must overcome a laissez-faire presumption. In the face of uncertainty about the costs and benefits of a regulation, the presumption would often cut against regulation. Opponents of regulatory intervention might grant that the market is highly imperfect. But they can always cast doubt on regulatory intervention by raising the specter of unintended consequences and distortive effects, as well as the costs of agency between society and the regulator. A singular focus on efficiency is therefore likely to terminate in an empirical debate over the relative distortions of the current market and regulatory alternatives. The ideological pull of the "free" market in an efficiency framework is likely to bias this debate toward inaction.

The norm of efficiency, further, has difficulty recognizing the force of other public values in justifying and delimiting the scope of administrative action. As a formal matter, values such as social equality, human dignity, or fairness can be plugged into an efficiency calculus as preferences held by individuals.[10] But, unlike monetary values, these considerations cannot be translated into a fungible quantitative medium such as money without being fundamentally distorted.[11] To ask what price one would be willing to accept to sacrifice elements of one's dignity, or how much one would pay to be treated as an equal regardless of one's race, sex, or disability, for example, is to misunderstand the distinction between human worth and exchange value. We need to ensure the integrity of the human agents who not only barter, truck, and trade in goods, but also reflect, evaluate, and act on principles. An administrative system that fails to recognize these core ethical concerns, or shunts them into a residual category unworthy of reasoned analysis, is likely to confront people as an inhospitable and oppressive form of rule—an iron cage that ignores rather than reflects their attachments and identities.

III. ARGUMENTS FROM CONSTITUTIONAL NORMS

Other accounts of administrative legitimacy proceed from arguments about the proper relationship between the constitutional allocation of power and the institutional position of agencies. These arguments rely on the constitutional separation of powers among the legislative, executive, and judicial branches as a normatively significant political arrangement, which secures values such as democracy, the rule of law, and individual liberty. The motivation for these theories is to address persistent concerns that administrative law is inconsistent with constitutional structure: that it grants legislative power to actors who should not wield it, that it adjudicates private rights through less-than-judicial process, or that it intrudes on the president's responsibility to ensure that the laws are faithfully executed.[12]

These kinds of concerns have been addressed at law by setting out conditions under which delegation of binding powers to administrative bodies is lawful. A statute must authorize an agency to act and must provide an "intelligible principle" to guide its conduct.[13] The agency must act within the scope of its statutory authority.[14] Judicial review of final agency action must generally be available.[15] Due process must be respected in administrative proceedings.[16] The legislature, executive, and judiciary must not intrude upon one another's core functions in overseeing administrative bodies.[17]

This set of legal protections has not resolved persistent doubts about the constitutional soundness of administrative power, however. Conservative scholars continue to raise foundational objections to vesting authority in bodies that are partially insulated from ordinary political or judicial control.[18] In response to these challenges, defenders of the administrative state have gone beyond positive judicial doctrine to make normative arguments for administrative power on the basis of structural-constitutional norms. The goal here is not merely to confirm that administrative power is formally lawful. Rather it is to demonstrate the continuity between fundamental constitutional norms and the procedures of agencies.

The first variety of such arguments is that administration is legitimate to the extent that it is an instrument of one or another constitutional authority. Administrative methods may be legitimate if they are "Necessary and Proper" to the exercise of legislative powers—if Congress determines that it requires some specialized and permanent body to carry its purposes into action.[19] Given the constraints on congressional time and attention, administrative agencies may be needed to perform the public functions the Constitution allocates to the legislature. Alternatively, administrative power may be legitimate if the president is able to direct and coordinate administrative decisions according to his or her political preferences.[20] Such instrumental arguments tend to interpret constitutional structure by reference to democratic values, maintaining that the legislative and executive powers have the electoral credentials to validate otherwise suspect administrative powers.

The second kind of argument is that administrative authority is legitimate to the extent that constitutional structures penetrate through administrative procedures. Some observe the way in which each of the three branches "shares the reins of control" over agencies, together ensuring that agencies remain within constitutional boundaries.[21] Others argue that statutes, judicial doctrine, and agency procedures replicate structural constitutional dynamics at the administrative level. These internal structures can ensure procedural fairness, constrain administrative discretion according to rules, mimic legislative procedures within the agency, or establish a separation of functions among various offices within the agency.[22] Such arguments tend to privilege the rule of law and individual liberty as the values secured by constitutional structure, arguing that second-order constitutionalism prevents arbitrariness and secures private parties against bureaucratic overreach.

The problem with these structural-constitutionalist defenses of administration is that they render one another vulnerable to attack. For example, administration cannot be seen both as an instrument of the legislature and the executive without the risk that one branch will undermine the other's control. Administrative law invariably concerns cases where statutory law is not self-executing or self-interpreting. Relying upon legislative control in these cases supposes that the legislature's current preferences should guide administrative action above and beyond what the plain terms of the statute oblige the agency to do.[23] A theorist of executive legitimacy will demur, arguing that it is the president's authority alone to faithfully execute the laws and that legislative preferences not unambiguously conveyed by the statute are irrelevant to the exercise of such authority. The theorist of legislative supremacy will answer back that structural-constitutional arrangements require the legislature's preferences at least to influence administrative choices, lest the executive authority arrogate to itself the core policymaking function that is properly Congress's. If one is trying to develop an overall account of administrative legitimacy, such conflicting claims fracture the grounds on which agencies might claim binding authority.

Similarly, it cannot be true that the administrative state conforms to constitutional norms both to the extent that it grants virtually unlimited discretion to the president and his or her officers and to the extent that administrative agencies internalize a system of separated powers that limit their discretion. Insofar as an agency is constrained by multiple and conflicting internal authorities, external influences, and durable procedural rules, it will not be subject to the discretionary preferences of the president. Whereas if the president can dictate the outcome of administrative policymaking, any other quasi-constitutional arrangements within the administrative system become mere fig leaves for the assertion of the chief executive's will. These kinds of structural trade-offs are as likely to undercut one another as they are to establish the legitimacy of the administrative system as a whole.

These structural conflicts are symptomatic of deeper normative disagreement. Privileging democracy as a political value appears to mean subordinating administration to the branch with the strongest democratic credentials or allocating oversight responsibilities in some mutually supportive way between each democratically accountable body. A focus on protecting individual rights against governmental interference will require intense judicial scrutiny of questions of law and fact, institutional fragmentation within agencies, and veto rights by political principals on administrative action. Concern with the rule-of-law will emphasize statutory precision, agency autonomy from political meddling, administrative rule-making, and rule-bound adjudication as methods of implementation, as well as judicial review focused on compliance with law rather than an agency's factual findings. It is not clear from the existing accounts how these conflicting normative priorities could be made consistent with one another. Each entails a starkly different institutional arrangement.

In a situation where constitutionalist theories of administration conflict so deeply with one another in conceptualizing the sources of legitimacy, and the structural conditions that flow from those sources, there is little reason to think that such constitutional theories, alone, can give us a satisfying account. Given the multiple constitutional norms at play within administrative law and the multiple institutional structures in which those norms are expressed, the regulatory state is perpetually open to the charge that it violates one fundamental value at the expense of another.[24]

In a constitutional system in which "[a]mbition must be made to counteract ambition," this normative and institutional fragmentation may have some appeal.[25] But its appeal stems from its capacity to restrain power, rather than positively to justify the exercise of power. The legitimacy of the administrative system cannot be secured solely on the basis of a constitutional theory in which suspicion of political action is the primary structural feature and normative consideration.[26] This is because the administrative system is principally a mechanism for the application of public authority. Arguments to the effect that this authority will be limited by institutional competition may give some assurance that regulation will be mild, limited in scope, and less prone to abuse. But this does not tell us why we should want, or why we might need, regulation in the first place.

A legislation-centered theory of constitutionalism may tell us we need expert regulation to achieve Congress's purposes. But that theory leaves the purpose of regulation strictly contingent on legislative enactment and does not give us a theory of what makes legislative enactment itself normatively significant. If it is answered that legislation embodies democratic purposes, the alternative democratic mandate of the president again presses its competing claims to represents the people, which then creates structural discontinuity rather than a coherent account of legitimacy. Furthermore, unlike the German Basic Law's designation of the Federal Republic as a "social state," the U.S. Constitution does not place any affirmative obligations on the government to provide for basic goods and services or to protect people from unjust social relationships.[27] It does not describe the normative relationship between government and society in any way. Without such affirmative obligations or principles of political-social orientation, constitutional theory is ill-equipped to legitimate administrative power on its own steam.

IV. ARGUMENTS FROM REPUBLICANISM

Another candidate to set out the conditions under which administrative power is legitimate is republican political theory. Republicanism includes a theory of social justice and a theory of political legitimacy, both premised on the norm of freedom as non-domination.[28] The Progressive account of administrative legitimacy I will offer overlaps with republicanism; indeed the Progressive scholar K. Sabeel Rahman has equated these two normative perspectives.[29] But republican theory offers only partial support for administrative institutions, in large part because it fails to offer an account of social justice that incorporates its own concern with political legitimacy.

Republican social justice requires that no person be subject to the uncontrolled interference, or domination, of another. The republican understanding of freedom requires an effective opportunity to choose between a set of options according to one's own will, rather than that of someone else. This understanding of social justice gives support for many of the services that the administrative state provides.[30] Public education, welfare provision, and social insurance may be necessary to ensure that individuals can exercise choice amongst a suitably wide menu of options. These functions of social provision reduce the danger that any individual will be dominated by others in his or her choice due to poverty or ignorance. Regulatory controls on the labor and financial markets are likewise necessary to prevent some private parties from dominating others by imposing arbitrary conditions on others' terms of employment, by controlling access to the resources through which others' choices are exercised, or by subjecting others to unaccountable power.

Republican political legitimacy, on the other hand, requires that the government not dominate the people, that is, interfere in their choices in an arbitrary or uncontrolled manner. The institutional means to secure this principle is a constitutional democracy, in which the people influence the government by voting for legislative representatives. This government must consist of multiple institutions that challenge and coordinate with one another to make and apply policy. Finally, policymaking must be governed and constrained by shared, deliberatively generated norms.[31] The combination of popular control, mixed constitutionalism, and deliberative policymaking ensure that, over the long run, government action tracks the common interests of those it binds.

Such a republican state includes administrative authorities insulated from the direct political control of elections or at-will removal.[32] Civic republican accounts of administrative legitimacy emphasize that some common interests, such as environmental protection or stable and equitable monetary policy, can only be managed with a long time horizon, requiring official insulation from short-term political incentives.[33] Legal scholars and political theorists in this tradition argue that agencies are capable of a high degree of rational deliberation and public engagement as a function of their organizational structures and procedural mechanisms.[34]

Republicanism remedies some of the deficits in efficiency-based and constitutional arguments. Even if it is not clear that the benefits of a regulation outweigh its costs in terms of net utility, republicanism can turn to the danger of social domination to justify it. There may be cases where the current market ordering increases overall welfare, and yet distributes resources in such a skewed way that some persons are able to exercise arbitrary authority over others. At-will employment, for example, may underwrite a flexible, efficiency-maximizing labor market and yet place some firms and persons in a position to dictate the conditions of their employees' existence.[35]

Republicanism also yields a unique ordering of constitutional structures in relation to administration that reduces the indeterminacy and mutual inconsistency of arguments from constitutional norms. The republican view places democratic control at the root of political legitimacy, requiring the development of shared policy norms based on reasoned argument. The republican view is averse to forms of control that are highly discretionary—that is, unpredictable, unconstrained by legal rules, or disconnected from shared norms. This view premises the legitimacy of agencies on their relationship to statutory norms, rule-bound administrative action within the scope of their discretion, and relatively intensive judicial review of questions of law.

Republicanism, however, has difficulty theorizing forms of injustice that are structural rather than individual in character.[36] Freedom as non-domination only requires that no external will have the capacity to interfere in the exercise of one's own. But what if the source of interference is not meaningfully "willed" at all? What if some individuals find themselves unable to exercise choice because others' choices have interacted systemically and incidentally to constrain these individuals' options? Or what if this same unconscious aggregation of social behavior produces unforeseen effects that can thwart rational expectations, with devastating consequences for life plans? Republicanism answers that these kind of situations are morally problematic to the extent they may make private domination more likely or severely limit an individual's menu of options. For example, an individual who has lost her house due to mortgage foreclosure after a financial crisis may find herself now at the mercy of capricious landlords, paternalistic charitable institutions, or predatory creditors. That is true enough. But this vision of freedom seems to obscure a more fundamental injustice. When the world we inhabit seems foreign or hostile to our rational decision-making, even where this state of affairs bears no proximate connection to the interference of a foreign will, we are determined by exogenous forces, rather than by ourselves.

A related issue is the limited conception of freedom offered by republicanism. Republicanism does not embrace a positive conception of freedom, which would require that the values, preferences, and plans that motivate our choice be truly "our own" and not determined by another will or external forces that are alien to our interests.[37] The threat of interference in the republican theory registers as a moral problem only where it affects the way we choose between options, not actual interference in the formation of the values, interests, and purposes by which we make the choice. The republican conception of freedom therefore cannot distinguish the levels of social justice that obtain when one's ends are formed against the background of social norms that are imposed without one's control, on the one hand, and cases where one's choices are formed against the background of social norms that are open to one's own evaluation, input, and proposal for amendment. From the perspective of republicanism, an authoritarian order could be as just as a democratic order, even though it was not as politically legitimate, so long as the two regimes had the same laws of social interaction.

This means the relationship between republican social justice and republican political legitimacy is entirely contingent, and the two might even run at cross purposes.[38] Suppose non-domination requires policy x. But the people do not believe they have an interest in x. A republican will simply have to choose between justice and legitimacy: either adopt a policy that departs from the people's will, or follow the people's will and allow social domination to continue unchecked. Progressivism, by contrast, treats questions of social justice and political legitimacy as intrinsically linked. Progressivism insists that a fair opportunity to exercise, and modify the exercise of, political power is part and parcel of social justice itself—not merely because democratic arrangements are more likely to generate just laws, but because we will remain subject to exogenous social forces unless we participate as equals in reworking the pattern of collective organization through law. Progressivism likewise maintains that social justice is part and parcel of democratic legitimacy, since no society will be truly democratic if its laws and policies do not actually guarantee the freedom and equality of its constituents. This is because democratic legitimacy cannot be perfected among a people who exercise vastly unequal social power.

Progressivism therefore conditions legitimacy and justice on one another across the full range of political values. Where neither the conditions of justice nor the conditions of legitimacy obtain, policies that advance either condition should be implemented in a way that also advances the other. If a policy tracks the current self-understandings of the people but is not completely substantively just, it should be implemented on the condition that future rounds of policymaking will enable dissenting voices to press on the moral failures of the policy. And where a policy meets the demands of social equality, but the people do not fully recognize those demands, it should be implemented in a way that allows public consciousness to come into line with the demands of justice. The policymaking apparatus must therefore allow multiple opportunities for public participation, contestation, specification, or reform. On this view, we become truly free by jointly authoring the social conditions that constitute our individual agency. And our politics becomes legitimate by creating the social conditions for the exercise of freedom. For this kind of a project, administrative intervention duly constituted by deliberative norms will be essential.

V. THE PROGRESSIVE CRITIQUE OF THE MARKET

To grasp this relationship between questions of justice and legitimacy, consider how the Progressives adopted Hegel's understanding and critique of the market economy. According to Hegel, rights of property and contract provide the building blocks of freedom, because they require each person to treat every other with formal respect. This is why Du Bois placed so much significance on the efforts of the Reconstruction Congress and the Freedmen's Bureau to furnish these rights to African Americans. At the same time, such rights are not purely atomistic. Rather, they establish a "system of needs" that allows each, in pursuing his own interest, to satisfy those of others.[39] Liberal rights do not merely protect isolated spheres of independence and binary agreements between willing parties. Hegel observes that the "private use of property has external relations with other individuals . . . which passes out of my control and can wrong or harm other people."[40] The division of labor and the differentiation of products and services increase the costs of "inquiries and negotiations" between buyers who know less about goods than sellers and increases the risk buyers will be "cheated."[41] Economies of scale lead to the growth of "large branches of industry" that are "dependent on external circumstances and remote combinations whose full implications cannot be grasped by the individuals who are tied to these spheres by occupation."[42] Finally, as the system of needs differentiates human desires and skills and assigns value according to the price mechanism, some persons find themselves dependent upon forces they cannot fully understand or meaningfully influence. Some are even unable to meet the fixed costs of daily existence without support. In this situation, "when a large mass of people sinks below the level of a certain standard of living . . . that feeling of right, integrity, and honor which comes from supporting oneself by one's own activity and work is lost."[43]

The thrust of these observations is that property and contract establish a social system that can undermine the form of freedom these institutions purport to establish. When the exchange of entitlements occurs within a complex network of other exchanges by persons with unequal knowledge, resources, and bargaining power, many individuals in the market do not determine their own purposive activity. Instead their agency is shaped by exogenous, unknown, and often averse circumstances. In this respect, the Hegelian critique of the marketplace is significantly broader than republicanism's. The claim is not merely that some persons in a capitalist economy dominate others, though this is certainly one prominent problem. Hegel is equally concerned with unintended consequences, systemic effects, and resource constraints that prevent people from recognizing their social world as one in which their own purposes may be pursued. The threat comes not only from the overweening power of some actors to interfere arbitrarily in the affairs of others but also from the emergence of supra-individual forces that are not willed by anyone in particular.[44] When these forces become highly unpredictable, or when they create deep hierarchies of wealth and status, many individuals will see the social world as an oppressive imposition or hostile power, rather than as facilitative or at least amenable to their plans.

The Progressives embraced this critique of the liberal market. They observed that the ideals that sustained a liberal legal framework did not match the social reality these entitlements produced. As Dewey observed, liberal law advertised an "individualistic philosophy of life" but produced "a collectivist scheme of interdependence."[45] This did not mean liberal ideals of autonomy were false or worthless but rather that new kinds of institutions would have to be contrived to vindicate them. What was needed was a form of "associated thought to take account of the realities and to frame policies in the common interest."[46] If each individual could recognize a shared purpose, and this purpose became efficacious within society, then each person would to that extent determine and control the social environment rather than be controlled by it. Freedom could be retained in a situation of deep social dependency if each person retained some authorship over the conditions of dependency.

Such collective authorship could itself be triggered by the social effects of the market. The disease might also generate the conditions for a cure. Dewey observed that "indirect, extensive, enduring and serious consequences of conjoint activity bring a public into existence having a common interest in controlling these consequences."[47] When a private transaction had significant external effects on those beyond the transaction, these effects became a matter of common—public—concern. Such effects could include an "externality" in the strict economic sense—namely an uncompensated cost imposed on persons who are not party to the transaction. But they could also include many other impositions that deprived individuals of the capacity to develop and pursue their purposes: price levels that prevented the acquisition of essential goods; undependable public utilities; labor contracts that subjected the seller to unsafe, unhealthy, or otherwise degrading working conditions; or financial or environmental crises that radically altered or thwarted life plans without warning. Any such conditions that affected persons jointly could become the object of a common purpose, such as the provision of goods and services or the regulation of labor and financial markets. The question this left was how such a common purpose might be formed.

VI. PUBLIC DELIBERATION

The Progressives fastened on public deliberation as the process through which disparate minds could focus on common problems and develop shared commitments. Wilson gestured at this deliberative ideal with his suggestion that political action be grounded in a "directive popular thought" that each person would contribute to.[48] Follett likewise emphasized a form of "power-with," as opposed to "power-over," in which individuals would generate collective agency in sorting through the common problems they diagnosed.[49] Dewey argued that the public could develop a shared understanding of jointly felt problems through "debate, discussion and persuasion."[50]

This emphasis on rationally formed public opinion marked the fundamental break between Hegelian and Progressive political theory. Hegelian freedom did not emerge from public deliberation about social conditions but rather from a mostly passive, customary, and habitual experience of equality, independence, and constitutional patriotism in the context of the universal laws and just administration of the state.[51] Discursive rationality in Hegel's system was for the most part performed from above by political officials. The Progressives modified this aspect of Hegel's political theory. Their audacious innovation was to meld Hegel's critique of civil society and his positive notion of freedom with democratic ideals. In this way, they provide a distinctive political philosophy that overlaps with but distinguishes itself from contemporary deliberative democratic theory.

The affinities between Progressivism and deliberative democracy have been noted by many prominent scholars in legal and political theory.[52] But contemporary theories have mostly settled on a particular conception of the relationship between deliberative norms and institutions that is more demanding and less practical than their Progressive forebears. In contemporary theories, the normative ideal of a debate between free and equal citizens concerning the common good provides a standard that political institutions are meant to "mirror."[53] We can assess institutions such as the legislature, the judiciary, administrative agencies, or the system as a whole according to the rationality, inclusiveness, and equality of its decision-making processes. And we can assess the rules that issue from these bodies according to whether the institutional author met the relevant criteria for deliberative rationality.

On the relatively narrow view advanced by Rawls, the Supreme Court is the "exemplar of public reason," since it deliberates over basic principles of justice that all members of society could assent to on the basis of their comprehensive moral views.[54] For Habermas, by contrast, the legislature enjoys pride of place as the institution "where lawmaking is interwoven with the formation of communicative power."[55] A number of scholars have also focused on the role of administrative agencies as deliberative institutions.[56] Some theorists take a more systematic approach and show how a network of institutions can together promote deliberative values, with each one playing a distinctive role through a specialized kind of discourse.[57] In each case, the relevant institutions are assessed by prior standards of deliberative quality.

The Progressive view retains deliberative norms of inclusiveness, rationality, and parity of participation as standards by which to assess institutional output. But the Progressive theory answers such questions of legitimation by looking forward towards consequences as well as backwards towards principles. Putting the principles of deliberation into practice informs our conception of what the principles entail for us. As Dewey puts it, the public is "amorphous and unarticulated" unless "indirect consequences are perceived, and . . . it is possible to project agencies which order their occurrence."[58] The systemic effects of social and economic activity at once create common perceptions of shared problems and prevent people from reaching rational judgments about those problems. The causes and consequences of issues such as poverty, discrimination, and financial crisis are often too multifaceted and contestable to be addressed according to a consensus reached by people reasoning in good faith. Information about these problems is diffuse, the persons affected by them are unequally situated, and the costs of collective problem-solving are quite high. It is therefore exceedingly difficult to settle on a fully determinate and deliberatively generated solution to the problem through individual speculation or joint discussion alone.

Deliberative problem-solving therefore requires the enactment and implementation of laws and regulations that are not completely justified ex ante but rather will help to guide future discussion. Common policies, refined by sustained and systematic investigation, are necessary to make social problems what Follett called an "articulate experience"—one that is readily communicable to others, subject to analysis, and capable of guiding action.[59] Progressive deliberation does not remain an abstract inquiry into shared norms but instead becomes an experiential examination into the felt consequences of rules.[60] Dewey thus emphasized that "policies and proposals for social action be treated as working hypotheses, not as programs to be rigidly adhered to and executed."[61] The burden is then taken off any given rule or rule-making body to meet exceedingly onerous demands of ex ante justification. We do not ask whether prior deliberations were adequate to fully justify the policy but whether the policy has allowed the next round of deliberations to be more informed and inclusive than the last. When it has, that is progress.

VII. THE PUBLIC'S LAW

Progressivism not only extends deliberative democracy from ex ante to ex post justification, but also from talk to rules. Deliberative democratic theory sometimes focuses so intently on the discursive and communicative elements of the political process that the institutional dimensions of democratic order fall from view. The Progressives, by contrast, provide us with a model of practical reason that is grounded not only in the reflective capacity of individual subjects or merely in arguments between persons, but in the social and political structures we share with one another and contribute to together. Progressivism thus invites consideration of "the state" as a source of normativity.

The Progressives did not understand the state in Weberian terms as an organization holding a monopoly on the legitimate means of violence within a given territory. Rather, the Progressives defined the state in a more relational sense. The Hegelian state the Progressives embraced encompassed subjective dispositions as well as the objective structures that mediated those habits and patterns of thought. Willoughby thus claimed that, for a state to exist, "an essential psychological element must first exist subjectively in the minds of the people, and then becomes objective in laws and institutions."[62] But the Progressives recognized that a state of this kind was necessarily bound by democratic norms. As Dewey put it, the state was "a public articulated."[63] It transformed general ideas, sentiments, and arguments expressed in the public sphere into the binding form of law. Unlike Hegel, the Progressives insisted that it was not possible for the state to realize the conditions of freedom unless the people actively determined the principles and policies by which they were bound.

Progressivism is therefore concerned not merely with the ways in which subjects develop common normative commitments through the medium of language but also with the way subjects engage with one another through the medium of institutions. The institutions embody implicit claims to justification as they implement the purposes of the past publics that brought them into being.[64] When individuals reconstruct the purpose of existing laws to argue for amendments to their provisions or for enacting new laws that match the older laws' spirit, the institution speaks through the individuals and individuals speak through the institution.[65] The state refers to this reciprocal relation between political discourse and institutional structure. Political discourse is the activity proper to the public sphere, in which individuals and groups exchange arguments and develop shared understandings, beliefs, and commitments. By contrast, I refer to the institutional dimension of the state as "the public's law"—the law that is produced by, and which in turn maintains, a condition of shared agency amongst individuals in society.

It is common in political and legal theory to repair immediately to constitutional rights and structures as the institutional analogue for the most fundamental ideals. Rawls's landmark theory of political liberalism defines "constitutional essentials" that set up the "basic structure" of society.[66] These essentials consist in fundamental civil and political rights guaranteed by the judiciary, leaving the legislature to further social welfare within the confines of such judicially enforced rights. For Ronald Dworkin, similarly, the rights of individual persons are elevated to the constitutional status of "principle" that the judiciary defends, whereas the regulatory authority of the legislature and executive is mere "policy" that a principle of right will always "trump."[67] These approaches tend to deprecate the policies and purposes enunciated by legislative norms, which arise out of a more inclusive and pluralistic process of democratic deliberation and negotiation than do judicial judgments.[68] And even deliberative democrats such as Habermas and Ackerman describe popular sovereignty as an only occasional occurrence, when public mobilization is sufficiently great to overtake the usual business of politics and dictate the policy of the state according to the rational discourse of the people as a whole.[69]

Much too much is left indeterminate in constitutional provisions or in sporadic moments of popular mobilization to merit the claim that "the people" genuinely governs. The people may determine that slavery is abolished or that all those born in the territory of the United States are its citizens. Or they may determine that the government should regulate the "private" sphere of property and contract. But if the people have little influence on what life after slavery shall mean, or what rights and obligations citizenship will entail, or what the ends and nature of market regulation are to be, then such moments of popular sovereignty are far too tenuous to maintain the people's grip on the rules that bind them.[70] If we take democracy to refer to "the *actual* collective authorization of laws and *policies* by the people subject to them"[71] and not merely to foundational moments when the political order is abstractly constituted, then we must turn our attention to institutions capable of identifying and specifying public purposes on a routine basis and at a fine-grained level. We must turn our gaze down from the heavens of constitutional law to the earthly activities of legislation and administration.

We live today in a "republic of statutes" where many of our political obligations, entitlements, and processes are set out not in "large 'C' Constitutional norms" but rather in legislation and its implementation by administrative agencies and the judiciary.[72] This public law system's legitimacy is tethered less than the grand constitutional order to norms of stability and permanence and is more geared toward adjusting the terms of political cooperation to people's current understandings of their needs and values. As David Mayhew observes, legislation is often a Deweyan, deliberative enterprise in which "presidents, members of Congress, and other relevant actors come to believe—sometimes quickly and surprisingly, that a 'problem' exists in some area and that it can and must be 'solved.' Agreement materializes on ends, more or less, and attention is given to means. A drive toward action builds from a pervasive view that something has to be done."[73] This pragmatic political mentality is not merely an elite affair but often triggered by "a certain kind of 'public mood' that favors government action"—a widely shared and intense political outlook that motivates elected officials to enact laws responsive to their constituents' expressed preferences, values, and criticisms concerning the existing social and legal order.[74] Wilson accordingly saw legislation as a privileged site of democratic legitimacy precisely because it could encapsulate the current understandings of the people. It was "deliberately formulated new law."[75]

"The public's law" refers to this evolving constellation of norms set out in the U.S. Code and implemented on a daily basis by officials of the federal government. I use the possessive to distinguish my meaning from the broad term, "public law," which generally refers to all laws concerning the relationship between the government and those subject to its authority. The possessive form expresses both an originating and a constitutive relationship between public discourse and legal norms. On the one hand, laws are enacted to address problems that individuals jointly perceive and communicate to one another. The law in this sense originates in public discourse. On the other hand, these laws make the democratic association what it is by concretizing its commitments into a legible and durable medium. Law constitutes the public.

The shared norms that law enacts may be shared in only a thin sense. At a minimum, they enjoy a presumption of validity among citizens and carry normative weight in argument. I do not assume that everyone agrees on the substantive terms of all laws but only that the existence of a law creates rebuttable reasons to believe that its norms are sound. Unlike the claims of a private person, a norm that has passed through the gauntlet of bicameralism and presentment represents a strong level of political agreement, which in turn can be relied upon by political actors for their own argumentative and tactical purposes. The enactment of a statute has a "moral impact" on private persons, as they must alter their normative assessments to take into account the fact that elected representatives in multiple chambers of government have settled on a particular set of requirements.[76] There is thus a world of difference between saying "I think it is wrong to discriminate on the basis of sex" and being able to say "the legislature has made it unlawful to discriminate on the basis of sex." The latter statement lays a claim on other citizens, as coauthors of the law, reminding them they are already (presumptively) committed to the norm in question, since the institutions who speak in their name have said so. The debate then tends to to center on the meaning of that preexisting commitment.

Some citizens might nonetheless say, "that may be the law, but I do not accept it as morally binding on me." But this dissenter will face an uphill battle in convincing others, in the face of a deliberatively generated and formally enacted commitment to sex equality.

The concept of the public's law sets out a normative standard to which the legal process ought to conform. To qualify as genuinely "public," the law must satisfy conditions of deliberative rationality. That is, it must arise out of and facilitate open, egalitarian, and reasoned discourse concerning jointly felt problems and shared values. To take legal form, on the other hand, the public discourse must satisfy conditions of institutional order. That is, it must yield relatively determinate and binding standards of conduct. The twin requirements of publicity and legality will rarely if ever be achieved through a single act of lawmaking. Public discourse will always be imperfectly precise, informed, and inclusive at a given moment in time or within a particular institution. For this reason, the public's law must arise from a diffuse process of normative elaboration, in which multiple actors specify the meaning of law in a way that enhances its deliberative credentials.

VIII. ADMINISTRATIVE AGENCIES AT THE INTERFACE OF LAW AND THE PUBLIC

For this process of specification to work, administrative agencies must mediate between statutory law and the public discourse it enacts. Such agencies therefore internalize the tension between the necessary rigidity of rules and the fluidity of argument. On the one hand, as Weber notes, public bureaucracies allow "a high degree of calculability of results for the heads of the organization and for those acting in relation to it."[77] This model of bureaucracy emphasizes organizational hierarchy as a means to realize programmatic goals, aggregate technical knowledge, and render consistent treatment.[78] The streamlined procedures of administrative agencies, as compared to legislative and judicial process, allow for the expeditious and uniform application of these statutory norms and executive priorities to the social sphere they regulate. Once the objectives have been determined, they must be administered neutrally to any party they bind or affect. As Goodnow argued, civil servants should maintain "a strictly impartial attitude towards the individuals with whom they have dealings" and provide "the most efficient possible administration."[79]

A chorus of scholars in American political theory and administrative law, on the other hand, emphasize agencies' capacity to engage in a polycentric form of policy reasoning. Agencies' particular competency, it is argued, is not merely to implement a predetermined policy goal in a cost-effective and impartial manner but also to specify the content of these goals in consultation with political institutions and affected groups.[80] This requires what Pierre Rosanvallon calls "interactive democracy," in which administration claims legitimacy by being "socially appropriated" and "subject to permanent and open debate."[81] This republican vision of administration treats bureaucracy as an institutional context for reasoning about the public good. More sensitive to political considerations than the courts but also more insulated from short-term electoral incentives than elected officials, agencies are able to reach decisions that are both well-reasoned and responsive to public needs, interests, and values.[82]

The intellectual and institutional history presented in chapters 2 and 3 has shown the way in which these two visions are both instinct in Progressive political thought and in tension with one another. Deliberative forms of administration will tend to increase the costs of administration, requiring that bureaucratic policymaking be undertaken with broad institutional and public input, reasoned explanation, and ample opportunity for judicial challenge. The costs of such wide popular engagement were on vivid display in the War on Poverty, as "maximum feasible participation" inhibited efficient delivery of material resources. Deliberative methods also increase the risk that the asymmetries of power and information in civil society will come to dominate the administrative process. When bureaucracies open up their doors to the influence of private actors, those actors who hold the most technical knowledge about the problem at hand and those who have the most resources to participate in administrative and judicial proceedings will tend to crowd out the voices of beneficiaries with less concrete understanding of the regulatory subject matter, higher costs of collective action, and fewer resources with which to vindicate their interests.[83] We saw these dynamics at play in the Tennessee Valley Authority and the Agricultural Adjustment Administration, as propertied farmers dominated deliberative processes around production controls and land-use planning.

On the other hand, purely instrumental, technocratic, efficiency-oriented forms of administration are likely to appear as alien, inscrutable, and dominating to those they affect. If agencies seal themselves off from the affected public and rely solely upon their professional training and detached analysis of social problems, they will be prone to ignore important values and empirical considerations that beneficiaries and regulated parties might be able to convey. As Dewey put it, "in the absence of an informed voice on the part of the masses, the wise cease to be wise."[84] We saw this threat of paternalism in the Farm Security Administration, which advanced its concerns for economic and racial equality without the input of the low-income farmers they were attempting to serve. Du Bois likewise recognized that the Freedmen's Bureau was unable to carry out its transformative egalitarian mission because national and local public opinion were not engaged to sustain it.

This is a tension between the efficient achievement of democratic ends and the use of democratic means to achieve those ends—between the material requisites the public needs to participate in democratic politics and the institutional contexts within government that enable them to participate. Progressivism is concerned not merely with having a conversation about politics but with changing society to promote collective interests and free and egalitarian forms of life.[85] It aims to implement public law as well as to countenance public opinion. But the efficient promulgation of rules often comes at the expense of thorough deliberation by all affected parties over the precise contours of those rules. To achieve statutory goals in the most efficient manner, the legislature may establish a bureaucratic organization capable of developing a workable, coherent system by which to implement them. But this organization's efficiency will ordinarily trade on the gains of hierarchy, discretion, and routine decision-making, all of which run counter to coordinate, reciprocal, and argument-based forms of collective action.

The tension between efficacious rules and inclusive reasoning is particularly acute within the administrative process, because bureaucracies are the most significant interface between the government and those it binds or affects. While the federal judiciary provides an important forum for resolving private disputes and challenging government action, the federal bureaucracy's provision of benefits, grants, and services; and its imposition of taxes, penalties, and regulations, represent a far more persistent and routine application of public power. At the same time as administrative organizations impact private life along this wide range of activity, the norms they implement are often highly general and abstract. Regulatory statutes invariably use terms that can be interpreted and applied in numerous ways, such as "harm" in the Endangered Species Act, or "stationary source" of pollution in the Clean Air Act, or "affirmatively further[] fair housing" in the Fair Housing Act.[86] The institutional demands of Progressivism require that these terms be specified clearly and expeditiously in the service of the underlying policy objective. Administration must, in Goodnow's words, function as the "deed" of the state, making the abstract "will" conveyed by statute a real public act.[87] The discursive demands of Progressivism, on the other hand, require that these terms be interpreted in a way that is rationally responsive to all affected interests and values. In Wilson's words, administration must be "intimately connected with the popular thought."[88]

The organizational life of the administrative system internalizes the tension between instrumental and discursive forms of decision-making. Administrative agencies are generally constructed as hierarchical institutions, with appointed leadership at the apex. In theory, all legal authority within the organization is delegated down from the chief, subject to any organizational requirements imposed by the statute.[89] But once this delegation is formalized into an organizational structure and becomes routinized as a matter of official behavior, the chief no longer exercises any kind of plenary and fully discretionary authority over the actions of her subordinates. Due process requires that an agency follow its own regulations, so an agency chief could not lawfully command her subordinates to disobey agency rules currently in force.[90] To change those rules, she would have to commence a lengthy process that would itself be deliberative and contested. Moreover, given the time constraints of the leadership, the informational advantages of career staff, the multiple external pressures on the agency, and its institutional habits and culture—given all of these obstacles to the seamless flow of commands down the hierarchical chain—coordination, persuasion, and a sense of shared organizational purpose will be as necessary to collective action as will orders.[91] Officials higher up in the organizational ladder will exercise greater influence over the determination of collective goals than any official further down. But bottom-up input will also play a prominent role, as "back and forth, up and down, the communications pass, reporting obstacles, difficulties, impossibilities, accomplishments; redefining, modifying purposes at every level."[92]

An ideal-typical Weberian bureaucracy would definitively favor instrumental efficiency over deliberative coordination. Though leaders would face organizational frictions, they would exercise decisive authority over organizational output. But the American public law system has institutionalized the discursive dimension of Progressive thought, thus securing a more prominent role for coordinate and deliberative models of governmental decision-making.[93] As I noted in chapter 3, the Administrative Procedure Act of 1946 codified the public participation practices which had been an aspect of American bureaucratic procedure since the Progressive Era.[94] The Act includes a procedure usually called "informal" or "notice-and-comment" rule-making, which requires public consultation before a rule is finalized. Before issuing a regulation, the agency must issue a "notice of proposed rule-making" that describes the "legal authority under which the rule is proposed" and "the terms or substance of the proposed rule."[95] The agency must then "give interested persons an opportunity to participate in the rule making through submission of written data, views, or arguments. After consideration of the relevant matter presented, the agency shall incorporate into the rules adopted a concise general statement of their basis and purpose."[96] Persons who suffer a legal wrong or who are adversely affected or aggrieved by an agency rule can challenge it in federal court, where the reviewing court must set the rule aside if it is "arbitrary, capricious, an abuse of discretion, or otherwise not in accordance with law."[97] These default procedures for informal rule-making establish a participatory process in which the public can shape the way administrative agencies interpret and apply the law. Administrative law scholar Kenneth Culp Davis accordingly describes the rule-making procedure as

> one of the greatest inventions of modern government. . . . Affected parties who know facts that the agency may not know or who have ideas or understandings that the agency may not share have opportunity by quick and easy means to transmit facts, ideas, or understandings to the agency at the crucial time when the agency's positions are still fluid. The procedure is both democratic and efficient.[98]

By allowing all interested parties to participate, rather than only those parties who are directly subjected to an adjudicatory determination, rule-making enables the democratic process to persist beyond legislative chambers. It institutionalizes Mary Follett's insight that participatory administrative processes can foster mutually reinforcing understanding between public officials and those they govern: "When the process of cooperation between expert and people is given its legitimate chance, the experience of the people may change the conclusions of the expert while the conclusions of the expert are changing the experience of the people."[99]

IX. DEEPENING DEMOCRATIC RULE-MAKING

The virtues of rule-making, however, should not be overstated. The notice-and-comment procedure is often a stylized rendering of a more opaque deliberative practice that goes on before a rule has even been proposed.[100] In these consultations, it is likely that powerful social groups will gain the upper hand, as they have the information and resources necessary to convince the agency of their position or to threaten litigation if the agency does not comply.[101] The problem lies not in the explicit costs of participation, but in the background information and opportunity costs faced by members of the public and all but the best-funded and most well-connected public interest groups. Though ordinary citizens are often deeply affected by the regulatory decisions of administrative agencies, they are rarely versed in the forms of technological and economic discourse in which agencies frame, consider, and ultimately respond to regulatory problems. The people often do not speak in the same register as the agency, and so they remain alienated from the state that is meant to articulate their common purposes. The democratic deficit in rule-making represents a broader problem with administrative policymaking that is hardly unique to the United States. When important policy choices are made "downstream" from legislation, private actors with more power and resources are often able to dominate the process.[102]

Administrative practice must respond to such imbalances of information and power if regulatory law is to lay a valid claim to being the public's law. Administrative officials must have a public-regarding consciousness that *aims* at the regulative ideal of a community of free and equal citizens rather than assuming that such a community has already been achieved. As John Forester has observed in regards to local land use planning, "where severe inequalities exist, treating the strong and the weak alike ensures only that the strong remain strong and the weak remain weak. The planner who pretends to act as a neutral regulator may sound egalitarian but is nevertheless acting, ironically, to perpetuate and ignore existing inequalities."[103] When officials consider particular regulatory problems, such as pollution, labor market discrimination, or financial regulation, they must use their discretion to rectify asymmetrical social relationships that leave certain social groups with arbitrary and unaccountable authority over others. It is in this sense that Hegel's description of public servants as a "universal class" can retain its vitality for present-day political theory. The officialdom should actively institute the general interest by remedying the maldistribution of power in the existing pattern of social organization. Administrative policies that reduce inequalities of resources, information, and access to the political process are therefore to be favored over those that worsen such inequalities or merely perpetuate the status quo.

Administrative procedures must also provide for public participation by all affected parties in order to ensure that decision-making remains sensitive to those elements of public reason that are not adequately recognized in civil society or the political process. It is not enough simply to open up the administrative process to all comers, for this approach will tend to privilege the better organized and equipped segments of society.[104] The organizational advantages of the more powerful must be kept in view, and efforts made to solicit and foster the participation of those groups who are equally affected, but are prevented by their social condition from full participation in administrative procedures. Agencies should thus be sensitive to differences in the participatory quality of public interest groups and private associations, giving greater weight to collective commenters who convey the deliberative judgment of a large numbers of citizens.[105] Agencies should also experiment with the "co-production" of public services by beneficiaries, as such persons could participate in designing, implementing, and monitoring welfare programs.[106]

Are these normative-procedural demands utopian? Do the same inequalities, asymmetries, and injustices that call for administrative intervention foreclose the development of a democratic mode of administrative policymaking? That possibility cannot be dismissed outright, but neither is such a result inevitable. One of the virtues of administrative law is that it opens up policy space within government—space to rethink the purposes of statutes, to reweigh the values that are implicated by regulatory decision-making, to introduce new voices into the conversation, or to empower actors in civil society who have been disenfranchised. My study of the New Deal and Civil Rights Era in chapter 3 shows that these openings are real, and they can have major social effects that extend beyond periods of great political mobilization. But we might also witness such openings in times that seem somewhat more "ordinary" and do not approach the heroic heights of constitutional change. This happens when public officials use their discretion for democratic ends; to reach out for the marginalized and equalize their social status. That kind of outreach can take the form of participation in a rule-making or more informal solicitude for social groups' claims of harm and rights to recognition.[107]

That is how I would characterize the Department of Education's Office for Civil Rights (OCR) recent effort to expand protections against sexual assault and harassment on university campuses. The Education Amendments of 1972 (Title IX) prohibit discrimination on the basis of sex by educational institutions that receive federal grants.[108] In 1975, the Department of Health, Education, and Welfare issued a regulation, in consideration of over four thousand comments, that implemented this requirement.[109] The regulation required, amongst other things, that grant recipients "adopt and publish grievance procedures providing for prompt and equitable resolution of student and employee complaints."[110] Responding to developments in Title IX case law and long-running pressure from feminist civil society groups, OCR issued a series of guidelines in the late 1990s and early 2000s that read this grievance procedure requirement to incorporate claims of sexual harassment and assault.[111] These guidelines in turn triggered an increase in student complaints alleging sex discrimination, and more intensive social movement mobilization and counter-mobilization around the topic.[112] Officials at the OCR thus built on the existing democratic credentials of the legislation and the regulation to extend protections for students on college campuses. The guidelines did not have the same ex ante democratic legitimacy as the 1972 law and the 1975 regulation, since they were not subject to the rigors of legislative process or notice-and-comment rule-making. But they served the ex post democratic function of contributing to public discourse around gender equality, and furthering conditions of sex equality on college campuses.

These moments are of course open to challenge, critique, and even reversal.[113] My normative assessment of OCR's implementation of Title IX may not be, and indeed is not, shared by all. That is in the nature of democratic politics. My point is that these cycles of bureaucratic intervention, social uptake and resistance, followed by bureaucratic revision, are and should be a fundamental part of our public life. Professors of law, public administration, and political science can make this process more salient by teaching their students to think about the administrative policy space as a site for political discourse and not merely for purely technical or economic reasoning. Members of social movements can seize on this potential by joining the civil service, taking up political appointments, or simply maximizing their existing opportunities to participate in rule-making and other less formal administrative processes. The substantive values that animate these movements will vary and may not reflect majoritarian opinion. But the point is that such substantive values are frequently at play in the administrative process. We disserve ourselves if we pretend they are not, and thus fail to take advantage of the opportunity to influence the development of regulatory norms.

Deepening an egalitarian administrative ethos and procedure would nonetheless have significant costs. Time and resources spent to consider the perspective of marginalized actors and groups, or to bring them to the table when they are not already there, are often not spent on implementing the policy in question. Problems may go unsolved or even worsen if an agency waits too long to issue a regulation. As it is, rule-making can often go on for years. Agencies have sometimes responded to this "ossification" of the regulatory process by avoiding notice-and-comment and instead issuing an "interim final rule" or a non-binding "guidance" document that communicates the agency's current policy position without actually imposing new requirements on the public.[114] Some scholars criticize these shortcuts as undermining democratic accountability; and indeed, they may, if agencies never engage the relevant stakeholders in policymaking.[115] But these developments also create the opportunity for reducing the cost of immediate action, while increasing the democratic credentials of more durable policy outputs. Agencies might issue interim regulations quickly and with limited or no participation, and subsequently commence an intensive, egalitarian, and deliberative rule-making process, which would result in a final rule to replace the interim rule. This way, the government would act and affected groups would see how the rule worked in practice before the agency settled on a long-term solution. In addition, agencies could then afford to engage in much more serious deliberative efforts than they often do—such as face-to-face conversations among regulated parties, public interest groups, and state officials; experimental trials within the margins of the current rule, listening sessions from affected stakeholders; expansion of advisory committees to include a wider range of viewpoints than the usual repeat players; randomly selected administrative juries composed of citizens who could learn about and assess the various policy proposals; or online platforms for broad-based public discussion of the regulatory problems at issue.[116]

If we were to allow agencies to act expeditiously, while at the same time requiring them to engage in some or all of these ambitious democratic practices, we might get some of our cake and eat much of it as well. We would get a more-or-less immediate intervention to address a social problem, as well as a thoughtful political assessment of that interim solution that was broad-based, egalitarian, and well-reasoned. To be sure, such a process would be quite costly. The direct costs would include the expense of providing all these opportunities for deliberation. There is no getting around the direct costs, though certain efficiencies may be in the offing.[117] Democracy in the modern world is expensive, and you get what you pay for. This study is meant to make a case that we should invest more in constructing an administrative state that lives up to the promise of political freedom. Whether that view wins the day is a question for us all to answer as a people.

The indirect costs would include harm to the reliance interests the interim solution induced, should the long-term rule-making undermine those interests. But these indirect costs might be managed. We might allow the other political branches, with their own democratic warrants and institutional competencies, to police administrative decision-making to ensure that it is adequately well-justified—including in its consideration for any interests the previous policy generated.[118]

X. JUDICIAL TECHNOCRACY IN THE REVIEW OF ADMINISTRATIVE ACTION

The purpose of administrative agencies in the Progressive theory is to refine public opinion and concretize it into political action. Progressive scholars such as Dickinson and Goodnow therefore proposed to enhance the procedural fairness of administrative bodies, giving affected persons notice and a hearing in exchange for judicial deference to administrative judgments. Agencies would gain respect from courts proportional to the adequacy of their decision-making process and the quality of their reasoning. Wilson, Dewey, Follett, and Comer emphasized that such procedures could discipline administrative action by public opinion, while at the same time articulating social interests in a more rational form. These insights cohere into a general principle of judicial review of administrative action: courts should require agencies to reason adequately with the affected public in the exercise of their discretion. Courts should at the same time take care not to displace or discourage participatory processes of which agencies are uniquely capable. In certain respects, current standards of review further these goals. But the judiciary nonetheless remains captivated by a Weberian image of administration that prizes instrumental reason and fails to recognize the legitimacy of discursive modes of justification.

Whereas a court will generally hold a statute constitutional if it has a "rational basis," administrative regulations are subject to more searching review.[119] American administrative law requires bureaucratic agencies to offer a "reasoned explanation" for their actions.[120] A reviewing court will not allow an agency to provide a "post hoc rationalization" for its decision, but must instead provide a "contemporaneous explanation" for its choice of policy that will allow the court to determine "whether the decision was based on the relevant factors."[121] An administrative regulation will be set aside as "arbitrary" or "capricious" if it "has relied on factors which Congress has not intended it to consider, entirely failed to consider an important aspect of the problem, offered an explanation of its decision that runs counter to the evidence before it, or is so implausible that it could not be ascribed to a difference in view or the product of agency expertise."[122] These standards of review lead agencies to write regulatory preambles often hundreds of pages in length, providing responses to all significant comments received, as well as laying out empirical assumptions, policy judgments, and interpretations of law the agency has relied upon.[123] To this extent, courts have encouraged a bureaucratic practice of thoughtful consideration, thorough justification, and at least minimal engagement with comments offered by the affected public.

The great failure of judicial review, however, is that the kind of reasoning courts expect and demand of administrative agencies is largely not deliberative, but rather instrumental. It is often assumed that the legitimate role of agencies is simply to identify the efficient means for realizing statutory objectives, as interpreted by the judiciary. At first, it seems unproblematic that agencies should identity a "rational connection between the facts found and the choice made."[124] But such instrumental rationality tends towards a purely calculative mindset that replicates market reasoning within the state and closes off the administrative process from a more serious engagement with public values other than efficiency. Courts have thus required agencies to meticulously quantify the costs and benefits of regulations, even where such a procedure has not been explicitly mandated by Congress.[125] As Jerry Mashaw notes, courts often assume that "administration is just implementation; its rationality is to be judged by means-ends convergence, not by cogent argument concerning the rightness of the ends pursued."[126] This approach simultaneously overburdens courts and agencies with requirements of technical explanation that are often extremely costly for agencies to offer, beyond courts' institutional competency to assess, and inscrutable to any member of the public without a graduate degree in the relevant subject matter. It is not surprising that courts have focused their energies on these quasi-scientific issues, since these are often an important component of the administrative determinations they are called upon to review. But by equating administrative legitimacy with economic and technological expertise, they have fostered a form of administrative explanation, and of public contestation of such decisions, in which questions of value must masquerade as questions of technique.

Take, for example, the famous administrative law case, *Motor Vehicle Manufacturers Association v. State Farm* (1983).[127] At issue was a decision of the National Highway Traffic Safety Administration (NHTSA) to rescind a "passive restraint" requirement for automobiles.[128] The passive restraint rule mandated the use of safety technologies that did not require an affirmative action on the part of the drivers, namely automatic seat belts or airbags. The agency explained its decision to rescind this rule on the grounds that manufacturers had overwhelmingly opted for automatic seat belts over airbags and that passengers had usually detached the automatic seat belts, such that they had little safety benefit. The Court found that the rescission of the rule was arbitrary because the agency had failed to explain why it did not simply change the rule to require airbags if automatic seat belts had proved ineffective, and because the agency did not have sufficient evidence for its claim that detachable automatic seat belts had no positive impact on public safety.

The Court's and the agency's focus on the technical aspects of the issue concealed important questions of value that lay under the surface. In their study of the federal effort to regulate automotive safety, Jerry Mashaw and David Harfst show that NHTSA was confronted by historically entrenched values of negative liberty.[129] The car had long been an embodiment of ideals of personal autonomy and mobility. When concerns about automobile deaths and injuries prompted the 1966 motor safety legislation, this moment of social consciousness therefore stood in tension with deeply held public norms. The agency's decision to rescind the passive restraint rule was motivated in part by the anti-regulatory stance of the Reagan administration and a growing recognition that the public resisted obvious intrusions on negative liberty, even if this took the modestly coercive form of the automatic seat belt. Mashaw and Harfst conclude the agency might have succeeded in *State Farm* if it had justified its rescission not in terms of economic analysis but in terms of these value-based concerns. The agency "needed to take the much more radical step of insisting on the relevance, indeed the crucial importance, of political sentiment when assessing 'need' and 'reasonableness' under the statute. . . . Although this would have been a high-risk strategy, we suspect that only a candid assertion of the political nature of the decision could have saved the rescission."[130]

This plea for a more value-conscious administrative law has largely fallen on deaf ears. Administrative agencies, the courts, and the public at large consequently suffer from a kind of false consciousness. We often treat the substance of administrative decisions as clerical matters when in fact they implicate deep and often conflicting political commitments. The Consumer Financial Protection Bureau regulations on mortgage lending disclosures implicate our collective understanding of fair relations between borrowers and creditors; the National Labor Relations Board's categorization of graduate students as "employees" impacts the relationship between the labor market and the system of higher education; the Federal Aviation Administration's regulations on the powers of airport personnel over travelers affect our dignity and even bodily integrity; Department of Education grantmaking priorities channel educational support to communities that participate in federal criminal justice and drug prevention programs; the Environmental Protection Agency's definition of "waters of the United States" sets the boundaries between a public space where common interests predominate and a private domain where they must struggle for a hearing.[131]

The profound value questions these regulatory actions raise cannot be adequately adjudicated solely by reliance on scientific studies or arguments from technological feasibility or efficiency. The administrative process can only claim legitimacy in the eyes of those it binds if it acknowledges its own moral and political character rather than concealing it in the apolitical language of expertise, technique, and procedure. As the Supreme Court once stated, "the administrative process will best be vindicated in the clarity of its exercise."[132] It might be argued that technocratic reasoning legitimates agency action by giving it the appearance of value neutrality. But this is a bad bet. When administrative decisions have major impacts on public life, and those decisions are reached through the exercise of discretionary judgment, the public is unlikely to be convinced for long that no ethical judgment calls were implicated in those decisions. This is why we often see commentators and citizens complain about "some bureaucrat in Washington" making policy—they do not believe that civil servants are just crunching the numbers. And they are right. Forthright engagement with the value choices the agency confronts provides the only way that political legitimacy can be sustained when so much authority rests with appointed officials. There is a risk that the public will divide deeply over these value questions and administrative legitimacy will suffer, in the short term at least. But if administrative and judicial reasoning can be reframed to offer a rational discussion of public values and if the people participate in this process, then social attachment to the policymaking process might be sustained even if the face of deep dissension.

Narrow judicial emphasis on agencies' scientific or economic reasoning has pushed agencies to explain themselves in purely technical terms even when normative judgments are at play. More recent trends in administrative law seem to confirm this tendency. In a series of cases, the Supreme Court has declined to defer to administrative judgments when they concern questions of "vast economic and political significance."[133] Most recently, in *King v. Burwell*,[134] the Court refused, despite an acknowledged statutory ambiguity, to defer to the Internal Revenue Service's determination that federal tax credits would be available for federally administered health insurance exchanges under the Affordable Care Act: "Whether those credits are available on Federal Exchanges is . . . a question of deep economic and political significance that is central to this statutory scheme; had Congress wished to assign that question to an agency, it surely would have done so expressly."[135] This emergent "major questions doctrine"[136] allows courts to avoid deferring to agency reasoning—irrespective of its deliberative democratic credentials—when judges deem the issue to be really important. If courts may deprive agencies of their deliberative discretion whenever they think the issue is a significant one, agencies will have strong incentives to treat every regulatory matter as clerical and noncontroversial. Agencies will then withdraw further into a technocratic mindset rather than growing into the role of public engagement. Important questions of political value will either be pushed beneath the surface or passed into the hands of judges.[137]

This is a recipe for an ironic and arbitrary form of statehood: ironic, because administrative agencies will say their interpretations are technical even if they are in fact political; arbitrary, because judges may supplant agency reasoning with their own when they reach a subjective determination that the issue actually matters. The solution is not for courts to abandon their insistence upon the rationality of agency action but rather to adjust the kind of rationality they are looking for. They should require agencies to state with greater clarity the various values that are at issue in their interpretation and application of statutory terms, to rank those values where possible, and to explain how those values contribute to the regulatory decisions and plans they have developed. Further, courts should permit and encourage agencies to explain their interpretation and application of values by reference to the opinions and information given by members of the public in the regulatory process. The quality of the process of deliberation leading up to a decision should count as a reason to defer to agency interpretations and applications of statutes. The basic framework for this kind of analysis already exists in the paradigm cases of administrative law, but it has been warped by the emphasis on technical questions and the failure to develop a justiciable conception of rational deliberation over contested values. What is needed is a language of judicial review that ensures the openness and integrity of public deliberation regarding the meaning and application of statutory terms.

XI. DEMOCRATIC VIRTUES AND AUTHORITARIAN DANGERS OF PRESIDENTIAL ADMINISTRATION

The president stands in a unique position with respect to administrative agencies. Because he is ultimately responsible for the execution of the laws, agencies that implement statutory provisions usually fall under his supervision. The accrual of administrative power to the state is, in this sense, an accrual of power to the president. To the extent that he is able to influence, direct, and control the decisions of administrative authorities, powers delegated to them are powers delegated to him. The key normative question is to what extent presidential power ought to advance in lockstep with administrative power. Should the president directly and pervasively determine the content of administrative action, or should administration retain some autonomy from presidential control, remaining instead subject to its own expert judgment, the control of the other coordinate branches, or to the public directly?

The early twentieth century saw the simultaneous elevation of the president as a national democratic representative and the growth of the Office of the President as an instrument of administrative control. Since then, modern presidents have recognized they cannot possibly personally supervise the swelling bureaucracy of the executive branch. But they nevertheless attempt to retain the capacity as chief executive to implement the laws in a way consonant with their vision of public values. The developmental dynamic has been defined by a continual effort of the White House to get a grip on the expansive administrative apparatus, and Congress rather feebly attempting to restrict this effort, resulting in the consolidation of policy control in the higher echelons of the executive.[138] Over time, once clear conceptual divisions between the executive's managerial soundness and the president's degree of political control have become more and more difficult to disentangle in the halls of the White House.[139]

The coup de grâce in breaking the wall within the presidency between politics and administration came with President Reagan's use of the White House's Office of Management and Budget (OMB) to review agency rule-making. Executive Order 12,291 essentially gave the Reagan White House a veto on agency regulations and thus enabled him to delay or prevent agency rule-making or significantly alter agency policy. [140] The centralized regulatory review process established by that order was used to subject administrative decision-making to public will as the president and his political staff conceived it.[141] These developments continued after Reagan, as Clinton combined regulatory review with public efforts to direct agency action and take ownership of regulatory outcomes.[142]

The institutional innovations that have increased the overlap between administrative and political dimensions of the executive have been complemented by jurisprudential and scholarly efforts to legitimate presidential power over administration by reference to democratic norms. In *Chevron v. Natural Resources Defense Council* (1984), the Court concluded that where statutory language is ambiguous, courts must generally defer to the interpretation of the agency charged with administering the statute so long as these interpretations are "reasonable."[143] In justifying this permissive standard of review, the Court emphasized that "while agencies are not directly accountable to the people, the Chief Executive is, and it is entirely appropriate for this political branch of the government to make such policy choices."[144] This democratic justification for presidential control of administration has found significant support in the scholarly literature. Justice Elena Kagan, for example, prior to her appointment to the Supreme Court, argued "the new presidentialization of administration renders the bureaucratic sphere more transparent and responsive to the public, while also better promoting important kinds of regulatory competence and dynamism."[145] More provocatively, Eric Posner and Adrian Vermeule have argued that American administrative law is necessarily "Schmittian," in the sense that the administrative state is controlled not by legal rules but rather by the political accountability of the president, who fills in abstract and ambiguous statutory authority with his democratically legitimate policy program.[146]

But the attempt to anchor the legitimacy of the administrative state fully in the democratic authority of the president founders upon the inability of presidents, despite a century's worth of institutional innovations, to achieve full and pervasive control over administrative decision-making and behavior. Presidential control remains to a large extent "sporadic and fortuitous," if only because the time and knowledge of the president and his staff are finite, and the regulatory terrain of the administrative state is vast.[147] The accretion of institutional heft within the executive branch has made it difficult even for presidents with democratic warrants for major reform to accomplish anything truly transformative in the face of stiff administrative, congressional, judicial, or public resistance. For example, while Reagan benefited from the resources of OMB to control administrative decisions and reduce government outlays, regulatory output, and enforcement, he was not able to undo the apparatus of the welfare state developed since the New Deal.[148] Nor was Obama, after winning a mandate for "change" in the midst of economic crisis, able to fundamentally shift the federal government's financial regulatory posture.[149] As of this writing, it remains to be seen how profoundly the Trump administration will "deconstruct[] the administrative state."[150] But judicial review of administrative action, as well as internal regulations on appointment and removal, have already placed some constraints on this political project.[151]

The fact that the president's control of administration remains limited by legislative control and administrative independence does not mean we have reached a stable equilibrium between the office's institutional power and its democratic legitimacy. The persistent calls to bolster presidential control, and the strong proclivity of presidents to do so, continue to represent a real threat to the deliberative integrity of the American administrative state. Whereas the legislature has strong incentives to delegate control to other actors, the president has strong incentives to overcome institutional obstacles and attempt to turn administration into his personal policy instrument. Nor does he face the same costs of reaching binding decisions as does the legislature—he alone exercises executive power.

As the discussion of German political development in chapter 1 goes to show, the modern state evinces a troubling tendency to concentrate power in the executive to the exclusion of the other branches and the public at large. If the state comes to draw all of its authority from the plebiscitary claims of the presidency, then the people will become subject to the will of the chief executive and identify its own power with his or hers. The descent of the Weimar Republic into National Socialist dictatorship shows the dangers of attempting to compensate for the decline in legislative control over administration with ever-greater executive power. The American Progressives offer us a far better alternative.

The great innovation of the Progressive vision of the state was to introduce new forms of deliberative democratic control within administration itself, rather than to hang all hopes upon the democratic warrant of the presidency. Even as president, Woodrow Wilson never bought into a strongly unitary conception of the executive, preferring to delegate power to the cabinet and solicit public input on regulation. But this vision has lost its purchase on the public imagination. We remain captivated by the aura of presidential authority. As Theodore Lowi has argued, today's "personal presidency" is "an office of tremendous personal power drawn from the people . . . based on the new democratic theory that the presidency with all powers is the necessary condition for governing a large nation."[152] When the president's policies reflect our own, we are exhilarated by the way in which our will seemingly has been transposed into and identified with the highest office in the land. When we vehemently oppose the president's policies, we are terrified by the great powers he has at his disposal to implement his vision, our deeply held objections notwithstanding. Politics in such a situation becomes a winner-take-all phenomenon. It becomes a clash of ideologies, represented by heroic figures, rather than a considered and constructive debate between representatives in whom we invest provisional confidence.

The increasing investment of institutional competencies and plebiscitary authority in the president thus threatens to supplant deliberative democratic government with an authoritarian administrative state. The growth of the managerial presidency, alongside the relative incapacity of Congress to detail substantive rules for administration, may facilitate a shift to Carl Schmitt's "governmental state, which finds its characteristic expression in the exalted personal will and authoritative command of a ruling head of state."[153] The danger in these developments is that the executive may become the sole unifying element within the constitutional and administrative structure. Arbitrary assertions of personal power would displace rational elaboration of policy between multiple actors. The public's law would then be replaced with the president's will.

XII. CONCLUSION

A profound ideological shift is therefore required, with accompanying institutional amendments. We must begin to think differently about the structure of the state—to understand administrative agencies not as instruments of presidential or legislative will but rather as agents of the people, directly. Public acknowledgment of the democratic authority of administrative agencies themselves would serve to ballast against the growth of presidential power. As I argued earlier in this chapter, the procedures Congress has set forth in the Administrative Procedure Act provide a framework for an administrative state that draws its legitimacy from direct public participation rather than merely from the majoritarian mandate of the president or from the laws enacted by Congress. But on its own, notice-and-comment rule-making is only a shadow of the more robust forms of public participation that were seen at work in the New Deal and the Second Reconstruction. A full renewal of the Progressive state would require deepening governmental intervention in society, coupled with participatory procedures calculated to redress the structural injustices that often characterize social and private life.

Conclusion

Progress in Times of Peril

This book has developed a Progressive conception of democracy to assess, critique, and ultimately fortify our current state's legitimacy. The Progressive conception is grounded in American thinkers' reception and transformation of German legal theory at the turn of the twentieth century. From the thought of Hegel and his progeny, the Progressives derived the notion that administrative government should have an emancipatory orientation toward civil society. This state would create the institutional and material conditions for the exercise of free agency where these had been undermined by the antagonisms and complexities of modern social life.

But the Progressives fundamentally altered the Hegelian conception of the state. They sought to empower the public to determine the meaning of freedom, rather than leave its definition up to philosophical speculation or official fiat. The state would therefore attempt both to furnish the conditions for rational and inclusive discourse and to empower this discourse by including affected persons and groups in the policymaking process. In consultation with these affected parties, administrative officials would exercise their interpretive discretion to dismantle social relationships characterized by servitude, domination, and exclusion, and support in their place equal, integrated, and reciprocal relationships between citizens.

The guiding norm is that the government must be structured in such a way as to render the democratic public sphere politically efficacious. Certain aspects of our constitutional order and our administrative process have realized this vision. Congress has expressed broadly conceived public purposes in the form of statutes. The president appoints leadership of executive agencies who are likely to act in accord with his popularly endorsed platform. The judiciary affords individuals and associations with an opportunity to challenge administrative actions that acutely affect them and requires agencies to act lawfully and rationally. The procedures for administrative decision-making within agencies open up their deliberations to the contributions of the private parties. All three branches of government, and the administrative organizations that are subject to their authority, contribute to a process of democratic will-formation, which is contested and concretized through interaction between the relevant institutions.

This system has at times brought the government into robust dialogue with the public sphere and achieved emancipatory alterations in the social order. In the New Deal, administrative agencies implemented agricultural policy in consultation with landowning farmers and sought to strengthen the democratic foundations of rural life with material support for low-income farmers. Despite exclusionary and paternalistic elements, these administrative labors wrought demographic changes and expansions in social capacity that helped to lay the groundwork for the Second Reconstruction. In this next milestone of Progressive democracy, federal agencies engaged the constitutional branches in dialogue over the content of the nation's commitment to racial equality. At the same time, the War on Poverty helped to foster the African American public sphere and its political power. The administrative dimensions of the twentieth century's constitutional moments thus demonstrate that the Progressive theory has some real purchase for understanding the the American state's development.

But this normative reconstruction does not deny that other forms of statehood are at work and compete for dominance within our current institutional matrix. I do not follow some Hegelians in suggesting that political development necessarily pushes forward toward the complete realization of freedom. There is much in the present to disabuse us of that confidence. The current combination of legislative inaction and increasingly intensive presidential control over administration undermines opportunities for public participation. The focus on instrumental rationality in the federal courts, and the suppression of value-based argument from administrative discourse, prevents the state from functioning as the deliberative democratic site it might be.

The Trump administration, in particular, represents the antithesis of Progressivism: it abandons reasoned argument, undermines the professional civil service, nurtures authoritarian habits, institutes social exclusion and hierarchy, and otherwise shows a general contempt for principles of transparent, egalitarian, and participatory government. This dangerous state of affairs has not emerged from a vacuum. As the institutions and ideologies of the state have diverged from the Progressive conception, competing theories of administrative legitimacy have gained prominence. Proponents of cost-benefit analysis argue that the state should analyze problems and justify solutions according to the metric of the perfectly competitively market. At the same time, the increasing predominance of the executive branch has led some to conclude we no longer inhabit a liberal democratic order, but rather a presidential state where the decisive will of the chief executive is the lodestone of democratic legitimacy. These trends coalesce into the businessman president who seeks to liberate private firms from regulation and wages war on the civil service. This reactionary political moment throws into relief the Progressive ideal of democratic regulation, which prizes public participation, social-egalitarian norms, and official practical judgment as the cornerstones of a lawful and just government. It is time to center our intellectual and political energies around this compelling alternative.

We live in an era in which what Hegel called the "sense of the state" is very much alive in the American mind; but what, precisely, this state is and ought to be remains in fierce dispute.[1] My argument has aimed to recover the Progressive vision so that it might reassert its claims against competing political programs, modes of discourse, and frameworks for guiding institutional development. The Progressives understood the state as a dynamic relationship between the structures of government and the claims of public opinion. Such a state would be legitimate where the law instituted the norms of a public sphere constituted by equal, inclusive, and rational deliberation. A law of this kind—the public's law—could arise from administrative efforts to enhance the social circumstances for rational discourse, and from social efforts to enhance the participatory features of government decision-making. But because the Progressive understanding of the state has often been cast as a defense of technocracy, its ethical orientation toward enhancing democratic life through administration has been obscured. If the argument up to this point has succeeded, then this Progressive understanding of the state should have again become a viable way to think about and to reconstruct our current institutions.

In this Conclusion, I want to sharpen the critical edge of this vision by showing how it reveals the inadequacies and dangers of competing frameworks. I will show how the Progressive theory contains what is true and insightful about cost-benefit analysis and presidentialism, while rejecting the more pernicious elements of each. The Progressive theory thus offers a unified conception of the administrative state, which is insulated against the pathologies of these other contemporary conceptions.

I. THE COST-BENEFIT STATE, OR MARKET MIMESIS

Cost-benefit analysis (CBA) asks whether the benefits of regulation justify its costs.[2] Beginning in the Carter administration as an attempt to increase governmental efficiency, CBA was employed as an anti-regulatory weapon by the Reagan administration through Executive Order 12,291, which directed the Office of Management and Budget (OMB) to review regulations and prevent their implementation if their costs exceeded their benefits.[3] Subsequent administrations have retained cost-benefit analysis as a lens through which to evaluate agency actions, adjusting the framework in an effort to include a wider set of considerations.[4] For the proponents of CBA, a fair accounting of regulatory effects is a universal requirement for effective administration and need not lead to conservative outcomes.[5] Critics of CBA, however, have pointed to serious problems with its practical operation and its normative suppositions: its indeterminateness, its susceptibility to political manipulation, and its failure to recognize non-market values adequately.[6]

Cost-benefit analysis assumes that the perfectly competitive market is the core metric by which to judge state activity. CBA attempts to simulate efficient economic transactions where there is a "market-failure" due to high transaction costs, asymmetries of information, or the market power of particular firms.[7] Frameworks such as "willingness to pay" and "shadow price" attempt to construct a "true value to society" for certain goods, behaviors, or other social outputs.[8] The thrust of this effort is to encourage the state to realize market logic where the market itself does not. It therefore posits contracts between individual property holders as the normative standard by which to evaluate administrative activity. As Elizabeth Anderson has observed, "the theory of market failure is a theory not of what is wrong with markets, but of what goes wrong when markets are not available: it is a theory of what goes wrong when goods are not commodified. . . . Cost benefit analysis is the state's way of mimicking the consequences of market transactions."[9] Cost-benefit analysis is therefore a kind of market mimesis, in the sense that it attempts to imitate in regulatory policy a world of fully informed, freely contracting agents.

The Hegelian Progressive theory does not reject cost-benefit analysis categorically. As I described in chapters 1 and 2, both Hegel and the Progressives understood many of the problems in civil society in terms similar to the logic of CBA: they argued that the growth of industrial organization had prevented individuals from fully understanding the social world in which they acted (incomplete information); that private transactions could create negative consequences for the public at large (externality); and that certain firms had amassed such strength that economic exchange could no longer be understood as a consensual agreement between similarly situated persons (market power).

CBA is an effective instrument for addressing aspects of these market pathologies. When the price mechanism has failed to create accurate information about social costs, the government can step in to craft regulatory responses that bend the market back toward an efficient outcome. For example, when contracts between consumers and producers of energy do not take into account the full societal cost of the pollution their transactions generate, administrators can design regulations that will measure and reduce these costs. By considering the comparative costs and benefits of different approaches—such as mandating various emission control technologies, capping total emissions from certain sources, taxing the production of pollutants, or auctioning exchangeable pollution permits—analysts can choose the policy response that most significantly reduces the harms caused by pollution at the lowest regulatory cost. Such a framework makes sense when the goal is for the government to make the market live up to its own normative criteria—the efficient allocation of resources through fully informed contracts.

CBA has an imperial tendency, however, to assert its jurisdiction beyond the limits of its authority. Once economic rationality becomes the centerpiece of regulatory analysis, it is tempting to equate the purpose of *all* regulation with the simulation of perfectly competitive markets. As Wendy Brown has observed, such indiscriminate use of CBA is a symptom of neoliberal governance, in which "the state is enfolded and animated by market rationality: that is, not simply profitability but a generalized calculation of cost and benefit becomes the measure of all state practice."[10] If universally and exclusively applied as a technique of regulatory analysis, CBA reduces the scope of state power to mere market mimicry. At the same time, it cultivates a form of life among citizens and reasoning among public officials that is inimical to political action. "A fully realized neo-liberal citizen would be the opposite of public-minded. The body politic ceases to be a body but is rather a group of individual entrepreneurs and consumers."[11] To avoid this dismal fate, it is no answer to abandon the state and attempt to form some kind of social movement without recourse to administrative forms.[12] A public sphere requires a public law to be efficacious. We need an alternative way to think about the state's functions that remains vital in our intellectual heritage and our institutional practices.

One of Hegel's most important insights, which the American Progressives adopted, was that the state cannot be "confused with civil society" or its purpose "equated with the security and protection of property and personal freedom."[13] The state is rightly oriented toward preserving this realm of private freedom, where individuals can form their identities on the basis of propertied attachments.[14] But the state also institutes a different, higher kind of *public freedom*. It ensures that people are more than formally equal, contracting persons, but also relational beings whose identities, interests, and values are formed in joint discourse and action. Whereas in the marketplace one person's ends may be satisfied by another's, in political life their ends can intertwine and coincide.[15] Though Hegel found this public freedom in life under the perfect monarchical constitution, the Progressives advanced a more active, participatory conception. They argued that individuals could engage in public discourse and agree to pursue common plans. The shared goals that gained salience in public opinion would become candidates for public law. They would be proposed and enacted, refined and challenged in interactions between the constitutional branches, administrative agencies, and affected members of society.

A purely market-driven perspective on regulation ignores the reality that, through this process, the public has advanced a variety of purposes that are at best only tangential to the function of the market: we redistribute income through the tax code; we provide for retirement savings and disability insurance; we proscribe forms of racial and gender discrimination even where purely economic rationality would hold them blameless; we subsidize homeownership and food production and consumption; we preserve natural beauty through the stewardship of public land. As Susan Rose-Ackerman observes, "a pure cost-benefit test, with its omission of distributive fairness, and procedural concerns, would not encompass the purposes of these statutory mandates."[16] In these cases, we do not take individual entitlements and interests as givens but rather attempt to shape the existing distribution of property and preference according to some shared idea about the society we want to live in.

The Obama administration's practice of CBA was not blind to the fact that there are non-market values that the administrative state has the authority to advance. A 2011 executive order on cost-benefit analysis allows that "each agency may consider (and discuss qualitatively) values that are difficult to quantify, including equity, human dignity, fairness, and distributive impacts."[17] OMB's circular describing how to use CBA describes two kinds of reasons for regulation: "market failure or other social purpose," with the latter including distribution, non-discrimination, privacy, personal freedom, and "other democratic aspirations."[18] CBA thus admitted a plurality of public purposes beyond the marketplace and allowed these purposes a place within the framework of regulatory analysis.

To see how this can work in practice, consider a 2015 rule from Department of Housing and Urban Development (HUD) implementing the Fair Housing Act of 1968.[19] The rule imposed information-gathering and public-participation requirements on local housing authorities in order to ensure that they "affirmatively further" racially integrated housing. HUD estimated that the total annual compliance cost of the rule would be $30 million. After citing the CBA executive order's provision on unquantifiable benefits, it reasoned: "If the rule prompts communities to promote a more racially and socio-economically equitable allocation of neighborhood services and amenities, residents would enjoy the mere sense of fairness from the new distribution. Elevating communities out of segregation revitalizes the dignity of residents who felt suppressed under previous housing regimes."[20]

If HUD had had to perform a pure cost-benefit analysis, it would have been forced to attempt to quantify the monetary consequences of decreasing residential segregation. This would have raised a host of questions that are irrelevant, or even repugnant, to the purposes of the Fair Housing Act: How much would wealthier white residents be "willing to pay" to maintain a segregated neighborhood? How much would less well-off, nonwhite residents be "willing to accept" to remain in segregated, subprime neighborhoods created by past federal policies and racial malice? Permitting agencies to consider unquantifiable, non-market purposes allows them to escape these kinds of inappropriate questions, which would thwart socially progressive purposes by assuming the justice of the existing distribution of entitlements and preferences.

The importance of unquantifiable benefits is not limited to such plain questions of public freedom as civil rights enforcement. Rather, market efficiency and other political objectives often intersect in agency policymaking. Consider the Securities and Exchange Commission's (SEC) rule implementing the Dodd-Frank Act's disclosure requirements for payments to governments by resource extraction companies.[21] The Commission recognized that the purposes behind this provision were not merely economic, though it expected economic benefits to accrue from greater transparency. SEC thus interpreted the statute as furthering complementary market and political objectives: "the rules that we are adopting require the disclosure of payment information involving resource extraction activities so that the citizens of each country and those acting on their behalf can help combat corruption in connection with the sale of their nation's oil, gas, and mineral resources, and can hold relevant actors accountable."[22] A pure cost-benefit analysis would exclude these kinds of non-monetary factors from consideration, except to the extent that they indirectly impacted economic utility. Such political values are often important elements of the public purposes Congress gives legal force, even in areas where market values are also appropriate considerations.

The problem with the Obama administration's framework for considering such questions of public freedom is that these purposes are presented as marginal, rather than central, to the project of justifying state action. OMB's circular on cost-benefit analysis provides that where there is some unquantifiable social purpose implicated in a regulation, the proper procedure is to determine the upper and lower bounds of its value and then to assess whether it would tip the scales in favor or against a regulatory proposal.[23] Even non-market values must therefore be quantified to the extent possible. This leads agencies to distort plainly ethical questions into dollar valuations. The Department of Justice, for example, sought to determine society's willingness-to-pay to avoid rape in justifying a rule that would reduce the incidence of prison rape.[24] Political values that cannot be reduced to monetary quantities (such as the enforcement of constitutional rights) are then lumped together into a residual category that is subordinated to the paramount work of identifying and remedying market failures.[25] Economists and efficiency-minded lawyers thus gain the upper hand over both the specialists who actually understand the problem at hand and lawyers who represent interests other than the optimal allocation of risk and capital.

The Progressive alternative would be to ask first: What is the public purpose expressed in the relevant statute? If the purpose is simply to increase economic efficiency, then ordinary cost-benefit is plainly appropriate. If the statute's purposes include both market and political values, these political values *must* be considered alongside economic factors. If the statute primarily aims to further a political value, such as public health, workplace safety, or environmental protection, consideration of this value should have serial *priority* over the consideration of monetary costs and benefits. Otherwise, there is an acute risk that the interests of public freedom enshrined in law may be under-enforced in order to guard the marketplace against democratic control.

Under the Clean Air Act, for example, the EPA is directed to regulate emissions from coal- and oil-fired power plants if, after performing a study as to their "hazards to public health," EPA determines that regulation is "appropriate and necessary."[26] In this case, the primary goal of the statutory provision is the protection of public health, even though costs may be important in determining the optimal degree of regulation. It would seem logical, then, first to determine whether regulation is appropriate and necessary, based on a consideration of detrimental public health effects and available technology, and then consider the most cost-effective means to do so at a later step in the regulatory process. But the Supreme Court has held that the EPA acted unreasonably by failing explicitly to consider cost in determining whether the regulation of power plants was "appropriate and necessary" in the first place.[27] As the dissent in that case pointed out, however, the EPA had indeed gone on to consider costs in determining pollution thresholds.[28]

The Court's decision shows the danger of CBA when it assumes a hegemonic position. It can undermine the statutory priority accorded to public purposes over and above market efficiency. If properly interpreted, the Clean Air Act would allow a tiered consideration, where "appropriateness" was first evaluated according to the causal relation between power plant emissions and health effects, the availability of control technologies, and a normative consideration of what "public health" in fact means and requires. In light of social-scientific research and consultations with the broader public, the EPA might find that the appropriateness of regulation should be understood according to the socioeconomic distribution of the health effects of pollution, or the effects of health on political participation, rather than solely on aggregate monetary costs and benefits.[29] Once the agency, in consultation with the public, has thought through what kind of public health it should promote and protect, it would be in a position to consider the relevance of market values to its regulatory output. It could determine, for example, that a regulatory option that imposed higher quantifiable costs than benefits was nonetheless justified by its likely effects on the health outcomes of low-income or otherwise marginalized communities. The Obama administration's approach to CBA allowed the consideration of these factors, but it failed to take significant steps to ensure that they were not overshadowed by a totalizing emphasis on efficiency. It is essential to carve out stages in the decision-making process where these ethical concerns gain the full attention of public officials rather than being tacked onto an analysis primarily concerned with quantifiable economic effects.

Under the Trump administration, CBA has gone in the opposite direction. President Trump ordered executive agencies to keep the "incremental costs" of new regulations beneath a prescribed allotment and rescind two regulations for every one they promulgate.[30] These requirements do not really aim to promote efficiency in the sense of net-utility improvement. Otherwise, they would mention *benefits* as well as costs and not take a ham-handed quantitative approach to reducing the numerical quantity of regulations. The purpose of these requirements is simply, as the title of the executive order indicates, "Reducing Regulation and Controlling Regulatory Costs."[31] It does not seem to matter to the president or his inferior officers what the economic and social consequences of that effort may be.

While this effort is not in keeping with the utilitarian spirit of CBA—or with reasoned decision-making more broadly—it is in another sense the natural and probable result of CBA's market fetishism. If you want government to behave like a business, you should not be surprised when a businessman grabs the reins and instructs the executive department to stay out of capital's way, the public interest be damned. The decades-long, bipartisan effort to transform the state's purpose and structure into those of the market has left genuinely public institutions and reasoning vulnerable to the arbitrary and rapacious practices of the current administration. As Jon Michaels has noted, "Trump represents the apotheosis of the businesslike government movement."[32] If CBA deserves a second chance, it must only be on the condition that it will respect the limits of its competence and not presume that economic efficiency is the primary value to animate government.

II. THE PRESIDENTIAL STATE, OR WEIMAR-ON-POTOMAC

The structural position of the president and the executive branch as a whole has strengthened exponentially since the Progressive Era. With the growth of the regulatory and welfare functions of the state and the concomitant delegation of rulemaking authority to executive agencies, the president has assumed a central role in policymaking and implementation, even as Congress remains an important if occasional player.[33] When Congress empowers an executive agency with broad powers to determine the content of policy, the president's constitutional prerogatives and budgetary supervision allow him or her to direct, constrain, and otherwise influence agency action to a greater extent than Congress.[34] This has led scholars to diagnose and in some cases to endorse a form of "presidential administration," where executive agencies are treated primarily as the agents of the president rather than of Congress.[35]

The long-term trend in the consolidation of presidential power has sometimes combined with divided party government to further concentrate power in the executive.[36] When Congress is unwilling to work with the president because of major ideological cleavages, or unable to because of internal divisions, the president retains the power to deploy his or her existing authority to act unilaterally. In the words of President Obama, "If Congress won't act, I will."[37] Obama was true to his word, using his authority to push forward his party's agenda without any new congressional authorization in areas such as gun control,[38] immigration,[39] labor,[40] and the environment.[41] And Trump has followed in Obama's procedural footsteps, taking unilateral actions to undo his predecessor's legacy.[42]

The situation is in some ways eerily reminiscent of the executive-centered politics of the late Weimar Republic. With the legislative branch paralyzed by ideological conflict, power steadily accrued to the executive branch. Democracy came to be associated with the decisive will of executive leaders rather than with parliamentary debate, legislation, or more participatory forms of public engagement. Politics became a winner-take-all affair—a struggle to the death among fascists, liberals, and communists rather than a matter of deliberating over common purposes.

Carl Schmitt's political thought remains the most vivid expression of that historical moment. Politics for Schmitt was not a matter of public discourse but rather of "the most intense and extreme antagonism" between "friend and enemy."[43] He argued that parliamentary debate had become a "facade," as the state became deeply involved in regulating society and thus had to abandon the forms of bourgeois liberal law.[44] The state would instead operate through emergency measures, broad delegations of power to the executive, and backroom deals between the great economic interests. With the collapse of the ideals of the *Rechtsstaat*, the alternative was to turn to the executive, which enjoyed plebiscitary democratic legitimacy. Here deliberation had no place, for "the perspective of a dialectic-dynamic process of discussion can certainly be applied to the legislative but scarcely to the executive."[45] Schmitt therefore hoped to liberate the Weimar Constitution from its liberal shell and place decisive power in the hands of the president, who "unites in himself lawmaking and legal execution and can enforce directly the norms he establishes, which the ordinary legislature of the parliamentary legislative state cannot do. . . ."[46]

To any engaged observer of early twenty-first-century American politics, Schmitt's critique of the Weimar Republic has purchase on the present. There has been a decline in genuine parliamentary deliberation, there are increasingly intense disputes between the Left and Right, and the executive has become more and more prominent, founding its authority on democratic acclamation.[47] It is nonetheless breathtaking to see some contemporary American administrative law scholars not only *diagnose* our situation in Schmitt's terms but enthusiastically *embrace* the plebiscitary executive rule he advocated. Most prominently, Eric Posner and Adrian Vermeule state that "Carl Schmitt's critical arguments against liberal legalism seem to us basically correct" and concur with him that the "legislature and courts . . . are continually behind the pace of events in the administrative state; they play an essentially reactive and marginal role. . . ."[48] They argue that "the major constraints on the executive, especially in crises, do not arise from law or from the separation-of-powers framework defended by liberal legalists, but from politics and public opinion. . . ."[49] In their view, the president's electoral mandate, rather than legal constraints, become the hallmark of administrative legitimacy. Political theorists, too, are not immune to Schmitt's charms, drawing on his thought to conceptualize democracy as a fundamentally agonistic, rather than deliberative, form of politics.[50]

The intellectual history of German and American public-legal thought shows that our ideas and institutions need not and should not take this Schmittian turn toward plebiscitary democracy. Schmitt, Posner, and Vermeule all mischaracterize "liberal legalism," suggesting that liberalism is categorically incompatible with delegations of legal authority to administrative agencies. This is not so. As I argued in chapter 1, while the German tradition of the *Rechtsstaat* maintained that administrative action must be authorized and constrained by law, it always left significant space for discretion in which indeterminate statutory commands could be interpreted and concretized by administrative officials. German public law scholars such as Hegel and Mohl understood that the stability and generality of legal norms could only be preserved by allowing their meaning and application to shift over time and according to context. Schmitt never grasped this mutually-reinforcing relationship between legislative generality and administrative particularity. He was eager to convert every institutional tension into an existential struggle, in which one side or the other must triumph.

In the context of early-twentieth-century Germany, Schmitt's faulty conceptual analysis nonetheless had some appeal as a description of recent institutional developments. This was in part because Germany attempted to graft democratic constitutionalism onto an authoritarian administrative structure. Under the old monarchical system, the tension between legislative norms and administrative discretion remained encapsulated within a relatively stable constitutional architecture wherein bourgeois liberal interests were represented in the legislature and *Staatsräson* had its place in the executive. With the turn to democratic constitutionalism, however, the executive gained democratic legitimacy at the same time parliament declined into conflict and inaction. The chief executive, then carrying a democratic mandate, had at his disposal a massive bureaucratic apparatus to implement his will, unconstrained by deliberative debate. Without a contrasting power to place constraints on executive administration, the executive power became truly unbound.

American political thought and development have furnished a different set of ideas and institutions to counterbalance executive power in the face of the decline in legislative control. We therefore have at our disposal modes of politics that the Weimar Republic did not. As I argued in chapter 2, Progressives such as Du Bois and Goodnow enthusiastically embraced the Hegelian notion of a state in which legislative will would be carried out by competent and ethically attuned administrators. But the Progressive vision required more than this. Dewey, Wilson, and Follett emphasized that the American Republic would have to be democratic in a deeper sense than the Weimar Republic: it would have to afford people the opportunity to deliberate with public officials as the coauthors of the rules that bound them. As I argued in chapters 3 and 4, the Administrative Procedure Act of 1946 codified a thin version of these Progressive ideals with its general notice-and-comment requirement for issuance of regulations. Judicial decisions have elaborated these statutory provisions into a mandate that administrative decision-making follow deliberative democratic principles, taking into account the arguments of all affected parties in giving rational explanations of their actions. The result is an administrative state that can gain democratic legitimacy not only by statutory authority and executive directive but also by the input of groups within civil society.

Why, then, does Schmitt's theory of plebiscitary democratic legitimacy continue to have such analytic purchase and normative appeal, when Progressive institutions of rational and inclusive administration remain an important part of American government? It is because the ethical significance of these institutions has been forgotten and distorted, and they have been left to languish at the margins of political discourse. The full democratic promise of rulemaking has not been fulfilled. Nor have we renewed the more extensive forms of participation and social provision that the state undertook in the New Deal and Second Reconstruction. Progressivism instead has been conscripted into the service of technocratic ideologies of administration. Legal scholars often encapsulate Progressivism brusquely as an appeal to bureaucratic expertise.[51] The

Supreme Court sometimes buttresses this trend by emphasizing that administrative reasoning must be instrumentally sound and justified solely on the basis of the scientific expertise of administrative agencies. While the justices recognize the importance of certain deliberative values—reasoned decision-making, responsiveness to relevant arguments, etc.—they often attempt to craft a form of deliberation that is restricted to technical questions and that brackets out the normative concerns that often underlie such instrumental disputes.[52] Such important questions, they argue, are best left to the courts, the legislature, and the president to answer, rather than to administrative agencies. Administrators often respond to such cues by concealing the political content of their action as value-neutral problem-solving. Cass Sunstein, who led the Office of Information and Regulatory Affairs (OIRA) for a time under President Obama, thus emphasized that "most of the OIRA process is technical, not political,"[53] even though there is significant evidence that OIRA's review process is indeed influenced by political pressure.[54]

This technocratic approach to democratic legitimation follows Weber in treating administration as a neutral and efficient means to implement purposes that have been identified elsewhere. It minimizes or dismisses the Progressive idea that administration can be a democratic forum in which to carry out substantive debate about regulatory goals. If we do not avail ourselves of the democratic channels that administration opens up, value contestation will become all the more intense at the apexes of political power. When the legislature abdicates its responsibilities to engage in constructive contestation with the executive, this value conflict condenses into struggles for control of the presidency. The embrace of Weber's instrumental conception of administration in this way complements the expansive conception of presidential power advanced by his "legitimate pupil," Carl Schmitt.[55] A politics of friend-and-enemy gains preeminence over a politics of inclusive and rational debate.

The threat we confront here is not necessarily a precipitous descent into fascism. More immediately, we face a highly unstable form of politics, where elections take on a zero-sum characteristic and social conflict is heightened rather than worked through.[56] As voters and political elites think in terms of either/or, they lose the capacity to engage with one another in rational argument, which might otherwise have led to new commonalities and constellations of interests. Opportunities dwindle for Follett's idea of integrated solution, where conflicts are resolved not by compromise but by identifying new alternatives that satisfy a wide range of interests.[57]

Nor can we expect presidential administration to deliver on all of its promises of popular legitimacy and programmatic performance. As I argued in chapter 4, the president is not able to shape all administrative outcomes in the way he or she would like. Though presidents have strong incentives to maximize their control over administration, agencies that are responsible to statutory commands, judicial rulings, and public constituencies are not perfectly responsive to presidential directive. The result of greater presidential control is thus likely to be greater arbitrariness rather than the truly uniform application of majoritarian preferences. If we wish to retain democratic control over administration, we therefore must seek solutions other than executive fiat.

The Progressive theory continues to offer a viable path forward out of the dangerous and ineffective politics of the plebiscitary administrative presidency. The Progressive understanding of the presidency does not dismiss his or her role as a political leader and supervisor of administration. But it rejects the notion that the president is—or ought to be—the primary source of legitimacy in the administrative state. Following Wilson, the Progressive theory understands the president as a spokesperson for public opinion. Presidents can and indeed should guide administration according to the policy preferences the public expresses by electing them. But presidents must do so in a way that transparently discloses their understanding of the public's policy priorities.

On its own, however, transparency is insufficient to ensure that public opinion remains efficacious beyond the time frame of national elections. More than this, we must ensure that presidential direction of the administrative apparatus does not squelch out further opportunities for affected parties to inform the experts about the problems at hand. Presidential policies should be the beginning of the process of interpreting statutory ambiguities, not the end. Because asymmetries of power and information in civil society prevent the formation of a fully rational public opinion, the president's authority to articulate public purposes is partial and attenuated. Presidents do not truly speak for the people as a whole, because the public remains inchoate. The people are blocked from expressing their interests by the imbalanced circulation of knowledge and influence within the world they inhabit. To fortify the legitimacy of state action, the people must be brought back into the administrative process when laws are concretized by administrative rules. In that process, the people must give the officials better information about their needs and values, and the officials must help work out the rational basis and programmatic entailments of popular commitments.

The live conflict between the Progressives' presidency and the Schmittian presidency can be seen in two of the Obama administration's programs. The implementation of the Climate Action Plan was an excellent example of Progressive ideals in action. His executive actions on immigration, by contrast, failed to take advantage of the discursive competencies of the administrative state and thus bred legitimate fear of executive aggrandizement. Moreover, because the Obama administration's immigration policies did not make use of inclusive and participatory procedures, the Trump administration may have an easier time displacing them.

Since 2001, Congress has considered but failed to pass various versions of a "DREAM Act," which would grant legal permanent residency to certain undocumented persons who entered the United States at a young age.[58] In the face of congressional inaction and increasing pressure from the Democratic Party's immigration-reform constituency, President Obama relied on his existing statutory authority to direct the Department of Homeland Security to take actions that approximated the provisions of such a DREAM Act. [59] In 2012, then-Secretary of Homeland Security Janet Napolitano instructed immigration officials not to remove certain young persons who had entered the United States unlawfully—the "Deferred Action for Childhood Arrivals" (DACA) policy.[60] Obama justified the action publicly at the time, explaining: "In the absence of any immigration action from Congress to fix our broken immigration system, what we've tried to do is focus our immigration enforcement resources in the right places. . . . We focus and use discretion about whom to prosecute, focusing on criminals who endanger our communities rather than students who are earning their education."[61]

In 2014, the Obama administration broadened its deferred action policy to cover a wider class of undocumented immigrants, including adults whose children were citizens or lawful permanent residents (the DAPA program).[62] The DAPA memorandum set forth certain threshold criteria under which an individual would be eligible for deferred action. The administration relied upon the advice of the Justice Department's Office of Legal Counsel, which found that this deferred action program was lawful because it was a reasonable response to scarce enforcement resources and was consistent with congressional policy favoring unification of lawful immigrants' families.[63] President Obama again explained his actions in an address to the nation:

> I want to work with both parties to pass a more permanent legislative solution. And the day I sign that bill into law, the actions I take will no longer be necessary. . . . Americans are tired of gridlock. What our country needs from us right now is a common purpose—a higher purpose. . . . Most Americans support the types of reforms I've talked about tonight. . . . [W]e are and always will be a nation of immigrants. We were strangers once, too. And whether our forebears were strangers who crossed the Atlantic, or the Pacific, or the Rio Grande, we are here only because this country welcomed them in, and taught them that to be an American is about something more than what we look like, or what our last names are, or how we worship. What makes us Americans is our shared commitment to an ideal—that all of us are created equal, and all of us have the chance to make of our lives what we will.[64]

The president thus took on the Wilsonian role of spokesman for public opinion to justify his unilateral action on immigration, relying both upon recent polling indicating support for immigration reform and a broader American ethic of a "nation of immigrants."

These executive actions did not, however, follow the Progressive principle that administrative action significantly affecting the public at large should proceed through deliberative democratic procedures. The enforcement guidelines did not go through any process approaching the minimal procedures of notice-and-comment rulemaking. The consultations that were undertaken were primarily intragovernmental, as with the Office of Legal Counsel's review of the memoranda. DHS did not publish the proposed enforcement principles in the Federal Register or make provisions for all interested parties to submit comments on a proposal.

The unilateral and procedurally abbreviated character of the president's actions was troubling because the memoranda seemed to function as rules of general applicability, which determined the allocation of public benefits. Though the 2014 memorandum was styled as "guidance for case-by-case deferred action,"[65] its purpose was to regularize and control the wide discretion of immigration enforcement officers. The Office of Legal Counsel thus justified the rule in part because the "establishment of threshold eligibility criteria can serve to avoid arbitrary enforcement decisions by individual officers, thereby furthering the goal of ensuring consistency across a large agency."[66] If the guidance actually functioned to avoid arbitrariness and ensure consistency, it had to effectively constrain prosecutorial discretion in the vast majority of cases, equitable exceptions notwithstanding. The success of the guidance therefore depended on its substitution of "case by case" exercises of discretion with general principles of decision-making.[67] Nor was the guidance merely a device of internal management without effect on private parties. While the memorandum disclaimed creating any substantive right, an individual granted deferred action under its criteria might win legal benefits, such as eligibility for employment authorization.[68] The guidance thus studiously evaded the appearance of a rule of general applicability while at the same time trading on its rule-like character to achieve the president's policy objectives.

Moreover, deferred action was far from a technical decision that could be removed from political input. Immigration enforcement policies raise a host of crucial questions about the substantive commitments of our public sphere, such as the humanitarian obligations of the people of the United States to individuals and families, including undocumented immigrants; the boundaries of our concept of "the people" that is the sovereign source of the Constitution and the laws; the expressive significance and incentive effect of tolerating unlawful entry and residence within the United States; the comparative weight of the distinction between violating immigration laws and violating serious domestic criminal laws; any obligations the United States carries toward nations from which immigrants came; the moral culpability of children; and social obligations to protect children and their familial attachments from instability and disruption.

Where such fundamental and contestable questions of political value are at issue, notice-and-comment procedures should be used, even if they are not legally mandatory. Such procedures, which do not discriminate between citizens and noncitizens, could have and should have been adapted in this case to ensure that the immigrants and families most affected by the proposed policies had a clear and distinct voice in the policy debate. The goal would be to ensure that not only citizens but all acutely affected by our immigration enforcement policy could contribute to the debate.[69] As Judge Richard Posner has stated in another context, "The greater the public interest in a rule, the greater reason to allow the public to participate in its formation."[70]

Because of the broad scope and the important political values it implicated, the guidance on deferred action should have been subject to greater public input and deliberation. I do not believe the DAPA guidance was procedurally invalid, though the Fifth Circuit Court of Appeals concluded that it probably was, and an equally divided Supreme Court affirmed that judgment.[71] My argument is rather that the agency should have gone through the notice-and-comment process even if it was not legally obliged to do so. That process would have exposed the important value questions implicated by deferred action and given the agency the opportunity to offer a cogent explanation for the policy that would have to be taken seriously in any effort to change it.

The choice to avoid rulemaking may have made it easier for the Trump administration to rescind the policies. Because DACA was issued as an enforcement memorandum rather than as a regulation with the force of law, the Trump administration can—and has—acted to rescind it without using the notice-and-comment rulemaking process.[72] As of this writing, that rescission has been held unlawful by several courts because of its weak legal justification and failure to consider the reliance interests generated by the previous policy.[73] No matter how that litigation turns out, the Obama administration's policies would likely have had longer staying power—and certainly more democratic legitimacy—if his Department of Homeland Security had used the participatory rulemaking procedure.

President Obama's executive actions on climate change exemplify this deliberative approach to administration, in stark contrast to the unilateral, plebiscitary leadership he pursued in immigration policy. In his second inaugural address, President Obama interpreted his electoral mandate by declaring that "We, the people, still believe that our obligations as Americans are not just to ourselves but to all posterity. We will respond to the threat of climate change, knowing that the failure to do so would betray our children and future generations."[74] When he made this declaration, the Environmental Protection Agency (EPA) had already published a notice of proposed rulemaking on regulating greenhouse gas emission from power plants.[75] With his environmental policy platform endorsed by the electorate, the president issued a memorandum to the EPA directing it to continue its deliberations with "labor leaders, nongovernmental organizations, other experts, tribal officials, other stakeholders, and members of the public on issues informing the design of the program."[76] The resulting 2015 final rule sets CO_2 emissions goals for each state to reach by 2030, based on its current energy mix. It allows states "broad flexibility and latitude" to develop their own plans to meet these standards, including an option to work with other states to develop regional plans.[77]

The president thus exercised leadership by giving renewed impetus, electoral legitimacy, and ethical purpose to the EPA's ongoing efforts to address climate change. He insisted the EPA engage with states and the public in general as it designed the program. The EPA took this emphasis on participation seriously. Prior to its promulgation of its proposed rule, the EPA had already engaged with states and stakeholders to get advice on how best to craft the greenhouse gas emission rule.[78] The EPA also held regional public hearings to receive comments on the proposal.[79] The rule itself further mandated that states conduct public hearings as they develop their emission reduction plans, with specific thematic focus:

> EPA is requiring states to demonstrate how they are meaningfully engaging all stakeholders, including workers and low-income communities, communities of color, and indigenous populations living near power plants and otherwise potentially affected by the state's plan. In their plan submittals, states must describe their engagement with their stakeholders, including their most vulnerable communities. The participation of these communities, along with that of ratepayers and the public, can be expected to help states ensure that plans maintain the affordability of electricity for all and preserve and expand jobs and job opportunities as they move forward to develop and implement their plans.[80]

The rule goes on to detail the agency's understanding of climate change as an "environmental justice issue," focusing on the unequal impact of pollution and climate change on low-income and minority communities.[81]

The implementation of the Climate Action Plan thus instituted core concerns of the Progressive conception of the state. While the president played an important role in directing and energizing agency action, the democratic content of the rule derives in large part from legislative authority, the ethical judgment of administrators, and the input of the affected public. The rule addresses highly technical issues, such as identifying the best systems of emission reduction for subcategories of power plants. It interprets the legislative plan under which it acts. It references the president's supervisory authority. But it goes beyond these considerations in ensuring that the public is able to participate in the policymaking process on equal terms. It attempts to provide the democratic requisites of public health and welfare in and through a collaborative administrative process that takes special note of disparate power and resources amongst members of the public. In this way, it recalls some of the best elements of the Farm Security Administration's emphasis on protecting the most vulnerable members of society during the New Deal, along with the Office of Economic Opportunity's effort to empower such groups to take political action during the War on Poverty.

The Trump EPA has proposed to rescind the Clean Power Plan.[82] But because the Obama EPA proceeded through rulemaking, it will be much more difficult for the Trump administration to rescind the plan than it will be for them to rescind deferred action on unlawful immigration. The EPA must hear public comments on the issue, and its final rule will inevitably be challenged in court by environmental groups and state governments. When the courts consider these challenges, they should keep in mind the principles of equality, rationality, and public participation that animate the democratic and administrative state. Rules are only lawful when they are formulated with due regard to the interests and arguments of all members of the affected public.

III. OUTLOOK

Strong crosscurrents of market logic and presidential authoritarianism challenge the Progressive legacy of deliberative democratic statehood. The Trump administration is doing its best to supplant the public interest with pecuniary interest. But precisely because the current administration stands opposite of the ideals of freedom, rationality, and public power that animated Progressivism, it throws these ideals into relief and shows their necessity for our health as a political community. At the nadir of presidential leadership and regulatory protection, we should contemplate the ideas and the institutions that can achieve a country adequate to the principles of liberty and equality that have underwritten our finest political institutions.

We need a state that emancipates the public sphere from the conditions of inequality and domination, rather than enhancing the power of already unaccountable private actors. We need laws that undermine social hierarchy and oppression, rather than replicating and entrenching the worst aspects of our history and culture. We need an administrative process that empowers the people to set the principles and polices that govern their collective life, rather than subjecting them to the whims of employers, the rents of monopolistic firms, and floods and droughts of a natural disaster of our own making. We need a freedom that is concrete and integral rather than abstract and isolated. With a better appreciation for the shared fates of bureaucracy and freedom, we can imagine and build a state in which the people finds itself truly at home.

NOTES

Introduction

1. James Morone, *The Democratic Wish: Popular Participation and the Limits of American Government* (New York: Basic Books, 1990), 29.
2. E.g., Gillian Metzger, "The Constitutional Duty to Supervise," *Yale Law Journal* 124, no. 6 (2015): 1836–933, 1847–48; Gregory A. Huber, *The Craft of Bureaucratic Neutrality: Interests and Influence in Governmental Regulation of Occupational Safety* (Cambridge: Cambridge University Press, 2007), 37–38; Edward L. Rubin, "Law and Legislation in the Administrative State," *Columbia Law Review* 89, no. 3 (1989): 369–429, 377–80; William J. Brennan Jr., "Reason, Passion, and 'The Progress of Law,'" *Cardozo Law Review* 10 (1988): 3–23, 19–20; James T. Kloppenberg, *Uncertain Victory: Social Democracy and Progressivism in European and American Thought, 1870–1920* (New York: Oxford University Press, 1986), 384–94; Peter D. Evans, Dietrich Rueschemeyer, and Theda Skocpol, eds., *Bringing the State Back In* (Cambridge: Cambridge University Press, 1985), 8, 50–59; Jerry L. Mashaw, *Bureaucratic Justice: Managing Social Security Disability Claims* (New Haven, CT: Yale University Press, 1983), 26; Louis L. Jaffe, "The Illusion of the Ideal Administration," *Harvard Law Review* 86, no. 7 (1973): 1183–99, 1186–87.
3. See generally James O. Freedman, *Crisis and Legitimacy: The Administrative Process and American Government* (Cambridge: Cambridge University Press, 1978).
4. This critique of Progressive Hegelianism ranges from the popular to the scholarly. See, e.g., Charles R. Kesler, *I Am the Change: Barack Obama and the Crisis of Liberalism* (New York: Broadside, 2012), 57; Jonah Goldberg, *Liberal Fascism: The Secret History of the American Left from Mussolini to the Politics of Meaning* (New York: Doubleday, 2007), 218; Ronald J. Pestritto, *Woodrow Wilson and the Roots of Modern Liberalism* (Lanham, MD: Rowman & Littlefield, 2005), 16–17; Ronald J. Pestritto, "The Progressive Origins of the Administrative State: Wilson, Goodnow, and Landis," *Social Philosophy and Policy* 24, no. 1 (2007): 16–54; Tiffany Jones Miller, "Freedom, History, and Race in Progressive Thought," in *Natural Rights, Individualism and Progressivism in American Political Philosophy*, ed. Ellen Frankel Paul, Fred D. Miller Jr., and Jeffrey Paul (Cambridge: Cambridge University Press, 2012), 220, 254; Philip Hamburger, *Is Administrative Law Unlawful*? (Chicago: University of Chicago Press, 2014),

447–78; Jean M. Yarbrough, *Theodore Roosevelt and American Political Thought* (Lawrence: University of Kansas Press, 2012), 19–24, 44–46.

5. Philip Rucker and Robert Costa, "Bannon Vows a Daily Fight for 'Deconstruction of the Administrative State,'" *Washington Post*, Feb. 23, 2017, https://perma.cc/Q7C2-5WDW.
6. Alexis de Tocqueville, *Democracy in America*, trans. Henry Reeve, ed. Francis Bowen, vol. 1, 6th ed. (Boston: John Allyn [1835] 1876), 536.
7. Ibid., 87.
8. Ibid., 268.
9. See, e.g., Daniel Ernst, *Tocqueville's Nightmare: The Administrative State Emerges in America, 1900–1940* (New York: Oxford University Press, 2014), 1.
10. Tocqueville, *Democracy in America*, 540.
11. Ibid., 328–9.
12. Alexis de Tocqueville, *The Old Regime and the Revolution*, trans. John Bonner (New York: Harper & Brothers, 1856), 19.
13. Ibid., 252.
14. Ibid., ix–x.
15. Hannah Arendt, *On Revolution* (New York: Penguin, [1963] 1990), 167.
16. Hannah Arendt, *The Human Condition* (Chicago: University of Chicago Press, 1958), 40.
17. Hannah Arendt, *The Origins of Totalitarianism* (New York: Harcourt, 1968), 185–221; Hannah Arendt, *Eichmann in Jerusalem: A Report on the Banality of Evil* (New York: Penguin, [1963] 2006), 286–94.
18. Arendt, *The Human Condition*, 199.
19. See generally Eric Posner and Adrian Vermeule, *The Executive Unbound: After the Madisonian Republic* (New York: Oxford University Press, 2011); Hamburger, *Is Administrative Law Unlawful?*. Seminally, A.V. Dicey, *Introduction to the Study of the Law of the Constitution*, 8th ed. (London: MacMillan, 1915), 324–26.
20. Michel Foucault, "Governmentality," in *The Foucault Effect: Studies in Governmentality*, ed. Graham Burchell, Colin Gordon, and Peter Miller (Chicago: University of Chicago Press, 1991), 87–104, 96.
21. Ibid., 95–96.
22. Ibid., 95.
23. Ibid.
24. Ibid., 100.
25. Bernardo Sordi, "*Révolution, Rechtsstaat* and the Rule of Law: Historical Reflections on the Emergence of Administrative Law," in *Comparative Administrative Law*, ed. Susan Rose-Ackerman, Peter L. Lindseth, and Blake Emerson, 2nd ed. (Cheltenham, UK: Northhampton, MA: Edward Elgar, 2017), 23–37.
26. Martin Loughlin, *Foundations of Public Law* (Oxford: Oxford University Press, 2010), 156.
27. Foucault, "Governmentality," 103.
28. Jürgen Habermas, *Structural Transformation of the Public Sphere: An Inquiry into a Category of Bourgeois Society*, trans. Thomas Burger (Cambridge, MA: MIT Press, 1991), 30–88.

29. Michel Foucault, "What Is Enlightenment?," in *The Foucault Reader*, ed. Paul Rabinow (New York: Random House, 1984), 32–50, 46.
30. Ibid., 50.
31. Immanuel Kant, "An Answer to the Question: 'What Is Enlightenment?,'" in *Practical Philosophy*, trans. and ed. Mary J. Gregor (Cambridge: Cambridge University Press, 1996), 11–22, 18.
32. Ibid.
33. Ibid.
34. My reconstructive method is similar to those of Jürgen Habermas and Axel Honneth. In Habermas's concept of "rational reconstruction," "the concept of practical reason . . . offers a guide for reconstructing the network of discourses that, aimed at forming opinions and preparing decisions, provides the matrix from which democratic authority emerges. . . [S]uch a reconstruction would provide a critical standard, against which actual practices—the opaque and perplexing reality of the constitutional state—could be evaluated." Jürgen Habermas, *Between Facts and Norms: Contributions to a Discourse Theory of Law and Democracy*, trans. Williams Rehg (Cambridge, MA: MIT Press, 1996), 3, 5. Honneth's idea of "normative reconstruction" is comparable but begins from institutional material rather than practical discourses. This procedure "throws into relief the essential features and particularities of . . . society by demonstrating the contribution that each respective social sphere makes to securing and realizing the values that have already been institutionalized in society. . . . In the course of normative reconstruction, the criterion of 'rationality' applied to those elements of social reality that contribute to the implementation of universal values not only asserts itself in the uncovering of already existing practices, but also in the critique of existing practices or in the attempt to anticipate other paths of development that have not yet been exhausted." Axel Honneth, *Freedom's Right: The Social Foundations of Democratic Life* (New York: Columbia University Press, 2014), 7–8. My method is to begin with an "intellectual reconstruction" of political norms through an exegesis of the Hegelian Progressive tradition, then proceed to an "institutional reconstruction" of the American state, and conclude with a "normative reconstruction" of that intellectual and institutional history.
35. See generally Amy Allen, *The End of Progress: Decolonizing the Normative Foundations of Critical Theory* (New York: Columbia University Press, 2017).
36. Karsten Harries, *The Ethical Function of Architecture* (Cambridge, MA: MIT Press, 1998), 287.
37. Henry S. Richardson, *Democratic Autonomy: Public Reasoning about the Ends of Policy* (New York: Oxford University Press, 2002).
38. Hamburger, *Is Administrative Law Unlawful?*, 447.
39. U.S. Const. pmbl.; S. Pac. Co. v. Jensen, 244 U.S. 205, 222 (1917) (Holmes, J., dissenting).
40. 244 U.S. at 222.
41. Anne M. Kornhauser, *Debating the American State: Liberal Anxieties and the New Leviathan, 1930–1970* (Philadelphia: University of Pennsylvania Press, 2015), 175–220.

42. Rawls articulates his "basic structure" into two principles: "First: each person is to have an equal right to the most extensive scheme of equal basic liberties compatible with a similar scheme of liberties for others. Second: social and economic inequalities are to be arranged so that they are both (a) reasonably expected to be to everyone's advantage and (b) attached to positions and offices open to all. . . . These principles are to be arranged in a serial order with the first principle prior to the second. This ordering means that *infringements of the basic equal liberties protected by the first principle cannot be justified, or compensated for, by greater social and economic advantages*." John Rawls, *A Theory of Justice*, 2nd ed. (Cambridge, MA: Harvard University Press 1999), 53–54 (emphasis added).
43. Jon D. Michaels, *Constitutional Coup: Privatization's Threat to the American Republic* (Cambridge, MA: Harvard University Press, 2017), 52.
44. Ibid., 58.
45. Adrian Vermeule, *Law's Abnegation: From Law's Empire to the Administrative State* (Cambridge, MA: Harvard University Press, 2016), 43–47.
46. Ibid., 8.
47. Ibid. 129.
48. Adrian Vermeule, "Our Schmittian Administrative Law," *Harvard Law Review* 122, no. 4 (2009): 1095–149.
49. Karen Orren and Stephen Skowronek, *The Policy State: An American Predicament* (Cambridge, MA: Harvard University Press, 2017).
50. Ibid., 27.
51. Ibid., 35.
52. Ibid., 195.
53. Richard Rorty, *Achieving Our Country: Leftist Thought in Twentieth Century America* (Cambridge, MA: Harvard University Press, 1998), 35.
54. Ibid., 60.
55. William J. Novak, "Beyond Max Weber: The Need for a Democratic (Not Aristocratic) Theory of the Modern State," *The Tocqueville Review* 36, no. 1 (2015): 43–91, 83.
56. K. Sabeel Rahman, *Democracy against Domination* (New York: Oxford University Press, 2016).
57. Ibid., 110.
58. Ibid., 141.
59. Ibid., 110.
60. 5 U.S.C. § 553(c) (2012).

Chapter 1

1. Novak, "Beyond Weber," 65–69. E.g., Metzger, "The Constitutional Duty to Supervise," 1847–48; Huber, *The Craft of Bureaucratic Neutrality*, 37–38; Edward L. Rubin, "Law and Legislation in the Administrative State," 377–80; William J. Brennan Jr., "Reason, Passion, and 'The Progress of Law,'" 19–20; Kloppenberg, *Uncertain* Victory, 384–94; Evans, *Bringing the State Back In*, 8, 50–59; Jerry L. Mashaw, *Bureaucratic Justice*, 26; Jaffe, "The Illusion of the Ideal Administration," 1186–87.

2. Ernst, *Tocqueville's Nightmare*, 9–15; Hamburger, *Is Administrative Law Unlawful?*, 447–78.
3. Robert D. Miewald, "The German Tradition and the Organic State," in *Politics and Administration: Woodrow Wilson and American Public Administration*, ed. Jack Rabin and James S. Bowman (New York: Marcel Dekker, 1984): 19–20; Pestritto, *Woodrow Wilson and the Roots of Modern Liberalism*, 16–17; Yarbrough, *Theodore Roosevelt and American Political Thought*, 19–24, 44–46.
4. Vermeule, "Our Schmittian Administrative Law," 1095–1149; Posner and Vermeule, *The Executive Unbound*, 3–18.
5. Hamburger, *Is Administrative Law Unlawful?*, 447–78.
6. Heinrich Triepel, "Law of the State and Politics" (1927), in *Weimar: A Jurisprudence of Crisis*, ed. Arthur J. Jacobson & Bernard Schlink (Berkeley: University of California Press, 2002), 176–88, 183.
7. G.W.F. Hegel, *Elements of the Philosophy of Right*, ed. Allen W. Wood, trans. H.B. Nisbet (Cambridge: Cambridge University Press, 1991), § 4.
8. G.W.F. Hegel, *Enzyklopädie der philosophischen Wissenschaften im Grundrisse* (1830*): Dritter Teil: Die Philosophie des Geistes* (Frankfurt-am-Main: Suhrkamp, 1970), § 469 (author's translation). See also Hegel, *Philosophy of Right*, § 21.
9. Herbert Marcuse, *Reason and Revolution: Hegel and the Rise of Social Theory* (Oxford: Oxford University Press: 1941), 206; Robert B. Pippin, *Hegel's Practical Philosophy: Rational Agency as Ethical Life* (Cambridge: Cambridge University Press, 2008), 205–9. As he says in the *Encyclopedia*, "right is to be taken comprehensively not only as limited juridical right, but as the being of all determinations of freedom." Hegel, *Enzyklopädie*, § 469 (author's translation).
10. G.W.F. Hegel, *Phenomenology of Spirit*, trans. A.V. Miller (New York: Oxford University Press, [1807] 1977), 111–19. In the *Philosophy of Right*, Hegel writes, "The point of view of the free will . . . is already beyond that false point of view whereby the human being exists as a natural being and as a concept which has being only in itself, and is therefore capable of enslavement. This earlier and false appearance is associated with the spirit that has not yet gone beyond the point of view of consciousness; the dialectic of the concept and of the as yet only immediate consciousness of freedom gives rise at this stage to the *struggle for recognition* and the relationship of *lordship* and *servitude* (see *Phenomenology*, pp. 115ff. and *Encyclopedia of the Philosophical Sciences*, §§ 325ff.). But that objective spirit, the content of right, should no longer be apprehended merely in its subjective concept, and consequently that the ineligibility of the human being in and for himself for slavery should no longer be apprehended merely as something which *ought* to be as, is an insight which comes only when we recognize that the idea of freedom is truly present only as *the state*." Hegel, *Philosophy of Right*, § 57A.
11. Seyla Benhabib, "Obligation, Contract, and Exchange: On the Significance of Hegel's Abstract Right," in *The State and Civil Society: Studies in Hegel's Political Philosophy*, ed. Z.A. Pelcynski (Cambridge: Cambridge University Press, 1984), 163.
12. G.W.F. Hegel, *Grundlinien der Philosophie des Rechts* (Hamburg: Felix Meiner, 1955), § 211. I have used my own translation in this case because Nisbet's translation does not capture the specifically statutory meaning of "*Gesetz*," translating it instead as "law." He also uses the verb "to become" whereas Hegel uses the verb

"to be" [*sein*], and gives the sentence a conditional form it lacks in the original. Further, his translation of *gelten* as "valid" seems to miss the thrust of the passage. Hegel is referring to the fact that, in positive law, right is in effect or in force. Right, for Hegel, is always "valid" in a purely normative sense, whether it is posited in statute or not.

13. Hegel, *Philosophy of Right*, §189–98.
14. Ibid., § 243.
15. Ibid., §§ 250–55.
16. Jean L. Cohen and Andrew Arato, *Civil Society and Political Theory* (Cambridge, MA: MIT Press, 1992), 100.
17. Hegel, *Philosophy of Right*, § 274.
18. Ibid., § 275, § 287, § 298.
19. Ibid., § 286. He describes the social organism in terms of institutional rationality elsewhere: "In the development of civil society, the ethical substance takes on its infinite form . . . the form of *universality* which is present in education, the form of *thought* whereby the spirit is objective to itself as an *organic* totality in laws and institutions, i.e. in its own will as *thought*." Ibid., § 256.
20. Contemporary commentators are right to find Hegel's defense of hereditary monarchy wanting. See, e.g., Pippin, *Hegel's Pratical Philosophy*, 261. His justification of the monarchy on the basis of its immediate connection with nature is particularly perplexing, given that Hegel's account of freedom always involves the mediation and transformation of natural endowments. Hegel, *Philosophy of Right*, §§ 279A, 280.
21. Hegel, *Philosophy of Right*, § 279A.
22. Ibid., §§ 317–18.
23. Ibid., § 315. See also Habermas, *Structural Transformation of the Public Sphere*, 117–23.
24. It is noteworthy that Hegel at one point compares the monarchical principle to public opinion: "We have considered subjectivity once already in connection with the monarch at the apex of the state. Its other aspect is its arbitrary appearance in public opinion as the most external manifestation." Hegel, *Philosophy of Right*, § 320A.
25. Ibid., § 299.
26. Ibid., § 280A.
27. As Carl Schmitt recognized, Hegel was an early exponent of the theory of the *Rechtsstaat*, though he did not use the term: "For Hegel, the law is the current truth in a general form. The legislative power expresses the general, the executive the particular." Carl Schmitt, *Constitutional Theory*, trans. Jeffrey Seitzer (Durham, NC: Duke University Press, [1928] 2008), 183.
28. Hegel, *Philosophy of Right*, § 299 (bracketed German in translated text omitted).
29. Hegel gives to the monarch the authority to appoint and dismiss the highest public officials and to make final decisions on law and policy. The monarch's power to appoint and dismiss high-ranking officials according to his "unrestricted arbitrary will" allows a potential for substantive influence over policy that is very hard to justify, especially given Hegel's own expressed doubts about the monarch's intellectual powers. Hegel, *Philosophy of Right*, §§ 281A, 283.

30. *Polizei* was a general term for the regulatory authority of the state in early modernity, beginning with the *Reichspolizeiordnungen* of the sixteenth century. *Polizei* included numerous regulatory activities including provision for the poor, price regulation, rent control, supervision of forests and agriculture, cultural and educational provisions, and criminal law. This encompassing regulatory authority of the early state was the forerunner of modern administration (*Verwaltung*), but it was not situated within modern constitutional distinction between the legislative creation of legal norms and the executive implementation of such norms. Nor did it presuppose the idea of a state standing above a society composed of independent and equal subjects. Norm creation and norm implementation, as well as state and society in general, stood in a more complex and fluid interrelationship in the early *Policeyrecht*. Michael Stolleis, "Was bedeutet 'Normdurchsetzung' bei Policeyordnungen der Frühen Neuzeit?," in *Ausgewählte Aufsätze und Beiträge* vol. 1, ed. Stefan Ruppert und Milos Vec (Frankfurt-am-Main: Vittorio Klostermann, 2011), 219–39, 221–22 (author's translation).
31. Hegel, *Philosophy of Right*, § 289.
32. Ibid, § 289A.
33. Ibid., § 236.
34. Ibid.
35. Ibid.
36. Ibid., § 205.
37. G.W.F. Hegel, "Proceedings of the Estates Assembly of the Kingdom of Württemberg," in *Heidelberg Writings*, trans. Brady Bowman and Allen Speight (Cambridge: Cambridge University Press, [1815–1816] 2009), 43.
38. Hegel, *Philosophy of Right*, § 21.
39. Ibid., § 303.
40. Ibid., § 296.
41. Carl K. Shaw, "Hegel's Theory of Modern Bureaucracy," *American Political Science Review* 86, no. 2 (1992): 381–89, 385.
42. Hegel, *Philosophy of Right*, § 336 (translation modified by author).
43. Gertrude Lübbe-Wolf, "Hegels Staatsrecht als Stellungnahme im ersten preußischen Verfassungskampf," *Zeitschrift für philosophische Forschung* 35, no. 3/4 (1981): 476–501.
44. The *Preussisches Allgemeines Landrecht* combined both liberal rights protecting the individual against state interference, as well as provisions for social welfare to be provided by the state. This combination was criticized by classical liberal commentators. "In Prussia, the General Land Law of 1794 united public and private law in a comprehensive codification. But with it there appeared Schlosser's criticism, which held that the two were so different that they could not be summarized in a single legal code. The goal of private law consisted in justice alone. Public law, by contrast, pursued political goals. If the possibility could not be foreclosed that the statute would be used as a means for politics, then one must at least neatly separate private from public law, so that the reflection of absolute justice would not idealize and strengthen political law." Dieter Grimm, *Das Öffentliche Recht vor der Frage nach seiner Identität* (Tübingen: Mohr Siebeck, 2012), 14–15. Hegel would not have countenanced such a distinction between

"absolute justice" and "political laws." The idea of an absolute justice, standing apart from the laws implemented by the state, was a reflection on an unhistorical moral consciousness and the errors of the philosophy of natural law. Law protecting the rights of individuals, as well as those "political" laws regarding the structure of the state, and its provision for the material betterment of individuals, were reflections of an underlying ideal of individual self-determination within the context of a common social, political, and economic life. For this reason, Hegel was famously in disagreement with Savigny over the need to codify private law in statutory form. Hegel thought that civil law, no less than public law, was an expression of the state's function as the ultimate guarantor of freedom. All legal rules required the rationality, clarity, and universality provided by the statutory form.

45. Hegel, *Philosophy of Right*, 19n18 (editor's note); Daniel Lee, "The Legacy of Medieval Constitutionalism in the *Philosophy of Right*: Hegel and the Prussian Reform Movement," *History of Political Thought* 29, no. 4 (2008): 601–34. As Lee observes, Hegel departed from some strands of the reform movement in attempting to preserve a role for guilds or "corporations" within the modern state. However, these institutional differences do not put in doubt Hegel's deeper commitment to uprooting feudal conceptions of political authority, in which public power is seen as the personal property of aristocrats and monarchs. For the same reason, he rejected the model of the social contract, which he thought incorrectly transplanted conceptions of private law into the public realm. Hegel, *Philosophy of Right*, § 75.
46. Paul Nolte, *Staatsbildung als Gesellschaftsreform: Politische Reformen in Preußen und den süddeutschen Staaten 1800–1820* (Frankfurt-am-Main: Campus, 1990), 55.
47. Mack Walker, *German Home Towns: Community, State, and General Estate*, 1648–1871 (Ithaca, NY: Cornell University Press, 1971), 147–216, 197.
48. Otto Hintze, "The Formation of States and Constitutional Development: A Study in History and Politics," in *The Historical Essays of Otto Hintze*, ed. Felix Gilbert (Oxford: Oxford University Press, 1975), 157–77, 175.
49. Reinhart Koselleck, *Preußen zwischen Reform und Revolution: Allgemeines Landrecht, Verwaltung und soziale Bewegung von 1791 bis 1848* (Munich: Deutscher Taschenbuch Verlag, [1967] 1989), 263.
50. Ibid., 51.
51. Hintze, "Formation of States," 175–76.
52. Koselleck, *Preußen*, 384.
53. James J. Sheehan, *German History, 1770–1866* (Oxford: Clarendon Press, 1989), 620.
54. Michael Stolleis, *Konstitution und Intervention: Studien zur Geschichte des öffentliches Rechts im 19. Jahrhundert* (Frankfurt-am-Main: Suhrkamp, 2001), 259.
55. Ernst Forsthoff, *Der Staat der Industriegesellschaft* (Munich: C.H. Beck, 1971), 23 (author's translation).
56. Robert von Mohl, *Die Polizeiwissenschaft nach den Grundsätzen des Rechtsstaates*, vol. 1, 3rd. ed. (Tübingen: Verlag H. Laupp'schen, 1866), 19 (author's translation).
57. Ibid., 5–6.

58. Dieter Langewiesche, "Republik, konstitutionelle Monarchie und 'soziale Frage.' Grundprobleme der deutschen Revolution 1848/49," *Historische Zeitschrift* 230, no. 1 (1980): 529–48, 547.
59. Karl Marx, *Critique of Hegel's 'Philosophy of Right'*, trans. Annette Jolin and Joseph O'Malley (Cambridge: Cambridge University Press, 1970), 77.
60. Ibid., 116.
61. Ibid., 119.
62. Ibid., 119.
63. Hegel, *Philosophy of Right*, § 280A (emphasis added).
64. "In the Frankfurt Parliament of 1848, 68 percent of all deputies were civil servants or other officials." Eric Hobsbawm, *The Age of Revolution: 1789–1848* (New York: Vintage, 1962), 192. Koselleck argues that "The great number of leading public officials in the Prussian National Assembly was . . . the last sign of an estate-state form of rule, which had reached its end, but remained deeply rooted in the social constitution. . . . The last President of the Prussian National Assembly, von Unruh, and the last Ministerial President in Frankfurt, Grävel, had both been Prussian government advisors, who in the *Vormärz* had quit their positions because of their liberal attitudes. They were not able to obtain in the revolution what they had striven for as administrators. Neither the attempt to remove all exemptions succeeded, nor did they succeed in their effort to disempower the aristocracy by expanding the state or the civil self-administration beyond the county and community level. Even the most modest demands, on which all delegates agreed despite the disputed questions concerning the new constitutional forms, were choked off by the counter-revolution. The administrative organization outlived the revolution, but since 1848 became more 'party-politically controlled,' and indeed not by liberals, but rather by conservatives, because of whom types such as Unruh or Grävel had abandoned the administrative class." Koselleck, *Preußen*, 396–97.
65. Peter Badura, *Staatsrecht: Systematische Erläuterung des Grundgesetz für die Bundesrepublik Deutschland* (Munich: C.H. Beck, 1986) § 24, p. 23.
66. Michael Stolleis, "Entwicklungsstufen der Verwaltungsrechtswissenschaft," in Wolfgang Hoffman-Riem, Eberhard Schmidt-Aßmann, and Andreas Voßkuhle, eds., *Grundlagen des Verwaltungsrechts* (Munich: C.H. Beck, 2006), para. 38.
67. Badura, *Staatsrecht*, § 26, p. 25.
68. Dieter Grimm, "Proportionality in Canadian and German Constitutional Jurisprudence," *University of Toronto Law Journal* 57, no. 2 (2007): 383–97, 384–85.
69. Peter Badura, *Das Verwaltungsrecht der liberalen Rechtsstaates* (Göttingen: Verlag Otto Schwarz, 1967), 18–25.
70. Peter C. Caldwell, *Popular Sovereignty and the Crisis of German Constitutional Law: The Theory and Practice of Weimar Constitutionalism* (Durham, NC: Duke University Press, 1997), 23.
71. Hajo Holborn, *A History of Modern Germany, 1840–1945* (Princeton, NJ: Princeton University Press, 1969), 108.
72. Fritz Stern, *Gold and Iron: Bismarck, Bleichröder, and the Building of the German Empire* (New York: Random House, 1977), 217–20.
73. Michael Stolleis, *Public Law in Germany, 1800–1914* (New York: Berghahn Books, 2001), 380.

74. The connections and differences between Hegel and Stein's conception of the state are explored in Stephan Koslowski, *Die Geburt des Sozialstaats aus dem Geist des deutschen Idealismus: Person und Gemeinschaft bei Lorenz von Stein* (Weinheim: VCH, Acta Humaniora, 1989). Koslowski argues that "Lorenz von Stein's apparently very Hegelian concept of the state takes up without much modification the fundamental concerns of Hegel's philosophy of law—to mediate the freedom of the individual with the substantial reason of the ideal of universal ethical life which appears in the state—so that one can easily overlook the independent foundations of the personal-state idea of Lorenz von Stein. . . . In place of Hegel's idea of the self-realizing absolute freedom or the freedom of the absolute in the state, personal freedom according to Stein refers to finite subjects, whose 'final end' does not lie in their sublation (*Aufhebung*) into the state, but rather the realization of the self-determination of the individual, which cannot be further determined." Ibid., 88–89 (author's translation).
75. Schmitt, *Constitutional Theory*, 62.
76. Lorenz von Stein, *Handbuch der Verwaltungslehre und des Verwaltungsrechts*, ed. Utz Schliesky (Tübingen: Mohr Siebeck, [1870] 2010), 6 (author's translation).
77. Lorenz von Stein, *Verwaltungslehre*, 1st ed. (1865), 78, quoted in Carl Schmitt, *Constitutional Theory*, 183.
78. Stein, *Handbuch der Verwaltungslehre*, 379.
79. Ibid.
80. Ernst-Wolfgang Böckenförde, "Lorenz von Stein als Theoretiker der Bewegung von Staat und Gesellschaft zum Sozialstaat," in *Lorenz von Stein: Gesellschaft-Staat-Recht*, ed. Ernst Forsthoff (Frankfurt-am-Main: Propyläen, 1972), 513–48, 514 (author's translation).
81. Stein, *Handbuch der Verwaltungslehre*, 16.
82. Badura, *Verwaltungsrecht des liberalen Rechtsstaates*, 13 (author's translation).
83. Gustav Schmoller, *Die Soziale Frage: Klassenbildung, Arbeiterfrage, Klassenkampf* (Munich: Leipzig: Duncker & Humblot, 1918), 648.
84. Rudolf Gneist, *Der Rechtsstaat und die Verwaltungsgerichte in Deutschland* (Berlin: Springer, 1879), 28.
85. Ibid., 34.
86. Ibid., 31.
87. Ibid., 271.
88. Stolleis, *Public Law in Germany*, 378–39.
89. Mahendra P. Singh, *German Administrative Law in Common Law Perspective* (Berlin: Springer, 2001), 23.
90. Ernst-Wolfgang Böckenförde, "The Origin and Development of the Concept of the *Rechtsstaat*," in *State, Society and Liberty: Studies in Political Theory and Constitutional Law* (New York: St. Martins, 1991), 55–56.
91. Gneist, *Der Rechtsstaat*, 286; Bernd Wunder, "Verwaltung, Amt, Beamter," in *Geschichtliche Grundbegriffe: Historisches Lexikon zur politisch-sozialen Sprache in Deutschland*, vol. 7, ed. Otto Brünner, Werner Conze, and Reinhart Koselleck (Stuttgart: Klett-Cotta, 1992), 84.
92. Gneist, *Der Rechtsstaat*, 317.

93. Otto Mayer, *Deutsches Verwaltungsrechts*, vol. 1, 1st ed. (Leipzig: Duncker & Humblot, 1896). See Dieter Grimm, *Recht und Staat der Bürgerlichen Gesellschaft* (Frankfurt-am-Main: Suhrkamp, 1987), 336; Armin von Bogdandy and Peter Huber, "Staat, Verwaltung, Verwaltungsrecht: Deutschland," in *Handbuch Ius Publicum Europaeum Band III, Verwaltungsrecht in Europa, Grundlagen*, ed. Armin von Bogdandy, Sabino Cassese, and Peter M. Huber (Heidelberg: C.F. Müller, 2010), 33–81, 52–56.
94. Triepel lists Otto Mayer alongside Romeo Maurenbrecher, Johann Stephan Pütter, August Wilhelm Heffer, and Carl Viktor Fricker as public law scholars influenced by Hegel. Triepel, "Law of the State and Politics," 183.
95. Otto Mayer, *Deutsches Verwaltungsrecht*, vol. 1, 2nd ed. (Munich: Leipzig, 1914), viii, quoted in Erk Volkmar Heyen, "Positivistische Staatsrechtslehre und politische Philosophie. Zur philosophischen Bildung Otto Mayers," *Quaderni Fiorentini* 8 (1979): 275–305, 280 (author's translation).
96. Otto Mayer, *Deutsches Verwaltungsrechts*, vol. 1, 1st ed. (Leipzig: Duncker & Humblot, 1896), 1 (author's translation).
97. Ibid., 14.
98. Ibid., 247.
99. Badura, *Das Verwaltungsrecht des liberalen Rechtsstaates*, 38.
100. Ibid., 19–20.
101. Ibid., 25.
102. See Georg Jellinek, *System der subjektiven öffentlichen Rechte* (Tübingen: J.C.B. Mohr [Paul Siebeck], 1905), 12–18.
103. While this understanding was positivist, in the sense that it sought to reconstruct an internally consistent system of legal norms, it betrayed a constitutional prioritization of the monarchical executive against the legislature and of the state against any external criteria of morality or justice. As Christoph Möllers notes, "in fact the theory enabled a historical and systematic prioritization of the monarchical bureaucracy against popular representation. . . . It is the monarchical administration, as the acting organ of the power state, which undertakes the act of self-obligation of the state and thus enables its juridification." Christoph Möllers, *Staat als Argument* (Munich: C.H. Beck, 2000), 19 (author's translation.).
104. On the relationship between Weber and Jellinek, see Guenther Roth, introduction to *Economy and Society*, trans. and ed. Guenther Roth and Claus Wittich (Berkeley: University of California Press, [1968] 1978), lxxxix.
105. Weber, *Economy and Society*, 217–18.
106. Ibid., 215.
107. Talcott Parsons, *Sociological Theory and Modern Society* (New York: Free Press, 1967), 94.
108. Weber, *Economy and Society*, 85, 657.
109. Ibid., 221.
110. Ibid., 225.
111. Ibid.
112. Wolfgang Mommsen, "Max Weber's Political Sociology and His Philosophy of World History," *International Social Science Journal* 17, no. 1 (1965): 23–45.

113. Weber, *Economy and Society*, 223.
114. Ibid., 987.
115. See Sheldon Wolin, "Democracy and the Welfare State: The Political and Theoretical Connections between *Staatsräson* and *Wohlfahrtstaatsräson*," *Political Theory* 15, no. 4 (1987): 467–500.
116. Otto Mayer, *Deutsches Verwaltungsrechts*, 3rd ed. (1923), foreword.
117. The Constitution of the German Empire of 1919, art. 7, 9, 109.
118. Michael Stolleis, *History of Social Law in Germany*, trans. Thomas Dunlap (Heidelberg: Springer, 2013), 95–134.
119. Franz L. Neumann, "Rechtsstaat, Gewaltenteilung, und Demokratie," in *Wirtschaft, Staat, Demokratie, Aufsätze, 1930–1954*, ed. Alfons Söllner (Frankfurt-am-Main: Suhrkamp, 1978), 124–33, 130. On Franz Neumann's critique of Max Weber's sociology of the *Rechtsstaat*, see William E. Scheuerman, *Between the Norm and the Exception: The Frankfurt School and the Rule of Law* (Cambridge, MA: MIT Press, 1994), 101–112.
120. Peter L. Lindseth, "The Paradox of Parliamentary Supremacy: Delegation, Democracy, and Dictatorship in Germany and France, 1920s–1950s," *Yale Law Journal* 113, no. 7 (2004), 1341–1415, 1361–72; Franz L. Neumann, "Der Niedergang der deutschen Demokratie," in *Wirtschaft, Staat, Demokratie, Aufsätze, 1930–1954*, ed. Alfons Söllner (Frankfurt-am-Main: Suhrkamp, 1978), 103–23, 112–13.
121. Karl Dietrich Bracher, *Die Auflösung der Weimarer Republik* (Düsseldorf: Droste Verlag, 1984), 165–66 (author's translation).
122. Max Weber, "Parliament and Government in a Reconstructed Germany" (1918), in *Economy and Society*, 1381–462, 1404.
123. Ibid.
124. Ibid.
125. Max Weber, "Politics as a Vocation," in *From Max Weber: Essays in Sociology*, trans. and ed. H.H. Girth and C. Wright Mills (New York: Oxford University Press, 1946), 77–128, 95.
126. Weber's concern to imbue the formal rational state with charismatic authority informed his influential proposals for the Weimar Constitution, published in the *Frankfurter Zeitung* in 1918. Weber called for a bicameral parliament led by a chancellor, the primary functions of which would be legislation, bureaucratic oversight, and the cultivation of political leadership for the post of president. This president would be popularly elected, with the power to appoint head ministers, to dissolve the lower house, to issue suspensive vetoes of legislative, and to intervene in legislative affairs through popular referenda. Parliamentary and presidential control of the bureaucracy could, he thought, prevent the stultifying effects of bureaucratic rule. Wolfgang Mommsen, *Max Weber and German Politics, 1890–1920*, trans. Michael S. Steinberg (Chicago: University of Chicago Press, [1959] 1984), 332–46.
127. Weber, "Politics as a Vocation," 152.
128. While deeply influenced by Nietzsche in his commitment to a form of aristocratic individualism, Weber departed from him in believing that the will to power worked with, not against, the masses, via charismatic authority. See Mommsen,

"Max Weber's Political Sociology," 37 and Robert Eden, *Political Leadership and Nihilism: A Study of Weber and Nietzsche* (Tampa: University Presses of Florida, 1983), 51, 53. Friedrich Nietzsche, *The Genealogy of Morals*, trans. Horace B. Samuel (New York: Boni and Liveright, 1918), 43. As Mark E. Warren argues in his analysis of this passage, "Weber politicizes Nietzsche's emphasis on responsibility by arguing for an 'ethics of responsibility,' an ethic that describes the rationality of an ideal political actor." Mark E. Warren, "Nietzsche and Weber: When Does Reason Become Power?" in *The Barbarism of Reason: Max Weber and the Twilight of Enlightenment*, ed. Asher Horowitz and Terry Maley (Toronto: University of Toronto Press, 1994), 68–90, 74.

129. Jürgen Habermas, "Discussion of Talcott Parsons' 'Value Freedom and Objectivity,'" in *Max Weber and Sociology Today*, ed. Otto Stammer, trans. Kathleen Morris (Oxford: Blackwell, 1971), 66. On Schmitt's effort to "radicalize[]" Weber's account of legitimacy, see Scheuerman, *Between the Norm and the Exception*, 78–9.

130. Schmitt, *Constitutional Theory*, 77.

131. See David Dyzenhaus, *Legality and Legitimacy: Carl Schmitt, Hans Kelsen and Hermann Heller in Weimar* (Oxford: Oxford University Press, 1997), 70–84.

132. Carl Schmitt, *Legality and Legitimacy*, trans. Jeffrey Seitzer (Durham, NC: Duke University Press, 2004), 93.

133. Carl Schmitt, *The Concept of the Political*, trans. George Schwab (Chicago: University of Chicago Press, [1932] 2007), 26.

134. Schmitt, *Legality and Legitimacy*, 14.

135. Ibid., 21.

136. "While the ordinary legislature of the parliamentary legislative state is only permitted to pass statutes and, according to the nature of the legislative state, is separated from the apparatus of applying the law, the extraordinary lawmaker of article 48 is able to confer on every individual measure he issues the character of a statute, with the entire priority that the statute unquestionably has in the parliamentary legislative state." Ibid., 70.

137. Ernst Forsthoff, *Der totale Staat*, 2nd ed. (Hamburg: Hanseatische Verlagsanstalt, 1935), 35 (author's translation).

138. Ibid., 45.

139. Karl Popper, *The Open Society and Its Enemies. Volume 2: Hegel and Marx* (New York: Routledge, [1945] 2003).

140. Franz Neumann, *Behemoth: The Structure and Practice of National Socialism* (New York: Oxford University Press, 1942), 78.

141. For the leading intellectual history on the origins of National Socialist ideology, see Fritz Stern, *The Politics of Cultural Despair:Aa Study in the Rise of the Germanic Ideology* (Berkeley: University of California Press, 1974).

142. See Hannah Arendt, *The Origins of Totalitarianism* (Boston: Houghton Mifflin Harcourt, 1973).

143. Basic Law for the Federal Republic of Germany, art. 20, par. 1.

144. Thursten Kingreen, "Rule of Law versus Welfare State," in *Debates in German Public Law*, ed. Hermann Pünder and Christian Waldhoff (Oxford: Hart, 2014), 95–115, 101.

145. Ernst Forsthoff, "Begriff und Wesen des sozialen Rechtsstaates," *Veröffentlichungen der Vereinigung der deutschen Staatsrechtslehrer*, 12 (1954), 8–36, 18 (author's translation).
146. Ibid., 19.
147. Wolfgang Abendroth, "Zum Begriff des demokratischen und sozialen Rechtsstaates im Grundgesetz der Bundesrepublik Deutschland," in *Rechtsstaatlichkeit und Sozialstaatlichkeit*, ed. Ernst Forsthoff (Darmstadt: Wissenschaftliche Buchgesellschaft, 1968), 114–44, 140 (author's translation).
148. Ibid., 119.
149. Ibid., 141–42.
150. Ibid., 125.
151. Fritz Werner, "Verwaltungsrecht als konkretisiertes Verfassungsrecht," *Deutsches Verwaltungsblatt*, 74 (1959): 527–33.
152. Ibid., 531.
153. Ibid., 532.
154. Rainer Wahl, *Herausforderungen und Antworten: Das Öffentliche Recht der letzten fünf Jahrzehnte* (Berlin: De Gruyter Recht, 2006), 37.
155. Christoph Möllers, "Scope and Legitimacy of Judicial Review in German Constitutional Law—The Court versus the Political Process," in *Debates in German Public Law*, ed. Hermann Pünder and Christian Waldhoff (Oxford: Hart, 2014), 3–27, 5.
156. Theodor Maunz and Reinhold Zippelius, *Deutsches Staatsrecht*, 30th ed., vol. 1 (Munich: C.H. Beck'schen Verlag, 1998) § 13.1, p. 93.
157. Basic Law, art. 80, para. 1; Claus Dieter Classen, "Gesetzvorbehalt und dritte Gewalt," *Juristen Zeitung* 58, no. 14 (2003): 693–701, 695.
158. Basic Law, art. 20, par. 2; Eberhardt Schmidt-Aßmann, "Verwaltungslegitimation als Rechtsbegriff," *Archiv des öffentlichen Rechts* 116, no. 3 (1991), 329–90, 349 ("the people, in the sense of Art. 20, Par. 2 of the Basic Law, does not mean an always identifiable group affected by state authority. Rather, what is meant is the constituted aggregate of persons [*Personengesamtheit*]. . . . Forms of participation, which are often found in administrative decisions, may facilitate the acceptance of decisions . . . but they do not mediate democratic legitimation, rather they can impair the elements of legitimation required by Art. 20, Par. 2") (author's translation).
159. Ernst-Wolfgang Böckenförde, "Demokratie als Verfassungsprinzip," in *Staat, Verfassung, Demokratie* (Frankfurt-am-Main: Suhrkamp, 1987), 289–378, 315.
160. Daniel Halberstam, "The Promise of Comparative Administrative Law: A Constitutional Perspective on Administrative Agencies," in *Comparative Administrative Law*, ed. Susan Rose Ackerman and Peter L. Lindseth (Cheltenham, UK: Edward Elgar, 2010), 185–205.
161. E.g., Lippeverband, 107 *Entscheidungen des Bundesverfassungsgerichts* (BVerfGE) 59 (German Federal Constitutional Court Dec. 5, 2002). For scholarly commentary, see Hans-Heinrich Trute, "Die demokratische Legitimation der Verwaltung," in *Grundlagen der Verwaltungsrechts*, vol. 1, 2nd ed. (Munich: C.H. Beck, 2012), 341–435; Matthias Jestaedt, "Democratic Legitimization of the Administrative Power—Exclusive versus Inclusive Democracy," in *Debates in German Public Law*, ed. Herman Pünder and Christian Waldhoff (Oxford: Hart, 2014), 181–203.

162. Jan Ross, "Hegel der Bundesrepublik," *Die Zeit* (October 11, 2001), https://www.zeit.de/2001/42/Hegel_der_Bundesrepublik.
163. Habermas, *Structural Transformation*, 222–35. See also Ernst Forsthoff, *Der Staat der Industriegesellschaft* (München: Verlag C.H. Beck, 1971).
164. Jürgen Habermas, *Legitimation Crisis*, trans. Thomas McCarthy (Boston: Beacon Press, 1975), 105.
165. Ibid., 70.
166. Jürgen Habermas, *A Theory of Communicative Action: Volume 2, A Critique of Functionalist Reason*, trans. Thomas McCarthy (Boston: Beacon Press, 1982), 365.
167. Habermas, *Between Facts and Norms*, 168.
168. Ibid., 306.
169. Ibid., 171–304.
170. Ibid., 192.
171. Ibid., 440.
172. Ibid.
173. Ibid., 191, quoting Jerry Mashaw, *Due Process in the Administrative State* (New Haven, CT: Yale University Press, 185), 26.
174. Hegel, *Philosophy of Right*, 21.
175. G.W.F. Hegel, *Introduction to the Philosophy of History*, trans. Leo Rauch (Indianapolis: Hackett, 1988), 90.

Chapter 2

1. Jerry L. Mashaw, *Creating the Administrative Constitution: The Lost One Hundred Years of American Administrative Law* (New Haven, CT: Yale University Press, 2012), 29–226; William J. Novak, *The People's Welfare: Law and Regulation in Nineteenth Century America* (Durham: University of North Carolina Press, 1996).
2. Michael Les Benedict, "Laissez-Faire and Liberty: A Re-evaluation of the Meaning and Origins of Laissez Faire Constitutionalism," *Law and History Review* 3, no. 2 (1985), 293–331; Julie Novkov, *Constituting Workers, Protecting Women: Gender, Law, and Labor in the Progressive Era and New Deal Years* (Ann Arbor: University of Michigan Press, 2001), 37–75.
3. Louis Hartz, *The Liberal Tradition in American: An Interpretation of American Political Thought since the Revolution* (New York: Harcourt, 1955), 3–34, 228–58.
4. Daniel T. Rogers, *Atlantic Crossings: Social Politics in a Progressive Age* (Cambridge, MA: Harvard University Press, 1998), 33.
5. Sylvia Fries, "*Staatstheorie* and the New American Science of Politics," *Journal of the History of Ideas* 34, no. 3 (1973): 391–404, 391 (describing W.W. Willoughby and John Burgess's adoption of nineteenth-century German public law's "postulates of organicism and process essential to Hegelian metaphysics, as well as the fundamental tenet of transcendentalism—that reality is ultimately spiritual"); Thomas I. Cook and Arnaud B. Leavelle, "German Idealism and American Theories of Democratic Community," *Journal of Politics* 5, no. 3 (1943): 213–36, 222 (showing that "German Idealism is . . . a recessive in American political and social thought, yet the traces of its influence in this country are many and

significant," including in the writings of Francis Lieber, Walt Whitman, W.T. Harris, Dewey, Dwight Woolsey, Burgess, and Willoughby); Morton G. White, "The Revolt against Formalism in the Social Thought of the Twentieth Century," *Journal of The History of Ideas* 8, no. 2 (1947): 131–52, 139 (noting how "Hegel provided [Dewey] with the concept of a universal consciousness which embraced everything and which provided the link between individual consciousness and the objects of knowledge. . . . The *objective mind* of idealism was made central."); Axel A. Schäfer, *American Progressives and German Social Reform, 1875–1920* (Stuttgart: Franz Steiner, 2000), 37–77 (arguing that American progressives such as Richard Ely, Simon Patten, W.E.B. Du Bois, Florence Kelley, and Dewey were influenced by Gustav Schmoller and the German historical school's "romanticism, Hegelian Idealism, and nineteenth century faith in progress"); Eldon Eisenach, "Progressivism as a National Narrative in Biblical Hegelian Time," *Social Philosophy and Policy* 24, no. 1 (2007): 55–83, 58 (arguing that Lyman Abbot, Albion Small, and Simon Patten attempted to develop a national narrative "grounded in Protestant evangelical theology and Hegelian philosophy, seeing the structural changes in American social and economic life as signs of an emerging morality and spirit that would lead to the reconstruction of American society.").

6. Hegel, *Philosophy of Right*, § 260.
7. Richard T. Ely, "Report of the Organization of the American Economic Association," *American Economic Review* 1, no. 1 (1886): 5–46, 6 quoted in Nancy Cohen, *The Reconstruction of American Liberalism, 1895–1914* (Charlotte: University of North Carolina Press, 2002), 165.
8. Friedrich A. Hayek, *The Road to Serfdom* (Chicago: University of Chicago Press, [1944] 2007), 74 (After 1870, "Germany became the center from which ideas destined to govern the world in the twentieth century spread east and west. Whether it was Hegel or Marx, List or Schmoller, Sombart or Mannheim, whether it was socialism in its more radical form or merely 'organization' or 'planning' of a less radical kind, German ideas were everywhere readily imported and German institutions imitated."); Hamburger, *Is Administrative Law Unlawful?*, 447–78 (arguing that Progressive legal theorists developed American administrative law from continental civil law, and particularly Hegelian conceptions of the *Rechtsstaat*). See also Miller, "Freedom, History, and Race," 221 (arguing that "the Progressives rejected the Founders' understanding of equality in favor of a new conception of freedom inspired by German idealism," which went hand in hand with ideologies of racial hierarchy and state paternalism); Pestritto, "The Progressive Origins of the Administrative State," 54 (attributing to Woodrow Wilson's Progressive adaptation of Hegelian ideas "the two pillars of today's liberal state: unelected judges who make law through constitutional interpretation, and unelected bureaucrats to whom significant policymaking power is delegated on the basis of their expertise"); Kesler, *I Am the Change: Barack Obama and the Future of Liberalism* 57, 236 (arguing that Hegel "laid the deepest underpinnings for modern American liberalism," which Kesler understands to have betrayed America's core constitutional values in favor of a fiscally and morally irresponsible "cult of the State."); see also Yarbrough, *Theodore Roosevelt and American Political Thought*, 6 (arguing that "it

was impossible to reconcile" John Burgess and Theodore Roosevelt's Hegelian views of freedom, history, and the state with "the political thought of the founders.")

9. Serious engagement with the Hegelian content of Progressivism must avoid the tendency toward caricature from which many of these polemics suffer. For example, it is not true, as Pestritto claims, that for Hegel, "there can be no principled universal notion of liberty or rights." Pestritto, *Woodrow Wilson and the Roots of Modern Liberalism*, 16–17. The *Philosophy of Right* deduces both liberal rights and the welfare state from the fundamental premise that "the will is free." Hegel, *Philosophy of Right*, §§ 3–4. Hamburger, similarly, ignores the constitutional structure Hegel elaborated when he asserts that his state would "govern through an administrative class." Hamburger, *Is Administrative Law Unlawful?*, 448. Hegel was indeed skeptical of popular government. But he nonetheless maintained that an elected legislature "has the power to determine and establish the universal" by enacting law, and that such statutes must govern administrative officials, who would apply their general rules to particular cases. Hegel, *Philosophy of Right*, §§ 273, 289–299.
10. Richard T. Hofstadter, *The Age of Reform: From Bryan to FDR* (New York: Alfred A. Knopf, 1955), 233 ("Since it has been common in recent years for ideologists of the extreme right to portray the growth of statism as the result of a sinister conspiracy of collectivists inspired by foreign ideologies, it is perhaps worth emphasizing that the first important steps toward the modern organization of society were taken by arch-individualists—the tycoons of the Gilded Age—and that the primitive beginning of modern statism was largely the work of men who were trying to save what they could of the eminently native Yankee values of individualism and enterprise.").
11. Kloppenberg, *Uncertain Victory*, 51; Marc Stears, *Progressives, Pluralists, and the Problems of the State: Ideologies of Reform in the United States and Britain, 1906–1926* (Oxford: Oxford University Press, 2002), 35.
12. Stephen B. Smith, *Hegel's Critique of Liberalism: Rights in Context* (Chicago: University of Chicago Press, 1989), 65–85, 103–14.
13. Herbert Croly, *Progressive Democracy* (New York: Macmillan, 1915), 353.
14. Robert Harrison, *Congress, Progressive Reform, the New American State* (Cambridge: Cambridge University Press, 2004), 44.
15. Robert H. Wiebe, *The Search for Order, 1877–1920* (New York: Farrar, Strauss, and Giroux, 1967), 12, 160.
16. Croly, *Progressive Democracy*, 373.
17. E.g., Mashaw, *Bureaucratic Justice*, 27.
18. E.g., Morton J. Horwitz, *The Transformation of American Law 1870-1960* (New York: Oxford University Press, 1992), 224–25; Marone, *The Democratic Wish*, 115–19.
19. Posner and Vermeule, *The Executive Unbound*, 3–18.
20. Vermeule, "Our Schmittian Administrative Law," 1095–149.
21. E.g., Eldon Eisenach, *The Lost Promise of Progressivism* (Lawrence: University of Kansas Press, 1994), 77–80.
22. William N. Novak, "The Legal Origins of the Modern American State," in *Looking Back at Law's Century*, ed. Austin Sarat, Bryant Garther, and Robert A. Kagan (Ithaca, NY: Cornell University Press, 2002), 260–72, 249–83.

23. Seminally, Richard B. Stewart, "The Reformation of American Administrative Law," *Harvard Law Review* 88, no. 8 (1975): 1667–813.
24. Rahman, *Democracy Against Domination*, 54–77.
25. See Eileen L. McDonagh, "The 'Welfare Rights State' and the 'Civil Rights State': Policy Paradox and State Building in the Progressive Era," *Studies in American Political Development* 7, no. 2 (1993): 225–74.
26. E.g, Richard A. Epstein, *How Progressives Rewrote the Constitution* (Washington, DC: Cato, 2006); Paul D. Moreno, *The American State from the Civil War to the New Deal: The Twilight of Constitutionalism and the Triumph of Progressivism* (Cambridge: Cambridge University Press, 2013).
27. Jeremy K. Kessler, "The Administrative Origins of Modern Civil Liberties Law," *Columbia Law Review* 14, no. 5 (2014): 1083–166; Karen M. Tani, *States of Dependency: Welfare, Rights, and American Governance* (Cambridge: Cambridge University Press, 2016); Novak, "The Legal Origins of the Modern American State," 264–65.
28. Honneth, *Freedom's Right*, 42–62.
29. Robert Gooding-Williams, "Philosophy of History and Social Critique in *The Souls of Black Folk*," *Social Science Information* 26, no. 1 (1987): 99–114, 105; Shamoon Zamir, *Dark Voices: W.E.B. Du Bois and American Thought, 1888–1903*, (Chicago: The University of Chicago Press, 1995), 114.
30. W.E.B. Du Bois, *The Souls of Black Folk* (New York: Penguin, [1903] 1989), 5.
31. Du Bois, *Souls of Black Folk*, 6–10; Robert Gooding-Williams, *In the Shadow of Du Bois: Afro-Modern Political Thought in America* (Cambridge, MA: Harvard University Press, 2009), 19–66.
32. Hegel, *Phenomenology of Spirit*, 116.
33. Hegel, *Philosophy of Right*, § 57A.
34. Herbert Aptheker, ed., *The Correspondence of W.E.B. Du Bois*, vol. 1 (Amherst: University of Massachusetts Press, 1973), 21. On the influence of Schmoller on Du Bois, see Gooding-Williams, *In the Shadow of Du Bois*, 19–66. As Paul Gottfried notes, Schmoller himself was influenced by Hegel in seeing an ethically oriented state bureaucracy as a means to address the antagonisms produced by conflict in civil society. Paul Gottfried, "Adam Smith and German Political Thought," *Modern Age* (Spring 1977): 146–52, 151.
35. Kenneth D. Barkin, "'Berlin Days,' 1892-1894: W.E.B. Du Bois and German Political Economy," *Boundary 2*, 27 no. 4 (2000: 79–101, 84, 88.
36. Aldon A. Morris, *The Scholar Denied: W. E. B. Du Bois and the Birth of Modern Sociology* (Berkeley, CA: University of California Press, 2015), 150.
37. An Act to Establish a Bureau for the Relief of Freedmen and Refugees, ch. 90, 13 Stat. 507 (1865).
38. John M. Bickers, "The Power to Do What Manifestly Must Be Done: Congress, the Freedmen's Bureau, and Constitutional Imagination," *Roger Williams University Law Review* 12, no. 70 (2017): 70–120, 85–87.
39. United States Bureau of Refugees, Freedmen, and Abandoned Lands. Circular No. 2 (May 19, 1865). Quoted in Bureau of Refugees, Freedmen, and Abandoned Lands, Fifth Semi-Annual Report on Schools for Freedmen, January 1, 1868, by J.W. Alvord (Washington, DC: U.S. Government Printing Office, 1868), 6.

40. Act of July 16, 1866 §§ 12, 13, ch. 200, 14 Stat. 173, 174 (1866).
41. Ibid., § 14; Amalia D. Kessler, *Inventing American Exceptionalism: The Origins of American Adversarial Legal Culture, 1800–1877* (New Haven, CT: Yale University Press, 2017), 263–322.
42. E.g., William Archibald Dunning, *Reconstruction: Political and Economic, 1865–1877* (New York: London: Harpers, 1907), 30–34. On Dunning and Du Bois, see David Levering Lewis, *W.E.B. Du Bois: The Fight for Equality in the American Century, 1919–1963* (New York: Henry Holt, 2000), 354..
43. Du Bois, *Souls of Black Folk*, 14.
44. Ibid., 21.
45. As a historical matter, Du Bois's description of the Freedmen's Bureau is neither the most negative nor the most positive. Compare John Cox and LaWanda Cox, "General O.O. Howard and the 'Misrepresented Bureau,'" *The Journal of Southern History* 19, no. 4 (1953): 427–56 with William S. McFeely, *Yankee Stepfather: General O.O. Howard and the Freedmen* (New York: W.W. Norton, [1968] 1994).
46. Du Bois, *Souls of Black Folk*, 31.
47. Mark A. Graber, "The Second Freedmen's Bureau Bill's Constitution," *Texas Law Review* 94, no. 7 (2016): 1361–402, 1367–68.
48. Ibid., 1384.
49. Melvin Rogers, "The People, Rhetoric, and Affect: On the Political Force of Du Bois' *The Souls of Black Folk*," *American Political Science Review* 106, no. 1 (2012): 188–203.
50. W.E.B. Du Bois, *The Philadelphia Negro: A Social Study* (Philadelphia: University of Pennsylvania Press, 1899), 395.
51. Ibid., 393.
52. Gregory P. Downs, *After Appomattox: Military Occupation and the Ends of War* (Cambridge, MA: Harvard University Press, 2015), 46–47, 121–22, 131–32.
53. Eric Foner, *Reconstruction: America's Unfinished Revolution, 1863–1877* (New York: Harper & Row 1988), 69–71, 153–70.
54. Chad Alan Goldberg, *Citizens and Paupers: Relief, Rights, and Race from the Freedmen's Bureau to Workfare* (Chicago: London: University of Chicago Press, 2007), 31–75.
55. W.E.B. Du Bois, *Black Reconstruction in America, 1860–1880* (New York: Free Press, [1935] 1998), 219.
56. W.E.B. Du Bois, "Federal Action Programs and Community Action in the South," *Social Forces* 19, no. 3 (1941): 375–80, 375.
57. Du Bois, *Black Reconstruction*, 708.
58. Ibid.
59. Eisenach argues that Wilson was not a true Progressive, given his conservative stances on constitutional issues such as the separation of powers, the judiciary, and the rule of law, as well as his defense of the party apparatus. Eisenach, *The Lost Promise of Progressivism*, 122–29. I present Wilson within the pantheon of Hegelian Progressives because of his pathbreaking work on administration, his roots in the Hegelian public law tradition, and his views on democratic influence in the administrative process, which were shared by Follett and Dewey. It is true that Wilson, particularly in *Constitutional Government in the United States*,

took some relatively conservative views about federalism, limited government, and judicial review. But he nonetheless adapted this perspective to Progressive conceptions of individual right. In this respect, Wilson's thought shows how elements of classical liberal constitutionalism and Progressivism can be brought into alignment.

60. Fritz Sager and Christian Rosser, "Weber, Wilson, and Hegel: Theories of Modern Bureaucracy," *Public Administration Review* 69, no. 6 (2009): 1136–47, 1143.
61. Dwight Waldo, *The Administrative State: A Study of the Political Theory of American Public Administration* (New Brunswick, NJ: Transaction, [1948] 2007), 91.
62. Pendleton Civil Service Reform Act, ch. 27, 22 Stat. 403 (1883).
63. Patricia Wallace Ingraham, *The Foundation of Merit: Public Service in American Democracy* (Baltimore: The Johns Hopkins University Press, 1995), 28.
64. Woodrow Wilson, "The Study of Administration," *Political Science Quarterly* 2, no. 2 (1887): 197–222.
65. Miewald, "The German Tradition and the Organic State," 19–20.
66. Wilson, "The Study of Administration," 198–99.
67. Ibid., 200.
68. In *The State*, Wilson elaborated on some of the functions social legislation can perform in industrial society: "By forbidding child labor, by supervising sanitary conditions of factories, by limiting the employment of women in occupations hurtful to their health, by instituting official tests of the purity or quality of goods sold, by limiting hours of labor in certain trades, by a hundred and one limitations of the power of unscrupulous and heartless men to out-do the scrupulous and merciful in trade or industry, government has assisted equity." Woodrow Wilson, *The State: Elements of Historical and Practical Politics* (Boston: D.C. Heath, [1898] 1901), 636.
69. Wilson, "The Study of Administration," 201.
70. Sager and Rosser, "Weber, Wilson, and Hegel," 1141n.10.
71. Lorenz von Stein, *Die Verwaltungslehre. Zweiter Theil. Die Lehre von Innern Verwaltung* (Stuttgart: J.G. Cotta'schen, 1866), 10 (author's translation).
72. Wilson, "The Study of Administration," 209–10.
73. Ibid., 217.
74. Ibid., 210.
75. Ibid., 212.
76. Wilson, *The State*, 576.
77. Woodrow Wilson, "The Modern Democratic State," in *The Papers of Woodrow Wilson, 1885–1888*, vol. 5, ed. Arthur S. Link (Princeton, NJ: Princeton University Press, 1969), 61–92, 74.
78. Jessica Blatt, *Race and the Making of American Political Science* (Philadelphia: University of Pennsylvania Press, 2018), 13–34.
79. Arthur S. Link, *Woodrow Wilson and the Progressive Era, 1910–1917* (New York: Harper, 1964), 63–66.
80. "Another Open Letter to President Wilson," *The Crisis* 6, no. 5 (Sept. 1913), 232–36, 233.
81. Ibid.

82. On the tension between these two aspects of democracy—"majority rule" and "equal self-determination"—see Robert A. Burt, *The Constitution in Conflict* (Cambridge, MA: Harvard University Press, 1992), 29, 81.
83. Wilson, "The Modern Democratic State," 74.
84. Woodrow Wilson, "Notes on Administration," in *The Papers of Woodrow Wilson, 1885–1888*, vol. 5, ed. Arthur S. Link (Princeton, NJ: Princeton University Press, 1968), 49–50, 50.
85. Eisenach, *The Lost Promise of Progressivism*, 131.
86. John G. Gunnell, *The Descent of Political Theory: The Genealogy of an American Vocation* (Chicago: University of Chicago Press), 50–57. Burgess's place in the Progressive pantheon might be questioned because he, like Wilson, emphasized limited government, individual rights, judicial control of legislative excess, and a racialized conception of national identity. His connection to the particular Progressive tradition I am describing is his Hegelian understanding of the state as a historically defined, ethical community that extended beyond government. See John Burgess, *Political Science and Comparative Constitutional Law* vol. 1, 2 (Boston: Ginn, 1890–1891). His concept of the state also influenced Frank Goodnow, whose views are described in detail below.
87. Wilson, *The State*, 587.
88. Hegel, *Philosophy of Right*, § 274.
89. W.W. Willoughby, *An Examination of the Nature of the State: A Study in Political Philosophy* (New York: MacMillan, [1896] 1992), 199.
90. Ajay K. Mehrotra, *Making the Modern American Fiscal State: Law, Politics, and the Rise of Progressive Taxation, 1877–1929* (Cambridge: Cambridge University Press, 2013), 113.
91. Henry C. Carter Adams, *Science of Finance* (New York: Henry Holt, 1898), 301–02, quoted in Mehrotra, *Making the Modern American Fiscal State*, 113.
92. Edwin Seligman, *Essays in Taxation* (New York: Macmillan, 1895), 72, quoted in Mehrotra, *Making the Modern American Fiscal State*, 113.
93. Hegel, *Philosophy of Right*, §§ 269, 273.
94. Wilson, "The Democratic State," 69.
95. Willoughby, *Examination of the Nature of the State*, 206.
96. Charles Edward Merriam, *A History of American Political Theories* (New York: MacMillan, 1920), 339, 343.
97. Ibid., 344.
98. Wilson, *Constitutional Government*, 4–5.
99. Ibid., 14.
100. Ibid., 22.
101. Ibid., 20, 22.
102. Ibid., 143.
103. Woodrow Wilson, "Notes for Lectures at the Johns Hopkins," *The Papers of Woodrow Wilson, 1890–1892*, vol. 7, ed. Arthur S. Link, (Princeton, NJ: Princeton University Press, 1969), 114–58, 153.
104. Roscoe Pound, "Common Law and Legislation," *Harvard Law Review*, 21, no. 6 (1908): 383–407, 403.
105. Ibid.

106. Wilson, *The State*, 591.
107. Ibid.
108. Wilson, "Notes for Lectures at the Johns Hopkins," 128–29.
109. Ibid., 138.
110. Willoughby, *Examination of the Nature of the State*, 214.
111. United States v. Eliason, 41 U.S. 291, 302 (1842); Gratiot v. United States, 45 U.S. 80, 117 (1846); *Ex parte* Reed, 100 U.S. 13, 22–23 (1879).
112. United States v. Eaton, 144 U.S. 677, 688 (1892).
113. E.g., United States v. Symonds, 120 U.S. 46, 50 (1887); Morrill v. Jones, 106 U.S. 466, 467 (1882).
114. U.S. Const. art. I, § 8, cl. 18.
115. Boske v. Comingore, 177 U.S. 459, 40 (1900).
116. San Diego Land & Town Co. v. Nat'l City, 174 U.S. 739, 752 (1899); San Diego Land & Town Co. v. Jasper, 189 U.S. 439, 442 (1903); So. Pacific R.R. Co. v. Campbell, 230 U.S. 537, 552 (1913). This approach was rejected in Ohio Valley Water Co. v. Ben Avon Borough, 253 U.S. 287, 289 (1919).
117. Louisville & Nashville R.R. Co. v. Garrett, 231 U.S. 298, 313 (1913).
118. John Dickinson, *Administrative Justice and the Supremacy of Law in the United States* (Cambridge, MA: Harvard University Press, 1927), 179.
119. U.S. Const. art. II, § 1.
120. Hegel, *Philosophy of Right*, § 320A.
121. Sidney M. Milkis, *Theodore Roosevelt, the Progressive Party, and the Transformation of American Democracy* (Lawrence: University of Kansas Press, 2009), 182–83.
122. Wilson, *Constitutional Government*, 60.
123. Ibid., 60.
124. Ibid., 68–73.
125. Ibid., 73.
126. Stephen Skowronek, "Conservative Insurgency and Presidential Power: A Developmental Perspective on the Unitary Executive," *Harvard Law Review* 122, no. 8 (2009): 2070–103, 2087.
127. Wilson, *Constitutional Government*, 66.
128. Ibid., 76.
129. Ibid., 67.
130. Ibid., 76.
131. Jeffrey K. Tulis, *The Rhetorical Presidency* (Princeton, NJ: Princeton University Press, 1987), 125
132. Stephen B. Wood, *Constitutional Politics in the Progressive Era: Child Labor and the Law* (Chicago: University of Chicago Press, 1968), 23.
133. Pub. L. No. 63-249, 39 Stat. 675 (Sept. 1, 1916), ruled unconstitutional in Hammer v. Dagenhart, 247 U.S. 251 (1918).
134. Pub. L. No. 63-43, 38 Stat. 251 (Dec. 23, 1913).
135. Pub. L. No. 63-203, 38 Stat. 717 (Sept. 26, 1914).
136. Arthur W. McMahon, "Woodrow Wilson: Political Leader and Administrator," in *The Philosophy and Policies of Woodrow Wilson*, ed. Earl Latham (Chicago: University of Chicago Press, 1958), 114.

137. John Dewey, *The Public and its Problems* (Athens: Swallow Press: Ohio University Press, [1927] 1954), 96.
138. Ibid., 97.
139. On Dewey and Du Bois, see David E. Price, "Community and Control: Critical Democratic Theory and the Progressive Theory," *American Political Science Review* 68, no. 4 (1974): 1663–78, 1670–72.
140. On the enduring Hegelian themes in Dewey, even after his turn to pragmatism, see generally James A. Good, *The Search for Unity in Diversity: The 'Permanent Hegelian Deposit' in the Philosophy of John Dewey* (New York: Rowman & Littlefield, 2006).
141. John Dewey, "From Absolutism to Experimentalism," in *John Dewey, The Later Works: 1925–1953.* vol. 5, 1929-1930, ed. Jon Ann Boydson (Carbondale: Southern Illinois University Press, 1984), 148–160, 154.
142. John Dewey, "Hegel's Philosophy of Spirit," in *John Dewey's Philosophy of Spirit, With the 1897 Lecture on Hegel,* ed. John R. Shook and James A. Good (New York: Fordham University Press, 2010), 159.
143. Dewey, "Hegel's Philosophy of Spirit," 159.
144. Ibid., 158.
145. John Dewey, "The Ethics of Democracy," in *John Dewey, The Early Works 1882–1898*, vol. 1, 1882–1888, ed. Jo Ann Boydston (Carbondale: Southern Illinois University Press, 1969), 227–249, 235.
146. Ibid.
147. Dewey cites Hegel's discussion on subjective freedom in *Philosophy of Right* § 124 in a section on "reflective conscience and the ethical world." In a footnote, he explains "I need hardly say how I am indebted in the treatment of this topic, and indeed, in the whole topic of the 'ethical world,' to Hegel." John Dewey, "Outlines of a Critical Theory of Ethics," in *John Dewey, The Early Works, 1882–1892,* vol. 3, 1889-1892, ed. Jo Ann Boyston (Carbondale: Southern Illinois University Press 1969), 357n.2.
148. Dewey, "Outlines," 322 (emphasis omitted).
149. Ibid., 347.
150. Ibid.
151. John Dewey and James H. Tufts, *Ethics* (New York: Henry Holt, 1908), 471. Dewey and Tufts cite Hegel's *Philosophy of Right* as a source for part III of the book "The World of Action." Ibid., 426. Throughout I refer to Dewey as the author of these claims because, as the preface states, he was the principal author of those sections of the book in which administration is discussed. Ibid., vi.
152. Dewey and Tufts, *Ethics*, 472.
153. Ibid., 474. Dewey describes the relationship between individualism and democracy in similar terms in *Philosophy and Democracy* (1918), "To say that what is specific and unique can be exalted and become forceful or actual only in relationship with other beings is merely, I take it, to give a metaphysical version to the fact that democracy is concerned not with freaks or geniuses or heroes or divine leaders but with associated individuals in which each by intercourse with others somehow makes the life of each more distinctive." John Dewey, "Philosophy and Democracy," in *The Middle Works, 1899–1924,* vol. 11, 1918–1919, ed. Jo Ann Boydston (Carbondale: Southern Illinois University Press, 1982), 53.

154. Dewey and Tufts, *Ethics*, 482.
155. Ibid., 471.
156. Ibid., *Ethics*, 473.
157. Hillary Putnam, "A Reconsideration of Deweyan Democracy," *Southern California Law Review* 63, no. 6 (1990): 1671–98, 1683.
158. Dewey, *The Public and Its Problems*, 202.
159. John Dewey, *Individualism Old and New* (New York: Prometheus, [1930] 1999), 8–9.
160. Ibid., 59.
161. Eisenach, *The Lost Promise of Progressivism*, 135.
162. Hegel, *Philosophy of Right*, §§ 251, 255.
163. Bernard S. Silberman, *Cages of Reason: The Rise of the Rational State in France, Japan, The United States and Great Britain* (Chicago: University of Chicago Press, 1993), 72; Daniel Carpenter, *The Forging Bureaucratic Autonomy: Reputations, Networks, and Policy Innovation in Executive Agencies, 1862–1928* (Princeton, NJ: Princeton University Press, 2001), 26–7, 32–33.
164. Dewey, *Individualism Old and New*, 54–56.
165. Hegel, *Philosophy of Right*, § 232.
166. Ibid., § 236.
167. Ibid.
168. Seminally, Ronald Coase, "The Problem of Social Cost," *Journal of Law and Economics* 3, no. 1 (1960): 1–4; James M. Buchanan and W.C. Stubblebine, "Externality," *Economica* 29, no. 116 (1962): 371–84.
169. Dewey, *The Public and Its Problems*, 65.
170. John Dewey, *The Public and Its Problems* (Athens: Ohio University Press, [1927] 1954), 109 (emphasis added).
171. Axel Honneth, "Democracy as Reflexive Cooperation: John Dewey and the Theory of Democracy Today," *Political Theory* 26, no. 6 (1998): 771.
172. Dewey's communicative transformation of Hegelian notions of collectivity is evident when he says that "[f]or beings who observe and think, and whose ideas are absorbed by impulses and become sentiments and interest, 'we' is as inevitable as 'I.' But 'we' and 'our' exist only when the consequences of combined action are perceived and become an object of desire and effort, just as 'I' and 'mine' appear on the scene only when a distinctive share in mutual action is consciously asserted or claimed. Dewey, *The Public and Its Problems*, 151 (1954). Compare with Hegel, *Phenomenology of Spirit*, where Hegel defines spirit as "that absolute substance which is the unity of the different self-consciousnesses which, in their opposition, enjoy perfect freedom and independence: 'I' that is 'We' and 'We' that is 'I.'" Hegel, *Phenomenology of Spirit*, 110.
173. Dewey, *The Public and Its Problems*, 71 (1954).
174. Gunnell, *The Descent of Political Theory*, 80. See e.g. W.W. Willoughby, "The Prussian Theory of the State," *American Journal of International Law* 12, no. 2 (1918): 251–65.
175. John Dewey, *German Philosophy and Politics* (New York: Henry Holt, 1915), 125.

176. Dewey, *The Public and Its Problems*, 67 (1954).
177. Elizabeth Anderson, "The Epistemology of Democracy," *Episteme: A Journal of Social Epistemology* 3, no. 1 (2006): 8–22, 13.
178. Quoted in Eisenach, *The Lost Promise of Progressivism*, 75.
179. Dewey, *The Public and Its Problems*, 177 (1954).
180. Melvin Rogers, *The Undiscovered Dewey: Religion, Morality, and the Ethos of Democracy* (New York: Columbia University Press, 2009), 22.
181. Novak, *The People's Welfare*, 235–48.
182. Munn v. Illinois, 94 U.S. 113, 126 (1877) (quoting Lord Matthew Hale, *De Portibus Maris*, 1 Harg. Law Tracts, 78).
183. 94 U.S. at 126.
184. Barbara H. Fried, *The Progressive Assault on Laissez Faire: Robert Hale and the First Law and Economics Movement* (Cambridge, MA: Harvard University Press, 1998), 160–61.
185. Robert Hale, "Rate Making and the Revision of the Property Concept," *Columbia Law Review* 22, no. 3 (1929): 209–17, 212.
186. Tyson & Bro.-United Theatre Ticket Offices v. Banton, 273 U.S. 418, 446 (1927) (Holmes, J., dissenting).
187. Thomas Reed Powell, "The Judiciality of Minimum Wage Legislation," *Harvard Law Review* 37 no. 5 (1924): 545–73, 556.
188. Dewey, *The Public and Its Problems*, 64–65 (1954).
189. John Dickinson, "Social Order and Political Authority," *American Political Science Review* 23, no. 2 (1929): 293–328, 294–95.
190. Ibid., 327.
191. Ibid., 328.
192. John Dickinson, *Administrative Justice and the Supremacy of Law in the United States* (Cambridge, MA: Harvard University Press, 1927), 13.
193. Ibid., 14.
194. Ibid., 55. On Dickinson's connection to the legal realist movement, see Robert Gordon, "Willis's American Counterparts: The Legal Realists' Defence of Administration," *University of Toronto Law Journal* 55, no. 3 (2005): 405–25.
195. Bruce Wyman, The *Principles of the Administrative Law concerning the Relations of Public Officers* (St. Paul, MN: Keefe-Davidson, 1903), 15.
196. Ibid., 4.
197. Dewey, *The Public and Its Problems*, 35 (1954).
198. Robert B. Westbrook, *John Dewey and American Democracy* (Ithaca, NY: Cornell University Press, 1991), 294–306; Walter Lippman, *Public Opinion* (New York: Harcourt, Brace, 1922).
199. Lippman, *Public Opinion*, 250–51.
200. Dewey, *The Public and Its Problems*, 206 (1954).
201. Ibid., 208.
202. Federal Water Power Act §4(g), Pub. L. No. 66–280, 41 Stat. 1063, 1065 (1920), discussed in John Preston Comer, *Legislative Functions of National Administrative Authorities* (New York: Columbia University Press, 1927), 240.

203. Plant Quarantine Act of 1912 § 8, Pub. L. No. 62-276, 37 Stat. 315, 318 (1912), discussed in Comer, *Legislative Functions of National Administrative Authorities*, 212–14.

204. Comer, *Legislative Functions of National Administrative Authorities*, 209–11. Comer's description of these extraordinary hearings deserves to be quoted at length:

> "The central office initiated the formal process of revising the rules for grazing by sending out a set of tentative regulations dealing with the more important problems of administration. The circular had a twofold purpose: setting the live-stock associations to thinking, and provoking criticism on the part of the various forest district officials. . . . The Chief Forester then sent invitations to all stockmen, chiefly through their organizations, to meet at Ogden the first week in March for the purpose of considering closely the tentative purpose of bringing order out of chaos. All of the local, state and national live-stock associations were represented; many of them had already been working together in framing their programs for presentation to the government officials. . . . The Forest Service men were divided into ten committees, each committee considering a different phase of the general question of forest grazing—such as grazing fees, supervision, and range improvements. . . . The work consisted largely of meetings at which the interested parties—some of whom were requested to appear and others of whom came of their own accord—testified.
>
> "On the fifth day of the hearing the Chief Forester, Col. Greely, had what was known as a free-for-all stockmen's meeting. He stated that while the committees were going over point by point the important features of the government's grazing policy and regulations, as well as the details of instruction, it would be well to hold an open meeting so that any stockman or group might elaborate particular views. The agenda for the day had been prepared but was not adhered to. Questions of principle and policy were discussed freely by the live-stock interest.
>
> "The various committees presented the results of their weeks work to a committee of the whole. Each report in which there had been a split vote gave both minority and majority views, together with supporting reasons; each report, for the sake of unity of policy and law, had the written approval (with comments) of the Chief Forester, who all the while had the solicitor at his elbow. The committee voted on the reports by sections; there was evidence in many case of differences of opinion. Two or three days were then spent by the proper committees in fitting the various recommendations into the Manual. When this had been done and order had been brought out of chaos, the chief inspector for the Service, Mr. Rachford, together with all the supervisors of grazing, met for three days in Denver with a committee representing all the stockmen for a careful review of the results of the conference. This committee for the most part approved the conference suggestions for revision of the Manual. The unchanged principle set forth by the government, viz. that 'the grazing interest is not a property right,' and the principle underlying the grazing

fees could not be agreed upon. The stockmen later had their opportunity to speak on these very points to the Sixty-ninth Congress." Ibid.

205. Ibid., 199.
206. Ibid., 210.
207. Felix Frankfurter, *The Public and Its Government* (Boston: Beacon Press, 1930).
208. Ibid., 158.
209. Ibid., 159.
210. Theodore Roosevelt, review of *The Speaker of the House of Representatives*, by M.P. Follett, *American Historical Review* 2, no. 1 (1896): 176–78; Stears, *Progressives, Pluralists, and the Problems of the State*, 146; Joan C. Tonn, *Mary P. Follett: Creating Democracy, Transforming Management* (New Haven, CT: Yale University Press, 2003), 1; Bryan R. Fry and Thomas R. Lotte, "Mary Parker Follett: Assessing the Contribution and Impact of Her Writings," *Journal of Management History* 2, no. 2 (1996): 11–19; Ricardo S. Morse, "Prophet of Participation: Mary Parker Follett and Public Participation in Public Administration," *Administrative Theory & Praxis* 28, no. 1 (2006): 1–32; Keith Snider, "Living Pragmatism: The Case of Mary Parker Follett," *Administrative Theory & Praxis* 20, no. 3 (1998): 274–86; James F. Wolf, *Refounding Democratic Public Administration: Modern Paradoxes, Postmodern Challenges* (Thousand Oaks, CA: Sage, 1997), 280–84.
211. Jane Mansbridge et al., "The Place of Self-Interest and the Role of Power in Deliberative Democracy," *The Journal of Political Philosophy* 18, no. 1 (2010): 64–100, 71; Benjamin Barber, "Mary Parker Follett: A Democratic Hero," preface to *The New State*, by Mary Parker Follett (University Park: Pennsylvania State University Press, 1998), xiii–xvi; Robert C. Post, *Citizens Divided: Campaign Finance Reform and the Constitution* (Cambridge, MA: Harvard University Press, 2014), 37.
212. Dwight Waldo, "Development of the Theory of Democratic Administration," *American Political Science Review* 46, no. 1 (1952): 94–97. Waldo reports that Lord Haldane once remarked that "had Hegel lived in Boston in 1920, 'he would probably . . . have said something not very different from what Miss Follett says.'" Ibid., 94–95n.31. See also James A. Stever, "Mary Parker Follett and the Quest for Pragmatic Administration," *Administration & Society* 18, no. 2 (1986): 159–77.
213. Mary Parker Follett, *The New State: Group Organization the Solution of Popular Government* (New York: Longmans, Green, 1918), 333.
214. See, e.g. Harold Laski, "Foundations of Sovereignty," *Foundations of Sovereignty and Other Essays* (New York: Harcourt, Brace, 1921), 1–29; Harold Laski, *Authority in the Modern State* (New Haven, CT: Yale University Press, 1919).
215. Follett, *The New State*, 19.
216. Ibid., 22.
217. Ibid., 70.
218. Ibid., 9.
219. For a comparison between American progressive nationalists such as Follett and British pluralists, see Stears, *Progressives, Pluralists, and the Problems of the State*, 156–66.

220. Follett, *The New State*, 306.
221. Ibid., 308.
222. Arendt distinguishes power, on the one hand, and force and violence, on the other, in a way that mirrors Follett's distinction between "power-with" and "power-over." For Arendt, "power springs up between men when they act together and vanishes the moment they disperse;" and "under the conditions of human life, the only alternative to power is . . . force, which indeed one man alone can exert against his fellow men and of which one or a few can possess a monopoly by acquiring the means of violence. But while violence can destroy power, it can never become a substitute for it." Arendt, *The Human Condition*, 200, 202.
223. Mary Parker Follett, *Creative Experience* (New York: Longmans, Green., 1924), 189.
224. Mary Parker Follett, "Power," in *Dynamic Administration: The Collected Papers of Mary Parker Follett*, ed. Henry C. Metcalf and L. Urwick (New York: Harper Brothers, 1940), 95–116, 101.
225. Ibid., 114.
226. Follett, *The New State*, 245.
227. As Joan C. Tonn points out, Follett contrasts true Hegelianism with the right-wing Hegelian ideology of the German state in World War I. Tonn argues that "the pluralists had responded to this distorted Hegelianism not only by rejecting the state as currently constituted but also by denying the possibility of collective sovereignty. Follett demurs, being firmly convinced that collective and distributive sovereignty can exist together." Tonn, *Mary P. Follett*, 294.
228. Follett, *The New State*, 267.
229. Follett, *Creative Experience*, 186.
230. Follett, *The New State*, 174–75.
231. Follett, *Creative Experience*, 197.
232. Ibid., 212–13.
233. Ibid., 213.
234. Ibid., 216.
235. Ibid.
236. Ibid., 218.
237. See Roscoe Pound, "The Scope and Purpose of Sociological Jurisprudence," *Harvard Law Review* 25, no. 2 (1911): 140–68. Pound himself had an ambivalent relationship to administrative law. Though he was initially skeptical that administration was a proper subject for legal scholarship, given his immersion in the Langdellian case method at Harvard, by 1919 Pound had acknowledged that the then-growing strength of the executive in the administration of justice was a functional evolution of the broadening of social interests governed by law. Roscoe Pound, "Administrative Application of Legal Standards," in *Reports of the American Bar Association* 44, reported by Charles A. Morrison (Baltimore: Lord Baltimore Press, 1919), 445–65. He saw administration as a setting in which flexible standards, rather than fixed logical rules, guided decision-making. He

nevertheless remained anxious about the possibility that administration would stray into ever-more particularistic decision-making, failing to create a stable body of precedent. For this reason he sought to retain and strengthen judicial supervision of administrative action. But Pound would later in life become an ardent critic of "administrative absolutism," as he believed the New Deal concentrated too much discretionary power in the executive branch. Walter Gelhorn, "The Administrative Procedure Act: The Beginnings," *Virginia Law Review* 72, no. 2 (1986): 219–33, 222. That stage of Pound's career is discussed in chapter 3.

238. Follett, *Creative Experience*, 265.
239. Ibid., 271.
240. Ibid., 292.
241. Federal Trade Commission, *Trade Practice Submittals*, (Washington DC: U.S. Government Printing Office, 1923), 21–22, quoted in Gerald C. Henderson, *The Federal Trade Commission: A Study in Administrative Law and Procedure* (New Haven, CT: Yale University Press, 1925), 79.
242. Henderson, *The Federal Trade Commission*, 79.
243. John Rohr, *To Run a Constitution: The Legitimacy of the Administrative State* (Lawrence: University Press of Kansas, 1986), 84.
244. Felix Frankfurter, "The Tasks of Administrative Law," *University of Pennsylvania Law Review* 75 no. 6 (1927): 614–21, 616. Freund and Goodnow both studied in Berlin under Rudolf von Gneist. Goodnow was Freund's teacher when Freund studied political science at Columbia University, where he would later serve on the law faculty. See Oliver Lepsius, *Verwaltungsrecht unter dem Common Law* (Tübingen: J.C.B. Mohr [Paul Siebeck], 1997), 10–12, 266. Freund took an approach to administrative law, much like Goodnow's, which emphasized the structure of the internal administrative process as a means for regulating the relation between the powers of government and the rights of citizens. More so than Goodnow, Freund was concerned with the dangers of administrative discretion and sought to limit it by more precise legislative guidance that could enable courts to review the substantive content of agency decisions. See Ernst Freund, "The Law of Administration in the United States," *Political Science Quarterly* 9, no. 3 (1894): 403–25, 419. Daniel R. Ernst, "Ernst Freund, Felix Frankfurter, and the American *Rechtsstaat*: A Transatlantic Shipwreck," *Studies in American Political Development* 23, no. 2 (2009): 171–88.
245. Frank J. Goodnow, *The Principles of the Administrative Law of the United States* (New York: Putnam, 1905), 17.
246. Ibid., 371.
247. Jerry Mashaw quotes at length from Goodnow to describe the domain of administrative law "from the perspective of nineteenth century experience." He argues that "Goodnow . . . got it almost right" in describing the three interests advanced by administrative law: governmental efficiency, individual rights, and democracy. But Mashaw says that Goodnow failed to understand "the degree to which any one of these three purposes can be served by techniques that he assigns to alternative forms of control." Jerry L. Mashaw, "Recovering American

Administrative Law: Federalist Foundations, 1787–1801," *Yale Law Journal* 115, no. 6 (2006): 1256–344, 1264–65. This characterization gives short shrift to Goodnow's recognition that political, administrative, and judicial functions could all be performed by executive agencies.

248. Frank J. Goodnow, *Social Reform and the Constitution* (New York: MacMillan, 1911), 16.
249. Ibid.
250. Hegel, *Philosophy of Right*, § 75.
251. Goodnow, *Social Reform an the Constitution*, 209.
252. U.S. Const. art. I, § 8, cl. 3.
253. Goodnow, *Social Reform and the Constitution*, 216.
254. Christian Rosser, "Examining Frank Goodnow's Hegelian Heritage: A Contribution to Understanding Progressive Administrative Theory," *Administration & Society* 45, no. 9 (2012): 1063–94, 1088.
255. Hegel, *Philosophy of Right*, § 273.
256. Ibid.
257. Stein, *Handbuch der Verwaltungslehre*, 14.
258. Gneist, *Der Rechtsstaat*, 65-66, 96, 127.
259. Frank Johnson Goodnow, *Politics and Administration: A Study in Government* (New York: MacMillan, 1900), 24. Goodnow's debt to Stein is clear not only from his adoption of the distinction between the "will" and the "deed" but also from this statement in his preface to *Comparative Administrative Law*: "While the age that has passed was one of constitutional, the present age is one of administrative reform." Goodnow, *Comparative Administrative Law*, iv. Stein in his *Handbuch der Verwaltungslehre und des Verwaltungsrechts* similarly writes: "we have essentially overcome the epoch of constitution formation, and the focus of further development lies in administration—not because the constitution has lost significance, but because we have, through the constitution, arrived at administration." Stein, *Handbuch der Verwaltungslehre*, 3 (author's translation).
260. Goodnow, *Politics and Administration*, 24.
261. Frank J. Goodnow, *The Principles of the Administrative Law of the United States* (New York: London: G.P. Putnam's Sons, 1905), 43.
262. Goodnow, *Politics and Administration*, 15.
263. Goodnow, *Administrative Law of the United States*, 46.
264. Goodnow, *Politics and Administration*, 91.
265. Ibid., 23.
266. Rohr, *To Run a Constitution*, 87–88.
267. Goodnow, *Administrative Law of the United States*, 329.
268. Goodnow, *Politics and Administration*, 39.
269. Ibid., 85.
270. Jonathan Kahn, *Budgeting Democracy: State Building and Citizenship in America, 1890–1928* (Ithaca, NY: Cornell University Press, 1997), 150; Skowronek, *Building A New American State*, 187–207.
271. See Mashaw, *Creating the Administrative Constitution*, 245–50; Aditaya Bamzai, "The Origins of Judicial Deference to Executive Interpretation," *Yale Law Journal* 126, no. 4 (2016): 908–1001, 955–58.

272. David S. Clark, "Tracing the Roots of American Legal Education: A Nineteenth Century German Connection," *Rabels Zeitschrift für ausländisches und internationales Privatrecht* 51, no. 3 (1987): 313–33, 313, excerpted in John H. Langbein, Renée Lettow Lerner, and Bruce P. Smith, *History of the Common Law: The Development of Anglo-American Legal Traditions* (Austin, TX: Wolters Kluwer, 2009), 960–61.
273. Butterworth v. United States, 112 U.S. 50, 59 (1884).
274. United States v. Duell, 172 U.S. 576, 581 (1899).
275. Wyman, *Administrative Law*, 84.
276. An Act to Regulate Commerce (Interstate Commerce Act), Sess. 1, ch. 103, 24 Stat. 379, 384, 385, §§ 14, 16 (1887).
277. Elizabeth Sanders, *Roots of Reform: Farmers, Workers, and the American State, 1877–1917* (Chicago: University of Chicago Press, 1999), 179–85.
278. An Act to Regulate Commerce (Hepburn Act) Sess. 1, ch. 3591, 34 Stat. 584, 592, § 6 (1906).
279. Thomas Merrill, "Article III, Agency Adjudication, and the Origins of the Appellate Review Model of Administrative Law," *Columbia Law Review* 111, no. 5 (2011): 939–1003, 959.
280. Interstate Commerce Comm'n v. Union Pacific R.R. Co., 222 U.S. 541, 546–48 (1912).
281. E.g., Murray's Lessee v. Hoboken Land & Improvement Co., 59 U.S. 272 (1856); See also Mashaw, *Creating the Administrative Constitution*, 217.
282. People *ex rel.* Copcutt v. Bd. of Health, 140 N.Y. 1 (1893); Commonwealth v. Sisson, 189 Mass. 247 (1905). See also Dickinson, *Administrative Justice*, 260–61, endorsing Frank Goodnow's criticism of such cases.
283. Goodnow, *Social Reform*, 230
284. E.g., Chicago M. & St. P. Ry. v. Minnesota, 134 U.S. 418, 457 (1890); New York *ex rel.* New York & Queens Gas Co. v. McCall, 245 U.S. 345, 348 (1917). This approach was already at work in some fields, such as licensing. See Ernst Freund, *The Police Power: Public Police and Constitutional Rights* (Chicago: Callaghan, 1904), § 20, 15; § 210, 199.
285. Goodnow, *Social Reform*, 231.
286. Adkins v. Children's Hosp., 261 U.S. 525, 562 (1923) (Taft, J., dissenting).
287. John Fabian Witt, *The Accidental Republic: Crippled Workingmen, Destitute Widows, and the Remaking of American Law* (Cambridge, MA: Harvard University Press 2004), 189.
288. Dickinson, *Administrative Justice*, 259–60.
289. Markus Dirk Dubber, *The Police Power: Patriarchy and the Foundations of American Government* (New York: Columbia University Press, 2005), 81–119.
290. Hermann Pünder, "German Administrative Procedure in Comparative Perspective: Observations on the Path to a Transnational *Ius Commune Proceduralis* in Administrative Law," *International Journal of Constitutional Law* 11, no. 4 (2013): 940–61, 942.
291. Gerald C. Henderson, *The Federal Trade Commission: A Study in Administrative Law and Procedure* (New Haven, CT: Yale University Press, 1924), 337, discussed in Ernst, *Tocqueville's Nightmare*, 20–22.

Chapter 3

1. On Hegel and Prussian administrative reform, see Koselleck, *Preußen*, 263. I discuss this historical background in greater detail in chapter 1.
2. Bogdandy and Huber, "Staat, Verwaltung, Verwaltungsrecht," § 30.
3. Lindseth, "The Paradox of Parliamentary Supremacy," 1361–72.
4. Du Bois, *The Souls of Black Folk*, 14; Goldberg, *Citizens and Paupers*, 31–75.
5. Wilson, "The Study of Administration," 210, 217.
6. Follett, *Creative Experience*, 197.
7. Woodrow Wilson, "The Reconstruction of the Southern States," *The Atlantic Monthly* 87, no. 519 (1901): 1–15.
8. Wilson, "The Study of Administration," 217.
9. 5 U.S.C. § 553 (c) (2012).
10. Henry Steele Commager, *The American Mind: An Interpretation of American Thought and Character since the 1880's* (New Haven, CT: Yale University Press, 1950), 342–43.
11. Tennessee Valley Authority Act of 1933, Pub. L. 73-17, 48 Stat. 59 (May 18, 1933).
12. Ibid., § 5.
13. Patrick Kline and Enrico Moretti, "Local Economic Development, Agglomeration Economies, and the Big Push: 100 Years of Evidence from the Tennessee Valley Authority," *Quarterly Journal of Economics* 129, no. 1 (2014): 275–331, 279.
14. David. E. Lilienthal, *TVA: Democracy on the March* (New York: Pocket Books, 1944), 204 (emphasis omitted).
15. Ibid. 216, quoting John Dewey, *Freedom and Culture* (New York: G.P. Putnam's Sons, 1939), 175–76.
16. Philip Selznick, *TVA and the Grass Roots: A Study in Politics and Organization* (Berkeley: University of California Press, [1949] 1984), 114, 166, 226.
17. Ibid., 231–38.
18. James C. Scott, "High Modernist Social Engineering: The Case of the Tennessee Valley Authority," in *Experiencing the State*, ed. Lloyd I. Rudolph and John Kurt Jacobsen (Oxford: Oxford University Press, 2006), 3–52, 30.
19. Agricultural Adjustment Act, Pub. L. 73-10, 48 Stat. 31 (May 12, 1933)
20. The latter taxation provision was ruled unconstitutional by the Supreme Court in *United States v. Butler*, 297 U.S. 1 (1936).
21. Theda Skocpol and Kenneth Feingold, "State Capacity and Economic Intervention in the Early New Deal," *Political Science Quarterly* 97, no. 2 (1982): 255–78, 257.
22. Richard S. Kendall, *Social Scientists and Farm Politics in the Age of Roosevelt* (Columbia: University of Missouri Press, 1966), 11–49.
23. Smith-Lever Act of 1914, Pub. L. 63-95, 38 Stat. 372 (1914); Kendrick A. Clements, "Woodrow Wilson and Administrative Reform," *Presidential Studies Quarterly* 28, no. 2 (1998): 320–36, 329; Marshall E. Dimock, "Woodrow Wilson as Legislative Leader," *The Journal of Politics* 19, no. 1 (1957): 3–19, 9; David E. Hamilton, "Building the Associative State: The Department of Agriculture and American State Building," *Agricultural History* 64, no. 2 (1990): 207–18.
24. Gladys A. Baker, *The County Agent* (Chicago: University of Chicago Press, 1939), 159; Alfred Charles True, *A History of Agricultural Extension Work in the United*

States, 1785–1923 (Washington, DC: U.S. Government Printing Office, 1928), 100–15.

25. Follett, *The New State*, 301, 256.
26. Sidney Baldwin, *Poverty and Politics: The Rinse and Decline of the Farm Security Administration* (Chapel Hill: University of North Carolina Press, 1968), 30–31, 287–88.
27. Dale Clark, "The Farmer as Co-administrator," *The Public Opinion Quarterly* 3, no. 3 (1939): 482–90.
28. John D. Lewis, "Democratic Planning in Agriculture I," *American Political Science Review* 35, no. 2 (1931): 232–39, 235.
29. Jess Gilbert, *Planning Democracy: Agrarian Intellectuals and the Intended New Deal* (New Haven, CT: Yale University Press, 2015), 115–141.
30. Ibid., 2.
31. M.L. Wilson, "The Democratic Processes in the Formation of Agricultural Policy," *Social Forces* 19, no. 1 (1940): 1–11, 8.
32. Gilbert, *Planning Democracy*, 161.
33. Gilbert, *Planning Democracy*, 162, quoting Agricultural Adjustment Administration, Division of Program Planning, *Schools for Extension Workers: What Is a Desirable Agricultural Action Program?* (Washington, DC: 1936) (on file with author).
34. AAA, "Schools for Extension Workers," 3.
35. Ibid.
36. Baldwin, *Poverty and Politics*, 31; Gilbert, *Planning Democracy*, 85.
37. Baldwin, *Poverty and Politics*, 31; Baker, *The County Agent*, 76, 206.
38. Donald H. Grubbs, *Cry from the Cotton: The Southern Tenant Farmers' Union and the New Deal* (Fayetteville: University of Arkansas Press, 2000), 17–61.
39. Gilbert, *Planning Democracy*, 85, 87, 182.
40. Baker, *The County Agent*, 135–44.
41. Gilbert, *Planning Democracy*, 214. Margaret Weir and Theda Skocpol, "State Structures and the Possibilities for 'Keynesian' Responses to the Great Depression in Sweden, Britain, and the United States," in *Bringing the State Back In*, ed. Peter B. Evans, Dietrich Rueschemeyer, and Theda Skocpol (Cambridge: Cambridge University Press, 1985), 144.
42. Emergency Relief Appropriation Act of 1935, 49 Stat. 115 (1935).
43. Exec. Order No. 7072, Establishing the Resettlement Administration (May 1, 1935).
44. The Bankhead-Jones Farm Tenant Act, Pub. L. 75-210, 50 Stat. 522 (1937)
45. The public investments of the FSA were significant: the Farm Security Administration's $180 million expenditures for fiscal year 1938 represented roughly one-quarter of the Department of Agriculture's total expenditures, 8 percent of federal social spending, and 2.5 percent of total federal expenditures. Baldwin, *Poverty and Politics*, 236. Edwin Amenta, *Bold Relief: Institution Politics and the Origins of Modern American Social Policy* (Princeton, NJ: Princeton University Press 1998), 4.
46. Grubbs, *Cry from the Cotton*, 157. Between 1937 and 1944, the FSA spent a total of $1.274 billion, $1.025 billion of which went to such rural rehabilitation programs. Baldwin, *Poverty and Politics*, 317.

47. Monroe Oppenheimer, "The Development of the Rural Rehabilitation Loan Program," *Law and Contemporary Problems* 4, no. 4 (1937): 473–88, 483. The official FSA staff guidebook distinguishes between "County TP [Tenant Purchase] Committees," composed of three local farmers, "whose function is to *certify* applicants and farms as specified in Title I of the Bankhead-Jones Farm Tenant Act," and "County RR [Rural Rehabilitation] Committees," a "committee of three farm men and women selected from the community whose function is to *assist* RR supervisors in all problems involving FSA families and applicants." Department of Agriculture, Farm Security Administration, *Toward Farm Security*, by Joseph Gaer (Washington, DC: U.S. Government Printing Office, 1941), 185 (emphasis added). Thus, in the Tenant Purchase program, the FSA followed the statutory mandate to delegate lending authority to local farmers, on the model of the AAA; whereas in the rural rehabilitation program, where it had no such legal obligation, the FSA chose to reserve decision-making power to FSA staff, giving the county committee only an advisory function. In addition, County Farm Debt Adjustment Committees composed of local farmers arbitrated voluntary debt adjustments between creditors and debtors. It seems likely that the FSA used committees in this case too because the Act said that the secretary of agriculture was only empowered to "assist in the voluntary adjustment of indebtedness" and "may cooperate and pay the whole or part of the expenses of State, territorial, and local agencies and committees engaged in such debt adjustment." Bankhead-Jones Act, § 22.
48. Baldwin, *Poverty and Politics*, 244.
49. Ibid., 245.
50. Paul Keith Conkin, *Tomorrow a New World: The New Deal Community Program* (Ithaca, NY: Cornell University Press, 1959), 221.
51. Department of Agriculture, *Toward Farm Security*, 62–63.
52. Ibid., 65-66.
53. Gunmar Myrdal, *An American Dilemma: The Negro Problem and Modern Democracy*, vol. 1 (New York: Harper & Row, 1944), 273–74; Donald Holley, "The Negro in the New Deal Resettlement Program," *Agricultural History* 45, no. 3 (1971): 179–93, 181. Greta de Jong, "'With the Aid of God and the F.S.A.': The Louisiana Farmers Union and the African American Freedom Struggle in the New Deal Era," *Journal of Social History* 34, no. 1 (2000): 105–39; Grubbs, *Cry from the* Cotton, 158.
54. Department of Agriculture, *Toward Farm Security*, 91.
55. Ibid., 118.
56. Charles Kenneth Roberts, "Client Failures and Supervised Credit in the Farm Security Administration," *Agricultural History* 83, no. 3 (2013): 368–90, 378–79.
57. Conkin, *Toward a New World*, 220–21.
58. Ibid., 220–33; Select Committee of the House Committee on Agriculture, *Report of the Select Committee of the House Committee on Agriculture to Investigate the Activities of the Farm Security Administration* (Washington, DC: United States: U.S. Government Printing Office, 1944), 2.
59. Baldwin, *Poverty and Politics*, 203.

60. Michael Grey, "The Medical Care Programs of the Farm Security Administration, 1932–1947: A Rehearsal for National Health Insurance?" *American Journal of Public Health* 84, no. 10 (1994): 1678–87.
61. Ibid., 1679.
62. Baldwin, *Poverty and Politics*, 204.
63. W.E.B. Du Bois, "Federal Action Programs and Community Action in the South," *Social Forces* 19, no. 3 (1940): 375–80, 377. Du Bois does not mention the FSA explicitly in the essay, focusing on the Works Progress Administration. But his analysis captures the spirit of the FSA's practice as well.
64. Ibid., 379.
65. Ibid., 380.
66. Baldwin, *Poverty and Politics*, 365–404.
67. Gilbert, *Planning Democracy*, 240–41.
68. George Shepherd, "Fierce Compromise: The Administrative Procedure Act Emerges from New Deal Politics," *Northwestern University Law Review* 90, no. 4 (1996): 1558–78, 1586–92; Joanna Grisinger, *The Unwieldy American State: Administrative Politics since the New Deal* (Cambridge: Cambridge University Press, 2012), 73–83.
69. Report of the Special Committee on Administrative Law, in *Reports of the American Bar Association* 63 (1938), 331–68, 364–68.
70. Roscoe Pound, "Executive Justice," *American Law Register* 55, no. 3 (1907): 137–46.
71. For a rich discussion of Pound's fraught relationship to the ABA and the Walter-Logan Bill, see Ernst, *Tocqueville's Nightmare*, 121–25.
72. S. 915, H.R. 6324, 76th Cong. 1st Sess. (1939).
73. Attorney General's Committee on Administrative Procedure, *Final Report* (Washington, DC: U.S. Government Printing Office, 1941), 103–4.
74. Ibid., 105.
75. 5 U.S.C. § 553 (c) (2012).
76. David Ciepley, *Liberalism in the Shadow of Totalitarianism* (Cambridge, MA: Harvard University Press, 2006), 129–46, 194–216; Reuel E. Schiller, "Reining in the Administrative State: World War II and the Decline of Expert Administration," in *Total War and the Law: The American Home Front in World War II*, ed. Daniel R. Ernst and Victor Jew (Westport, CT: Praeger, 2002), 185–206, 188–90.
77. Theodore J. Lowi, *The End of Liberalism: The Second Republic of the United States* 2nd ed. (New York: W.W. Norton, 1979), 40.
78. Brown v. Bd. of Educ., 347 U.S. 483, 494 n.11 (1954).
79. Myrdal, *An American Dilemma*, 278.
80. Lester M. Salamon, "The Time Dimension in Policy Evaluation," *Public Policy* 27, no. 2 (Spring 1979): 129–82.
81. Spencer D. Wood, *The Roots of Black Power: Land, Civil Society, and State in the Mississippi Delta*, (PhD. diss., University of Wisconsin-Madison, 2006), 5
82. Ibid., 5.
83. On the relationship between the Southern Tenant Farmers Union, the FSA, and early civil rights mobilization, see Nan Elizabeth Woodruff, *American Congo: The*

African American Freedom Struggle in the Delta (Cambridge, MA: Harvard University Press, 2003), 198–227.

84. Grey, "The Medical Care Programs of the Farm Security Administration, 1932–1947," 1686.
85. Richard A. Couto. "Heroic Bureaucracies," *Administration & Society* 23, no. 1 (1991): 123–47.
86. Michael L. Gillette, *Launching the War on Poverty: An Oral History*, 2nd ed. (New York: Oxford University Press, 2010), 307–10.
87. Warren C. Whatley, "Labor for the Picking: The New Deal in the South," *Journal of Economic History* 43, no. 4 (1983): 905–29.
88. Leah Platt Boustan, "Was Postwar Suburbanization 'White Flight'? Evidence from the Black Migration," *The Quarterly Journal of Economics*, 125, no. 1 (2010): 417–43.
89. Reuel Schiller, *Forging Rivals: Race, Class, Law, and the Collapse of Postwar Liberalism* (New York: Cambridge University Press, 2015), 144–48; Louis Jaffe, "The Public Right Dogma in Labor Board Cases," *Harvard Law Review* 59, no. 5 (1946): 720–45, 739.
90. Du Bois, *Souls of Black Folk*, 31.
91. Bruce Ackerman, *We the People 3: The Civil Rights Revolution* (Cambridge, MA: Harvard University Press, 2014), 2.
92. E.g., N.L.R.B. v. Hearst Pub'ns, 322 U.S. 111, 130–31 (1944).
93. Brown v. Bd. of Educ., 347 U.S. 483, 493 (1954).
94. United States Commission on Civil Rights, *Survey of School Desegregation in the Southern and Border States, 1965-66* (1966), 1.
95. Brown v. Bd. of Educ., 349 U.S. 294, 301 (1955); See also Richard W. Brown, "Freedom of Choice in the South: A Constitutional Perspective," *Louisiana Law Review* 28, no. 3 (1968): 455–68, 456 and Alexander Bickel, "The Decade of School Desegregation: Progress and Prospects," *Columbia Law Review* 64, no. 2 (1964): 193–229, 199.
96. Civil Rights Act of 1964, Pub. L. 88-432, 78 Stat. 241-267 (July 2, 1964).
97. Ibid., § 601.
98. Ibid., § 602.
99. Department of Health, Education, and Welfare, *Non-discrimination in Federally Assisted Programs of the Department of Health Education and Welfare—Effectuation of Title VI of the Civil Rights Act of 1964*, 29 Fed. Reg. 16,298, 16,300 (1964).
100. Responses to the proposed guidelines showed their potential to win the qualified support of even hostile politicians as a flexible administrative remedy. Senator Richard Russell of Georgia, for example, "expressed deep opposition to the whole idea of integration and to using the power of the Federal Government to force a region to do something distasteful. But then he said graciously that he realized he was resisting the inevitable, that HEW had handled things extremely well 'so far,' and that we were trying to be fair and reasonable." Douglas S. Cater, *Memorandum to the President* (February 26, 1966) with attached *Interviews and Reactions concerning New Title VI Guidelines for Elementary and Secondary*

Schools (February 26, 1966), Lyndon Baines Johnson Library, Papers of Lyndon Baines Johnson, Files of S. Douglass Cater, box 14.

101. By August 17, 1965, as HEW Secretary John W. Gardner wrote in a memorandum to White House aide Douglass Cater, in Georgia and South Carolina "hundreds of school districts signed HEW Form 441 [indicating compliance with requirements of Title VI] . . . despite the fact that it is well known the districts operate a dual system. The motives for signing probably ranged from good intent coupled with misunderstanding to deliberate intention to evade the Act." Department of Health, Education and Welfare, *Memorandum from John W. Gardner, Secretary of Health, Education, and Welfare for Honorable Douglass Cater* (March 23, 1965), Lyndon Baines Johnson Library, Papers of Lyndon Baines Johnson, Files of S. Douglass Cater, Box 51. See also Department of Health Education and Welfare, *Memorandum for Honorable Douglas Cater, Special Assistant to the President, Subject: Report on HEW Departmental Activities in Regard to Implementation of Title VI in the State of Virginia* (April 6, 1965), Lyndon Baines Johnson Library, Papers of Lyndon Baines Johnson, Files of S. Douglass Cater, Box 51; See also Department of Health Education and Welfare, *Letter from Francis Keppel, U.S. Commissioner of Education, to Claude Percell, Georgia State Department of Schools* (March 31, 1965), Lyndon Baines Johnson Library, Papers of Lyndon Baines Johnson, Files of S. Douglass Cater, Box 51.

102. As White House Aid Douglas Cater explained in a memo to the president, "After a great deal of deliberation between HEW and the Justice Department, it was decided to draft a detailed set of specifications to guide school districts in their desegregation plans submitted under provisions of Title VI of the Civil Rights Act. The problem was simply this: approximately 500 districts have submitted plans, most of them considered by the Commissioner of Education to be unacceptable. It would be impossible to negotiate with each on an ad hoc basis. . . . The decision reached was that specific guidelines would be the only way to break this impasse." Douglass Cater, *Memorandum to the President from Douglas Cater* (April 23, 1965), Lyndon Baines Johnson Library, Papers of Lyndon Baines Johnson, Files of S. Douglas Cater, Box 51.

103. "No regulation, rule, or order shall become effective unless and until approved by the President." Civil Rights Act of 1964 § 602.

104. "The question was raised whether to issue them as guidelines bearing only the authority of HEW. Secretary Celebrezze decided that HEW should bear the political burden and issue them as guidelines," Cater, *Memorandum to the President* (April 23, 1965).

105. Department of Health, Education, and Welfare, *Statement of Policies for School Desegregation Plans under Title VI of the Civil Rights Act of 1964*, 45 C.F.R. § 181.54(a) (1967). This provision reflected an understanding of the problem of discrimination and school desegregation that the agency had adopted as early as April 1965. A draft of the Office of Education's "Interpretive Bulletin No. 1" stated that "To comply with Title VI and the HEW Regulations . . . elementary and secondary school authorities have a duty to take positive action to remove

discrimination grounded on race, color, or national origin. This duty is not discharged by adopting rules or practices which shift the burden of removing discrimination to the class or classes of persons previously discriminated against. The right not to be subject to discrimination, which Title VI . . . secures, is the right to a system of schools which operate without discrimination. Where pupils, teachers, or staff personnel have been assigned to schools on the basis of race, color, or national origin, school officials must take the actions necessary to eliminate customs and practices characteristic of such dual or segregated school systems. The prohibition of discrimination in Title VI . . . does not, however, prevent the use of race, color, or national origin as a factor in actions designed to prevent, ameliorate, or eliminate either *de jure* or *de facto* racial segregation." Department of Housing Education and Welfare, Office of Education, *Interpretive Bulletin No. 1, Elementary and Secondary Schools: Standards for Compliance with Title VI of the Civil Rights Act; Nondiscrimination in Federally Assisted Programs* (April 19, 1965), Lyndon Baines Johnson Library, Papers of Lyndon Baines Johnson, Files of S. Douglas Cater, Box 51.

106. 45 C.F.R. 181.54 (b), (f), and (i) (1967).

107. Ibid., 181.54(a).

108. As Edwin Yourman, Assistant General Counsel at HEW, noted in the Department's 1968 Administrative History, during 1966 and 1967, "both the courts and administrative policies and 'guidelines,' concerned at first with mechanisms to break down rigidly racial assignment patterns, have moved gradually but surely toward an insistence on attainment of the ultimate objective, elimination of the dual school system. . . . School officials and community groups originally opposed the right of a Negro child to choose a school established for whites. When experience showed that in most cases only a limited number of such choices would be made, they stoutly defended this type of arrangement as though it constituted a fundamental natural right." Department of Health, Education, and Welfare, Office of the General Counsel, "School Desegregation under the Regulation," by Edwin Yourman, Lyndon Baines Johnson Library, Papers of Lyndon Baines Johnson, Administrative History, Department of Health, Education, and Welfare Vol. I, Part III, Box 2, pp. 15–16. See also Gary Orfield, *The Reconstruction of Southern Education: The Schools and the 1964 Civil Rights Act* (New York: Wiley, 1969), 340.

109. Interview with Elaine Heffernan, May 20, 1968, in "Office Of Civil Rights, OCR Historical Record, Title VI Implementation DHEW," by Elaine Heffernan, Lyndon Baines Johnson Library, Papers of Lyndon Baines Johnson, *Administrative History, Department of Health, Education, and Welfare* Vol. I, Part III, Box 2 (1968), Ch. II, p. 163. Derrick Bell would go on to become the first African American full professor of law at Harvard Law School and would later become a famous critic of school integration, once efforts to do so stalled. See Derrick A. Bell Jr., "*Brown v. Board of Education* and the Interest-Convergence Dilemma," *Harvard Law Review* 93, no. 3 (1980): 518–33.

110. Elaine Heffernan, who was an administrative assistant to Director of OCR Peter Libassi, argued in her Administrative History of the Office that "[c]onsiderably older than Title VI is its governing principle, which may be formulated on broad terms as follows: *the practice of and participation in racial discrimination*

by the Federal government is improper. . . . We recognize that the 'principle' we have posited is very broad. We recognize also that it does not stand alone, but rather, is grounded in fundamental principles of public administration, constitutional law, and morality," including the norm that "[p]ublic funds spent for the common good should be distributed equitably among the members of the public for whose benefit they are intended." Heffernan, *Office of Civil Rights, OCR Historical Record,* 1–2.

111. Librassi "had spent virtually his entire career as a civil rights specialist in New York with the Civil Rights Commission." Orfield, *Reconstruction of Southern Education*, 329. Derrick Bell was one of the plaintiffs' attorneys in *Singleton v. Jackson Municipal School District*, 348 F.2d 729 (5th Cir. 1965), to be discussed in the next paragraph, before he joined HEW.

112. Gary Orfield, "The 1964 Civil Rights Act and American Education," in *Legacies of the 1964 Civil Rights Act*, ed. Bernard Grofman (Charlottesville: University of Virginia Press, 2002) 89–129, 102.

113. 348 F.2d. 729 (1965).

114. United States v. Jefferson County Bd. of Educ. 372 F.2d 836 (5th Cir. 1966), quoting Singleton v. Jackson Municipal Separate Sch. Dist. 348 F.2d 729, 731 (5th Cir. 1965), *aff'd en banc*, United States v. Jefferson Cty. Bd. of Educ. 380 F.2d 385 (5th Cir. 1967).

115. 348 F.2d at 731.

116. Scripps-Howard Radio v. FCC, 316 U.S. 4, 15 (1942).

117. United States v. Jefferson Cty. Bd. of Educ. 380 F.2d 385 (5th Cir. 1967); Green v. County Sch. Bd., 391 U.S. 430 (1968).

118. Ackerman credits Judge Wisdom in *Jefferson County* with moving "beyond technocracy to ultimate constitutional values." Ackerman, *We the People 3*, 236. While it is true that Judge Wisdom applied HEW's statutory interpretation of the Civil Rights Act to his interpretation of the requirements of the Fourteenth Amendment, it is important not to cast the agency in the role of mere technocracy, and to valorize the courts as the sole voice of values. HEW's 1966 Guidelines did not merely pronounce a set of numerical guidelines, but explained why such a statistical approach was necessary given the agency's sophisticated understanding of the social constraints on individual choice. As I have argued, HEW officials' judgment that free choice was limited by community prejudice emerged from their mediation of egalitarian principles and administrative experience.

119. Jacqueline Dowd Hall, "The Long Civil Rights Movement and the Political Uses of the Past," *The Journal of American History* 91, no. 4 (2005): 1252–53.

120. Martin Luther King, *"I Have a Dream . . ." Speech by the Rev. Martin Luther King at the "March on Washington"* (August 28, 1963), available at: https://perma.cc/H78Z-2RKR.

121. Civil Rights Act of 1964, § 703(a)(1) (1964).

122. Congress's intent on this issue remains a matter of scholarly disputation. See Hugh Davis Graham, *The Civil Rights Era, Origins and Development of National Policy* (New York: Oxford University Press, 1990), 246, 150–52; John David Skrentny, *Ironies of Affirmative Action: Politics, Culture, and Justice in America* (Chicago: Chicago University Press, 1997), 121; Ackerman, *We the People 3*, 177.

123. Nicholas Pedriana and Robin Stryker, "The Strength of a Weak Agency: Enforcement of Title VII of the 1964 Civil Rights Act and the Expansion of State Capacity, 1965–1971," *American Journal of Sociology* 110, no. 3 (2004): 709–60, 725.
124. Equal Employment Opportunity Commission, "Equal Employment Opportunity Commission: Administrative History," microformed on *Civil Rights During the Johnson Administration*, 1963–1969 part II, Steven F. Lawson ed., reel 1, frame 0249 (Univ. Publications Am. [1968] 1984).
125. Civil Rights Act § 703(h) (1964).
126. *Griggs*, 401 U.S. at 433 n. 9 (quoting EEOC Guidelines on Employment Testing Procedures, CCH EMPL. PRAC. GUIDE, ¶ 17,304.53 (EEOC Dec. 2, 1966)).
127. Alfred Blumrosen, *Black Employment and the Law* (New Brunswick, NJ: Rutgers University Press, 1971), 52.
128. Erbin Crowell Jr., "EEOC's Image—Remedy for Job Discrimination?," *Civil Rights Digest* 1, no. 1 (1968): 29–34, 30.
129. Equal Employment Opportunity Commission, "They Have the Power—We Have the People": The Status of Equal Employment Opportunity in Houston, Texas, 1970 (Washington, DC: EEOC, 1970), i.
130. Commissioner Brown's public statement that "discrimination is a condition of pervasive exclusion," and Commissioner Jackson's suggestion that discrimination had become less a matter of an "evil state of mind" than an "institutionalized" condition, cast serious doubt on John David Skrentny's claim that "there was no ideological or ethical attachment to the affirmative action model" amongst EEOC officials who developed it. Skrentny, *Ironies of Affirmative Action*, 223. In reconceiving discrimination as a pernicious pattern of social behavior, rather than the isolated, irrational act of the bigot, EEOC began piecing together a new critique of the injustices of civil society and an ethical vision for its reconstruction. EEOC's petition to FCC to intervene in AT&T's rate increase petition provides yet another example of the moral content of EEOC's effects-based arguments. EEOC's petition emphasized, in its analysis of black employment at the company, that the "present situation with respect to blacks represents historic exclusionary practices," indicating EEOC's reliance on a conception of discrimination as a state of social exclusion rather than intentional malice. EEOC's assessment of AT&T was laced with moral reprobation, describing the company's statistical employment record as "appalling" and arguing that "AT&T has violated the fair employment laws so flagrantly as to shock the conscience." Equal Employment Opportunity Commission, *Memorandum in Support of EEOC Petition to Intervene from Stanley P. Hebert, General Council, & David A. Copus, Attorney, EEOC, to FCC* (Dec. 10, 1970), (EEOC v. AT&T, NAACP Papers, Part V, Box 353, Folder 1), 3–4, 24 (on file with author). See also Sophia Z. Lee, "Race, Sex, and Rulemaking: Administrative Constitutionalism and the Workplace, 1960 to the Present," *Virginia Law Review* 96, no. 4 (2010): 799–886, 810–44. While Skrentny is right to emphasize that considerations of "administrative pragmatism" and "crisis management" influenced EEOC and other government agencies in developing effects-based arguments, these statements show that EEOC officials were also beginning to rethink the very meaning of

racism in America, rather than merely using whatever administrative tools were available to address black unemployment and urban unrest. Their innovative interpretations of the Civil Rights Act were reminiscent of Stokely Carmichael and Charles Hamilton's concept of "institutional racism" and anticipated Iris Marion Young's concept of "structural injustice," meaning injustice "embedded in unquestioned norms, habits, symbols, in the assumptions underlying institutional rules and the collective consequences of following those rules." Iris Marion Young, *Justice and the Politics of Difference* (Princeton, NJ: Princeton University Press, 1990), 41; Stokely Carmichael and Charles Hamilton, *Black Power: The Politics of Liberation in American* (New York: Random House, 1967). Skrentny's implication that administrative rationality and ethical judgment cannot coexist and that moral arguments only legitimately originate in persons and groups within civil society, rather than in the deliberations of public officials, bespeaks his Weberian sociological assumptions about the nature of the state, which has difficulty recognizing the Progressive Hegelian practices that are the focus of my study.

131. Equal Employment Opportunity Commission, *The Role of the EEO-1 Reporting System in Commission Operations* (1967), in EEOC, Administrative History, Reel 2, Frames 0633–0659.
132. See generally The White House Conference on Equal Employment Opportunity. *Panel 1—First Session: "Patterns of Discrimination."* Washington DC: August 19, 1965 (Washington, DC: Ward & Paul, 1965).
133. Equal Employment Opportunity Commission, *The Role of the EEO-1 Reporting System in Commission Operations* (1967). In EEOC Administrative History, reel 1, frames 0150–0151.
134. Douglas Robinson, "Business Job Bias in City Is Charged," *New York Times*, January 16, 1968, at 1.
135. Ibid.
136. Crowell, "EEOC," 32.
137. Equal Employment Opportunity Commission and Dana Whitaker, eds., *Recollections of Luther Holcomb, Vice-Chairman of the Equal Employment Opportunity Commission from 1964-1974*, https://perma.cc/2UXX-224X.
138. Ackerman, *We the People 3*, 181; Graham, *The Civil Rights Era*, 468–70.
139. Nicholas Pedriana and Robin Stryker note that "the early EEOC was populated by an ideologically and professionally diverse senior staff that, as a collectivity, was initially unsure about the Commission's central objectives or how they might be accomplished." Pedriana and Stryker, "The Strength of a Weak Agency," 721.
140. Napoleon Johnson of the National Urban League argued at the Commission's 1965 White House Conference that "social statistics with racial designations are subject to possible misuse and bigots and the uninformed have used racial statistics to encourage the erroneous but widespread belief that race itself is a significant causal factor in delinquency, crime and other social pathology. . . . We reaffirm our opposition to the identification of race and religion of the individual." Equal Employment Opportunity Commission, *White House Conference on Equal Employment Opportunity*, 10. Clarence Mitchell of the NAACP voiced similar objections. Skrentny, *Ironies of Affirmative Action*, 128.

141. Robert C. Lieberman, "Ideas, Institutions and Political Order: Explaining Political Change," *American Political Science Review* 96, no. 4 (2002): 697–712, 708.
142. 401 U.S. 424 (1971).
143. 401 U.S. at 427.
144. Civil Rights Act of 1964 § 703(h) (1964).
145. 401 U.S. at 429.
146. 401 U.S. at 431.
147. 401 U.S. at 427.
148. 401 U.S. at 435.
149. Economic Opportunity Act of 1964, Pub. L. 88-452, 78 Stat. 503 (1964).
150. John F. Kennedy, "Letter to the President of the Senate and to the Speaker of the House Proposing the Establishment of a National Service Corps.," (April 10, 1963), online at *The American Presidency Project*, ed. Gerhard Peters and John T. Woolley, https://perma.cc/T7TE-C2CA. Several best-selling books came out in the late 1950s and early 1960s highlighting the problem of poverty, including Michael Harrington, *The Other America: Poverty in the United States* (New York: MacMillan, 1962) and John Kenneth Galbraith, *The Affluent Society* (New York: The New American Library, 1958). President Kennedy and Johnson after him subsequently took up the call to address poverty. James L. Sundquist, *Politics and Policy: The Eisenhower, Kennedy, and Johnson Years* (Washington, DC: The Brookings Institution, 1968), 111–45. Johnson's proposed legislation won added support because of contemporaneous urban unrest, which commentators saw as inextricably linked with the civil rights struggles of the same year. For example, in the midst of rioting in New York City in August 1964, as the bill was before Congress, the *New York Times* Editorial Board wrote: "In New York and all the other many Northern cities with large Negro populations what is called the civil rights struggle is also a movement inspired by resentment at mass unemployment and lack of access to other than menial jobs. Though misguided and self-defeating, the disturbances of recent weeks are as much demonstrations against Negro poverty as against discrimination and what some call 'police brutality.' The anti-poverty bill, in the new perspective given by the disturbances of this long, hot summer, is also an anti-riot bill. The members of the House of Representatives will do well to bear that in mind when the time comes for a vote." Editorial, *New York Times*, August 4, 1964.
151. S.M. Miller and Martin Rein, "Participation, Poverty, and Administration," *Public Administration Review* 29, no. 1 (1969): 15–25; Morone, *The Democratic Wish*, 219.
152. Lyndon B. Johnson, "Address on Voting Rights to Joint Session of Congress," Public Papers of the Presidents of the United States: Lyndon B. Johnson, 1965. Volume I, entry 107, pp. 281–87. Washington, DC: U.S. Government Printing Office, 1966.
153. Economic Opportunity Act of 1964, § 202.
154. Ibid., § 202(a)(4).

155. Probably by Harold Horowitz, associate general counsel at HEW before he was assigned to the Task Force. Gillette, *Launching the War on Poverty*, 59, 98.
156. Ibid., 95–104.
157. James L. Sundquist, who was on the Task Force, argues that "the bill was deliberately drafted to grant the broadest possible discretion to the administrator." Sundquist, *Politics and Policy*, 145.
158. Daniel P. Moynihan, *Maximum Feasible Misunderstanding: Community Action in the War on Poverty* (New York: Free Press, 1969), 87.
159. Economic Opportunity Act § 202(a)(4) (emphasis added).
160. S. Rep. No. 88-1218 at 19 (1964).
161. H. Rep. No. 88-1458 at 10 (1964).
162. Morone, *The Democratic Wish*, 227–28; John H. Wheeler, "Civil Rights Groups—Their Impact upon the War on Poverty," *Law and Contemporary Problems* 31, no. 1 (1966): 152–58.
163. Office of Economic Opportunity, *Community Action Program Guide* vol. 1 (Washington, DC, 1965), 18, quoted in Paul E. Peterson, "Forms of Representation: Participation of the Poor in the Community Action Program," *American Political Science Review* 64, no. 2 (1970): 491–507, 494.
164. Office of Economic Opportunity, *Administrative History*, 117–18.
165. J. David Greenstone and Paul E. Peterson, *Race and Authority in Urban Politics: Community Action and the War on Poverty* (Chicago: London University of Chicago Press, 1973), 306.
166. Morone, *The Democratic Wish*, 233–35.
167. Greenstone and Peterson, *Race and Authority*, 307.
168. Robert Halpern, *Rebuilding the Inner City: A History of Neighborhood Initiatives to Address Poverty in the United States* (New York: Columbia University Press, 1995), 113–15.
169. Greenstone and Peterson, *Race and Authority*, 9–10, 111–62.
170. See, e.g., Mandi Isaacs Jackson, *Model City Blues: Urban Space and Organized Resistance in New Haven* (Philadelphia: Temple University Press, 2008), 82–84; Greenstone and Peterson, *Race and Authority*, 309.
171. Mandi Isaacs Jackson, *Model City Blues: Urban Space and Organized Resistance in New Haven* (Philadelphia: Temple University Press, 2008), 82–84; Greenstone and Peterson, *Race and Authority*, 7, 309. See also Robert C. Smith, "Black Power and the Transformation of Protest into Policies," *Political Science Quarterly* 96, no. 3 (1981): 431–43.
172. S.M. Miller and Martin Rein, "Participation, Poverty, and Administration," *Public Administration Review* 29, no. 1 (1969): 15–25, 17.
173. Halpern, *Rebuilding the Inner City*, 113.
174. Head Start, an early childhood education program, was a brainchild of the chief of the Office of Economic Opportunity, Sargent Shriver. While the plan initially worked through the community action programs, and thus involved parents to varying degrees in implementation, it was eventually removed to HEW, where it took on a more conventional, bureaucratic shape. Kathryn R.

Kuntz, "A Lost Legacy: Head Start's Origins in Community Action," in *Critical Perspective on Head Start: Revisioning the Hope and the Challenge*, ed. Jeanne Ellsworth and Lynda L. James (Albany, NY: SUNY Press, 1998), 1–48. The success of the early, more participatory program is a matter of some dispute, but observable educational gains were decidedly mixed where measured. Walter Williams and John W. Evans "The Politics of Evaluation: The Case of Head Start," *Annals of the American Academy of Political and Social Science* 385, no. 1 (1969): 118–35.

175. Moynihan, *Maximum Feasible Misunderstanding*, 148, 152.

176. Paul Bernstein and Kathleen Monaghan, "Equal Opportunity and the Mobilization of Law," *Law & Society Review* 20, no. 3 (1986): 355–88.

177. See B. Dan Wood, "Does Politics Make a Difference at the EEOC?" *American Journal of Political Science* 34, no. 2 (1990): 503–30, 509. Thomas criticized the work of the Commission under his predecessor, Eleanor Holmes Norton, for "concentrat[ing] on prospective relief in the form of numerical goals and time tables rather than full relief for the party actually filing charge. . . . [T]he emphasis was on obtaining broad remedies for a theoretical group that had not filed charges. I find it ironic that anyone would put in place a policy that provided less relief for those who were actually hurt than for those who may have been hurt as a result of some attenuated, historical events. . . . [W]e have, unfortunately, permitted sociological and demographic realities to be manipulated to the point of surreality by convenient legal theories such as 'adverse impact' and 'prima facie cases.'" Clarence Thomas, "The Equal Employment Opportunity Commission: Reflections on a New Philosophy," *Stetson Law Review* 15, no. 1 (1985): 29–36, 33, 36.

178. See, e.g., Wards Cove Packing Co., Inc. v. Atonio, 490 U.S. 642, 661 (1989) ("any alternative practices which respondents offer up in . . . must be equally effective as petitioners' chosen hiring procedures in achieving petitioners' legitimate employment goals," considerations of cost included).

179. Pub. L. No. 102-166, 105 Stat. 1071 (1991).

180. Ibid. § 2(2).

181. Ibid. § 2(3).

182. Reginald C. Govan, "Honorable Compromises and the Moral High Ground: The Conflict between the Rhetoric and the Content of the Civil Rights Act of 1991," *Rutgers Law Review* 46 no. 1 (1993): 1–242.

183. Texas Dept. of Housing and Comm. Affairs v. Inclusive Communities Project, Inc., 135 S. Ct. 2507 (2015).

184. Pub. L. 90-284, 82 Stat. 73, 42 U.S.C. § 3601 et. seq. (2012).

185. *Inclusive Communities*, 135 S. Ct. at 2511.

186. Department of Housing and Urban Development, *Implementation of the Fair Housing Act's Discriminatory Effects Standard*, 78 Fed. Reg. 11,460 (2013).

187. *Inclusive Communities*, 135 S. Ct. at 2523; 78 Fed. Reg. 11460, 11,466 (2013).

188. 135 S. Ct. at 2524, 2525.

189. Id. at 2528 (Thomas, J., dissenting).

190. *Griggs*, 401 U.S. at 432 (1971).
191. 391 U.S. 430 (1968).
192. Ackerman, *We the People 3*, 240.
193. Department of Housing and Urban Development, *Non-discrimination in Federally Assisted Programs*, 45 C.F.R. § 181.54 (1967).
194. Parents Involved in Community Schs. v. Seattle Sch. Dist. No. 1, 551 U.S. 701 (2007).
195. 551 U.S. at 748.
196. Gary Orfield and Chungmei Lee report that "executive branch enforcement under President Johnson made the South the nation's most integrated region with just a few years of serious enforcement." Gary Orfield and Chugmei Lei, *Historic Reversals, Accelerating Resegregation, and the Need for New Integration Strategies* (UCLA Civil Rights Project, 2007), 13, https://perma.cc/WQA2-5339. The trends continued for the next two decades as courts continued to provide injunctive relief to the victims of segregation: though only 2 percent of Southern schools were integrated at all in 1965, by 1968 19 percent of African Americans in the South attended majority white schools; by 1991, 40 percent attended majority white schools. Ibid., 28.
197. Compare Richard H. Thaler and Cass R. Sunstein, *Nudge: Improving Decisions about Health, Welfare, and Happiness* (New York: Penguin, 2008).

Chapter 4

1. Seminally, James O. Freedman, *Crisis and Legitimacy: The Administrative Process and American Government* (Cambridge: Cambridge University Press, 1980).
2. E.g., Susan Rose-Ackerman, *Rethinking the Progressive Agenda: The Reform of the American Regulatory State* (New York: The Free Press, 1992), 6–7.
3. Office of Management and Budget, *Circular A-4, To the Heads of Executive Agencies and Establishments, Subject: Regulatory Analysis* (September 17, 2003), https://perma.cc/8FU4-SV5W.
4. Ibid.
5. E.g., Oren Bar-Gill and Elizabeth Warren, "Making Credit Safer," *University of Pennsylvania Law Review* 157, no. 1 (2008): 1–102.
6. E.g., James Landis, *The Administrative Process* (New Haven, CT: Yale University Press, 1938), 16.
7. Matthew D. McCubbins, "The Legislative Design of Regulatory Structure," *American Journal of Political Science* 29, no. 4 (1985): 729–48, 742.
8. Matthew D. McCubbins, Roger G. Noll, and Barry Weingast, "Administrative Procedures as Instruments of Political Control," *Journal of Law, Economics & Organization* 3, no. 2 (1987): 243–77, 247; John Ferejohn and Charles Shippan, "Congressional Influence on Bureaucracy," special issue, *Journal of Law, Economics & Organization* 6 (1990): 1–20, 18–19.
9. F. A. Hayek, "The Use of Knowledge in Society," *American Economic Review* 35, no. 4 (1945): 519–30.
10. Exec. Order No. 13,563, Improving Regulation and Regulatory Review, Section 1(c) (July 18, 2011).

11. Elizabeth Anderson, *Value in Ethics and Economics* (Cambridge, MA: Harvard University Press, 1993), 147–67.
12. E.g., Dept. of Transp. v. Am. Ass'n of Railroads, 135 S. Ct. 1225, 1242 (2015) (Thomas, J., concurring in the judgment); PHH Corp. v. Consumer Fin. Protection Bureau, 881 F.3d 75, 164 (D.C. Cir. 2018) (Kavanaugh, J., dissenting).
13. J.W. Hampton, Jr., & Co. v. United States, 276 U.S. 394, 409 (1928).
14. 5 U.S.C. § 706 (2012).
15. Louis Jaffe, *Judicial Control of Administrative Action* (1965), 320.
16. Mathews v. Eldrige, 424 U.S. 319, 333 (1976).
17. INS v. Chadha, 462 U.S. 919, 962–63 (1983) (Powell, J., concurring in the judgment); Commodity Futures Trading Comm'n v. Schor, 478 U.S. 833, 837 (1986).
18. E.g., Hamburger, *Is Administrative Law Unlawful?*; Jennifer Mascott, "Who Are 'Officers of the United States'?," *Stanford Law Review* 70, no. 2 (2018): 443–564.
19. Henry P. Monaghan, "*Marbury* and the Administrative State," *Columbia Law Review* 83, no. 1 (1983): 25–26; Stephen Breyer, *Active Liberty: Interpreting Our Democratic Constitution* (New York: Alfred A. Knopf, 2005), 103.
20. E.g., Brett Kavanaugh, "Separation of Powers during the Forty-Fourth Presidency and Beyond," *Minnesota Law Review* 93, no. 5 (2009): 1454–86, 1475.
21. Peter Strauss, "The Place of Agencies in Government: Separation of Powers and the Fourth Branch," *Columbia Law Review* 84, no. 3 (1984): 573–669, 580.
22. E.g., Michaels, *Constitutional Coup*, 57–75.
23. E.g., Robert A. Katzman, *Judging Statutes* (New York: Oxford University Press, 2014), 23–28.
24. Blake Emerson, "The Administration of Constitutional Conflict: Structural Transformations in American Public Law, 1877–1946," *Quaderni Fiorentini* 46 (2017): 385–415, 414.
25. James Madison, "The Federalist, 51" in Alexander Hamilton, James Madison, and John Jay, *The Federalist Papers*, ed. Lawrence Goldman (Oxford: Oxford University Press [1787–1788] 2008), 256–60, 257.
26. Peter Crane, *Controlling Administrative Power: An Historical Comparison* (Cambridge: Cambridge University Press, 2016), 111.
27. Basic Law for the Federal Republic of Germany art. 20, 28.
28. In this section, I primarily follow Philip Pettit, who has offered the most comprehensive and sustained defense of republican political theory. See generally, Philip Pettit, *On the People's Terms: A Republican Theory and Model of Democracy* (Cambridge: Cambridge University Press, 2012). The other prominent contemporary theorist of republicanism is Quentin Skinner. See, e.g., Quentin Skinner, "The Republican Ideal of Political Liberty," in *Machiavelli and Republicanism*, ed. Gisela Block, Quentin Skinner, and Maurizio Viroli (Cambridge, UK: Cambridge University Press, 1990), 293–309. Both Skinner and Pettit shy away from the positive conception of freedom endorsed by Hegel and the Progressives.
29. Rahman, *Democracy Against Domination*, 81–92.
30. Philip Pettit, *On the People's Terms*, 111–17.
31. Philip Pettit, *Republicanism: A Theory of Freedom and Government* (Oxford: Oxford University Press, 1997), 188–89.

32. Pettit, *On The People's Terms*, 232.
33. Ibid.
34. Mark Seidenfeld, "A Civic-Republican Justification for the Bureaucratic State," *Harvard Law Review* 105, no. 7 (1992): 1511–76; William N. Eskridge Jr. and John Ferejohn, *A Republic of Statutes: The New American Constitution* (New Haven, CT: Yale University Press, 2010), 29–74; Richardson, *Democratic Autonomy*, 214–30; Glen Staszewski, "Statutory Interpretation as Contestatory Democracy," *William & Mary Law Review* 55, no. 1 (2013): 221–304, 259–60.
35. Elizabeth Anderson, *Private Government: How Employers Rule Our Lives (And Why We Don't Talk about It)* (Princeton, NJ: Princeton University Press, 2017), 45–46.
36. On structural injustice, see Young, *Justice and the Politics of Difference*, 41. Rahman's friendly amendment of republicanism to include Young's notion of structural injustice addresses some of my critiques of the republican theory. But his account seems to stretch the republican notion of domination beyond what it can reasonably bear. It is not clear how a structure, which lacks a will, could be seen as "dominating" in the sense with which the republican tradition is concerned. Republicanism's critical bite is best at diagnosing cases where some powerful figure or concerted group is able to assert their will over others, thus subjecting them to arbitrary interference. But where the social system exposes people to unfair or degrading conditions, without proximate intentionality, republicanism core concerns have less intuitive traction. As Rahman acknowledges, Progressives such as Dewey analyzed those cases in which a "condition of unfreedom is a product of a set of social and economic systems and the individual's position in those system." Rahman, *Democracy against Domination*, 85. Here, Progressivism's critique of the market goes beyond republicanism's, and demands different institutional and discursive resources to develop a solution. Moreover, the potential mismatch between republican social justice and republican political legitimacy go unaddressed in Rahman's account, which does not make use of deliberative rationality to draw an intrinsic link between democratic ends and democratic means.
37. Pettit, *The People Themselves*, 48-49.
38. Ibid., 130.
39. Hegel, *Philosophy of Right*, § 189.
40. Ibid., § 233.
41. Ibid., § 235.
42. Ibid., § 236.
43. Ibid., § 244
44. Compare Raymond Plant, *The Neoliberal State* (New York: Oxford University Press, 2004), 82.
45. Dewey, *Individualism Old and New*, 24.
46. Ibid., 58.
47. Dewey, *The Public and Its Problems*, 126.
48. Wilson, "Notes on Administration," 50.
49. Mary Parker Follett, "Power," in *Dynamic Administration: The Collected Papers of Mary Parker Follett*, ed. Henry C. Metcalf and L. Urwick (New York: London: Harper Brothers, 1940), 95–116, 101.

50. Dewey, *The Public and Its Problems*, 208.
51. Michael Theunissen, trans. Eric Watkins and Fred Dallmayr, "The Repressed Intersubjectivity in Hegel's Philosophy of Right," in *Hegel and Legal Theory*, ed. Drucilla Cornell, Michel Rosenfeld, and David Gray Carlson (New York: Routledge, 1991), 3–64.
52. Habermas, *Between Facts and Norms*, 301; James Bohman, *Public Deliberation: Pluralism, Complexity, and Democracy* (Cambridge, MA: MIT Press, 1996), 2; Jane Mansbridge et al., "The Place of Self-Interest and the Role of Power in Deliberative Democracy," 71; Eskridge and Ferejohn, *A Republic of Statutes*, 114; Post, *Citizens Divided*, 37.
53. Joshua Cohen, "Deliberation and Democratic Legitimacy," in *Deliberation and Democracy: Essays on Reason and Politics*, ed. James Bohman and William Rehg (Cambridge, MA: MIT Press, 1997), 67–92, 24.
54. John Rawls, *Political Liberalism*, expanded ed. (New York: Columbia University Press, 1993), 231–40.
55. Habermas, *Between Facts and Norms*, 162.
56. E.g. Amy Guttman and Dennis Thompson, *Democracy and Disagreement: Why Moral Conflict Cannot Be Avoided in Politics, and What We Should Do About It* (Cambridge, MA: Harvard University Press, 1996), 18, 165–78; Henry Richardson, *Democratic Autonomy*; Archong Fung and Erik Olin Wright, eds., *Deepening Democracy: Institutional Innovations in Empowered Participatory Governance* (London: Verson, 2003); Bohman, *Public Deliberation*, 188–90.
57. E.g. John Parkinson and Jane Mansbridge, eds., *Deliberative Systems* (Cambridge: Cambridge University Press, 2012); Mark E. Warren, "Deliberative Democracy and Authority," *American Political Science Review* 90, no. 1 (1996): 46–60.
58. Dewey, *The Public and Its Problems*, 131.
59. Follett, *Creative Experience*, 216.
60. Michael C. Dorf and Charles F. Sabel, "A Constitution of Democratic Experimentalism," *Columbia Law Review* 98, no. 2 (1998): 267–473, 283, 345–58.
61. Dewey, *The Public and Its Problems*, 203.
62. Willoughby, *An Examination of the Nature of the State*, 199.
63. Dewey, *The Public and Its Problems*, 67.
64. Rainer Forst, *Justification and Critique*, trans. Ciaran Cronin (Malden, MA: Polity Press, 2014), 39, 2.
65. Seyla Benhabib, *Another Cosmopolitanism* (Oxford: Oxford University Press, 2006), 48.
66. John Rawls, "The Idea of Public Reason," in *Deliberative Democracy: Essays on Reason and Politics*, ed. James Bohman and William Rehg (Cambridge, MA: MIT Press, 1997), 93–130, 106–07.
67. Ronald Dworkin, *Taking Rights Seriously* (Cambridge, MA: Harvard University Press, 1978), 90–92.
68. Jeremy Waldron, *The Dignity of Legislation* (Cambridge: Cambridge University Press, 1999), 63–91.

69. Bruce Ackerman, *We The People 1: Foundations* (Cambridge, MA: Harvard University Press, 1991), 6–10; Habermas, *Between Facts and Norms*, 373–80.
70. Christopher Zurn, *Deliberative Democracy and the Institutions of Judicial Review* (Cambridge: Cambridge University Press, 2007), 139.
71. David M. Estlund, *Democratic Authority: A Philosophical Framework* (Princeton, NJ: Princeton University Press, 2009), 38 (emphasis added).
72. Eskridge and Ferejohn, *A Republic of Statutes*, 5.
73. David R. Mayhew, *Divided We Govern: Party Control, Lawmaking, and Investigations, 1946–2002*, 2nd ed. (New Haven, CT: Yale University Press, 2005), 130–31.
74. Ibid., 159–60.
75. Wilson, *The State*, 591.
76. Mark Greenberg, "The Moral Impact Theory of Law," *Yale Law Journal* 123, no. 5 (2014): 1288–342, 1313.
77. Weber, *Economy and Society*, 223.
78. Mirjan R. Damaska, *The Faces of Justice and State Authority: A Comparative Approach to the Legal Process* (New Haven, CT: Yale University Press), 18–22.
79. Goodnow, *Politics and Administration*, 85.
80. E.g., Elizabeth Fisher, *Risk Regulation and Administrative Constitutionalism* (Oxford: Hart, 2007), 26–34; Michaels, *Constitutional Coup*, 59–65; Rahman, *Democracy against Domination*, 164; Richardson, *Democratic Autonomy*, 222.
81. Pierre Rosanvallon, *Democratic Legitimacy: Impartiality, Reflexivity, Proximity*, trans. Arthur Goldhammer (Princeton, NJ: Princeton University Press, 2011), 210–16, 103.
82. Jerry L. Mashaw, "Norms, Practices, and the Paradox of Deference: A Preliminary Inquiry into Agency Statutory Interpretation," *Administrative Law Review* 57, no. 2 (2005): 501–42.
83. E.g., Wendy Wagner, "Administrative Law, Filter Failure, and Information Capture," *Duke Law Journal* 59, no. 7 (2010): 1321–432.
84. Dewey, *The Public and Its Problems*, 206.
85. Alexander Livingston, "Between Means and Ends: Reconstructing Coercion in Dewey's Democratic Theory," *American Political Science Review* 111, no. 3 (2017): 522–34; Marc Stears, *Demanding Democracy: American Radicals In Search of a New Politics* (Princeton, NJ: Princeton University Press, 2010), 95–97.
86. 16 U.S.C § 703(a) (2012); 42 U.S.C. § 7411(a)(2) (2012); 42 U.S.C. § 3608(d) (2012).
87. Goodnow, *Politics and Administration*, 24.
88. Wilson, "The Study of Administration," 217.
89. Bruce Wyman, *The Principles of the Administrative Law Governing the Relations of Public Officers* (St. Paul, MN: Keefe-Davidson, 1903), 17.
90. United States *ex rel.* Accardi v. Shaughnessy, 347 U.S. 260, 266–68 (1954).
91. Herbert A. Simon, *Administrative Behavior*, 4th ed. (New York: Free Press, [1945] 1997), 33, 180–81, 185–86, 211–17; Herbert Kaufman, *The Administrative Behavior of Federal Bureau Chiefs* (Washington, DC: Brookings, 1981), 20, 114, 167.

92. Chester I. Barnard, *The Functions of the Executive* (Cambridge, MA: Harvard University Press, 1938), 232.
93. Michaels, *Constitutional Coup*, 39–50.
94. Attorney General's Committee on Administrative Procedure, Final Report, 103–08.
95. 5 U.S.C. § 553(b) (2012).
96. Ibid., § 553(c).
97. Ibid., § 706(2)(A).
98. Kenneth Culp Davis, *Administrative Law Text*, 3rd ed. (St. Paul: West, 1972), 142.
99. Follett, *Creative Experience*, 212–13.
100. Donald Elliot, "Re-inventing Rulemaking," *Duke Law Journal* 41, no. 6 (1992): 1490–96.
101. Jason Webb Yackee and Susan Webb Yackee, "A Bias towards Business? Assessing Interest Group Influence on the U.S. Bureaucracy," *Journal of Politics* 68, no. 1 (2006): 128–39.
102. John Boswell, "Deliberating Downstream: Countering Democratic Distortions in the Policy Process," *Perspectives on Politics* 14, no. 1 (2016): 724–37.
103. John Forester, *Planning in the Face of Power* (Berkeley: University of California Press, 1989), 101.
104. Yackee and Yackee, "A Bias toward Business?," 128–39.
105. See Miriam Seifter, "Second-Order Participation in Administrative Law," *UCLA Law Review* 63, no. 5 (2016): 1300–65.
106. E.g., Tony Bovaird, "Beyond Engagement and Participation: User and Community Coproduction of Public Services," *Public Administration Review* 67, no. 5 (2007): 846–60.
107. See generally Nancy Fraser and Axel Honneth, *Redistribution or Recognition? A Political Philosophical Exchange* (London: Verso, 2003).
108. 20 U.S.C. § 1681 (2012).
109. Alexandra Brodsky, "A Rising Tide: Learning about Fair Disciplinary Process from Title IX," *Journal of Legal Education* 66, no. 4 (2016): 822–49, 822–23.
110. 40 Fed. Reg. 24,128, 24,139 (June 4, 1975); 34 C.F.R. 106.8 (2012).
111. U.S. Department of Education, Office for Civil Right, Sexual Harassment Guidance: Harassment of Students by School Employees, Other Students, or Third Parties, 62 Fed. Reg. 12,034 (March 13, 1997); U.S. Department of Education, Office for Civil Rights, Revised Sexual Harassment Guidance: Harassment of Students by School Employees, Other Students, or Third Parties, iii–iv (Jan. 2001), https://perma.cc/PV9P-FRQB; U.S. Department of Education, Office for Civil Rights, Dear College Letter (April 4, 2011), https://perma.cc/FVV3-DQZT.
112. Celene Reynolds, "The Mobilization of Title IX across Colleges and Universities, 1994-2014," *Social Problems* (2018), available at: https://doi.org/10.1093/socpro/spy005.
113. Indeed, the Trump administration has rescinded the 2011 Guidance and commenced rule-making on the topic. U.S. Department of Education, Office for Civil Rights, Dear Colleague Letter (Sept. 22, 2017), https://perma.cc/8CLQ-SHZ3; U.S. Department of Education, Title IX of the Education Amendents of 1972, Notice of Proposed Rulemaking, 34 CFR Part 106 (Nov. 16, 2018), https://perma.cc/DHK9-L5XC.

114. Richard J. Pierce, "Seven Ways to Deossify Agency Rulemaking," *Administrative Law Review* 47, no. 1 (1995): 59–95, 60–62; Daniel A. Farber and Anne Joseph O'Connell, "The Lost World of Administrative Law," *Texas Law Review* 92 (2014): 1137–89, 1161; Abbe R. Gluck, Anne Joseph O'Connell, and Rosa Po, "Unorthodox Lawmaking, Unorthodox Rulemaking," *Columbia Law Review* 115, no. 7 (2015), 1789–1866, 1801–02, 1809–11.
115. Robert A. Anthony, "Interpretive Rules, Policy Statements, Guidances, Manuals, and the Like—Should Federal Agencies Use Them to Bind the Public?" *Duke Law Journal* 41, no. 6 (1991): 1311–84.
116. E.g., Mariano-Florentino Cuéllar, "Rethinking Regulatory Democracy," *Administrative Law Review* 57 (2005): 411–99; Beth Simone Noveck, *Smart Citizens, Smarter State: The Technologies of Expertise and the Future of Governing* (Cambridge, MA: Harvard University Press, 2015); Cynthia R. Farina et al., "Rulemaking 2.0," *University of Miami Law Review* 65 (2011): 365–447.
117. Nicholas Parrillo, *Federal Agency Guidance: An Institutional Perspective*, Final Report for the Administrative Conference of the United States (Oct. 2017), https://perma.cc/5K9C-RPWG, 33–34.
118. Encino Motorcars, LLC v. Navarro, 136 S. Ct. 2117, 2126 (2016); FCC. v. Fox Television Stations, Inc., 556 U.S. 502, 515 (2009).
119. Jerry Mashaw, "Small Things Like Reasons Are Put in a Jar: Reason and Legitimacy in the Administrative State," *Fordham Law Review* 70, no. 1 (2001): 17–35.
120. FCC v. Fox Television Stations, Inc. 556 U.S. 502, 515 (2009).
121. Overton Park v. Volpe, 401 U.S. 402, 416 (1971).
122. 463 U.S. 29, 43 (1983).
123. Richard J. Pierce, *Administrative Law Treatise*, vol. 1, 5th ed. (Austin, TX; Wolters Kluwer, 2010), 593.
124. Burlington Truck Lines, Inc. v. United States, 371 U.S. 156, 168 (1962).
125. Michigan v. EPA, 135 S. Ct. 2699, 2707 (2015); Bus. Roundtable v. SEC, 647 F.3d 1144, 1151 (D.C. Cir. 2011).
126. Mashaw, "Small Things Like Reasons," 32.
127. Motor Vehicle Mfrs. Ass'n v. State Farm Mut. Auto. Ins. Co., 463 U.S. 29, 43 (1983).
128. National Highway Traffic Safety Administration, *Federal Motor Vehicle Safety Standards; Occupant Crash Protection*, 46 Fed. Reg. 53419 (Oct. 29, 1981).
129. Jerry L. Mashaw and David L. Harfst, *The Struggle for Auto Safety* (Cambridge, MA: Harvard University Press, 1990).
130. Ibid., 221.
131. Consumer Financial Protection Bureau, Integrated Mortgage Disclosures under the Real Estate Settlement Procedures Act (Regulation X) and the Truth in Lending Act (Regulation Z), 78 Fed. Reg. 79,730 (Dec. 31, 2013); The Trustees of Columbia University in the City of New York and Graduate Workers of Columbia—GWC, UAW, N.L.R.B. Case No. 02-RC-143012, Decision on Review and Order (Aug. 23, 2016); Federal Aviation Administration, Operating Requirements: Domestic, Flag, and Supplemental Operations, 14 C.F.R. pt. 121 (2017); Federal Aviation Administration, Economic Regulations: Oversales, 14 C.F.R. pt. 250 (2017); Department of Education, Application for New Awards; Promise Neighborhoods Program, 82 Fed. Reg. 33,881 (Jul7 21, 2017);

Environmental Protection Agency, Clean Water Rule: Definition of Waters of the United States, 80 Fed. Reg. 37,053 (June 29, 2015).

132. Phelps Dodge Corp. v. N.L.R.B., 313 U.S. 177, 197, 61 S. Ct. 845, 853 (1941).
133. Utility Regulatory Air Group v. EPA, 134 S. Ct. 2427, 2444 (2014), quoting FDA v. Brown & Williamson Tobacco Corp., 529 U.S. 120, 160 (2000). See also MCI Telecomms. Corp. v. Am. Tel. & Tel. Co., 512 U.S. 218, 231 (1994).
134. 135 S. Ct. 2480 (2014).
135. 135 S. Ct. at 2483.
136. Cass R. Sunstein, "Chevron Step Zero," *Virginia Law Review* 92, no. 2 (2006): 187–249, 240–42.
137. Blake Emerson, "Administrative Answers to 'Major Questions,' On the Democratic Legitimacy of Agency Statutory Interpretation," *Minnesota Law Review* 102, no. 5 (2018): 2019–99, 2085–86.
138. Kenneth Mayer, *With the Stroke of a Pen: Executive Orders and Presidential Power* (Princeton, NJ: Princeton University Press, 2001), 121.
139. Peri E. Arnold, *The Managerial Presidency: Comprehensive Reorganization Planning, 1905–1996*, 2nd ed. (Lawrence: University Press of Kansas, [1986] 1998) 351–61.
140. Exec. Order No. 12,291, Federal Regulation, § 3(f) (Feb. 17, 1981).
141. Ibid. at § 2(b) and (c), § (3).
142. Elana Kagan, "Presidential Administration," *Harvard Law Review* 114, no. 8 (2001), 2245–385, 2281–303.
143. 467 U.S. 837, 844 (1984).
144. 467 U.S. at 865.
145. Kagan, "Presidential Administration," 2252.
146. Posner and Vermeule, *The Executive Unbound,* 113–27.
147. Cynthia Farina, "The 'Chief Executive' and the Quiet Constitutional Revolution," *Administrative Law Review* 49, no. 1 (1997): 179–86, 185.
148. Stephen Skowronek, *The Politics Presidents Make: Leadership from John Adams to Bill Clinton* (Cambridge, MA: Harvard University Press, 1993), 414–29.
149. Daniel Carpenter, "Institutional Strangulation: Bureaucratic Politics and Financial Reform in the Obama Administration," *Perspectives on Politics* 8, no. 3 (2010): 825–39.
150. Phillip Rucker and Robert Costa, "'Deconstruction of the Administrative State,'" *Washington Post*, Feb. 23, 2017.
151. E.g. Regents of Univ. of California v. United States Dep't of Homeland Sec., 279 F. Supp. 3d 1011 (N.D. Cal. 2018); General Powers of Special Counsel—Conduct and Accountability, 28 C.F.R. 600.7 (2012).
152. Theodore Lowi, *The Personal Presidency: Power Invested, Promise Unfulfilled* (Ithaca, NY: Cornell University Press, 1985), 20.
153. Schmitt, *Legality and Legitimacy*, 5.

Conclusion

1. Compare Hegel, "Proceedings of the State Assembly of the Kingdom Württemberg," 43 and Skowronek, *Building a New American State*, 1.

2. Cass R. Sunstein, *The Cost-Benefit State: The Future of Regulatory Protection* (Chicago: American Bar Association, 2002), ix.
3. 46 Fed. Reg. 13193 (February 17, 1981).
4. Executive Order 12,866, 58 Fed. Reg. 51735 (Oct. 4, 1993); Executive Order 13,563 76 Fed. Reg. 3821 (Jan. 21, 2011).
5. Cass R. Sunstein, *Valuing Life: Humanizing the Regulatory State* (Chicago: University of Chicago Press, 2014); Richard A. Revesz and Michael A. Livermore, *Retaking Rationality: How Cost-Benefit Analysis Can Better Protect the Environment and Our Health* (Oxford: Oxford University Press, 2011).
6. Anderson, *Value in Ethics and Economics*, 190–210; Thomas O. McGarity, "Professor Sunstein's Fuzzy Math," *Georgetown Law Journal* 90, no. 7 (2002): 2341–77.
7. White House Office of Management and Budget, *Circular A-4*.
8. Ibid.
9. Anderson, *Value in Ethics and Economics*, 192.
10. Wendy Brown, *Edgework: Critical Essays on Knowledge and Politics* (Princeton, NJ: Princeton University Press, 2009), 42.
11. Ibid., 43.
12. Mitchell Dean and Kaspar Villadsen, *State Phobia and Civil Society: The Political Legacy of Michel Foucault* (Stanford, CA: Stanford University Press, 2016), 9–22.
13. Hegel, *Philosophy of Right*, § 257.
14. Margaret Jane Radin, "Property and Personhood," *Stanford Law Review* 34, no. 5 (1982): 957–1015.
15. Axel Honneth, trans. Blake Emerson, "Three, Not Two, Concepts of Liberty: A Proposal to Enlarge Our Moral Self-Understanding," in *Hegel and Philosophy and History*, ed. Rachel Zuckert and James Kreines (Cambridge: Cambridge University Press, 2017), 177–92.
16. Susan Rose-Ackerman, "Putting Cost-Benefit Analysis in Its Place: Rethinking Regulatory Review," *University of Miami Law Review* 65 (2011): 347.
17. Exec. Order No. 13,563, 76 Fed. Reg. 14,3821 (2011).
18. Office of Management and Budget, *Circular A-4*.
19. Department of Housing and Urban Development, "Affirmatively Further Fair Housing, Final Rule," 80 Fed. Reg. 42,349 (2015).
20. Securities and Exchange Commission, *Disclosure of Payments by Resource Extraction Issuers, Final Rule* (June 27, 2016), https://perma.cc/7PZU-KHY8.
21. Dodd-Frank Wall Street Reform and Consumer Financial Protection Act, Pub. L. 111-203, § 1504, 124 Stat. 1376, 2220 (2010), 15 U.S.C. § 78m(q)(2)(A) (2012).
22. Securities and Exchange Commission, *Disclosure of Payments by Resource Extraction Issuers*, 83n.294.
23. Office of Management and Budget, *Circular A*-4, 2.
24. United States Department of Justice, *Regulatory Impact Assessment, National Standards to Prevent, Detect, and Respond to Prison Rape under the Prison Rape Elimination Act (PREA)*, 28 C.F.R. 115, Docket No. OAG-131, RIN 1105-AB34 (May 17, 2012), 40–42, https://perma.cc/A8P6-3E2R.
25. Ibid., 66-69.

26. 42 U. S. C. § 7412(n)(1)(A) (2012).
27. Michigan v. EPA, 135 S. Ct. 2699 (2015).
28. 135 S. Ct. at 2714 (Kagan, J., dissenting).
29. J.M. Samet et al., "Fine Particulate Air Pollution and Mortality in Twenty U.S. Cities, 1987–1994," *New England Journal of Medicine* 343 (2000): 1742–49; Tony A. Blakely, Bruce P. Kennedy, and Ichiro Kawachi, "Socioeconomic Inequality in Voting Participation and Self-Rated Health," *American Journal of Public Health* 91, no. 1 (2001): 99–104.
30. Exec. Order No. 13,771, 82 Fed. Reg. 9339 (Jan. 30, 2017).
31. Ibid.
32. Michaels, *Constitutional Coup*, 13.
33. Keith E. Whittington and Daniel P. Carpenter, "Executive Power in American Institutional Development," *Perspectives of Politics* 1, no. 3 (2003): 495–513, 498–502; William G. Howell and David E. Lewis, "Agencies by Presidential Design," *The Journal of Politics* 64, no. 4 (2002): 1095–114.
34. William N. Eskridge Jr. and John Ferejohn, "The Article I, Section 7 Game," *Georgetown Law Journal* 80 (1992): 523–64.
35. Kagan, "Presidential Administration," 2245–385.
36. Abbé Gluck, Anne Joseph O'Connel, and Rosa Po, "Unorthodox Lawmaking, Unorthodox Rulemaking," 1828–30; William G. Howell, *Power without Persuasion: The Politics of Direct Presidential Action* (Princeton, NJ: Princeton University Press, 2003).
37. Barack Obama, "Working When Congress Won't Act," Remarks of President Obama, Weekly Address, The White House (May 17, 2014), https://perma.cc/7QT3-PM3U.
38. David Nakamura and Juliet Eilperin, "Obama Details Executive Action on Gun Restrictions," *Washington Post*, Jan. 4, 2016, https://perma.cc/2RUB-9UKJ.
39. Michael D. Shear, "Obama, Daring Congress, Acts to Overhaul Immigration," *New York Times* (Nov. 20, 2014), https://www.nytimes.com/2014/11/21/us/obama-immigration-speech.html.
40. Executive Order 13,658, "Establishing a Minimum Wage for Contractors," 79 Fed. Reg. 9849 (Feb. 12, 2014); Peter Baker, "Obama Orders Federal Contractors to Provide Workers Paid Sick Leave," *New York Times* (Sept. 7, 2015), https://www.nytimes.com/2015/09/08/us/politics/obama-to-require-federal-contractors-to-provide-paid-sick-leave.html.
41. The While House, Office of the Press Secretary, Presidential Memorandum: Power Sector Carbon Pollution Standards (June 25, 2013), https://perma.cc/4GHD-QYVU.
42. Lisa Friedman and Brad Plumer, "E.P.A. Announces Repeal of Major Obama-Era Carbon Emissions Rule," *New York Times* (Oct. 9, 2017), https://www.nytimes.com/2017/10/09/climate/clean-power-plan.html; Michael D. Shear and Julia Hirschfeld Davis, "Trump Moves to End DACA and Calls on Congress to Act," *New York Times* (Sept. 5, 2017), https://www.nytimes.com/2017/09/05/us/politics/trump-daca-dreamers-immigration.html.
43. Schmitt, *The Concept of the Political*, 29, 26.

44. Carl Schmitt, *The Crisis of Parliamentary Democracy*, trans. Ellen Kennedy (Cambridge, MA: MIT Press, 1988), 49.
45. Ibid., 48.
46. Schmitt, *Legality and Legitimacy*, 71.
47. Bruce Ackerman, *The Decline and Fall of the American Republic* (Cambridge, MA: Harvard University Press, 2012), 6–10; Geoffrey C. Layman, Thomas M. Carsey, and Juliana Menasce Horowitz, "Party Polarization in American Politics," *Annual Review of Political Science* 9 (2006): 83–110; Marc J. Hetherington, "Resurgent Mass Partisanship: The Role of Elite Polarization," *American Political Science Review* 95, no. 3 (2001): 619–31; Terry M. Moe and William G. Howell, "Unilateral Action and Presidential Power: A Theory," *Presidential Studies Quarterly* 29, no. 4 (1999): 850–72.
48. Posner and Vermeule, *The Executive Unbound*, 5.
49. Ibid.
50. For a review of this literature, see John P. McCormick, "Irrational Choice and Mortal Combat as Political Destiny: The Essential Carl Schmitt," *Annual Review of Political Science* 10 (2007): 315–39.
51. See, e.g., Martin Shapiro, "On Predicting the Future of Administrative Law," *American Enterprise Institute Journal on Government and Society* 6 (1982): 18–25; David B. Spence, "A Public Choice Progressivism, Continued," *Cornell Law Review* 87 (2002): 398–446; Mark Tushnet, "Administrative Law in the 1930s: The Supreme Court's Accommodation of Progressive Legal Theory," *Duke Law Journal* 60 (2011): 1565–637.
52. See, e.g., Motor Vehicle Mfrs. Ass'n of U.S., Inc. v. State Farm Mut. Auto. Ins. Co., 463 U.S. 29 (1983); King v. Burwell, 135 S.Ct. 2480 (2015).
53. Cass R. Sunstein, "The Office of Information and Regulatory Affairs: Myths and Realities," *Harvard Law Review* 126 (2013): 1839–78, 1871.
54. Simon F. Haeder and Susan Webb Yackee, "Influence and the Administrative Process: Lobbying the President's Office of Management and Budget," *American Political Science Review* 109, no. 3 (2015): 507–22.
55. Habermas, "Discussion of Talcott Parsons' 'Value Freedom and Objectivity,'" 66.
56. Juan Linz, "The Perils of Presidentialism," *The Journal of Democracy* 1, no. 1 (1999): 51–69, 52.
57. Mary Parker Follett, "Constructive conflict," in *Dynamic Administration: The Collected Papers of Mary Parker Follett*, ed. H. C. Metcalf and L. Urwick (New York: Harper, [1925] 1942), 32–33.
58. For a history of the legislative developments, see Congressional Research Service, "Unauthorized Alien Students: Issues and 'Dream Act' Legislation" (Jan. 30, 2007), https://perma.cc/2RXQ-XZ53.
59. Julia Preston and John H. Cushman Jr., "Obama to Permit Young Migrants to Remain in U.S.," *New York Times* (June 25, 2012), http://www.nytimes.com/2012/06/16/us/us-to-stop-deporting-some-illegal-immigrants.html.
60. U.S. Department of Homeland Security, *Memorandum from Janet Napolitano, Secretary of Homeland Security for David Aguilar et al.* (June 15, 2012), https://www.dhs.gov/xlibrary/assets/s1-exercising-prosecutorial-discretion-individuals-who-came-to-us-as-children.pdf.

61. The White House, Office of the Press Secretary, "Remarks by the President on Immigration," (June 15, 2012), https://perma.cc/W7QG-WPSX.
62. U.S. Department of Homeland Security, *Memorandum from Jeh Charles Jonhson, Director, U.S. Citizenship and Immigration Service, for Léon Rodríguez et al.*, Nov. 20, 2016. https://perma.cc/JHL9-WFSQ.
63. U.S. Department of Justice, Office of Legal Counsel, *Memorandum Opinion for the Secretary of Homeland Security and the Counsel to the President*, 10 (Nov. 19, 2014), https://perma.cc/XV3M-Z6GB.
64. The White House, Office of the Press Secretary, "Remarks by the President in Address to the Nation on Immigration," (Nov. 20, 2014) https://perma.cc/R4A7-YV3R.
65. U.S. Department of Homeland Sec., *Memorandum of Jeh Charles Johnson*, 2.
66. U.S. Department of Justice, *Memorandum from the Office of Legal Counsel*, 23.
67. Adam B. Cox and Cristina M. Rodríguez, "The President and Immigration Law Redux," *Yale Law Journal* 125 (2015): 104–225, 175–82.
68. U.S. Department of Justice, Office of Legal Counsel, *Memorandum Opinion*, 2.
69. Robert E. Goodin, "Enfranchising All Affected Interests, and Its Alternatives," *Philosophy & Public Affairs* 35, no. 1 (2007): 40–68; Benhabib, *Another Cosmopolitanism*, 45–88.
70. Hoctor v. U.S. Dep't of Agric., 82 F.3d 165, 171 (7th Cir. 1996).
71. Texas v. United States, 809 F.3d. 134 (5th Cir. 2015), affirmed by an equally divided Court, United States v. Texas, 136 S. Ct. 2271 (2016).
72. U.S. Department of Homeland Security, Memorandum of Elaine C. Duke, "Memorandum on Rescission of Deferred Action For Childhood Arrivals (DACA)," (Sept. 5, 2017).
73. Nat'l Ass'n for the Advancement of Colored People v. Trump, 298 F. Supp. 3d 209, 2018 WL 1920079 (D.D.C. 2018); Regents of Univ. of California v. U.S. Dep't of Homeland Sec., 279 F. Supp. 3d 1011 (N.D. Cal. 2018), affirmed by Regents of the Univ. of California v. U.S. Dep't of Homeland Sec., 908 F.3d 476 (9th Cir. 2018).
74. The White House, Office of the Press Secretary, *Inaugural Address by President Barack Obama* (Jan. 21, 2013), https://perma.cc/CJ35-H3K7.
75. Environmental Protection Agency, *Standards of Performance for Greenhouse Gas Emissions from New Stationary Sources: Electric Utility Generating Units*, 77 Fed. Reg. 22,392 (2012).
76. The White House, Office of the Press Secretary, *Presidential Memorandum: Power Sector Carbon Pollution Standards* (June 25, 2013), https://perma.cc/RP93-YUAZ.
77. Environmental Protection Agency, *Carbon Pollution Emission Guidelines for Existing Stationary Sources: Electric Utility Generating Units*, Final Rule, 80 Fed. Reg. 64,662, 64,665–64,666 (Oct. 23, 2015).
78. Environmental Protection Agency, *Standards of Performance for Greenhouse Gas Emissions for New Stationary Sources: Electricity Generated Units, Proposed Rule*, 77 Fed. Reg. 22,392, 22,405 (April 13, 2012).
79. See, e.g., Environmental Protection Agency, *Carbon Pollution Emission Guidelines for Existing Stationary Sources and Standards for Modified and Reconstructed Stationary Sources, Proposed Rule, Notice of Additional Public Hearings*, 79 Fed. Reg. 37,981 (Oct. 16, 2014).

80. Environmental Protection Agency, *Carbon Pollution Emission Guidelines*, 80 Fed. Reg. 64,662, 64,667 (Oct. 23, 2015).
81. Ibid., 64,670.
82. Environmental Protection Agency, *State Guidelines for Greenhouse Gas Emissions from Existing Electric Utility Generating Units: Advanced Notice of Proposed Rulemaking*, 82 Fed. Reg. 61,507 (Dec. 28, 2017).

INDEX

The Public's Law. Blake Emerson.